The Religion
Of
The Ancient Celts

By
J. A.
MacCulloch

The Religion Of The Ancient Celts
by J. A. MacCulloch

Copyright © 2023

All Rights reserved.
No part of this publication may be reproduced, stored in a retrieval system, or transmitted in any form or by any means, electronic, mechanical, photocopying or Otherwise, without the written permission of the publisher.

The author/editor asserts the moral right to be identified as the author/editor of this work.

ISBN: 978-93-60465-38-4

Published by

DOUBLE 9 BOOKS

2/13-B, Ansari Road, Daryaganj
New Delhi – 110002
info@double9books.com
www.double9books.com
Tel. 011-40042856

This book is under public domain

ABOUT THE AUTHOR

James Alexander MacCulloch, known as J. A. MacCulloch, was a distinguished British scholar and author, born in Edinburgh, United Kingdom, in 1868, and passing away in 1950. He made significant contributions to the fields of literature, folklore, and religious studies during his lifetime. MacCulloch's diverse body of work reflects his wide-ranging intellectual interests. "The Misty Isle of Skye" showcases his literary talents and fascination with the Scottish landscape, offering readers a vivid portrayal of the Isle of Skye. In "The Childhood of Fiction, " he delved into the origins and development of storytelling and fiction, demonstrating his interest in the evolution of narrative traditions. However, MacCulloch is perhaps best known for his scholarly contributions in the realm of religion. "The Religion of the Ancient Celts" stands as a seminal work in the study of Celtic religion and mythology. His meticulous research and insightful analysis shed light on the spiritual beliefs and practices of the ancient Celtic peoples, enriching our understanding of this important historical and cultural aspect. Throughout his career, J. A. MacCulloch's dedication to rigorous research and his ability to present complex subjects in a readable manner earned him recognition as a respected scholar.

CONTENTS

PREFACE 7

CHAPTER I
   INTRODUCTORY 9

CHAPTER II
   THE CELTIC PEOPLE 14

CHAPTER III
   THE GODS OF GAUL AND THE CONTINENTAL CELTS 25

CHAPTER IV
   THE IRISH MYTHOLOGICAL CYCLE 46

CHAPTER V
   THE TUATHA DÉ DANANN 57

CHAPTER VI
   THE GODS OF THE BRYTHONS 83

CHAPTER VII
   THE CÚCHULAINN CYCLE 108

CHAPTER VIII
   THE FIONN SAGA. 119

CHAPTER IX
   GODS AND MEN 130

CHAPTER X
   THE CULT OF THE DEAD 135

CHAPTER XI
   PRIMITIVE NATURE WORSHIP 140

CHAPTER XII
   RIVER AND WELL WORSHIP 149

CHAPTER XIII
TREE AND PLANT WORSHIP 163

CHAPTER XIV
ANIMAL WORSHIP 171

CHAPTER XV
COSMOGONY 185

CHAPTER XVI
SACRIFICE, PRAYER, AND DIVINATION 190

CHAPTER XVII
TABU 206

CHAPTER XVIII
FESTIVALS 209

CHAPTER XIX
ACCESSORIES OF CULT 226

CHAPTER XX
THE DRUIDS 237

CHAPTER XXI
MAGIC 257

CHAPTER XXII
THE STATE OF THE DEAD 268

CHAPTER XXIII
REBIRTH AND TRANSMIGRATION 279

CHAPTER XXIV
ELYSIUM 290

INDEX 312

PREFACE

The scientific study of ancient Celtic religion is a thing of recent growth. As a result of the paucity of materials for such a study, earlier writers indulged in the wildest speculative flights and connected the religion with the distant East, or saw in it the remains of a monotheistic faith or a series of esoteric doctrines veiled under polytheistic cults. With the works of MM. Gaidoz, Bertrand, and D'Arbois de Jubainville in France, as well as by the publication of Irish texts by such scholars as Drs. Windisch and Stokes, a new era may be said to have dawned, and a flood of light was poured upon the scanty remains of Celtic religion. In this country the place of honour among students of that religion belongs to Sir John Rh[^y]s, whose Hibbert Lectures On the Origin and Growth of Religion as illustrated by Celtic Heathendom (1886) was an epoch-making work. Every student of the subject since that time feels the immense debt which he owes to the indefatigable researches and the brilliant suggestions of Sir John Rh[^y]s, and I would be ungrateful if I did not record my indebtedness to him. In his Hibbert Lectures, and in his later masterly work on The Arthurian Legend, however, he took the standpoint of the "mythological" school, and tended to see in the old stories myths of the sun and dawn and the darkness, and in the divinities sun-gods and dawn-goddesses and a host of dark personages of supernatural character. The present writer, studying the subject rather from an anthropological point of view and in the light of modern folk survivals, has found himself in disagreement with Sir John Rh[^y]s on more than one occasion. But he is convinced that Sir John would be the last person to resent this, and that, in spite of his mythological interpretations, his Hibbert Lectures must remain as a source of inspiration to all Celtic students. More recently the studies of M. Salomon Reinach and of M. Dottin, and the valuable little book on Celtic Religion, by Professor Anwyl, have broken fresh ground. 1

In this book I have made use of all the available sources, and have endeavoured to study the subject from the comparative point of view and in the light of the anthropological method. I have also interpreted the earlier cults by means of recent folk-survivals over the Celtic area wherever it has seemed legitimate to do so. The results are summarised in the introductory chapter of the work, and students of religion, and especially of Celtic religion, must judge how far they form a true interpretation of the earlier faith of our Celtic forefathers, much of which resembles primitive religion and folk-belief everywhere.

Unfortunately no Celt left an account of his own religion, and we are left to our own interpretations, more or less valid, of the existing materials, and to the light shed on them by the comparative study of religions. As this book was written during a long residence in the Isle of Skye, where the old language of the people still survives, and where the genius loci speaks everywhere of things remote and strange, it may have been easier to attempt to realise the ancient religion there than in a busier or more prosaic place. Yet at every point I have felt how much would have been gained could an old Celt or Druid have revisited his former haunts, and permitted me to question him on a hundred matters which must remain obscure. But this, alas, might not be!

I have to thank Miss Turner and Miss Annie Gilchrist for valuable help rendered in the work of research, and the London Library for obtaining for me several works not already in its possession. Its stores are an invaluable aid to all students working at a distance from libraries.

J.A. MACCULLOCH.

THE RECTORY,

BRIDGE OF ALLAN,

October 1911.

Footnote 1: See also my article "Celts" in Hastings' Encyclopædia of Religion and Ethics, vol. iii.

CHAPTER I
INTRODUCTORY

To summon a dead religion from its forgotten grave and to make it tell its story, would require an enchanter's wand. Other old faiths, of Egypt, Babylon, Greece, Rome, are known to us. But in their case liturgies, myths, theogonies, theologies, and the accessories of cult, remain to yield their report of the outward form of human belief and aspiration. How scanty, on the other hand, are the records of Celtic religion! The bygone faith of a people who have inspired the world with noble dreams must be constructed painfully, and often in fear and trembling, out of fragmentary and, in many cases, transformed remains.

We have the surface observations of classical observers, dedications in the Romano-Celtic area to gods mostly assimilated to the gods of the conquerors, figured monuments mainly of the same period, coins, symbols, place and personal names. For the Irish Celts there is a mass of written material found mainly in eleventh and twelfth century MSS. Much of this, in spite of alteration and excision, is based on divine and heroic myths, and it also contains occasional notices of ritual. From Wales come documents like the Mabinogion, and strange poems the personages of which are ancient gods transformed, but which tell nothing of rite or cult. 2 Valuable hints are furnished by early ecclesiastical documents, but more important is existing folk-custom, which preserves so much of the old cult, though it has lost its meaning to those who now use it. Folk-tales may also be inquired of, if we discriminate between what in them is Celtic and what is universal. Lastly, Celtic burial-mounds and other remains yield their testimony to ancient belief and custom.

From these sources we try to rebuild Celtic paganism and to guess at its inner spirit, though we are working in the twilight on a heap of fragments. No Celt has left us a record of his faith and practice, and the unwritten poems of the Druids died with them. Yet from these fragments we see the Celt as the seeker after God, linking himself by strong ties to the unseen, and eager to conquer the unknown by religious rite or magic art. For the things of the spirit have never appealed in vain to the Celtic soul, and long ago classical observers were struck with the religiosity of the Celts. They neither forgot nor transgressed the law of the gods, and they thought that no good befell men apart from their will. 3 The submission of the Celts to the Druids shows how they welcomed authority in matters of religion, and all Celtic regions have been characterised by religious devotion, easily passing over to superstition, and by loyalty to ideals and lost causes. The Celts were born dreamers, as their exquisite Elysium belief will show, and much that is spiritual and romantic in more than one European literature is due to them.

The analogy of religious evolution in other faiths helps us in reconstructing that of the Celts. Though no historic Celtic group was racially pure, the profound influence of the Celtic temperament soon "Celticised" the religious contributions of the non-Celtic element which may already have had many Celtic parallels. Because a given Celtic rite or belief seems to be "un-Aryan," it need not necessarily be borrowed. The Celts had a savage past, and, conservative as they were, they kept much of it alive. Our business, therefore, lies with Celtic religion as a whole. These primitive elements were there before the Celts migrated from the old "Aryan" home; yet since they appear in Celtic religion to the end, we speak of them as Celtic. The earliest aspect of that religion, before the Celts became a separate people, was a cult of nature spirits, or of the life manifested in nature. But men and women probably had separate cults, and, of the two, perhaps that of the latter is more important. As hunters, men worshipped the animals they slew, apologising to them for the slaughter. This apologetic attitude, found with all primitive hunters, is of the nature of a cult. Other animals, too sacred to be slain, would be preserved and worshipped, the cult giving rise to domestication and pastoral life, with totemism as a probable factor. Earth, producing vegetation, was the fruitful mother; but since the origin of agriculture is mainly due to women, the Earth cult would be practised by them, as well as, later, that of vegetation and corn spirits, all regarded as female. As men began to interest themselves in agriculture, they would join in the female cults, probably with the result of changing the sex of the spirits worshipped. An Earth-god would take the place of the Earth-mother, or stand as her consort or son. Vegetation and corn spirits would often become male, though many spirits, even when they were exalted into divinities, remained female.

With the growth of religion the vaguer spirits tended to become gods and goddesses, and worshipful animals to become anthropomorphic divinities, with the animals as their symbols, attendants, or victims. And as the cult of vegetation spirits centred in the ritual of planting and sowing, so the cult of the divinities of growth centred in great seasonal and agricultural festivals, in which the key to the growth of Celtic religion is to be found. But the migrating Celts, conquering new lands, evolved divinities of war; and here the old female influence is still at work, since many of these are female. In spite of possessing so many local war-gods, the Celts were not merely men of war. Even the equites engaged in war only when occasion arose, and agriculture as well as pastoral industry was constantly practised, both in Gaul and Britain, before the conquest. 4 In Ireland, the belief in the dependence of fruitfulness upon the king, shows to what extent agriculture flourished there. 5 Music, poetry, crafts, and trade gave rise to culture divinities, perhaps evolved from gods of growth, since later myths attributed to them both the origin of arts and crafts, and the introduction of domestic animals among men. Possibly some culture gods had been worshipful animals, now worshipped as gods, who had given these animals to man. Culture-goddesses still held their place among culture-gods, and were regarded as their mothers. The prominence of these divinities shows that the Celts were more than a race of warriors.

The pantheon was thus a large one, but on the whole the divinities of growth were more generally important. The older nature spirits and divine animals were never quite forgotten, especially by the folk, who also preserved the old rituals of vegetation spirits, while the gods of growth were worshipped at the great festivals. Yet in essence the lower and the higher cults were one and the same, and, save where Roman influence destroyed Celtic religion, the older primitive strands are everywhere apparent. The temperament of the Celt kept him close to nature, and he never quite dropped the primitive elements of his religion. Moreover, the early influence of female cults of female spirits and goddesses remained to the end as another predominant factor.

Most of the Celtic divinities were local in character, each tribe possessing its own group, each god having functions similar to those of other groups. Some, however, had or gained a more universal character, absorbing divinities with similar functions. Still this local character must be borne in mind. The numerous divinities of Gaul, with differing names—but, judging by their assimilation to the same Roman divinity, similar functions, are best understood as gods of local groups. This is probably true also of Britain and Ireland. But those gods worshipped far and wide over the Celtic area may be gods of the undivided Celts, or gods of some dominant Celtic group extending their influence on all sides, or, in some cases, popular gods whose cult passed beyond the tribal bounds. If it seem precarious to see such close similarity in the local gods of a people extending right across Europe, appeal can be made to the influence of the Celtic temperament, producing everywhere the same results, and to the homogeneity of Celtic civilisation, save in local areas, e.g. the South of Gaul. Moreover, the comparison of the various testimonies of onlookers points to a general similarity, while the permanence of the primitive elements in Celtic religion must have tended to keep it everywhere the same. Though in Gaul we have only inscriptions and in Ireland only distorted myths, yet those testimonies, as well as the evidence of folk-survivals in both regions, point to the similarity of religious phenomena. The Druids, as a more or less organised priesthood, would assist in preserving the general likeness.

Thus the primitive nature-spirits gave place to greater or lesser gods, each with his separate department and functions. Though growing civilisation tended to separate them from the soil, they never quite lost touch with it. In return for man's worship and sacrifices, they gave life and increase, victory, strength, and skill. But these sacrifices, had been and still often were rites in which the representative of a god was slain. Some divinities were worshipped over a wide area, most were gods of local groups, and there were spirits of every place, hill, wood, and stream. Magic rites mingled with the cult, but both were guided by an organised priesthood. And as the Celts believed in unseen gods, so they believed in an unseen region whither they passed after death.

Our knowledge of the higher side of Celtic religion is practically a blank, since no description of the inner spiritual life has come down to us. How far the Celts cultivated religion in our sense of the term, or had glimpses of Monotheism, or were troubled by a deep sense of sin, is unknown. But a people whose spiritual influence has later been so great, must have had glimpses of these things. Some of them must have known the thirst of the soul for God, or sought a higher ethical standard than that of their time. The enthusiastic reception of Christianity, the devotion of the early Celtic saints, and the character of the old Celtic church, all suggest this.

The relation of the Celtic church to paganism was mainly intolerant, though not wholly so. It often adopted the less harmful customs of the past, merging pagan festivals in its own, founding churches on the sites of the old cult, dedicating sacred wells to a saint. A saint would visit the tomb of a pagan to hear an old epic rehearsed, or would call up pagan heroes from hell and give them a place in paradise. Other saints recall dead heroes from the Land of the Blessed, and learn the nature of that wonderland and the heroic deeds

"Of the old days, which seem to be

Much older than any history

That is written in any book."

Reading such narratives, we gain a lesson in the fine spirit of Christian tolerance and Christian sympathy.

Footnote 2: Some writers saw in the bardic poetry a Druidic-esoteric system and traces of a cult practised secretly by the bards—the "Neo-Druidic heresy"; see Davies, Myth. of the Brit. Druids, 1809; Herbert, The Neo-Druidic Heresy, 1838. Several French writers saw in "Druidism" a monotheistic faith, veiled under polytheism.

Footnote 3: Livy, v. 46; Cæsar, vi. 16; Dion. Hal. vii. 70; Arrian, Cyneg. xxxv. 1.

Footnote 4: Cæsar, vi. 15, cf. v. 12, "having waged war, remained there and cultivated the lands."

Footnote 5: Cf. Pliny, HN xvii. 7, xviii. 18 on the wheeled ploughs and agricultural methods of Gauls and Britons. Cf. also Strabo, iv. 1. 2, iv. 5. 5; Girald. Camb. Top. Hib. i. 4, Descr. Camb. i. 8; Joyce, SH ii. 264.

CHAPTER II
THE CELTIC PEOPLE

Scrutiny reveals the fact that Celtic-speaking peoples are of differing types—short and dark as well as tall and fairer Highlanders or Welshmen, short, broad-headed Bretons, various types of Irishmen. Men with Norse names and Norse aspect "have the Gaelic." But all alike have the same character and temperament, a striking witness to the influence which the character as well as the language of the Celts, whoever they were, made on all with whom they mingled. Ethnologically there may not be a Celtic race, but something was handed down from the days of comparative Celtic purity which welded different social elements into a common type, found often where no Celtic tongue is now spoken. It emerges where we least expect it, and the stolid Anglo-Saxon may suddenly awaken to something in himself due to a forgotten Celtic strain in his ancestry.

Two main theories of Celtic origins now hold the field:

(1) The Celts are identified with the progenitors of the short, brachycephalic "Alpine race" of Central Europe, existing there in Neolithic times, after their migrations from Africa and Asia. The type is found among the Slavs, in parts of Germany and Scandinavia, and in modern France in the region of Cæsar's "Celtæ," among the Auvergnats, the Bretons, and in Lozère and Jura. Representatives of the type have been found in Belgian and French Neolithic graves. 6 Professor Sergi calls this the "Eurasiatic race," and, contrary to general opinion, identifies it with the Aryans, a savage people, inferior to the dolichocephalic Mediterranean race, whose language they Aryanised. 7 Professor Keane thinks that they were themselves an Aryanised folk before reaching Europe, who in turn gave their acquired Celtic and Slavic speech to the preceding masses. Later came the Belgæ, Aryans, who acquired the Celtic speech of the people they conquered. 8

Broca assumed that the dark, brachycephalic people whom he identified with Cæsar's "Celtæ," differed from the Belgæ, were conquered by them, and acquired the language of their conquerors, hence wrongly called Celtic by philologists. The Belgæ were tall and fair, and overran Gaul, except Aquitaine, mixing generally with the Celtæ, who in Cæsar's time had thus an infusion of Belgic blood. 9 But before this conquest, the Celtæ had already mingled with the aboriginal dolichocephalic folk of Gaul, Iberians, or Mediterraneans of Professor Sergi. The latter had apparently remained comparatively pure from admixture in Aquitaine, and are probably the Aquitani of Cæsar. 10

But were the short, brachycephalic folk Celts? Cæsar says the people who call themselves "Celtæ" were called Gauls by the Romans, and Gauls, according to classical writers, were tall and fair. 11 Hence the Celtæ were not a short, dark race, and Cæsar himself says that Gauls (including Celtæ) looked with contempt on the short Romans. 12 Strabo also says that Celtæ and Belgæ had the same Gaulish appearance, i.e. tall and fair. Cæsar's statement that Aquitani, Galli, and Belgæ differ in language, institutions, and laws is vague and unsupported by evidence, and may mean as to language no more than a difference in dialects. This is also suggested by Strabo's words, Celtæ and Belgæ "differ a little" in language. 13 No classical writer describes the Celts as short and dark, but the reverse. Short, dark people would have been called Iberians, without respect to skulls. Classical observers were not craniologists. The short, brachycephalic type is now prominent in France, because it has always been so, eliminating the tall, fair Celtic type. Conquering Celts, fewer in number than the broad and narrow-headed aborigines, intermarried or made less lasting alliances with them. In course of time the type of the more numerous race was bound to prevail. Even in Cæsar's day the latter probably outnumbered the tall and fair Celts, who had, however, Celticised them. But classical writers, who knew the true Celt as tall and fair, saw that type only, just as every one, on first visiting France or Germany, sees his generalised type of Frenchman or German everywhere. Later, he modifies his opinion, but this the classical observers did not do. Cæsar's campaigns must have drained Gaul of many tall and fair Celts. This, with the tendency of dark types to out-number fair types in South and Central Europe, may help to explain the growing prominence of the dark type, though the tall, fair type is far from uncommon. 14

(2) The second theory, already anticipated, sees in Gauls and Belgæ a tall, fair Celtic folk, speaking a Celtic language, and belonging to the race which stretched from Ireland to Asia Minor, from North Germany to the Po, and were masters of Teutonic tribes till they were driven by them from the region between Elbe and Rhine. 15 Some Belgic tribes claimed a Germanic ancestry, 16 but "German" was a word seldom used with precision, and in this case may not mean Teutonic. The fair hair of this people has made many suppose that they were akin to the Teutons. But fairness is relative, and the dark Romans may have called brown hair fair, while they occasionally distinguished between the "fair" Gauls and fairer Germans.

Their institutions and their religions (pace Professor Rh[^y]s) differed, and though they were so long in contact the names of their gods and priests are unlike. 17 Their languages, again, though of "Aryan" stock, differ more from each other than does Celtic from Italic, pointing to a long period of Italo-Celtic unity, before Italiotes and Celts separated, and Celts came in contact with Teutons. 18 The typical German differs in mental and moral qualities from the typical Celt. Contrast an east country Scot, descendant of Teutonic stock, with a West Highlander, and the difference leaps to the eyes. Celts and Germans of history differ, then, in relative fairness, character, religion, and language.

The tall, blonde Teutonic type of the Row graves is dolichocephalic. Was the Celtic type (assuming that Broca's "Celts" were not true Celts) dolicho or brachy? Broca thinks the Belgæ or "Kymri" were dolichocephalic, but all must agree with him that the skulls are too few to generalise from. Celtic iron-age skulls in Britain are dolichocephalic, perhaps a recrudescence of the aboriginal type. Broca's "Kymric" skulls are mesocephalic; this he attributes to crossing with the short round-heads. The evidence is too scanty for generalisation, while the Walloons, perhaps descendants of the Belgæ, have a high index, and some Gauls of classical art are broad-headed. 19

Skulls of the British round barrows (early Celtic Bronze Age) are mainly broad, the best specimens showing affinity to Neolithic brachycephalic skulls from Grenelle (though their owners were 5 inches shorter), Selaigneaux, and Borreby. 20 Dr. Beddoe thinks that the narrow-skulled Belgæ on the whole reinforced the meso- or brachycephalic round barrow folk in Britain. Dr. Thurnam identifies the latter with the Belgæ (Broca's Kymri), and thinks that Gaulish skulls were round, with beetling brows. 21 Professors Ripley and Sergi, disregarding their difference in stature and higher cephalic index, identify them with the short Alpine race (Broca's Celts). This is negatived by Mr. Keane. 22 Might not both, however, have originally sprung from a common stock and reached Europe at different times? 23

But do a few hundred skulls justify these far-reaching conclusions regarding races enduring for thousands of years? At some very remote period there may have been a Celtic type, as at some further period there may have been an Aryan type. But the Celts, as we know them, must have mingled with the aborigines of Europe and become a mixed race, though preserving and endowing others with their racial and mental characteristics. Some Gauls or Belgæ were dolichocephalic, to judge by their skulls, others were brachycephalic, while their fairness was a relative term. Classical observers probably generalised from the higher classes, of a purer type; they tell us nothing of the people. But the higher classes may have had varying skulls, as well as stature and colour of hair, 24 and Irish texts tell of a tall, fair, blue-eyed stock, and a short, dark, dark-eyed stock, in Ireland. Even in those distant ages we must consider the people on whom the Celts impressed their characteristics, as well as the Celts themselves. What happened on the Eurasian steppe, the hypothetical cradle of the "Aryans," whence the Celts came "stepping westwards," seems clear to some, but in truth is a book sealed with seven seals. The men whose Aryan speech was to dominate far and wide may already have possessed different types of skull, and that age was far from "the very beginning."

Thus the Celts before setting out on their Wanderjahre may already have been a mixed race, even if their leaders were of purer stock. But they had the bond of common speech, institutions, and religion, and they formed a common Celtic type in Central and Western Europe. Intermarriage with the already mixed Neolithic folk of Central Europe produced further removal from the unmixed Celtic racial type; but though both reacted on each other as far as language, custom, and belief were concerned, on the whole the Celtic elements predominated in these respects. The Celtic migration into Gaul produced further racial mingling with descendants of the old palæolithic stock, dolichocephalic Iberians and Ligurians, and brachycephalic swarthy folk (Broca's Celts). Thus even the first Celtic arrivals in Britain, the Goidels, were a people of mixed race, though probably relatively purer than the late coming Brythons, the latest of whom had probably mingled with the Teutons. Hence among Celtic-speaking folk or their descendants—short, dark, broad-beaded Bretons, tall, fair or rufous Highlanders, tall chestnut-haired Welshmen or Irishmen, Highlanders of Norse descent, short, dark, narrow-headed Highlanders, Irishmen, and Welshmen—there is a common Celtic facies, the result of old Celtic characteristics powerful enough so to impress themselves on such varied peoples in spite of what they gave to the Celtic incomers. These peoples became Celtic, and Celtic in speech and character they have remained, even where ancestral physical types are reasserting themselves. The folk of a Celtic type, whether pre-Celtic, Celtic, or Norse, have all spoken a Celtic language and exhibit the same old Celtic characteristics—vanity, loquacity, excitability, fickleness, imagination, love of the romantic, fidelity, attachment to family ties, sentimental love of their country, religiosity passing over easily to superstition, and a comparatively high degree of sexual morality. Some of these traits were already noted by classical observers.

Celtic speech had early lost the initial p of old Indo-European speech, except in words beginning with pt and, perhaps, ps. Celtic pare (Lat. præ) became are, met with in Aremorici, "the dwellers by the sea," Arecluta, "by the Clyde," the region watered by the Clyde. Irish athair, Manx ayr, and Irish iasg, represent respectively Latin pater and piscis. P occurring between vowels was also lost, e.g. Irish caora, "sheep," is from kaperax; for, "upon" (Lat. super), from uper. This change took place before the Goidelic Celts broke away and invaded Britain in the tenth century B.C., but while Celts and Teutons were still in contact, since Teutons borrowed words with initial p, e.g. Gothic fairguni, "mountain," from Celtic percunion, later Ercunio, the Hercynian forest. The loss must have occurred before 1000 B.C. But after the separation of the Goidelic group a further change took place. Goidels preserved the sound represented by qu, or more simply by c or ch, but this was changed into p by the remaining continental Celts, who carried with them into Gaul, Spain, Italy, and Britain (the Brythons) words in which q became p. The British Epidii is from Gaulish epos, "horse," which is in Old Irish ech (Lat. equus). The Parisii take their name from Qarisii, the Pictones or Pictavi of Poictiers from Pictos (which in the plural Pidi gives us "Picts"), derived from quicto. This change took place after the Goidelic invasion of Britain in the tenth century B.C. On the other hand, some continental Celts may later have regained the power of pronouncing q. In Gaul the q of Sequana (Seine) was not changed to p, and a tribe dwelling on its banks was called the Sequani. This assumes that Sequana was a pre-Celtic word, possibly Ligurian. 25 Professor Rh[^y]s thinks, however, that Goidelic tribes, identified by him with Cæsar's Celtæ, existed in Gaul and Spain before the coming of the Galli, and had preserved q in their speech. To them we owe Sequana, as well as certain names with q in Spain. 26 This at least is certain, that Goidelic Celts of the q group occupied Gaul and Spain before reaching Britain and Ireland. Irish tradition and archæological data confirm this. But whether their descendants were represented by Cæsar's "Celtæ" must be uncertain. Celtæ and Galli, according to Cæsar, were one and the same, 28 and must have had the same general form of speech.

The dialects of Goidelic speech—Irish, Manx, Gaelic, and that of the continental Goidels—preserved the q sound; those of Gallo-Brythonic speech—Gaulish, Breton, Welsh, Cornish—changed q into p. The speech of the Picts, perhaps connected with the Pictones of Gaul, also had this p sound. Who, then, were the Picts? According to Professor Rh[^y]s they were pre-Aryans, 29 but they must have been under the influence of Brythonic Celts. Dr. Skene regarded them as Goidels speaking a Goidelic dialect with Brythonic forms. 30 Mr. Nicholson thinks they were Goidels who had preserved the Indo-European p. 31 But might they not be descendants of a Brythonic group, arriving early in Britain and driven northwards by newcomers? Professor Windisch and Dr. Stokes regard them as Celts, allied to the Brythons rather than to the Goidels, the phonetics of their speech resembling those of Welsh rather than Irish. 32

The theory of an early Goidelic occupation of Britain has been contested by Professor Meyer, 33 who holds that the first Goidels reached Britain from Ireland in the second century, while Dr. MacBain 34 was of the opinion that England, apart from Wales and Cornwall, knew no Goidels, the place-names being Brythonic. But unless all Goidels reached Ireland from Gaul or Spain, as some did, Britain was more easily reached than Ireland by migrating Goidels from the Continent. Prominent Goidelic place-names would become Brythonic, but insignificant places would retain their Goidelic form, and to these we must look for decisive evidence. 35 A Goidelic occupation by the ninth century B.C. is suggested by the name "Cassiterides" (a word of the q group) applied to Britain. If the Goidels occupied Britain first, they may have called their land Qretanis or Qritanis, which Pictish invaders would change to Pretanis, found in Welsh "Ynys Pridain," Pridain's Isle, or Isle of the Picts, "pointing to the original underlying the Greek [Greek: Pretanikai Nêsoi] or Pictish Isles," 36 though the change may be due to continental p Celts trading with q Celts in Britain. With the Pictish occupation would agree the fact that Irish Goidels called the Picts who came to Ireland Cruithne=Qritani=Pre-tani. In Ireland they almost certainly adopted Goidelic speech.

Whether or not all the Pictish invaders of Britain were called "Pictavi," this word or Picti, perhaps from quicto (Irish cicht, "engraver"), 37 became a general name for this people. Q had been changed into p on the Continent; hence "Pictavi" or "Pictones," "the tattooed men," those who "engraved" figures on their bodies, as the Picts certainly did. Dispossessed and driven north by incoming Brythons and Belgæ, they later became the virulent enemies of Rome. In 306 Eumenius describes all the northern tribes as "Caledonii and other Picts," while some of the tribes mentioned by Ptolemy have Brythonic names or names with Gaulish cognates. Place-names in the Pictish area, personal names in the Pictish chronicle, and Pictish names like "Peanfahel," 38 have Brythonic affinities. If the Picts spoke a Brythonic dialect, S. Columba's need of an interpreter when preaching to them would be explained. 39 Later the Picts were conquered by Irish Goidels, the Scotti. The Picts, however, must already have mingled with aboriginal peoples and with Goidels, if these were already in Britain, and they may have adopted their supposed non-Aryan customs from the aborigines. On the other hand, the matriarchate seems at one time to have been Celtic, and it may have been no more than a conservative survival in the Pictish royal house, as it was elsewhere. Britons, as well as Caledonii, had wives in common. 41 As to tattooing, it was practised by the Scotti ("the scarred and painted men"?), and the Britons dyed themselves with woad, while what seem to be tattoo marks appear on faces on Gaulish coins. 42 Tattooing, painting, and scarifying the body are varieties of one general custom, and little stress can be laid on Pictish tattooing as indicating a racial difference. Its purpose may have been ornamental, or possibly to impart an aspect of fierceness, or the figures may have been totem marks, as they are elsewhere. Finally, the description of the Caledonii, a Pictish people, possessing flaming hair and mighty limbs, shows that they differed from the short, dark pre-Celtic folk. 43

The Pictish problem must remain obscure, a welcome puzzle to antiquaries, philologists, and ethnologists. Our knowledge of Pictish religion is too scanty for the interpretation of Celtic religion to be affected by it. But we know that the Picts offered sacrifice before war—a Celtic custom, and had Druids, as also had the Celts.

The earliest Celtic "kingdom" was in the region between the upper waters of the Rhine, the Elbe, and the Danube, where probably in Neolithic times the formation of their Celtic speech as a distinctive language began. Here they first became known to the Greeks, probably as a semi-mythical people, the Hyperboreans—the folk dwelling beyond the Ripœan mountains whence Boreas blew—with whom Hecatæus in the fourth century identifies them. But they were now known as Celts, and their territory as Celtica, while "Galatas" was used as a synonym of "Celtæ," in the third century B.C. 44 The name generally applied by the Romans to the Celts was "Galli" a term finally confined by them to the people of Gaul. 45 Successive bands of Celts went forth from this comparatively restricted territory, until the Celtic "empire" for some centuries before 300 B.C. included the British Isles, parts of the Iberian peninsula, Gaul, North Italy, Belgium, Holland, great part of Germany, and Austria. When the German tribes revolted, Celtic bands appeared in Asia Minor, and remained there as the Galatian Celts. Archæological discoveries with a Celtic facies have been made in most of these lands but even more striking is the witness of place-names. Celtic dunon, a fort or castle (the Gaelic dun), is found in compound names from Ireland to Southern Russia. Magos, "a field," is met with in Britain, France, Switzerland, Prussia, Italy, and Austria. River and mountain names familiar in Britain occur on the Continent. The Pennine range of Cumberland has the same name as the Appenines. Rivers named for their inherent divinity, devos, are found in Britain and on the Continent—Dee, Deva, etc.

Besides this linguistic, had the Celts also a political unity over their great "empire," under one head? Such a unity certainly did not prevail from Ireland to the Balkan peninsula, but it prevailed over a large part of the Celtic area. Livy, following Timagenes, who perhaps cited a lost Celtic epos, speaks of king Ambicatus ruling over the Celts from Spain to Germany, and sending his sister's sons, Bellovesus and Segovesus, with many followers, to found new colonies in Italy and the Hercynian forest. 46 Mythical as this may be, it suggests the hegemony of one tribe or one chief over other tribes and chiefs, for Livy says that the sovereign power rested with the Bituriges who appointed the king of Celticum, viz. Ambicatus. Some such unity is necessary to explain Celtic power in the ancient world, and it was made possible by unity of race or at least of the congeries of Celticised peoples, by religious solidarity, and probably by regular gatherings of all the kings or chiefs. If the Druids were a Celtic priesthood at this time, or already formed a corporation as they did later in Gaul, they must have endeavoured to form and preserve such a unity. And if it was never so compact as Livy's words suggest, it must have been regarded as an ideal by the Celts or by their poets, Ambicatus serving as a central figure round which the ideas of empire crystallised. The hegemony existed in Gaul, where the Arverni and their king claimed power over the other tribes, and where the Romans tried to weaken the Celtic unity by opposing to them the Aedni. 47 In Belgium the hegemony was in the hands of the Suessiones, to whose king Belgic tribes in Britain submitted. 48 In Ireland the "high king" was supreme over other smaller kings, and in Galatia the unity of the tribes was preserved by a council with regular assemblies. 49

The diffusion of the Ambicatus legend would help to preserve unity by recalling the mythic greatness of the past. The Boii and Insubri appealed to transalpine Gauls for aid by reminding them of the deeds of their ancestors. 50 Nor would the Druids omit to infuse into their pupils' minds the sentiment of national greatness. For this and for other reasons, the Romans, to whom "the sovereignty of all Gaul" was an obnoxious watch-word, endeavoured to suppress them. 51 But the Celts were too widely scattered ever to form a compact empire. 52 The Roman empire extended itself gradually in the consciousness of its power; the cohesion of the Celts in an empire or under one king was made impossible by their migrations and diffusion. Their unity, such as it was, was broken by the revolt of the Teutonic tribes, and their subjugation was completed by Rome. The dreams of wide empire remained dreams. For the Celts, in spite of their vigour, have been a race of dreamers, their conquests in later times, those of the spirit rather than of the mailed fist. Their superiority has consisted in imparting to others their characteristics; organised unity and a vast empire could never be theirs.

Footnote 6: Ripley, Races of Europe; Wilser, L'Anthropologie, xiv. 494; Collignon, ibid. 1-20; Broca, Rev. d'Anthrop. ii. 589 ff.

Footnote 7: Sergi, The Mediterranean Race, 241 ff., 263 ff.

Footnote 8: Keane, Man, Past and Present, 511 ff., 521, 528.

Footnote 9: Broca, Mem. d'Anthrop. i. 370 ff. Hovelacque thinks, with Keane, that the Gauls learned Celtic from the dark round-heads. But Galatian and British Celts, who had never been in contact with the latter, spoke Celtic. See Holmes, Cæsar's Conquest of Gaul, 311-312.

Footnote 10: Cæsar, i. 1; Collignon, Mem. Soc. d'Anthrop. de Paris, 3me ser. i. 67.

Footnote 11: Cæsar, i. 1.

Footnote 12: Cæsar, ii. 30.

Footnote 13: Cæsar, i. 1; Strabo, iv. 1. 1.

Footnote 14: Cf. Holmes, 295; Beddoe, Scottish Review, xix. 416.

Footnote 15: D'Arbois, Les Celtes, 175.

Footnote 16: Cæsar, ii. 4; Strabo, vii. 1. 2. Germans are taller and fairer than Gauls; Tacitus, Agric. ii. Cf. Beddoe, JAI xx. 354-355.

Footnote 17: D'Arbois, PH ii. 374. Welsh Gwydion and Teutonic Wuotan may have the same root, . Celtic Taranis has been compared to Donar, but there is no connection, and Taranis was not certainly a thunder-god. Much of the rrrfolk-religion was alike, but this applies to folk-religion everywhere.

Footnote 18: D'Arbois, ii. 251.

Footnote 19: Beddoe, L'Anthropologie, v. 516. Tall, fair, and highly brachycephalic types are still found in France, ibid. i. 213; Bortrand-Reinach, Les Celtes, 39.

Footnote 20: Beddoe, 516; L'Anthrop., v. 63; Taylor, 81; Greenwell, British Barrows, 680.

Footnote 21: Fort. Rev. xvi. 328; Mem. of London Anthr. Soc., 1865.

Footnote 22: Ripley, 309; Sergi, 243; Keane, 529; Taylor, 112.

Footnote 23: Taylor, 122, 295.

Footnote 24: The Walloons are both dark and fair.

Footnote 25: D'Arbois, PH ii. 132.

Footnote 26: Rh[^y]s, Proc. Phil. Soc. 1891; "Celtæ and Galli," Proc. Brit. Acad. ii. D'Arbois points out that we do not know that these words are Celtic (RC xii, 478).

Footnote 28: Cæsar, i. 1.

Footnote 29: CB 4 160.

Footnote 30: Skene, i. ch. 8; see p. 135.

Footnote 31: ZCP iii. 308; Keltic Researches.

Footnote 32: Windisch, "Kelt. Sprachen," Ersch-Gruber's Encylopädie; Stokes, Linguistic Value of the Irish Annals.

Footnote 33: THSC 1895-1896, 55 f.

Footnote 34: CM xii. 434.

Footnote 35: In the Isle of Skye, where, looking at names of prominent places alone, Norse derivatives are to Gaelic as 3 to 2, they are as 1 to 5 when names of insignificant places, untouched by Norse influence, are included.

Footnote 36: Rh[^y]s, CB 4 241.

Footnote 37: D'Arbois, Les Celtes, 22.

Footnote 38: Bede, Eccl. Hist. i. 12.

Footnote 39: Adamnan, Vita S. Col.

Footnote 41: Dio Cass. lxxvi. 12; Cæsar, v. 14. See p. 223.

Footnote 42: Isidore, Etymol. ix. 2, 103; Rh[^y]s, CB 242-243; Cæsar, v. 14; Nicholson, ZCP in. 332.

Footnote 43: Tacitus, Agric. ii.

Footnote 44: If Celtæ is from qelo, "to raise," it may mean "the lofty," just as many savages call themselves "the men," par excellence. Rh[^y]s derives it from qel, "to slay," and gives it the sense of "warriors." See Holder, s.v.; Stokes, US 83. Galatæ is from gala (Irish gal), "bravery." Hence perhaps "warriors."

Footnote 45: "Galli" may be connected with "Galatæ," but D'Arbois denies this. For all these titles see his PH ii. 396 ff.

Footnote 46: Livy, v. 31 f.; D'Arbois, PH ii. 304, 391.

Footnote 47: Strabo, iv. 10. 3; Cæsar, i. 31, vii. 4; Frag. Hist. Græc. i. 437.

Footnote 48: Cæsar, ii. 4.

Footnote 49: Strabo, xii. 5. 1.

Footnote 50: Polybius, ii. 22.

Footnote 51: Cæsar, i. 2, 1-3.

Footnote 52: On the subject of Celtic unity see Jullian, "Du patriotisme gaulois," RC xxiii. 373.

CHAPTER III
THE GODS OF GAUL AND THE CONTINENTAL CELTS

The passage in which Cæsar sums up the Gaulish pantheon runs: "They worship chiefly the god Mercury; of him there are many symbols, and they regard him as the inventor of all the arts, as the guide of travellers, and as possessing great influence over bargains and commerce. After him they worship Apollo and Mars, Juppiter and Minerva. About these they hold much the same beliefs as other nations. Apollo heals diseases, Minerva teaches the elements of industry and the arts, Juppiter rules over the heavens, Mars directs war.... All the Gauls assert that they are descended from Dispater, their progenitor." 53

As will be seen in this chapter, the Gauls had many other gods than these, while the Roman gods, by whose names Cæsar calls the Celtic divinities, probably only approximately corresponded to them in functions. As the Greeks called by the names of their own gods those of Egypt, Persia, and Babylonia, so the Romans identified Greek, Teutonic, and Celtic gods with theirs. The identification was seldom complete, and often extended only to one particular function or attribute. But, as in Gaul, it was often part of a state policy, and there the fusion of cults was intended to break the power of the Druids. The Gauls seem to have adopted Roman civilisation easily, and to have acquiesced in the process of assimilation of their divinities to those of their conquerors. Hence we have thousands of inscriptions in which a god is called by the name of the Roman deity to whom he was assimilated and by his own Celtic name—Jupiter Taranis, Apollo Grannus, etc. Or sometimes to the name of the Roman god is added a descriptive Celtic epithet or a word derived from a Celtic place-name. Again, since Augustus reinstated the cult of the Lares, with himself as chief Lar, the epithet Augustus was given to all gods to whom the character of the Lares could be ascribed, e.g. Belenos Augustus. Cults of local gods became cults of the genius of the place, coupled with the genius of the emperor. In some cases, however, the native name stands alone. The process was aided by art. Celtic gods are represented after Greco-Roman or Greco-Egyptian models.

Sometimes these carry a native divine symbol, or, in a few cases, the type is purely native, e.g. that of Cernunnos. Thus the native paganism was largely transformed before Christianity appeared in Gaul. Many Roman gods were worshipped as such, not only by the Romans in Gaul, but by the Gauls, and we find there also traces of the Oriental cults affected by the Romans. 54

There were probably in Gaul many local gods, tribal or otherwise, of roads and commerce, of the arts, of healing, etc., who, bearing different names, might easily be identified with each other or with Roman gods. Cæsar's Mercury, Mars, Minerva, etc., probably include many local Minervas, Mars, and Mercuries. There may, however, have been a few great gods common to all Gaul, universally worshipped, besides the numerous local gods, some of whom may have been adopted from the aborigines. An examination of the divine names in Holder's Altceltischer Sprachschatz will show how numerous the local gods of the continental Celts must have been. Professor Anwyl reckons that 270 gods are mentioned once on inscriptions, 24 twice, 11 thrice, 10 four times, 3 five times, 2 seven times, 4 fifteen times, 1 nineteen times (Grannos), and 1 thirty-nine times (Belenos). 55

The god or gods identified with Mercury were very popular in Gaul, as Cæsar's words and the witness of place-names derived from the Roman name of the god show. These had probably supplanted earlier names derived from those of the corresponding native gods. Many temples of the god existed, especially in the region of the Allobrogi, and bronze statuettes of him have been found in abundance. Pliny also describes a colossal statue designed for the Arverni who had a great temple of the god on the Puy de Dôme. 56 Mercury was not necessarily the chief god, and at times, e.g. in war, the native war-gods would be prominent. The native names of the gods assimilated to Mercury are many in number; in some cases they are epithets, derived from the names of places where a local "Mercury" was worshipped, in others they are derived from some function of the gods. 57 One of these titles is Artaios, perhaps cognate with Irish art, "god," or connected with artos, "bear." Professor Rh[^y]s, however, finds its cognate in Welsh âr, "ploughed land," as if one of the god's functions connected him with agriculture. 58 This is supported by another inscription to Mercurius Cultor at Wurtemberg. Local gods of agriculture must thus have been assimilated to Mercury. A god Moccus, "swine," was also identified with Mercury, and the swine was a frequent representative of the corn-spirit or of vegetation divinities in Europe. The flesh of the animal was often mixed with the seed corn or buried in the fields to promote fertility. The swine had been a sacred animal among the Celts, but had apparently become an anthropomorphic god of fertility, Moccus, assimilated to Mercury, perhaps because the Greek

Hermes caused fertility in flocks and herds. Such a god was one of a class whose importance was great among the Celts as an agricultural people.

Commerce, much developed among the settled Gauls, gave rise to a god or gods who guarded roads over which merchants travelled, and boundaries where their transactions took place. Hence we have an inscription from Yorkshire, "To the god who invented roads and paths," while another local god of roads, equated with Mercury, was Cimiacinus. 59

Another god, Ogmíos, a native god of speech, who draws men by chains fastened to the tip of his tongue, is identified in Lucian with Heracles, and is identical with the Goidelic Ogma. 60 Eloquence and speech are important matters among primitive peoples, and this god has more likeness to Mercury as a culture-god than to Heracles, Greek writers speaking of eloquence as binding men with the chains of Hermes.

Several local gods, of agriculture, commerce, and culture, were thus identified with Mercury, and the Celtic Mercury was sometimes worshipped on hilltops, one of the epithets of the god, Dumias, being connected with the Celtic word for hill or mound. Irish gods were also associated with mounds.

Many local gods were identified with Apollo both in his capacity of god of healing and also that of god of light. 61 The two functions are not incompatible, and this is suggested by the name Grannos, god of thermal springs both in Britain and on the Continent. The name is connected with a root which gives words meaning "burning," "shining," etc., and from which comes also Irish grian, "sun." The god is still remembered in a chant sung round bonfires in Auvergne. A sheaf of corn is set on fire, and called "Granno mio," while the people sing, "Granno, my friend; Granno, my father; Granno, my mother." 62 Another god of thermal springs was Borvo, Bormo, or Bormanus, whose name is derived from borvo, whence Welsh berw, "boiling," and is evidently connected with the bubbling of the springs. 63 Votive tablets inscribed Grannos or Borvo show that the offerers desired healing for themselves or others.

The name Belenos found over a wide area, but mainly in Aquileia, comes from belo-s, bright, and probably means "the shining one." It is thus the name of a Celtic sun-god, equated with Apollo in that character. If he is the Belinus referred to by Geoffrey of Monmouth, 64 his cult must have extended into Britain from the Continent, and he is often mentioned by classical writers, while much later Ausonius speaks of his priest in Gaul. 65 Many place and personal names point to the popularity of his cult, and inscriptions show that he, too, was a god of health and of healing-springs. The plant Belinuntia was called after him and venerated for its healing powers. 66 The sun-god's functions of light and fertility easily passed over into those of health-giving, as our study of Celtic festivals will show.

A god with the name Maponos, connected with words denoting "youthfulness," is found in England and Gaul, equated with Apollo, who himself is called Bonus Puer in a Dacian inscription. Another god Mogons or Mogounos, whose name is derived from Mago, "to increase," and suggests the idea of youthful strength, may be a form of the sun-god, though some evidence points to his having been a sky-god. 67

The Celtic Apollo is referred to by classical writers. Diodorus speaks of his circular temple in an island of the Hyperboreans, adorned with votive offerings. The kings of the city where the temple stood, and its overseers, were called "Boreads," and every nineteenth year the god appeared dancing in the sky at the spring equinox. 68 The identifications of the temple with Stonehenge and of the Boreads with the Bards are quite hypothetical. Apollonius says that the Celts regarded the waters of Eridanus as due to the tears of Apollo—probably a native myth attributing the creation of springs and rivers to the tears of a god, equated by the Greeks with Apollo. 69 The Celtic sun-god, as has been seen, was a god of healing springs.

Some sixty names or titles of Celtic war-gods are known, generally equated with Mars. 70 These were probably local tribal divinities regarded as leading their worshippers to battle. Some of the names show that these gods were thought of as mighty warriors, e.g. Caturix, "battle-king," Belatu-Cadros—a common name in Britain—perhaps meaning "comely in slaughter," 71 and Albiorix, "world-king." 72 Another name, Rigisamus, from rix and samus, "like to," gives the idea of "king-like." 73

Toutatis, Totatis, and Tutatis are found in inscriptions from Seckau, York, and Old Carlisle, and may be identified with Lucan's Teutates, who with Taranis and Esus mentioned by him, is regarded as one of three pan-Celtic gods. 74 Had this been the case we should have expected to find many more inscriptions to them. The scholiast on Lucan identifies Teutates now with Mars, now with Mercury. His name is connected with teuta, "tribe," and he is thus a tribal war-god, regarded as the embodiment of the tribe in its warlike capacity.

Neton, a war-god of the Accetani, has a name connected with Irish nia, "warrior," and may be equated with the Irish war-god Nét. Another god, Camulos, known from British and continental inscriptions, and figured on British coins with warlike emblems, has perhaps some connection with Cumal, father of Fionn, though it is uncertain whether Cumal was an Irish divinity. 75

Another god equated with Mars is the Gaulish Braciaca, god of malt. According to classical writers, the Celts were drunken race, and besides importing quantities of wine, they made their own native drinks, e.g. [Greek: chourmi], the Irish cuirm, and braccat, both made from malt (braich). 76 These words, with the Gaulish brace, "spelt," 77 are connected with the name of this god, who was a divine personification of the substance from which the drink was made which produced, according to primitive ideas, the divine frenzy of intoxication. It is not clear why Mars should have been equated with this god.

Cæsar says that the Celtic Juppiter governed heaven. A god who carries a wheel, probably a sun-god, and another, a god of thunder, called Taranis, seem to have been equated with Juppiter. The sun-god with the wheel was not equated with Apollo, who seems to have represented Celtic sun-gods only in so far as they were also gods of healing. In some cases the god with the wheel carries also a thunderbolt, and on some altars, dedicated to Juppiter, both a wheel and a thunderbolt are figured. Many races have symbolised the sun as a circle or wheel, and an old Roman god, Summanus, probably a sun-god, later assimilated to Juppiter, had as his emblem a wheel. The Celts had the same symbolism, and used the wheel symbol as an amulet, 78 while at the midsummer festivals blazing wheels, symbolising the sun, were rolled down a slope. Possibly the god carries a thunderbolt because the Celts, like other races, believed that lightning was a spark from the sun.

Three divinities have claims to be the god whom Cæsar calls Dispater — a god with a hammer, a crouching god called Cernunnos, and a god called Esus or Silvanus. Possibly the native Dispater was differently envisaged in different districts, so that these would be local forms of one god.

1. The god Taranis mentioned by Lucan is probably the Taranoos and Taranucnos of inscriptions, sometimes equated with Juppiter. 79 These names are connected with Celtic words for "thunder"; hence Taranis is a thunder-god. The scholiasts on Lucan identify him now with Juppiter, now with Dispater. This latter identification is supported by many who regard the god with the hammer as at once Taranis and Dispater, though it cannot be proved that the god with the hammer is Taranis. On one inscription the hammer-god is called Sucellos; hence we may regard Taranis as a distinct deity, a thunder-god, equated with Juppiter, and possibly represented by the Taran of the Welsh tale of Kulhwych. 80

Primitive men, whose only weapon and tool was a stone axe or hammer, must have regarded it as a symbol of force, then of supernatural force, hence of divinity. It is represented on remains of the Stone Age, and the axe was a divine symbol to the Mycenæans, a hieroglyph of Neter to the

Egyptians, and a worshipful object to Polynesians and Chaldeans. The cult of axe or hammer may have been widespread, and to the Celts, as to many other peoples, it was a divine symbol. Thus it does not necessarily denote a thunderbolt, but rather power and might, and possibly, as the tool which shaped things, creative might. The Celts made ex voto hammers of lead, or used axe-heads as amulets, or figured them on altars and coins, and they also placed the hammer in the hand of a god. 81

The god with the hammer is a gracious bearded figure, clad in Gaulish dress, and he carries also a cup. His plastic type is derived from that of the Alexandrian Serapis, ruler of the underworld, and that of Hades-Pluto. 82 His emblems, especially that of the hammer, are also those of the Pluto of the Etruscans, with whom the Celts had been in contact. 83 He is thus a Celtic Dispater, an underworld god, possibly at one time an Earth-god and certainly a god of fertility, and ancestor of the Celtic folk. In some cases, like Serapis, he carries a modius on his head, and this, like the cup, is an emblem of chthonian gods, and a symbol of the fertility of the soil. The god being benevolent, his hammer, like the tool with which man forms so many things, could only be a symbol of creative force. 84 As an ancestor of the Celts, the god is naturally represented in Celtic dress. In one bas-relief he is called Sucellos, and has a consort, Nantosvelta. 85 Various meanings have been assigned to "Sucellos," but it probably denotes the god's power of striking with the hammer. M. D'Arbois hence regards him as a god of blight and death, like Balor. 86 But though this Celtic Dispater was a god of the dead who lived on in the underworld, he was not necessarily a destructive god. The underworld god was the god from whom or from whose kingdom men came forth, and he was also a god of fertility. To this we shall return.

2. A bearded god, probably squatting, with horns from each of which hangs a torque, is represented on an altar found at Paris. 87 He is called Cernunnos, perhaps "the horned," from cerna, "horn," and a whole group of nameless gods, with similar or additional attributes, have affinities with him.

(a) A bronze statuette from Autun represents a similar figure, probably horned, who presents a torque to two ram's-headed serpents. Fixed above his ears are two small heads. 88 On a monument from Vandoeuvres is a squatting horned god, pressing a sack. Two genii stand beside him on a serpent, while one of them holds a torque. 89

(b) Another squatting horned figure with a torque occurs on an altar from Reims. He presses a bag, from which grain escapes, and on it an ox and stag are feeding. A rat is represented on the pediment above, and on either side stand Apollo and Mercury. 90 On the altar of Saintes is a squatting but headless god with torque and purse. Beside him is a goddess with a cornucopia, and a smaller divinity with a cornucopia and an apple. A similar squatting figure, supported by male and female deities, is represented on the other side of the altar. 91 On the altar of Beaune are three figures, one horned with a cornucopia, another three-headed, holding a basket. 92 Three figures, one female and two male, are found on the Dennevy altar. One god is three-faced, the other has a cornucopia, which he offers to a serpent. 93

(c) Another image represents a three-faced god, holding a serpent with a ram's head. 94

(d) Above a seated god and goddess on an altar from Malmaison is a block carved to represent three faces. To be compared with these are seven steles from Reims, each with a triple face but only one pair of eyes. Above some of these is a ram's head. On an eighth stele the heads are separated. 95

Cernunnos may thus have been regarded as a three-headed, horned, squatting god, with a torque and ram's-headed serpent. But a horned god is sometimes a member of a triad, perhaps representing myths in which Cernunnos was associated with other gods. The three-headed god may be the same as the horned god, though on the Beaune altar they are distinct. The various representations are linked together, but it is not certain that all are varying types of one god. Horns, torque, horned snake, or even the triple head may have been symbols pertaining to more than one god, though generally associated with Cernunnos.

The squatting attitude of the god has been differently explained, and its affinities regarded now as Buddhist, now as Greco-Egyptian. 96 But if the god is a Dispater, and the ancestral god of the Celts, it is natural, as M. Mowat points out, to represent him in the typical attitude of the Gauls when sitting, since they did not use seats. 97 While the horns were probably symbols of power and worn also by chiefs on their helmets, 98 they may also show that the god was an anthropomorphic form of an earlier animal god, like the wolf-skin of other gods. Hence also horned animals would be regarded as symbols of the god, and this may account for their presence on the Reims monument. Animals are sometimes represented beside the divinities who were their anthropomorphic forms. 99 Similarly the ram's-headed serpent points to animal worship. But its presence with three-headed and horned gods is enigmatic, though, as will be seen later, it may have been connected with a cult of the dead, while the serpent was a chthonian animal. 100 These gods were gods of fertility and of the underworld of the dead. While the bag or purse (interchangeable with the cornucopia) was a symbol of Mercury, it was also a symbol of Pluto, and this may point to the fact that the gods who bear it had the same character as Pluto. The significance of the torque is also doubtful, but the Gauls offered torques to the gods, and they may have been regarded as vehicles of the warrior's strength which passed from him to the god to whom the victor presented it.

Though many attempts have been made to prove the non-Celtic origin of the three-headed divinities or of their images, 101 there is no reason why the conception should not be Celtic, based on some myth now lost to us. The Celts had a cult of human heads, and fixed them up on their houses in order to obtain the protection of the ghost. Bodies or heads of dead warriors had a protective influence on their land or tribe, and myth told how the head of the god Bran saved his country from invasion. In other myths human heads speak after being cut off. 102 It might thus easily have been believed that the representation of a god's head had a still more powerful protective influence, especially when it was triplicated, thus looking in all directions, like Janus.

The significance of the triad on these monuments is uncertain but since the supporting divinities are now male, now female, now male and female, it probably represents myths of which the horned or three-headed god was the central figure. Perhaps we shall not be far wrong in regarding such gods, on the whole, as Cernunnos, a god of abundance to judge by his emblems, and by the cornucopia held by his companions, probably divinities of fertility. In certain cases figures of squatting and horned goddesses with cornucopia occur. 103 These may be consorts of Cernunnos, and perhaps preceded him in origin. We may also go further and see in this god of abundance and fertility at once an Earth and an Under-earth god, since earth and under-earth are much the same to primitive thought, and fertility springs from below the earth's surface. Thus Cernunnos would be another form of the Celtic Dispater. Generally speaking, the images of Cernunnos are not found where those of the god with the hammer (Dispater) are most numerous. These two types may thus be different local forms of Dispater. The squatting attitude of Cernunnos is natural in the image of the ancestor of a people who squatted. As to the symbols of plenty, we know that Pluto was confounded with Plutus, the god of riches, because corn and minerals came out of the earth, and were thus the gifts of an Earth or Under-earth god. Celtic myth may have had the same confusion.

On a Paris altar and on certain steles a god attacks a serpent with a club. The serpent is a chthonian animal, and the god, called Smertullos, may be a Dispater. 104 Gods who are anthropomorphic forms of earlier animal divinities, sometimes have the animals as symbols or attendants, or are regarded as hostile to them. In some cases Dispater may have outgrown the serpent symbolism, the serpent being regarded locally as his foe; this assumes that the god with the club is the same as the god with the hammer. But in the case of Cernunnos the animal remained as his symbol.

Dispater was a god of growth and fertility, and besides being lord of the underworld of the dead, not necessarily a dark region or the abode of "dark" gods as is so often assumed by writers on Celtic religion, he was ancestor of the living. This may merely have meant that, as in other mythologies, men came to the surface of the earth from an underground region, like all things whose roots struck deep down into the earth. The lord of the underworld would then easily be regarded as their ancestor. 105

3. The hammer and the cup are also the symbols of a god called Silvanus, identified by M. Mowat with Esus, 106 a god represented cutting down a tree with an axe. Axe and hammer, however, are not necessarily identical, and the symbols are those of Dispater, as has been seen. A purely superficial connection between the Roman Silvanus and the Celtic Dispater may have been found by Gallo-Roman artists in the fact that both wear a wolf-skin, while there may once have been a Celtic wolf totem-god of the dead. 107 The Roman god was also associated with the wolf. This might be regarded as one out of many examples of a mere superficial assimilation of Roman and Celtic divinities, but in this case they still kept certain symbols of the native Dispater — the cup and hammer. Of course, since the latter was also a god of fertility, there was here another link with Silvanus, a god of woods and vegetation. The cult of the god was widespread — in Spain, S. Gaul, the Rhine provinces, Cisalpine Gaul, Central Europe and Britain. But one inscription gives the name Selvanos, and it is not impossible that there was a native god Selvanus. If so, his name may have been derived from selva, "possession," Irish sealbh, "possession," "cattle," and he may have been a chthonian god of riches, which in primitive communities consisted of cattle. 108 Domestic animals, in Celtic mythology, were believed to have come from the god's land. Selvanus would thus be easily identified with Silvanus, a god of flocks.

Thus the Celtic Dispater had various names and forms in different regions, and could be assimilated to different foreign gods. Since Earth and Under-earth are so nearly connected, this divinity may once have been an Earth-god, and as such perhaps took the place of an earlier Earth-mother, who now became his consort or his mother. On a monument from Salzbach, Dispater is accompanied by a goddess called Aeracura, holding a basket of fruit, and on another monument from Ober-Seebach, the companion of Dispater holds a cornucopia. In the latter instance Dispater holds a hammer and cup, and the goddess may be Aeracura. Aeracura is also associated with Dispater in several inscriptions. 109 It is not yet certain that she is a Celtic goddess, but her presence with this evidently Celtic god is almost sufficient proof of the fact. She may thus represent the old Earth-goddess, whose place the native Dispater gradually usurped.

Lucan mentions a god Esus, who is represented on a Paris altar as a woodman cutting down a tree, the branches of which are carried round to the next side of the altar, on which is represented a bull with three cranes— Tarvos Trigaranos. The same figure, unnamed, occurs on another altar at Trèves, but in this case the bull's head appears in the branches, and on them sit the birds. M. Reinach applies one formula to the subjects of these altars— "The divine Woodman hews the Tree of the Bull with Three Cranes." 110 The whole represents some myth unknown to us, but M. D'Arbois finds in it some allusion to events in the Cúchulainn saga. To this we shall return. 111 Bull and tree are perhaps both divine, and if the animal, like the images of the divine bull, is three-horned, then the three cranes (garanus, "crane") may be a rebus for three-horned (trikeras), or more probably three-headed (trikarenos). 112 In this case woodman, tree, and bull might all be representatives of a god of vegetation. In early ritual, human, animal, or arboreal representatives of the god were periodically destroyed to ensure fertility, but when the god became separated from these representatives, the destruction or slaying was regarded as a sacrifice to the god, and myths arose telling how he had once slain the animal. In this case, tree and bull, really identical, would be mythically regarded as destroyed by the god whom they had once represented. If Esus was a god of vegetation, once represented by a tree, this would explain why, as the scholiast on Lucan relates, human sacrifices to Esus were suspended from a tree. Esus was worshipped at Paris and at Trèves; a coin with the name Æsus was found in England; and personal names like Esugenos, "son of Esus," and Esunertus, "he who has the strength of Esus," occur in England, France, and Switzerland. 113 Thus the cult of this god may have been comparatively widespread. But there is no evidence that he was a Celtic Jehovah or a member, with Teutates and Taranis, of a pan-Celtic triad, or that this triad, introduced by Gauls, was not accepted by the Druids. 114 Had such a great triad existed, some instance of the occurrence of the three names on one inscription would certainly have been found. Lucan does not refer to the gods as a triad, nor as gods of all the Celts, or even of one tribe. He lays stress merely on the fact that they were worshipped with human sacrifice, and they were apparently more or less well-known local gods. 115

The insular Celts believed that some of their gods lived on or in hills. We do not know whether such a belief was entertained by the Gauls, though some of their deities were worshipped on hills, like the Puy de Dôme. There is also evidence of mountain worship among them. One inscription runs, "To the Mountains"; a god of the Pennine Alps, Poeninus, was equated with

Juppiter; and the god of the Vosges mountains was called Vosegus, perhaps still surviving in the giant supposed to haunt them. 116

Certain grouped gods, Dii Casses, were worshipped by Celts on the right bank of the Rhine, but nothing is known regarding their functions, unless they were road gods. The name means "beautiful" or "pleasant," and Cassi appears in personal and tribal names, and also in Cassiterides, an early name of Britain, perhaps signifying that the new lands were "more beautiful" than those the Celts had left. When tin was discovered in Britain, the Mediterranean traders called it [Greek: chassiteros], after the name of the place where it was found, as cupreus, "copper," was so called from Cyprus. 117

Many local tutelar divinities were also worshipped. When a new settlement was founded, it was placed under the protection of a tribal god, or the name of some divinised river on whose banks the village was placed, passed to the village itself, and the divinity became its protector. Thus Dea Bibracte, Nemausus, and Vasio were tutelar divinities of Bibracte, Nimes, and Vaison. Other places were called after Belenos, or a group of divinities, usually the Matres with a local epithet, watched over a certain district. 118 The founding of a town was celebrated in an annual festival, with sacrifices and libations to the protecting deity, a practice combated by S. Eloi in the eighth century. But the custom of associating a divinity with a town or region was a great help to patriotism. Those who fought for their homes felt that they were fighting for their gods, who also fought on their side. Several inscriptions, "To the genius of the place," occur in Britain, and there are a few traces of tutelar gods in Irish texts, but generally local saints had taken their place.

The Celtic cult of goddesses took two forms, that of individual and that of grouped goddesses, the latter much more numerous than the grouped gods. Individual goddesses were worshipped as consorts of gods, or as separate personalities, and in the latter case the cult was sometimes far extended. Still more popular was the cult of grouped goddesses. Of these the Matres, like some individual goddesses, were probably early Earth-mothers, and since the primitive fertility-cults included all that might then be summed up as "civilisation," such goddesses had already many functions, and might the more readily become divinities of special crafts or even of war. Many individual goddesses are known only by their names, and were of a purely local character. 119 Some local goddesses with different names but similar functions are equated with the same Roman goddess; others were never so equated.

The Celtic Minerva, or the goddesses equated with her, "taught the elements of industry and the arts," 120 and is thus the equivalent of the

Irish Brigit. Her functions are in keeping with the position of woman as the first civiliser—discovering agriculture, spinning, the art of pottery, etc. During this period goddesses were chiefly worshipped, and though the Celts had long outgrown this primitive stage, such culture-goddesses still retained their importance. A goddess equated with Minerva in Southern France and Britain is Belisama, perhaps from qval, "to burn" or "shine." 121 Hence she may have been associated with a cult of fire, like Brigit and like another goddess Sul, equated with Minerva at Bath and in Hesse, and in whose temple perpetual fires burned. 122 She was also a goddess of hot springs. Belisama gave her name to the Mersey, 123 and many goddesses in Celtic myth are associated with rivers.

Some war-goddesses are associated with Mars—Nemetona (in Britain and Germany), perhaps the same as the Irish Nemon, and Cathubodua, identical with the Irish war-goddess Badb-catha, "battle-crow," who tore the bodies of the slain. 124 Another goddess Andrasta, "invincible," perhaps the same as the Andarta of the Voconces, was worshipped by the people of Boudicca with human sacrifices, like the native Bellona of the Scordisci. 125

A goddess of the chase was identified with Artemis in Galatia, where she had a priestess Camma, and also in the west. At the feast of the Galatian goddess dogs were crowned with flowers, her worshippers feasted and a sacrifice was made to her, feast and sacrifice being provided out of money laid aside for every animal taken in the chase. 126 Other goddesses were equated with Diana, and one of her statues was destroyed in Christian times at Trèves. 127 These goddesses may have been thought of as rushing through the forest with an attendant train, since in later times Diana, with whom they were completely assimilated, became, like Holda, the leader of the "furious host" and also of witches' revels. 128 The Life of Cæsarius of Arles speaks of a "demon" called Diana by the rustics. A bronze statuette represents the goddess riding a wild boar, 129 her symbol and, like herself, a creature of the forest, but at an earlier time itself a divinity of whom the goddess became the anthropomorphic form.

Goddesses, the earlier spirits of the waters, protected rivers and springs, or were associated with gods of healing wells. Dirona or Sirona is associated with Grannos mainly in Eastern Gaul and the Rhine provinces, and is sometimes represented carrying grapes and grain. 130 Thus this goddess may once have been connected with fertility, perhaps an Earth-mother, and if her name means "the long-lived," 131 this would be an appropriate title for an Earth-goddess. Another goddess, Stanna, mentioned in an inscription at Perigueux, is perhaps "the standing or abiding one," and thus may also have been Earth-goddess. 132 Grannos was also associated with the local goddesses Vesunna and Aventia, who gave their names to

Vesona and Avanche. His statue also stood in the temple of the goddess of the Seine, Sequana. 133 With Bormo were associated Bormana in Southern Gaul, and Damona in Eastern Gaul—perhaps an animal goddess, since the root of her name occurs in Irish dam, "ox," and Welsh dafad, "sheep." Dea Brixia was the consort of Luxovius, god of the waters of Luxeuil. Names of other goddesses of the waters are found on ex votos and plaques which were placed in or near them. The Roman Nymphæ, sometimes associated with Bormo, were the equivalents of the Celtic water-goddesses, who survived in the water-fairies of later folk-belief. Some river-goddesses gave their names to many rivers in the Celtic area—the numerous Avons being named from Abnoba, goddess of the sources of the Danube, and the many Dees and Dives from Divona. Clota was goddess of the Clyde, Sabrina had her throne "beneath the translucent wave" of the Severn, Icauna was goddess of the Yonne, Sequana of the Seine, and Sinnan of the Shannon.

In some cases forests were ruled by goddesses—that of the Ardennes by Dea Arduinna, and the Black Forest, perhaps because of the many waters in it, by Dea Abnoba. 134 While some goddesses are known only by being associated with a god, e.g. Kosmerta with Mercury in Eastern Gaul, others have remained separate, like Epona, perhaps a river-goddess merged with an animal divinity, and known from inscriptions as a horse-goddess. 135 But the most striking instance is found in the grouped goddesses.

Of these the Deoe Matres, whose name has taken a Latin form and whose cult extended to the Teutons, are mentioned in many inscriptions all over the Celtic area, save in East and North-West Gaul. 136 In art they are usually represented as three in number, holding fruit, flowers, a cornucopia, or an infant. They were thus goddesses of fertility, and probably derived from a cult of a great Mother-goddess, the Earth personified. She may have survived as a goddess Berecynthia; worshipped at Autun, where her image was borne through the fields to promote fertility, or as the goddesses equated with Demeter and Kore, worshipped by women on an island near Britain. 137 Such cults of a Mother-goddess lie behind many religions, but gradually her place was taken by an Earth-god, the Celtic Dispater or Dagda, whose consort the goddess became. She may therefore be the goddess with the cornucopia on monuments of the horned god, or Aeracura, consort of Dispater, or a goddess on a monument at Epinal holding a basket of fruit and a cornucopia, and accompanied by a ram's-headed serpent. 138 These symbols show that this goddess was akin to the Matres. But she sometimes preserved her individuality, as in the case of Berecynthia and the Matres, though it is not quite clear why she should have been thus triply multiplied. A similar phenomenon is found in the close connection of Demeter and Persephone, while the Celts regarded three as a sacred number. The primitive division of the year into three seasons—spring, summer, and winter—may have had its effect in triplicating a goddess of fertility with which the course of the seasons was connected. 139 In other mythologies groups of three goddesses are found, the Hathors in Egypt, the Moirai, Gorgons, and Graiæ of Greece, the Roman Fates, and the Norse Nornæ, and it is noticeable that the Matres were sometimes equated with the Parcæ and Fates. 140

In the Matres, primarily goddesses of fertility and plenty, we have one of the most popular and also primitive aspects of Celtic religion. They originated in an age when women cultivated the ground, and the Earth was a goddess whose cult was performed by priestesses. But in course of time new functions were bestowed on the Matres. Possibly river-goddesses and others are merely mothers whose functions have become specialised. The Matres are found as guardians of individuals, families, houses, of towns, a province, or a whole nation, as their epithets in inscriptions show. The Matres Domesticæ are household goddesses; the Matres Treveræ, or Gallaicæ, or Vediantæ, are the mothers of Trèves, of the Gallaecæ, of the Vediantii; the Matres Nemetiales are guardians of groves. Besides presiding over the fields as Matres Campestræ they brought prosperity to towns and people. 141 They guarded women, especially in childbirth, as ex votos prove, and in this aspect they are akin to the Junones worshipped also in Gaul and Britain. The name thus became generic for most goddesses, but all alike were the lineal descendants of the primitive Earth-mother. 142

Popular superstition has preserved the memory of these goddesses in the three bonnes dames, dames blanches, and White Women, met by wayfarers in forests, or in the three fairies or wise women of folk-tales, who appear at the birth of children. But sometimes they have become hateful hags. The Matres and other goddesses probably survived in the beneficent fairies of rocks and streams, in the fairy Abonde who brought riches to houses, or Esterelle of Provence who made women fruitful, or Aril who watched over meadows, or in beings like Melusine, Viviane, and others. 143 In Gallo-Roman Britain the cult of the Matres is found, but how far it was indigenous there is uncertain. A Welsh name for fairies, Y Mamau, "the Mothers," and the phrase, "the blessing of the Mothers" used of a fairy benediction, may be a reminiscence of such goddesses. 144 The presence of similar goddesses in Ireland will be considered later. 145 Images of the Matres bearing a child have sometimes been taken for those of the Virgin, when found accidentally, and as they are of wood blackened with age, they are known as Vierges Noires, and occupy an honoured place in Christian sanctuaries. Many churches of Nôtre Dame have been built on sites where an image of the Virgin is said to have been miraculously found—the image probably being that of a pagan Mother. Similarly, an altar to the Matres at Vaison is now dedicated to the Virgin as the "good Mother." 146

In inscriptions from Eastern and Cisalpine Gaul, and from the Rhine and Danube region, the Matronæ are mentioned, and this name is probably indicative of goddesses like the Matres. 147 It is akin to that of many rivers, e.g. the Marne or Meyrone, and shows that the Mothers were associated with rivers. The Mother river fertilised a large district, and exhibited the characteristic of the whole group of goddesses.

Akin also to the Matres are the Suleviæ, guardian goddesses called Matres in a few inscriptions; the Comedovæ, whose name perhaps denotes guardianship or power; the Dominæ, who watched over the home, perhaps the Dames of mediæval folk-lore; and the Virgines, perhaps an appellative of the Matres, and significant when we find that virgin priestesses existed in Gaul and Ireland. 148 The Proxumæ were worshipped in Southern Gaul, and the Quadriviæ, goddesses of cross-roads, at Cherbourg. 149

Some Roman gods are found on inscriptions without being equated with native deities. They may have been accepted by the Gauls as new gods, or they had perhaps completely ousted similar native gods. Others, not mentioned by Cæsar, are equated with native deities, Juno with Clivana, Saturn with Arvalus, and to a native Vulcan the Celts vowed spoils of war. 150 Again, many native gods are not equated with Roman deities on inscriptions. Apart from the divinities of Pyrenæan inscriptions, who may not be Celtic, the names of over 400 native deities, whether equated with Roman gods or not, are known. Some of these names are mere epithets, and most of the gods are of a local character, known here by one name, there by another. Only in a very few cases can it be asserted that a god was worshipped over the whole Celtic area by one name, though some gods in Gaul, Britain, and Ireland with different names have certainly similar functions. 151

The pantheon of the continental Celts was a varied one. Traces of the primitive agricultural rites, and of the priority of goddesses to gods, are found, and the vaguer aspects of primitive nature worship are seen behind the cult of divinities of sky, sun, thunder, forests, rivers, or in deities of animal origin. We come next to evidence of a higher stage, in divinities of culture, healing, the chase, war, and the underworld. We see divinities of Celtic groups—gods of individuals, the family, the tribe. Sometimes war-gods assumed great prominence, in time of war, or among the aristocracy, but with the development of commerce, gods associated with trade and the arts of peace came to the front. 152 At the same time the popular cults of agricultural districts must have remained as of old. With the adoption of Roman civilisation, enlightened Celts separated themselves from the lower aspects of their religion, but this would have occurred with growing civilisation had no Roman ever entered Gaul. In rural districts the more savage aspects of the cult would still have remained, but that these were entirely due to an aboriginal population is erroneous. The Celts must have brought such cults with them or adopted cults similar to their own wherever they came. The persistence of these cults is seen in the fact that though Christianity modified them, it could not root them out, and in out-of-the-way corners, survivals of the old ritual may still be found, for everywhere the old religion of the soil dies hard.

Footnote 53: Cæsar, de Bell. Gall. vi. 17, 18.

Footnote 54: Bloch (Lavisse), Hist, de France, i. 2, 419; Reinaoh, BF 13, 23.

Footnote 55: Trans. Gaelic Soc. of Inverness, xxvi. p. 411 f.

Footnote 56: Vallentin, Les Dieux de la cité des Allobroges, 15; Pliny, HN xxxiv. 7.

Footnote 57: These names are Alaunius, Arcecius, Artaius, Arvernorix, Arvernus, Adsmerius, Canetonensis, Clavariatis, Cissonius, Cimbrianus, Dumiatis, Magniacus, Moecus, Toeirenus, Vassocaletus, Vellaunus, Visuoius, Biausius, Cimiacinus, Naissatis. See Holder, s.v.

Footnote 58: Rh[^y]s, HL 6.

Footnote 59: Hübner, vii. 271; CIL iii. 5773.

Footnote 60: Lucian, Heracles, 1 f. Some Gaulish coins figure a head to which are bound smaller heads. In one case the cords issue from the mouth (Blanchet, i. 308, 316-317). These may represent rrrLucian's Ogmíos, but other interpretations have been put upon them. See Robert, RC vii. 388; Jullian, 84.

Footnote 61: The epithets and names are Anextiomarus, Belenos, Bormo, Borvo, or Bormanus, Cobledulitavus, Cosmis (?), Grannos, Livicus, Maponos, Mogo or Mogounos, Sianus, Toutiorix, Viudonnus, Virotutis. See Holder, s.v.

Footnote 62: Pommerol, Ball. de Soc. d'ant. de Paris, ii. fasc. 4.

Footnote 63: See Holder, s.v. Many place-names are derived from Borvo, e.g. Bourbon l'Archambaut, which gave its name to the Bourbon dynasty, thus connected with an old Celtic god.

Footnote 64: infra.

Footnote 65: Jul. Cap. Maxim. 22; Herodian, viii. 3; Tert. Apol. xxiv. 70; Auson. Prof. xi. 24.

Footnote 66: Stokes derives belinuntia from beljo-, a tree or leaf, Irish bile, US 174.

Footnote 67: Holder, s.v.; Stokes, US 197; Rh[^y]s, HL 23; see p. 180, infra.

Footnote 68: Diod. Sic. ii. 47.

Footnote 69: Apoll. Rhod. iv. 609.

Footnote 70: Albiorix, Alator, Arixo, Beladonnis, Barrex, Belatucadros, Bolvinnus, Braciaca, Britovis, Buxenus, Cabetius, Camulus, Cariocecius, Caturix, Cemenelus, Cicollius, Carrus, Cocosus, Cociduis, Condatis, Cnabetius, Corotiacus, Dinomogetimarus, Divanno, Dunatis, Glarinus, Halamardus, Harmogius, Ieusdriuus, Lacavus, Latabius, Leucetius, Leucimalacus, Lenus, Mullo, Medocius, Mogetius, Nabelcus, Neton, Ocelos, Ollondios, Rudianus, Rigisamus, Randosatis, Riga, Segomo, Sinatis, Smertatius, Toutates, Tritullus, Vesucius, Vincius, Vitucadros, Vorocius. See Holder, s.v.

Footnote 71: D'Arbois, ii. 215; Rh[^y]s, HL 37.

Footnote 72: So Rh[^y]s, HL 42.

Footnote 73: Hübner, 61.

Footnote 74: Holder, s.v.; Lucan, i. 444 f. The opinions of writers who take this view are collected by Reinach, RC xviii. 137.

Footnote 75: Holder, s.v. The Gaulish name Camulogenus, "born of Cumel," represents the same idea as in Fionn's surname, MacCumall.

Footnote 76: Athen. iv. 36; Dioscorides, ii. 110; Joyce, SH ii. 116, 120; IT i. 437, 697.

Footnote 77: Pliny, HN xviii. 7.

Footnote 78: Gaidoz, Le Dieu Gaulois de Soleil; Reinach, CS 98, BF 35; Blanchet, i. 27.

Footnote 79: Lucan, Phar. i. 444. Another form, Tanaros, may be simply the German Donar.

Footnote 80: Loth, i. 270.

Footnote 81: Gaidoz, RC vi. 457; Reinach, OS 65, 138; Blanchet, i. 160. The hammer is also associated with another Celtic Dispater, equated with Sylvanus, who was certainly not a thunder-god.

Footnote 82: Reinach, BF 137 f.; Courcelle-Seneuil, 115 f.

Footnote 83: Barthelemy, RC i. 1 f.

Footnote 84: See Flouest, Rev. Arch. v. 17.

Footnote 85: Reinach, RC xvii. 45.

Footnote 86: D'Arbois, ii. 126. He explains Nantosvelta as meaning "She who is brilliant in war." The goddess, however, has none of the attributes of a war-goddess. M. D'Arbois also saw in a bas-relief of the hammer-god, a female figure, and a child, the Gaulish equivalents of Balor, Ethne, and Lug (RC xv. 236). M. Reinach regards Sucellos, Nantosvelta, and a bird which is rrrfigured with them, as the same trio, because pseudo-Plutarch (de Fluv. vi. 4) says that lougos means "crow" in Celtic. This is more than doubtful. In any case Ethne has no warlike traits in Irish story, and as Lug and Balor were deadly enemies, it remains to be explained why they appear tranquilly side by side. See RC xxvi. 129. Perhaps Nantosvelta, like other Celtic goddesses, was a river nymph. Nanto Gaulish is "valley," and nant in old Breton is "gorge" or "brook." Her name might mean "shining river." See Stokes, US 193, 324.

Footnote 87: RC xviii. 254. Cernunnos may be the Juppiter Cernenos of an inscription from Pesth, Holder, s.v.

Footnote 88: Reinach, BF 186, fig. 177.

Footnote 89: Rev. Arch. xix. 322, pl. 9.

Footnote 90: Bertrand, Rev. Arch. xv. 339, xvi. pl. 12.

Footnote 91: Ibid. xv. pl. 9, 10.

Footnote 92: Ibid. xvi. 9.

Footnote 93: Ibid. pl. 12 bis.

Footnote 94: Bertrand, Rev. Arch. xvi. 8.

Footnote 95: Ibid. xvi. 10 f.

Footnote 96: Ibid. xv., xvi.; Reinach, BF 17, 191.

Footnote 97: Bull. Epig. i. 116; Strabo, iv. 3; Diod. Sic. v. 28.

Footnote 98: Diod. Sic. v. 30; Reinach, BF 193.

Footnote 99: infra.

Footnote 100: infra.

Footnote 101: e.g., Mowat, Bull. Epig. i. 29; de Witte, Rev. Arch. ii. 387, xvi. 7; Bertrand, ibid. xvi. 3.

Footnote 102: infra; Joyce, SH ii. 554; Curtin, 182; RC xxii. 123, xxiv. 18.

Footnote 103: Dom Martin, ii. 185; Reinach, BF 192, 199.

Footnote 104: however, infra; and for another interpretation of this god as equivalent of the Irish Lug slaying Balor, see D'Arbois, ii. 287.

Footnote 105: infra.

Footnote 106: Reinach, BF 162, 184; Mowat, Bull. Epig. i. 62, Rev. Epig. 1887, 319, 1891, 84.

Footnote 107: Reinach, BF 141, 153, 175, 176, 181; , infra. Flouest, Rev. Arch. 1885, i. 21, thinks that the identification was with an earlier chthonian Silvanus. Cf. Jullian, 17, note 3, who observes that the Gallo-Roman assimilations were made rrr"sur le doinaine archaisant des faits populaires et rustiques de l'Italie." For the inscriptions, see Holder, s.v.

Footnote 108: Stokes, US 302; MacBain, 274; RC xxvi. 282.

Footnote 109: Gaidoz, Rev. Arch. ii. 1898; Mowat, Bull. Epig. i. 119; Courcelle-Seneuil, 80 f.; Pauly-Wissowa, Real. Lex. i. 667; Daremberg-Saglio, Dict. ii., s.v. "Dispater."

Footnote 110: Lucan, i. 444; RC xviii. 254, 258.

Footnote 111: infra.

Footnote 112: For a supposed connection between this bas-relief and the myth of Geryon, see Reinach, BF 120; RC xviii. 258 f.

Footnote 113: Coins of the Ancient Britons, 386; Holder, i. 1475, 1478.

Footnote 114: For these theories see Dom Martin, ii. 2; Bertrand, 335 f.

Footnote 115: Cf. Reinach, RC xviii. 149.

Footnote 116: Orelli, 2107, 2072; Monnier, 532; Tacitus, xxi. 38.

Footnote 117: Holder, i. 824; Reinach, Rev. Arch. xx. 262; D'Arbois, Les Celtes, 20. Other grouped gods are the Bacucei, Castoeci, Icotii, Ifles, Lugoves, Nervini, and Silvani. See Holder, s.v.

Footnote 118: For all these see Holder, s.v.

Footnote 119: Professor Anwyl gives the following statistics: There are 35 goddesses mentioned once, 2 twice, 3 thrice, 1 four times, 2 six times, 2 eleven times, 1 fourteen times (Sirona), 1 twenty-one times (Rosmerta), 1 twenty-six times (Epona) (Trans. Gael. Soc. Inverness, xxvi. 413).

Footnote 120: Cæsar, vi. 17.

Footnote 121: D'Arbois, Les Celtes, 54; Rev. Arch. i. 201. See Holder, s.v.

Footnote 122: Solinus, xxii. 10; Holder, s.v.

Footnote 123: Ptolemy, ii. 2.

Footnote 124: infra.

Footnote 125: Dio Cass. lxii. 7; Amm. Marc. xxvii. 4. 4.

Footnote 126: Plutarch, de Vir. Mul. 20; Arrian, Cyneg. xxxiv. 1.

Footnote 127: S. Greg. Hist. viii. 15.

Footnote 128: Grimm, Teut. Myth. 283, 933; Reinach, RC xvi. 261.

Footnote 129: Reinach, BF 50.

Footnote 130: Holder, i. 1286; Robert, RC iv. 133.

Footnote 131: Rh[^y]s, HL 27.

Footnote 132: Anwyl, Celt. Rev. 1906, 43.

Footnote 133: Holder, s.v.; Bulliot, RC ii. 22.

Footnote 134: Holder, i. 10, 89.

Footnote 135: Holder, s.v.;infra.

Footnote 136: Holder, ii. 463. They are very numerous in South-East Gaul, where also three-headed gods are found.

Footnote 137: infra.

Footnote 138: Courcelle-Seneuil, 80-81.

Footnote 139: See my article "Calendar" in Hastings' Encyclop. of Religion and Ethics, iii. 80.

Footnote 140: CIL v. 4208, 5771, vii. 927; Holder, ii. 89.

Footnote 141: For all these titles see Holder, s.v.

Footnote 142: There is a large literature devoted to the Matres. See De Wal, Die Mæder Gottinem; Vallentin, Le Culte des Matræ; Daremberg-Saglio, Dict. s.v. Matres; Ihm, Jahrbuch. des Vereins von Alterth. in Rheinlande, No. 83; Roscher, Lexicon, ii. 2464 f.

Footnote 143: See Maury, Fées du Moyen Age; Sébillot, i. 262; Monnier, 439 f.; Wright, Celt, Roman, and Saxon, 286 f.; Vallentin, RC iv. 29. The Matres may already have had a sinister aspect in Roman times, as they appear to be intended by an inscription Lamiis Tribus on an altar at Newcastle. Hübner, 507.

Footnote 144: Anwyl, Celt. Rev. 1906, 28. Cf. Y Foel Famau, "the hill of the Mothers," in the Clwydian range.

Footnote 145: infra.

Footnote 146: Vallentin, op. cit. iv. 29; Maury, Croyances du Moyen Age, 382.

Footnote 147: Holder, s.v.

Footnote 148: infra.

Footnote 149: For all these see Holder, s.v.; Rh[^y]s, HL 103; RC iv. 34.

Footnote 150: Florus, ii. 4.

Footnote 151: See the table of identifications, infra.

Footnote 152: We need not assume with Jullian, 18, that there was one supreme god, now a war-god, now a god of peace. Any prominent god may have become a war-god on occasion.

CHAPTER IV
THE IRISH MYTHOLOGICAL CYCLE

Three divine and heroic cycles of myths are known in Ireland, one telling of the Tuatha Dé Danann, the others of Cúchulainn and of the Fians. They are distinct in character and contents, but the gods of the first cycle often help the heroes of the other groups, as the gods of Greece and India assisted the heroes of the epics. We shall see that some of the personages of these cycles may have been known in Gaul; they are remembered in Wales, but, in the Highlands, where stories of Cúchulainn and Fionn are still told, the Tuatha Dé Danann are less known now than in 1567, when Bishop Carsewell lamented the love of the Highlanders for "idle, turbulent, lying, worldly stories concerning the Tuatha Dédanans." 153

As the new Achæan religion in Greece and the Vedic sacred books of India regarded the aboriginal gods and heroes as demons and goblins, so did Christianity in Ireland sometimes speak of the older gods there. On the other hand, it was mainly Christian scribes who changed the old mythology into history, and made the gods and heroes kings. Doubtless myths already existed, telling of the descent of rulers and people from divinities, just as the Gauls spoke of their descent from Dispater, or as the Incas of Peru, the Mikados of Japan, and the kings of Uganda considered themselves offspring of the gods. This is a universal practice, and made it the more easy for Christian chroniclers to transmute myth into history. In Ireland, as elsewhere, myth doubtless told of monstrous races inhabiting the land in earlier days, of the strife of the aborigines and incomers, and of their gods, though the aboriginal gods may in some cases have been identified with Celtic gods, or worshipped in their own persons. Many mythical elements may therefore be looked for in the euhemerised chronicles of ancient Ireland. But the chroniclers themselves were but the continuers of a process which must have been at work as soon as the influence of Christianity began to be felt. 154 Their passion, however, was to show the descent of the Irish and the older peoples from the old Biblical personages, a process dear to the modern Anglo-Israelite, some of whose arguments are based on the wild romancing of the chroniclers.

Various stories were told of the first peopling of Ireland. Banba, with two other daughters of Cain, arrived with fifty women and three men, only to die of the plague. Three fishermen next discovered Ireland, and "of the island of Banba of Fair Women with hardihood they took possession." Having gone to fetch their wives, they perished in the deluge at Tuath Inba. 155 A more popular account was that of the coming of Cessair, Noah's granddaughter, with her father, husband, a third man, Ladru, "the first dead man of Erin," and fifty damsels. Her coming was the result of the advice of a laimh-dhia, or "hand-god," but their ship was wrecked, and all save her husband, Finntain, who survived for centuries, perished in the flood. 156 Cessair's ship was less serviceable than her grandparent's! Followed the race of Partholan, "no wiser one than the other," who increased on the land until plague swept them away, with the exception of Tuan mac Caraill, who after many transformations, told the story of Ireland to S. Finnen centuries after. 157 The survival of Finntain and Tuan, doubles of each other, was an invention of the chroniclers, to explain the survival of the history of colonists who had all perished. Keating, on the other hand, rejecting the sole survivor theory as contradictory to Scripture, suggests that "aerial demons," followers of the invaders, revealed all to the chroniclers, unless indeed they found it engraved with "an iron pen and lead in the rocks." 158

Two hundred years before Partholan's coming, the Fomorians had arrived, 159 and they and their chief Cichol Gricenchos fought Partholan at Mag Itha, where they were defeated. Cichol was footless, and some of his host had but one arm and one leg. 160 They were demons, according to the chroniclers, and descendants of the luckless Ham. Nennius makes Partholan and his men the first Scots who came from Spain to Ireland. The next arrivals were the people of Nemed who returned to Spain, whence they came (Nennius), or died to a man (Tuan). They also were descendants of the inevitable Noah, and their sojourn in Ireland was much disturbed by the Fomorians who had recovered from their defeat, and finally overpowered the Nemedians after the death of Nemed. 161 From Tory Island the Fomorians ruled Ireland, and forced the Nemedians to pay them annually on the eve of Samhain (Nov. 1st) two-thirds of their corn and milk and of the children born during the year. If the Fomorians are gods of darkness, or, preferably, aboriginal deities, the tribute must be explained as a dim memory of sacrifice offered at the beginning of winter when the powers of darkness and blight are in the ascendant. The Fomorians had a tower of glass in Tory Island. This was one day seen by the Milesians, to whom appeared on its battlements what seemed to be men. A year after they attacked the tower and were overwhelmed in the sea. 162 From the survivors of a previously wrecked vessel of their fleet are descended the Irish. Another version makes the Nemedians the assailants. Thirty of them survived their defeat, some of them going to Scotland or Man (the Britons), some to Greece (to return as the Firbolgs), some to the north, where they learned magic and returned as the Tuatha Dé Danann. 163 The Firbolgs, "men of bags," resenting their ignominious treatment by the Greeks, escaped to Ireland. They included the Firbolgs proper, the Fir-Domnann, and the Galioin. 164 The Fomorians are called their gods, and this, with the contemptuous epithets bestowed on them, may point to the fact that the Firbolgs were the pre-Celtic folk of Ireland and the Fomorians their divinities, hostile to the gods of the Celts or regarded as dark deities. The Firbolgs are vassals of Ailill and Medb, and with the Fir Domnann and Galioin are hostile to Cúchulainn and his men, 165 just as Fomorians were to the Tuatha Dé Danann. The strifes of races and of their gods are inextricably confused.

The Tuatha Dé Danann arrived from heaven — an idea in keeping with their character as beneficent gods, but later legend told how they came from the north. They reached Ireland on Beltane, shrouded in a magic mist, and finally, after one or, in other accounts, two battles, defeated the Firbolgs and Fomorians at Magtured. The older story of one battle may be regarded as a euhemerised account of the seeming conflict of nature powers. 166 The first battle is described in a fifteenth to sixteenth century MS., 167 and is referred to in a fifteenth century account of the second battle, full of archaic reminiscences, and composed from various earlier documents. 168 The Firbolgs, defeated in the first battle, join the Fomorians, after great losses. Meanwhile Nuada, leader of the Tuatha Dé Danann, lost his hand, and as no king with a blemish could sit on the throne, the crown was given to Bres, son of the Fomorian Elatha and his sister Eri, a woman of the Tuatha Dé Danann. One day Eri espied a silver boat speeding to her across the sea. From it stepped forth a magnificent hero, and without delay the pair, like the lovers in Theocritus, "rejoiced in their wedlock." The hero, Elatha, foretold the birth of Eri's son, so beautiful that he would be a standard by which to try all beautiful things. He gave her his ring, but she was to part with it only to one whose finger it should fit. This was her child Bres, and by this token he was later, as an exile, recognised by his father, and obtained his help against the Tuatha Dé Danann. Like other wonderful children, Bres grew twice as quickly as any other child until he was seven. 169 Though Elatha and Eri are brother and sister, she is among the Tuatha Dé Danann. 170 There is the usual inconsistency of myth here and in other accounts of Fomorian and Tuatha Dé Danann unions. The latter had just landed, but already had united in marriage with the Fomorians. This inconsistency escaped the chroniclers, but it points to the fact that both were divine not human, and that, though in conflict, they united in marriage as members of hostile tribes often do.

The second battle took place twenty-seven years after the first, on Samhain. It was fought like the first on the plain of Mag-tured, though later accounts made one battle take place at Mag-tured in Mayo, the other at Mag-tured in Sligo. 171 Inconsistently, the conquering Tuatha Dé Danann in the interval, while Bres is their king, must pay tribute imposed by the Fomorians. Obviously in older accounts this tribute must have been imposed before the first battle and have been its cause. But why should gods, like the Tuatha Dé Danann, ever have been in subjection? This remains to be seen, but the answer probably lies in parallel myths of the subjection or death of divinities like Ishtar, Adonis, Persephone, and Osiris. Bres having exacted a tribute of the milk of all hornless dun cows, the cows of Ireland were passed through fire and smeared with ashes—a myth based perhaps on the Beltane fire ritual. 172 The avaricious Bres was satirised, and "nought but decay was on him from that hour," 173 and when Nuada, having recovered, claimed the throne, he went to collect an army of the Fomorians, who assembled against the Tuatha Dé Danann. In the battle Indech wounded Ogma, and Balor slew Nuada, but was mortally wounded by Lug. Thereupon the Fomorians fled to their own region.

The Tuatha Dé Danann remained masters of Ireland until the coming of the Milesians, so named from an eponymous Mile, son of Bile. Ith, having been sent to reconnoitre, was slain, and the Milesians now invaded Ireland in force. In spite of a mist raised by the Druids, they landed, and, having met the three princes who slew Ith, demanded instant battle or surrender of the land. The princes agreed to abide by the decision of the Milesian poet Amairgen, who bade his friends re-embark and retire for the distance of nine waves. If they could then effect a landing, Ireland was theirs. A magic storm was raised, which wrecked many of their ships, but Amairgen recited verses, fragments, perhaps, of some old ritual, and overcame the dangers. After their defeat the survivors of the Tuatha Dé Danann retired into the hills to become a fairy folk, and the Milesians (the Goidels or Scots) became ancestors of the Irish.

Throughout the long story of the conquests of Ireland there are many reduplications, the same incidents being often ascribed to different personages. 174 Different versions of similar occurrences, based on older myths and traditions, may already have been in existence, and ritual practices, dimly remembered, required explanation. In the hands of the chroniclers, writing history with a purpose and combining their information with little regard to consistency, all this was reduced to a more or less connected narrative. At the hands of the prosaic chroniclers divinity passed from the gods, though traces of it still linger.

> "Ye are gods, and, behold, ye shall die, and the waves be upon you at last.
>
> In the darkness of time, in the deeps of the years, in the changes of things,
>
> Ye shall sleep as a slain man sleeps, and the world shall forget you for kings."

From the annalistic point of view the Fomorians are sea demons or pirates, their name being derived from muir, "sea," while they are descended along with other monstrous beings from them. Professor Rh[^y]s, while connecting the name with Welsh foawr, "giant" (Gaelic famhair), derives the name from fo, "under," and muir, and regards them as submarine beings. 175 Dr. MacBain connected them with the fierce powers of the western sea personified, like the Muireartach, a kind of sea hag, of a Fionn ballad. 176 But this association of the Fomorians with the ocean may be the result of a late folk-etymology, which wrongly derived their name from muir. The Celtic experience of the Lochlanners or Norsemen, with whom the Fomorians are associated, 177 would aid the conception of them as sea-pirates of a more or less demoniacal character. Dr. Stokes connects the second syllable mor with mare in "nightmare," from moro, and regards them as subterranean as well as submarine. 178 But the more probable derivation is that of Zimmer and D'Arbois, from fo and morio (mor, "great "), 179 which would thus agree with the tradition which regarded them as giants. They were probably beneficent gods of the aborigines, whom the Celtic conquerors regarded as generally evil, perhaps equating them with the dark powers already known to them. They were still remembered as gods, and are called "champions of the síd," like the Tuatha Dé Danann. 180 Thus King Bres sought to save his life by promising that the kine of Ireland would always be in milk, then that the men of Ireland would reap every quarter, and finally by revealing the lucky days for ploughing, sowing, and reaping. 181 Only an autochthonous god could know this, and the story is suggestive of the true nature of the Fomorians. The hostile character attributed to them is seen from the fact that they destroyed corn, milk, and fruit. But in Ireland, as elsewhere, this destructive power was deprecated by begging them not to destroy "corn nor milk in Erin beyond their fair tribute." 182 Tribute was also paid to them on Samhain, the time when the powers of blight feared by men are in the ascendant. Again, the kingdom of Balor, their chief, is still described as the kingdom of cold. 183 But when we remember that a similar "tribute" was paid to Cromm Cruaich, a god of fertility, and that after the conquest of the Tuatha Dé Danann they also were regarded as hostile to agriculture, 184 we realise that the Fomorians must have been aboriginal gods of fertility whom the conquering Celts regarded as hostile to them and their gods.

Similarly, in folk-belief the beneficent corn-spirit has sometimes a sinister and destructive aspect. 185 Thus the stories of "tribute" would be distorted reminiscences of the ritual of gods of the soil, differing little in character from that of the similar Celtic divinities. What makes it certain that the Fomorians were aboriginal gods is that they are found in Ireland before the coming of the early colonist Partholan. They were the gods of the pre-Celtic folk — Firbolgs, Fir Domnann, and Galioin 186 — all of them in Ireland before the Tuatha Dé Danaan arrived, and all of them regarded as slaves, spoken of with the utmost contempt. Another possibility, however, ought to be considered. As the Celtic gods were local in character, and as groups of tribes would frequently be hostile to other groups, the Fomorians may have been local gods of a group at enmity with another group, worshipping the Tuatha Dé Danaan.

The strife of Fomorians and Tuatha Dé Danann suggests the dualism of all nature religions. Demons or giants or monsters strive with gods in Hindu, Greek, and Teutonic mythology, and in Persia the primitive dualism of beneficent and hurtful powers of nature became an ethical dualism — the eternal opposition of good and evil. The sun is vanquished by cloud and storm, but shines forth again in vigour. Vegetation dies, but undergoes a yearly renewal. So in myth the immortal gods are wounded and slain in strife. But we must not push too far the analogy of the apparent strife of the elements and the wars of the gods. The one suggested the other, especially where the gods were elemental powers. But myth-making man easily developed the suggestion; gods were like men and "could never get eneuch o' fechtin'." The Celts knew of divine combats before their arrival in Ireland, and their own hostile powers were easily assimilated to the hostile gods of the aborigines.

The principal Fomorians are described as kings. Elatha was son of Nét, described by Cormac as "a battle god of the heathen Gael," i.e. he is one of the Tuatha Dé Danann, and has as wives two war-goddesses, Badb and Nemaind. 187 Thus he resembles the Fomorian Tethra whose wife is a badb or "battle-crow," preying on the slain. 188 Elatha's name, connected with words meaning "knowledge," suggests that he was an aboriginal culture-god. 189 In the genealogies, Fomorians and Tuatha Dé Danann are inextricably mingled. Bres's temporary position as king of the Tuatha Déa may reflect some myth of the occasional supremacy of the powers of blight. Want and niggardliness characterise his reign, and after his defeat a better state of things prevails. Bres's consort was Brigit, and their son Ruadan, sent to spy on the Tuatha Dé Danann, was slain. His mother's wailing for him was the first mourning wail ever heard in Erin. 190 Another god, Indech, was son of Déa Domnu, a Fomorian goddess of the deep, i.e. of the underworld and probably also of fertility, who may hold a position among the Fomorians similar to that of Danu among the Tuatha Dé Danann. Indech was slain by Ogma, who himself died of wounds received from his adversary.

Balor had a consort Cethlenn, whose venom killed Dagda. His one eye had become evil by contact with the poisonous fumes of a concoction which his father's Druids were preparing. The eyelid required four men to raise it, when his evil eye destroyed all on whom its glance fell. In this way Balor would have slain Lug at Mag-tured, but the god at once struck the eye with a sling-stone and slew him. 191 Balor, like the Greek Medusa, is perhaps a personification of the evil eye, so much feared by the Celts. Healthful influences and magical charms avert it; hence Lug, a beneficent god, destroys Balor's maleficence.

Tethra, with Balor and Elatha, ruled over Erin at the coming of the Tuatha Dé Danann. From a phrase used in the story of Connla's visit to Elysium, "Thou art a hero of the men of Tethra," M. D'Arbois assumes that Tethra was ruler of Elysium, which he makes one with the land of the dead. The passage, however, bears a different interpretation, and though a Fomorian, Tethra, a god of war, might be regarded as lord of all warriors. Elysium was not the land of the dead, and when M. D'Arbois equates Tethra with Kronos, who after his defeat became ruler of a land of dead heroes, the analogy, like other analogies with Greek mythology, is misleading. He also equates Bres, as temporary king of the Tuatha Dé Danann, with Kronos, king of heaven in the age of gold. Kronos, again, slain by Zeus, is parallel to Balor slain by his grandson Lug. Tethra, Bres, and Balor are thus separate fragments of one god equivalent to Kronos. 193 Yet their personalities are quite distinct. Each race works out its mythology for itself, and, while parallels are inevitable, we should not allow these to override the actual myths as they have come down to us.

Professor Rh[^y]s makes Bile, ancestor of the Milesians who came from Spain, a Goidelic counterpart of the Gaulish Dispater, lord of the dead, from whom the Gauls claimed descent. But Bile, neither a Fomorian nor of the Tuatha Dé Danann, is an imaginary and shadowy creation. Bile is next equated with a Brythonic Beli, assumed to be consort of Dôn, whose family are equivalent to the Tuatha Dé Danann. 194 Beli was a mythic king whose reign was a kind of golden age, and if he was father of Dôn's children, which is doubtful, Bile would then be father of the Tuatha Dé Danann. But he is ancestor of the Milesians, their opponents according to the annalists. Beli is also equated with Elatha, and since Dôn, reputed consort of Beli, was grandmother of Llew, equated with Irish Lug, grandson of Balor, Balor is equivalent to Beli, whose name is regarded by Professor Rh[^y] s as related etymologically to Balor's. 195 Bile, Balor, and Elatha are thus Goidelic equivalents of the shadowy Beli. But they also are quite distinct personalities, nor are they ever hinted at as ancestral gods of the Celts, or gods of a gloomy underworld. In Celtic belief the underworld was probably a fertile region and a place of light, nor were its gods harmful and evil, as Balor was.

On the whole, the Fomorians came to be regarded as the powers of nature in its hostile aspect. They personified blight, winter, darkness, and death, before which men trembled, yet were not wholly cast down, since the immortal gods of growth and light, rulers of the bright other-world, were on their side and fought against their enemies. Year by year the gods suffered deadly harm, but returned as conquerors to renew the struggle once more. Myth spoke of this as having happened once for all, but it went on continuously. 196 Gods were immortal and only seemed to die. The strife was represented in ritual, since men believe that they can aid the gods by magic, rite, or prayer. Why, then, do hostile Fomorians and Tuatha Dé Danann intermarry? This happens in all mythologies, and it probably reflects, in the divine sphere, what takes place among men. Hostile peoples carry off each the other's women, or they have periods of friendliness and consequent intermarriage. Man makes his gods in his own image, and the problem is best explained by facts like these, exaggerated no doubt by the Irish annalists.

The Tuatha Dé Danann, in spite of their euhemerisation, are more than human. In the north where they learned magic, they dwelt in four cities, from each of which they brought a magical treasure—the stone of Fal, which "roared under every king," Lug's unconquerable spear, Nuada's irresistible sword, the Dagda's inexhaustible cauldron. But they are more than wizards or Druids. They are re-born as mortals; they have a divine world of their own, they interfere in and influence human affairs. The euhemerists did not go far enough, and more than once their divinity is practically acknowledged. When the Fian Caoilte and a woman of the Tuatha Dé Danann appear before S. Patrick, he asks, "Why is she youthful and beautiful, while you are old and wrinkled?" And Caoilte replies, "She is of the Tuatha Dé Danann, who are unfading and whose duration is perennial. I am of the sons of Milesius, that are perishable and fade away." 197

After their conversion, the Celts, sons of Milesius, thought that the gods still existed in the hollow hills, their former dwellings and sanctuaries, or in far-off islands, still caring for their former worshippers. This tradition had its place with that which made them a race of men conquered by the Milesians—the victory of Christianity over paganism and its gods having been transmuted into a strife of races by the euhemerists. The new faith, not the people, conquered the old gods. The Tuatha Dé Danann became the Daoine-sidhe, a fairy folk, still occasionally called by their old name, just as individual fairy kings or queens bear the names of the ancient gods. The euhemerists gave the Fomorians a monstrous and demoniac character, which they did not always give to the Tuatha Dé Danann; in this continuing the old tradition that Fomorians were hostile and the Tuatha Dé Danann beneficent and mild.

The mythological cycle is not a complete "body of divinity"; its apparent completeness results from the chronological order of the annalists. Fragments of other myths are found in the Dindsenchas; others exist as romantic tales, and we have no reason to believe that all the old myths have been preserved. But enough remains to show the true nature of the Tuatha Dé Danann—their supernatural character, their powers, their divine and unfailing food and drink, their mysterious and beautiful abode. In their contents, their personages, in the actions that are described in them, the materials of the rrr"mythological cycle," show how widely it differs from the Cúchulainn and Fionn cycles. 198 "The white radiance of eternity" suffuses it; the heroic cycles, magical and romantic as they are, belong far more to earth and time.

Footnote 153: For some Highland references to the gods in saga and Märchen, see Book of the Dean of Lismore, 10; Campbell, WHT ii. 77. The sea-god Lir is probably the Liur of Ossianic ballads (Campbell, LF 100, 125), and his son Manannan is perhaps "the Son of the Sea" in a Gaelic song (Carmichael, CG ii. 122). Manannan and his daughters are also known (Campbell, witchcraft, 83).

Footnote 154: The euhemerising process is first seen in tenth century poems by Eochaid hua Flainn, but was largely the work of Flainn Manistrech, ob. 1056. It is found fully fledged in the Book of Invasions.

Footnote 155: Keating, 105-106.

Footnote 156: Keating, 107; LL 4b. Cf. RC xvi. 155.

Footnote 157: LL 5.

Footnote 158: Keating, 111. Giraldus Cambrensis, Hist. Irel. c. 2, makes Roanus survive and tell the tale of Partholan to S. Patrick. He is the Caoilte mac Ronan of other tales, a survivor of the Fians, who held many racy dialogues with the Saint. Keating abuses Giraldus for equating Roanus with Finntain in his "lying history," and for calling him

Roanus instead of Ronanus, a mistake in which he, "the guide bull of the herd," is followed by others.

Footnote 159: Keating, 164.

Footnote 160: LL 5a.

Footnote 161: Keating, 121; LL 6a; RC xvi. 161.

Footnote 162: Nennius, Hist. Brit. 13.

Footnote 163: LL 6, 8b.

Footnote 164: LL 6b, 127a; IT iii. 381; RC xvi. 81.

Footnote 165: LL 9b, 11a.

Footnote 166: See Cormac, s.v. "Nescoit," LU 51.

Footnote 167: Harl. MSS. 2, 17, pp. 90-99. Cf. fragment from Book of Invasions in LL 8.

Footnote 168: Harl. MS. 5280, translated in RC xii. 59 f.

Footnote 169: RC xii. 60; D'Arbois, v. 405 f.

Footnote 170: For Celtic brother-sister unions .

Footnote 171: O'Donovan, Annals, i. 16.

Footnote 172: RC xv. 439.

Footnote 173: RC xii. 71.

Footnote 174: Professor Rh[^y]s thinks the Partholan story is the aboriginal, the median the Celtic version of the same event. Partholan, with initial p cannot be Goidelic (Scottish Review, 1890, "Myth. Treatment of Celtic Ethnology").

Footnote 175: HL 591.

Footnote 176: CM ix. 130; Campbell LF 68.

Footnote 177: RC xii. 75.

Footnote 178: US 211.

Footnote 179: D'Arbois, ii. 52; RC xii. 476.

Footnote 180: RC xii. 73.

Footnote 181: RC xii. 105.

Footnote 182: RC xxii. 195.

Footnote 183: Larmime, "Kian, son of Kontje."

Footnote 184: LL 245b.

Footnote 185: Mannhardt, Mythol. Forsch. 310 f.

Footnote 186: "Fir Domnann," "men of Domna," a goddess (Rh[^y]s, HL 597), or a god (D'Arbois, ii. 130). "Domna" is connected with Irish-words meaning "deep" (Windisch, IT i. 498; Stokes, US 153). Domna, or Domnu, may therefore have been a goddess of the deep, not the sea so much as the underworld, and so perhaps an Earth-mother from whom the Fir Domnann traced their descent.

Footnote 187: Cormac, s.v. "Neith"; D'Arbois, v. 400; RC xii. 61.

Footnote 188: LU 50. Tethra is glossed badb (IT i. 820).

Footnote 189: IT i. 521; Rh[^y]s, HL 274 f.

Footnote 190: RC xii. 95.

Footnote 191: RC xii. 101.

Footnote 193: D'Arbois, ii. 198, 375.

Footnote 194: HL 90-91.

Footnote 195: HL 274, 319, 643. For Beli, infra.

Footnote 196: Whatever the signification of the battle of Mag-tured may be, the place which it was localised is crowded with Neolithic megaliths, dolmens, etc. To later fancy these were the graves of warriors slain in a great battle fought there, and that battle became the fight between Fomorians and Tuatha Dé Dananns. Mag-tured may have been the scene of a battle between their respective worshippers.

Footnote 197: O'Grady, ii. 203.

Footnote 198: It should be observed that, as in the Vedas, the Odyssey, the Japanese Ko-ji-ki, as well as in barbaric and savage mythologies, Märchen formulæ abound in the Irish mythological cycle.

CHAPTER V
THE TUATHA DÉ DANANN

The meaning formerly given to Tuatha Dé Danann was "the men of science who were gods," danann being here connected with dán, "knowledge." But the true meaning is "the tribes or folk of the goddess Danu," 199 which agrees with the cognates Tuatha or Fir Dea, "tribes or men of the goddess." The name was given to the group, though Danu had only three sons, Brian, Iuchar, and Iucharbar. Hence the group is also called fir tri ndea, "men of the three gods." 200 The equivalents in Welsh story of Danu and her folk are Dôn and her children. We have seen that though they are described as kings and warriors by the annalists, traces of their divinity appear. In the Cúchulainn cycle they are supernatural beings and sometimes demons, helping or harming men, and in the Fionn cycle all these characteristics are ascribed to them. But the theory which prevailed most is that which connected them with the hills or mounds, the last resting-places of the mighty dead. Some of these bore their names, while other beings were also associated with the mounds (síd)—Fomorians and Milesian chiefs, heroes of the sagas, or those who had actually been buried in them. 201 Legend told how, after the defeat of the gods, the mounds were divided among them, the method of division varying in different versions. In an early version the Tuatha Dé Danann are immortal and the Dagda divides the síd. 202 But in a poem of Flann Manistrech (ob. 1056) they are mortals and die. 203 Now follows a regular chronology giving the dates of their reigns and their deaths, as in the poem of Gilla Coemain (eleventh century). 204 Hence another legend told how, Dagda being dead, Bodb Dearg divided the síd, yet even here Manannan is said to have conferred immortality upon the Tuatha Dé Danann. 205 The old pagan myths had shown that gods might die, while in ritual their representatives were slain, and this may have been the starting-point of the euhemerising process. But the divinity of the Tuatha Dé Danann is still recalled. Eochaid O'Flynn (tenth century), doubtful whether they are men or demons, concludes, "though I have treated of these deities in order, yet have I not adored them." 206 Even in later times they were still thought of as gods in exile, a view which appears in the romantic tales and sagas existing side by side with the notices of the annalists. They were also regarded as fairy kings and queens, and yet fairies of a different order from those of ordinary tradition. They are "fairies or sprites with corporeal forms, endowed with immortality," and yet also dei terreni or síde worshipped by the folk before the coming of S. Patrick. Even the saint and several bishops were called by the fair pagan daughters of King Loegaire, fir síde, "men of the síd," that is, gods. 207 The síd were named after the names of the Tuatha Dé Danann who reigned in them, but the tradition being localised in different places, several mounds were sometimes connected with one god. The síd were marvellous underground palaces, full of strange things, and thither favoured mortals might go for a time or for ever. In this they correspond exactly to the oversea Elysium, the divine land.

But why were the Tuatha Dé Danann associated with the mounds? If fairies or an analogous race of beings were already in pagan times connected with hills or mounds, gods now regarded as fairies would be connected with them. Dr. Joyce and O'Curry think that an older race of aboriginal gods or síd-folk preceded the Tuatha Déa in the mounds. 208 These may have been the Fomorians, the "champions of the síd," while in Mesca Ulad the Tuatha Déa go to the underground dwellings and speak with the síde already there. We do not know that the fairy creed as such existed in pagan times, but if the síde and the Tuatha Dé Danann were once distinct, they were gradually assimilated. Thus the Dagda is called "king of the síde"; Aed Abrat and his daughters, Fand and Liban, and Labraid, Liban's husband, are called síde, and Manannan is Fand's consort. 209 Labraid's island, like the síd of Mider and the land to which women of the síde invite Connla, differs but little from the usual divine Elysium, while Mider, one of the síde, is associated with the Tuatha Dé Danann. 210 The síde are once said to be female, and are frequently supernatural women who run away or marry mortals. 211 Thus they may be a reminiscence of old Earth goddesses. But they are not exclusively female, since there are kings of the síde, and as the name Fir síde, "men of the síde," shows, while S. Patrick and his friends were taken for síd-folk.

The formation of the legend was also aided by the old cult of the gods on heights, some of them sepulchral mounds, and now occasionally sites of Christian churches. 212 The Irish god Cenn Cruaich and his Welsh equivalent Penn Cruc, whose name survives in Pennocrucium, have names meaning "chief or head of the mound." 213 Other mounds or hills had also a sacred character. Hence gods worshipped at mounds, dwelling or revealing themselves there, still lingered in the haunted spots; they became fairies, or were associated with the dead buried in the mounds, as fairies also have been, or were themselves thought to have died and been buried there. The haunting of the mounds by the old gods is seen in a prayer of S. Columba's, who begs God to dispel "this host (i.e. the old gods) around the cairns that reigneth." 214 An early MS also tells how the Milesians allotted the underground part of Erin to the Tuatha Déa who now retired within the hills; in other words, they were gods of the hills worshipped by the Milesians on hills. 215 But, as we shall see, the gods dwelt elsewhere than in hills. 216

Tumuli may already in pagan times have been pointed out as tombs of gods who died in myth or ritual, like the tombs of Zeus in Crete and of Osiris in Egypt. Again, fairies, in some aspects, are ghosts of the dead, and haunt tumuli; hence, when gods became fairies they would do the same. And once they were thought of as dead kings, any notable tumuli would be pointed out as theirs, since it is a law in folk-belief to associate tumuli or other structures not with the dead or with their builders, but with supernatural or mythical or even historical personages. If síde ever meant "ghosts," it would be easy to call the dead gods by this name, and to connect them with the places of the dead. 217

Many strands went to the weaving of the later conception of the gods, but there still hung around them an air of mystery, and the belief that they were a race of men was never consistent with itself.

Danu gave her name to the whole group of gods, and is called their mother, like the Egyptian Neith or the Semitic Ishtar. 218 In the annalists she is daughter of Dagda, and has three sons. She may be akin to the goddess Anu, whom Cormac describes as "mater deorum hibernensium. It was well she nursed the gods." From her name he derives ana, "plenty," and two hills in Kerry are called "the Paps of Anu." 219 Thus as a goddess of plenty Danu or Anu may have been an early Earth-mother, and what may be a dim memory of Anu in Leicestershire confirms this view. A cave on the Dane Hills is called "Black Annis' Bower," and she is said to have been a savage woman who devoured human victims. 220 Earth-goddesses usually have human victims, and Anu would be no exception. In the cult of Earth divinities Earth and under-Earth are practically identical, while Earth-goddesses like Demeter and Persephone were associated with the underworld, the dead being Demeter's folk. The fruits of the earth with their roots below the surface are then gifts of the earth- or under-earth goddess. This may have been the case with Danu, for in Celtic belief the gifts of civilisation came from the underworld or from the gods. Professor Rh[^y]s finds the name Anu in the dat. Anoniredi, "chariot of Anu," in an inscription from Vaucluse, and the identification is perhaps established by the fact that goddesses of fertility were drawn through the fields in a vehicle. 221 Cormac also mentions Buanann as mother and nurse of heroes, perhaps a goddess worshipped by heroes. 222

Danu is also identified with Brigit, goddess of knowledge (dán), perhaps through a folk-etymology. She was worshipped by poets, and had two sisters of the same name connected with leechcraft and smithwork. 223 They are duplicates or local forms of Brigit, a goddess of culture and of poetry, so much loved by the Celts. She is thus the equivalent of the Gaulish goddess equated with Minerva by Cæsar, and found on inscriptions as Minerva Belisama and Brigindo. She is the Dea Brigantia of British inscriptions. 224 One of the seats of her worship was the land of the Brigantes, of whom she was the eponymous goddess, and her name (cf. Ir. brig, "power" or "craft"; Welsh bri, "honour," "renown") suggests her high functions. But her popularity is seen in the continuation of her personality and cult in those of S. Brigit, at whose shrine in Kildare a sacred fire, which must not be breathed on, or approached by a male, was watched daily by nineteen nuns in turn, and on the twentieth day by the saint herself. 225 Similar sacred fires were kept up in other monasteries, 226 and they point to the old cult of a goddess of fire, the nuns being successors of a virgin priesthood like the vestals, priestesses of Vesta. As has been seen, the goddesses Belisama and Sul, probably goddesses of fire, resembled Brigit in this. 227 But Brigit, like Vesta, was at once a goddess of fire and of fertility, as her connection with Candlemas and certain ritual survivals also suggest. In the Hebrides on S. Bride's day (Candlemas-eve) women dressed a sheaf of oats in female clothes and set it with a club in a basket called "Briid's bed." Then they called, "Briid is come, Briid is welcome." Or a bed was made of corn and hay with candles burning beside it, and Bride was invited to come as her bed was ready. If the mark of the club was seen in the ashes, this was an omen of a good harvest and a prosperous year. 228 It is also noteworthy that if cattle cropped the grass near S. Brigit's shrine, next day it was as luxuriant as ever.

Brigit, or goddesses with similar functions, was regarded by the Celts as an early teacher of civilisation, inspirer of the artistic, poetic, and mechanical faculties, as well as a goddess of fire and fertility. As such she far excelled her sons, gods of knowledge. She must have originated in the period when the Celts worshipped goddesses rather than gods, and when knowledge—leechcraft, agriculture, inspiration—were women's rather than men's. She had a female priesthood, and men were perhaps excluded from her cult, as the tabued shrine at Kildare suggests. Perhaps her fire was fed from sacred oak wood, for many shrines of S. Brigit were built under oaks, doubtless displacing pagan shrines of the goddess. 229 As a goddess,

Brigit is more prominent than Danu, also a goddess of fertility, even though Danu is mother of the gods.

Other goddesses remembered in tradition are Cleena and Vera, celebrated in fairy and witch lore, the former perhaps akin to a river-goddess Clota, the Clutoida (a fountain-nymph) of the continental Celts; the latter, under her alternative name Dirra, perhaps a form of a goddess of Gaul, Dirona. 230 Aine, one of the great fairy-queens of Ireland, has her seat at Knockainy in Limerick, where rites connected with her former cult are still performed for fertility on Midsummer eve. If they were neglected she and her troops performed them, according to local legend. 231 She is thus an old goddess of fertility, whose cult, even at a festival in which gods were latterly more prominent, is still remembered. She is also associated with the waters as a water-nymph captured for a time as a fairy-bride by the Earl of Desmond. 232 But older legends connect her with the síd. She was daughter of Eogabal, king of the síd of Knockainy, the grass on which was annually destroyed at Samhain by his people, because it had been taken from them, its rightful owners. Oilill Olomm and Ferchus resolved to watch the síd on Samhain-eve. They saw Eogabal and Aine emerge from it. Ferchus killed Eogabal, and Oilill tried to outrage Aine, who bit the flesh from his ear. Hence his name of "Bare Ear." 233 In this legend we see how earlier gods of fertility come to be regarded as hostile to growth. Another story tells of the love of Aillén, Eogabal's son, for Manannan's wife and that of Aine for Manannan. Aine offered her favours to the god if he would give his wife to her brother, and "the complicated bit of romance," as S. Patrick calls it, was thus arranged. 234

Although the Irish gods are warriors, and there are special war-gods, yet war-goddesses are more prominent, usually as a group of three—Morrigan, Neman, and Macha. A fourth, Badb, sometimes takes the place of one of these, or is identical with Morrigan, or her name, like that of Morrigan, may be generic. 235 Badb means "a scald-crow," under which form the war-goddesses appeared, probably because these birds were seen near the slain. She is also called Badbcatha, "battle-Badb," and is thus the equivalent of -athubodua, or, more probably, Cathubodua, mentioned in an inscription from Haute-Savoie, while this, as well as personal names like Boduogenos, shows that a goddess Bodua was known to the Gauls. 236 The badb or battle-crow is associated with the Fomorian Tethra, but Badb herself is consort of a war-god Nét, one of the Tuatha Dé Danann, who may be the equivalent of Neton, mentioned in Spanish inscriptions and equated with Mars. Elsewhere Neman is Nét's consort, and she may be the Nemetona of inscriptions, e.g. at Bath, the consort of Mars. Cormac calls Nét and Neman "a venomous couple," which we may well believe them to have been. 237 To Macha were devoted the heads of slain enemies, "Macha's mast," but she, according to the annalists, was slain at Mag-tured, though she reappears in the Cúchulainn saga as the Macha whose ill-treatment led to the "debility" of the Ulstermen. 238 The name Morrigan may mean "great queen," though Dr. Stokes, connecting mor with the same syllable in "Fomorian," explains it as "nightmare-queen." 239 She works great harm to the Fomorians at Mag-tured, and afterwards proclaims the victory to the hills, rivers, and fairy-hosts, uttering also a prophecy of the evils to come at the end of time. 240 She reappears prominently in the Cúchulainn saga, hostile to the hero because he rejects her love, yet aiding the hosts of Ulster and the Brown Bull, and in the end trying to prevent the hero's death.

The prominent position of these goddesses must be connected with the fact that women went out to war—a custom said to have been stopped by Adamnan at his mother's request, and that many prominent heroines of the heroic cycles are warriors, like the British Boudicca, whose name may be connected with boudi, "victory." Specific titles were given to such classes of female warriors—bangaisgedaig, banfeinnidi, etc. 242 But it is possible that these goddesses were at first connected with fertility, their functions changing with the growing warlike tendencies of the Celts. Their number recalls that of the threefold Matres, and possibly the change in their character is hinted in the Romano-British inscription at Benwell to the Lamiis Tribus, since Morrigan's name is glossed lamia. 243 She is also identified with Anu, and is mistress of Dagda, an Earth-god, and with Badb and others expels the Fomorians when they destroyed the agricultural produce of Ireland. 244 Probably the scald-crow was at once the symbol and the incarnation of the war-goddesses, who resemble the Norse Valkyries, appearing sometimes as crows, and the Greek Keres, bird-like beings which drank the blood of the slain. It is also interesting to note that Badb, who has the character of a prophetess of evil, is often identified with the "Washer at the Ford," whose presence indicates death to him whose armour or garments she seems to cleanse. 245

The Matres, goddesses of fertility, do not appear by name in Ireland, but the triplication of such goddesses as Morrigan and Brigit, the threefold name of Dagda's wife, or the fact that Arm, Danu, and Buanan are called "mothers," while Buanan's name is sometimes rendered "good mother," may suggest that such grouped goddesses were not unknown. Later legend knows of white women who assist in spinning, or three hags with power over nature, or, as in the Battle of Ventry, of three supernatural women who fall in love with Conncrithir, aid him in fight, and heal his wounds. In this document and elsewhere is mentioned the "síd of the White Women." 246

Goddesses of fertility are usually goddesses of love, and the prominence given to females among the síde, the fact that they are often called Be find, "White Women," like fairies who represent the Matres elsewhere, and that they freely offer their love to mortals, may connect them with this group of goddesses. Again, when the Milesians arrived in Ireland, three kings of the Tuatha Déa had wives called Eriu, Banba, and Fotla, who begged that Ireland should be called after them. This was granted, but only Eriu (Erin) remained in general use. 247 The story is an ætiological myth explaining the names of Ireland, but the three wives may be a group like the Matres, guardians of the land which took its name from them.

Brian, Iuchar, and Iucharba, who give a title to the whole group, are called tri dee Donand, "the three gods (sons of) Danu," or, again, "gods of dán" (knowledge), perhaps as the result of a folk-etymology, associating dân with their mother's name Danu. 248 Various attributes are personified as their descendants, Wisdom being son of all three. 249 Though some of these attributes may have been actual gods, especially Ecne or Wisdom, yet it is more probable that the personification is the result of the subtleties of bardic science, of which similar examples occur. 250 On the other hand, the fact that Ecne is the son of three brothers, may recall some early practice of polyandry of which instances are met with in the sagas. 251 M. D'Arbois has suggested that Iuchar and Iucharba are mere duplicates of Brian, who usually takes the leading place, and he identifies them with three kings of the Tuatha Déa reigning at the time of the Milesian invasion—MacCuill, MacCecht, and MacGrainne, so called, according to Keating, because the hazel (coll), the plough (cecht), and the sun (grian) were "gods of worship" to them. Both groups are grandsons of Dagda, and M. D'Arbois regards this second group as also triplicates of one god, because their wives Fotla, Banba, and Eriu all bear names of Ireland itself, are personifications of the land, and thus may be "reduced to unity." 252 While this reasoning is ingenious, it should be remembered that we must not lay too much stress upon Irish divine genealogies, while each group of three may have been similar local gods associated at a later time as brothers. Their separate personality is suggested by the fact that the Tuatha Dé Danann are called after them "the Men of the Three Gods," and their supremacy appears in the incident of Dagda, Lug, and Ogma consulting them before the fight at Mag-tured—a natural proceeding if they were gods of knowledge or destiny. 253 The brothers are said to have slain the god Cian, and to have been themselves slain by Lug, and on this seems to have been based the story of The Children of Tuirenn, in which they perish through their exertions in obtaining the eric demanded by Lug. 254 Here they are sons of Tuirenn, but more usually their mother Danu or Brigit is mentioned.

Another son of Brigit's was Ogma, master of poetry and inventor of ogham writing, the word being derived from his name. 255 It is more probable that Ogma's name is a derivative from some word signifying "speech" or "writing," and that the connection with "ogham" may be a mere folk-etymology. Ogma appears as the champion of the gods, 256 a position given him perhaps from the primitive custom of rousing the warriors' emotions by eloquent speeches before a battle. Similarly the Babylonian Marduk, "seer of the gods," was also their champion in fight. Ogma fought and died at Mag-tured; but in other accounts he survives, captures Tethra's sword, goes on the quest for Dagda's harp, and is given a síd after the Milesian victory. Ogma's counterpart in Gaul is Ogmíos, a Herakles and a god of eloquence, thus bearing the dual character of Ogma, while Ogma's epithet grianainech, "of the smiling countenance," recalls Lucian's account of the "smiling face" of Ogmíos. 257 Ogma's high position is the result of the admiration of bardic eloquence among the Celts, whose loquacity was proverbial, and to him its origin was doubtless ascribed, as well as that of poetry. The genealogists explain his relationship to the other divinities in different ways, but these confusions may result from the fact that gods had more than one name, of which the annalists made separate personalities. Most usually Ogma is called Brigit's son. Her functions were like his own, but in spite of the increasing supremacy of gods over goddesses, he never really eclipsed her.

Among other culture gods were those associated with the arts and crafts—the development of Celtic art in metal-work necessitating the existence of gods of this art. Such a god is Goibniu, eponymous god of smiths (Old Ir. goba, "smith"), and the divine craftsman at the battle of Mag-tured, making spears which never failed to kill. 258 Smiths have everywhere been regarded as uncanny—a tradition surviving from the first introduction of metal among those hitherto accustomed to stone weapons and tools. S. Patrick prayed against the "spells of women, smiths, and Druids," and it is thus not surprising to find that Goibniu had a reputation for magic, even among Christians. A spell for making butter, in an eighth century MS. preserved at S. Gall, appeals to his "science." 259 Curiously enough, Goibniu is also connected with the culinary art in myth, and, like Hephaistos, prepares the feast of the gods, while his ale preserves their immortality. 260 The elation produced by heady liquors caused them to be regarded as draughts of immortality, like Soma, Haoma, or nectar. Goibniu survives in tradition as the Gobhan Saer, to whom the building of round towers is ascribed.

Another god of crafts was Creidne the brazier (Ir. cerd, "artificer"; cf. Scots caird, "tinker"), who assisted in making a silver hand for Nuada, and supplied with magical rapidity parts of the weapons used at Mag-tured. 261 According to the annalists, he was drowned while bringing golden ore from Spain. 262 Luchtine, god of carpenters, provided spear-handles for the battle, and with marvellous skill flung them into the sockets of the spear-heads. 263

Diancecht, whose name may mean "swift in power," was god of medicine, and, with Creidne's help, fashioned a silver hand for Nuada. 264 His son Miach replaced this by a magic restoration of the real hand, and in jealousy his father slew him—a version of the Märchen formula of the jealous master. Three hundred and sixty-five herbs grew from his grave, and were arranged according to their properties by his sister Airmed, but Diancecht again confused them, "so that no one knows their proper cures." 265 At the second battle of Mag-tured, Diancecht presided over a healing-well containing magic herbs. These and the power of spells caused the mortally wounded who were placed in it to recover. Hence it was called "the spring of health." 266 Diancecht, associated with a healing-well, may be cognate with Grannos. He is also referred to in the S. Gall MS., where his healing powers are extolled.

An early chief of the gods is Dagda, who, in the story of the battle of Mag-tured, is said to be so called because he promised to do more than all the other gods together. Hence they said, "It is thou art the good hand" (dag-dae). The Cóir Anmann explains Dagda as "fire of god" (daig and déa). The true derivation is from dagos, "good," and deivos, "god," though Dr. Stokes considers Dagda as connected with dagh, whence daghda, "cunning." 267 Dagda is also called Cera, a word perhaps derived from kar and connected with Lat. cerus, "creator" and other names of his are Ruad-rofhessa, "lord of great knowledge," and Eochaid Ollathair, "great father," "for a great father to the Tuatha Dé Danann was he." 268 He is also called "a beautiful god," and "the principal god of the pagans." 269 After the battle he divides the brugs or síd among the gods, but his son Oengus, having been omitted, by a stratagem succeeded in ousting his father from his síd, over which he now himself reigned 270 — possibly the survival of an old myth telling of a superseding of Dagda's cult by that of Oengus, a common enough occurrence in all religions. In another version, Dagda being dead, Bodb Dearg divides the síd, and Manannan makes the Tuatha Déa invisible and immortal. He also helps Oengus to drive out his foster-father Elemar from his brug, where Oengus now lives as a god. 271 The underground brugs are the gods' land, in all respects resembling the oversea Elysium, and at once burial-places of the euhemerised gods and local forms of the divine land. Professor Rh[^y]s regards Dagda as an atmospheric god; Dr. MacBain sees in him a sky-god. More probably he is an early Earth-god and a god of agriculture. He has power over corn and milk, and agrees to prevent the other gods from destroying these after their defeat by the Milesians—former beneficent gods being regarded as hurtful, a not uncommon result of the triumph of a new faith. 272 Dagda is called "the god of the earth" "because of the greatness of his power." 273 Mythical objects associated with him suggest plenty and fertility—his cauldron which satisfied all comers, his unfailing swine, one always living, the other ready for cooking, a vessel of ale, and three trees always laden with fruit. These were in his síd, where none ever tasted death; 274 hence his síd was a local Elysium, not a gloomy land of death, but the underworld in its primitive aspect as the place of gods of fertility. In some myths he appears with a huge club or fork, and M. D'Arbois suggests that he may thus be an equivalent of the Gaulish god with the mallet. 275 This is probable, since the Gaulish god may have been a form of Dispater, an Earth or under-Earth god of fertility.

If Dagda was a god of fertility, he may have been an equivalent of a god whose image was called Cenn or Cromm Cruaich, "Head or Crooked One of the Mound," or "Bloody Head or Crescent." 276 Vallancey, citing a text now lost, says that Crom-eocha was a name of Dagda, and that a motto at the sacrificial place at Tara read, "Let the altar ever blaze to Dagda." 277 These statements may support this identification. The cult of Cromm is preserved in some verses:

> "He was their god,
>
> The withered Cromm with many mists...
>
> To him without glory
>
> They would kill their piteous wretched offspring,
>
> With much wailing and peril,
>
> To pour their blood around Cromm Cruaich.
>
> Milk and corn
>
> They would ask from him speedily
>
> In return for a third of their healthy issue,
>
> Great was the horror and fear of him.
>
> To him noble Gaels would prostrate themselves." 278

Elsewhere we learn that this sacrifice in return for the gifts of corn and milk from the god took place at Samhain, and that on one occasion the violent prostrations of the worshippers caused three-fourths of them to die. Again, "they beat their palms, they pounded their bodies ... they shed falling showers of tears." 279 These are reminiscences of orgiastic rites in which pain and pleasure melt into one. The god must have been a god of fertility; the blood of the victims was poured on the image, the flesh, as in analogous savage rites and folk-survivals, may have been buried in the fields to promote fertility. If so, the victims' flesh was instinct with the power of the divinity, and, though their number is obviously exaggerated, several victims may have taken the place of an earlier slain representative of the god. A mythic Crom Dubh, "Black Crom," whose festival occurs on the first Sunday in August, may be another form of Cromm Cruaich. In one story the name is transferred to S. Patrick's servant, who is asked by the fairies when they will go to Paradise. "Not till the day of judgment," is the answer, and for this they cease to help men in the processes of agriculture. But in a variant Manannan bids Crom ask this question, and the same result follows. 280 These tales thus enshrine the idea that Crom and the fairies were ancient gods of growth who ceased to help men when they deserted them for the Christian faith. If the sacrifice was offered at the August festival, or, as the texts suggest, at Samhain, after harvest, it must have been on account of the next year's crop, and the flesh may have been mingled with the seed corn.

Dagda may thus have been a god of growth and fertility. His wife or mistress was the river-goddess, Boand (the Boyne), 281 and the children ascribed to him were Oengus, Bodb Dearg, Danu, Brigit, and perhaps Ogma. The euhemerists made him die of Cethlenn's venom, long after the battle of Mag-tured in which he encountered her. 282 Irish mythology is remarkably free from obscene and grotesque myths, but some of these cluster round Dagda. We hear of the Gargantuan meal provided for him in sport by the Fomorians, and of which he ate so much that "not easy was it for him to move and unseemly was his apparel," as well as his conduct with a Fomorian beauty. Another amour of his was with Morrigan, the place where it occurred being still known as "The Couple's Bed." 283 In another tale Dagda acts as cook to Conaire the great. 284

The beautiful and fascinating Oengus is sometimes called Mac Ind Oc, "Son of the Young Ones," i.e. Dagda and Boand, or In Mac Oc, "The Young Son." This name, like the myth of his disinheriting his father, may point to his cult superseding that of Dagda. If so, he may then have been affiliated to the older god, as was frequently done in parallel cases, e.g. in Babylon. Oengus may thus have been the high god of some tribe who assumed supremacy, ousting the high god of another tribe, unless we suppose that Dagda was a pre-Celtic god with functions similar to those of Oengus, and that the Celts adopted his cult but gave that of Oengus a higher place. In one myth the supremacy of Oengus is seen. After the first battle of Mag-tured, Dagda is forced to become the slave of Bres, and is much annoyed by a lampooner who extorts the best pieces of his rations. Following the advice of Oengus, he not only causes the lampooner's death, but triumphs over the Fomorians. 285 On insufficient grounds, mainly because he was patron of Diarmaid, beloved of women, and because his kisses became birds which whispered love thoughts to youths and maidens, Oengus has been called the Eros of the Gaels. More probably he was primarily a supreme god of growth, who occasionally suffered eclipse during the time of death in nature, like Tammuz and Adonis, and this may explain his absence from Mag-tured. The beautiful story of his vision of a maiden with whom he fell violently in love contains too many Märchen formulæ to be of any mythological or religious value. His mother Boand caused search to be made for her, but without avail. At last she was discovered to be the daughter of a semi-divine lord of a síd, but only through the help of mortals was the secret of how she could be taken wrung from him. She was a swan-maiden, and on a certain day only would Oengus obtain her. Ultimately she became his wife. The story is interesting because it shows how the gods occasionally required mortal aid. 286

Equally influenced by Märchen formulæ is the story of Oengus and Etain. Etain and Fuamnach were wives of Mider, but Fuamnach was jealous of Etain, and transformed her into an insect. In this shape Oengus found her, and placed her in a glass grianan or bower filled with flowers, the perfume of which sustained her. He carried the grianan with him wherever he went, but Fuamnach raised a magic wind which blew Etain away to the roof of Etair, a noble of Ulster. She fell through a smoke-hole into a golden cup of wine, and was swallowed by Etair's wife, of whom she was reborn. 287 Professor Rh[^y]s resolves all this into a sun and dawn myth. Oengus is the sun, Etain the dawn, the grianan the expanse of the sky. 288 But the dawn does not grow stronger with the sun's influence, as Etain did under that of Oengus. At the sun's appearance the dawn begins

"to faint in the light of the sun she loves,

To faint in his light and to die."

The whole story is built up on the well-known Märchen formulæ of the "True Bride" and the "Two Brothers," but accommodated to well-known mythic personages, and the grianan is the Celtic equivalent of various objects in stories of the "Cinderella" type, in which the heroine conceals herself, the object being bought by the hero and kept in his room. 289 Thus the tale reveals nothing of Etain's divine functions, but it illustrates the method of the "mythological" school in discovering sun-heroes and dawn-maidens in any incident, mythical or not.

Oengus appears in the Fionn cycle as the fosterer and protector of Diarmaid. 290 With Mider, Bodb, and Morrigan, he expels the Fomorians when they destroy the corn, fruit, and milk of the Tuatha Dé Danann. 291 This may point to his functions as a god of fertility.

Although Mider appears mainly as a king of the síde and ruler of the brug of Bri Léith, he is also connected with the Tuatha Déa. 292 Learning that Etain had been reborn and was now married to King Eochaid, he recovered her from him, but lost her again when Eochaid attacked his brug. He was ultimately avenged in the series of tragic events which led to the death of Eochaid's descendant Conaire. Though his síd is located in Ireland, it has so much resemblance to Elysium that Mider must be regarded as one of its lords. Hence he appears as ruler of the Isle of Falga, i.e. the Isle of Man regarded as Elysium. Thence his daughter Bláthnat, his magical cows and cauldron, were stolen by Cúchulainn and Curoi, and his three cranes from Bri Léith by Aitherne 293 — perhaps distorted versions of the myths which told how various animals and gifts came from the god's land. Mider may be the Irish equivalent of a local Gaulish god, Medros, depicted on bas-reliefs with a cow or bull. 294

The victory of the Tuatha Déa at the first battle of Mag-tured, in June, their victory followed, however, by the deaths of many of them at the second battle in November, may point to old myths dramatising the phenomena of nature, and connected with the ritual of summer and winter festivals. The powers of light and growth are in the ascendant in summer; they seem to die in winter. Christian euhemerists made use of these myths, but regarded the gods as warriors who were slain, not as those who die and revive again. At the second battle, Nuada loses his life; at the first, though his forces are victorious, his hand was cut off by the Fomorian Sreng, for even when victorious the gods must suffer. A silver hand was made for him by Diancecht, and hence he was called Nuada Argetlám, "of the silver hand." Professor Rh[^y]s regards him as a Celtic Zeus, partly because he is king of the Tuatha Dé Danann, partly because he, like Zeus or Tyr, who lost tendons or a hand through the wiles of evil gods, is also maimed. 295 Similarly in the Rig-Veda the Açvins substitute a leg of iron for the leg of Vispala, cut off in battle, and the sun is called "golden-handed" because Savitri cut off his hand and the priests replaced it by one of gold. The myth of Nuada's hand may have arisen from primitive attempts at replacing lopped-off limbs, as well as from the fact that no Irish king must have any bodily defect, or possibly because an image of Nuada may have lacked a hand or possessed one of silver. Images were often maimed or given artificial limbs, and myths then arose to explain the custom. 296 Nuada appears to be a god of life and growth, but he is not a sun-god. His Welsh equivalent is Llûd Llawereint, or "silver-handed," who delivers his people from various scourges. His daughter Creidylad is to be wedded to Gwythur, but is kidnapped by Gwyn. Arthur decides that they must fight for her yearly on 1st May until the day of judgment, when the victor would gain her hand. 297 Professor Rh[^y]s regards Creidylad as a Persephone, wedded alternately to light and dark divinities. 298 But the story may rather be explanatory of such ritual acts as are found in folk-survivals in the form of fights between summer and winter, in which a Queen of May figures, and intended to assist the conflict of the gods of growth with those of blight. 299 Creidylad is daughter of a probable god of growth, nor is it impossible that the story of the battle of Mag-tured is based on mythic explanations of such ritual combats.

The Brythons worshipped Nuada as Nodons in Romano-British times. The remains of his temple exist near the mouth of the Severn, and the god may have been equated with Mars, though certain symbols seem to connect him with the waters as a kind of Neptune. 300 An Irish mythic poet Nuada Necht may be the Nechtan who owned a magic well whence issued the Boyne, and was perhaps a water-god. If such a water-god was associated with Nuada, he and Nodons might be a Celtic Neptune. 301 But the relationship and functions of these various personages are obscure, nor is it certain that Nodons was equated with Neptune or that Nuada was a water-god. His name may be cognate with words meaning "growth," "possession," "harvest," and this supports the view taken here of his functions. 302 The Welsh Nudd Hael, or "the Generous," who possessed a herd of 21,000 milch kine, may be a memory of this god, and it is possible that, as a god of growth, Nuada had human incarnations called by his name. 303

Ler, whose name means "sea," and who was a god of the sea, is father of Manannan as well as of the personages of the beautiful story called The Children of Lir, from which we learn practically all that is known of him. He resented not being made ruler of the Tuatha Déa, but was later reconciled when the daughter of Bodb Dearg was given to him as his wife. On her death, he married her sister, who transformed her step-children into swans. 304 Ler is the equivalent of the Brythonic Llyr, later immortalised by Shakespeare as King Lear.

The greatness of Manannan mac Lir, "son of the sea," is proved by the fact that he appears in many of the heroic tales, and is still remembered in tradition and folk-tale. He is a sea-god who has become more prominent than the older god of the sea, and though not a supreme god, he must have had a far-spreading cult. With Bodb Dearg he was elected king of the Tuatha Dé Danann. He made the gods invisible and immortal, gave them magical food, and assisted Oengus in driving out Elemar from his síd. Later tradition spoke of four Manannans, probably local forms of the god, as is suggested by the fact that the true name of one of them is said to be Orbsen, son of Allot. Another, the son of Ler, is described as a renowned trader who dwelt in the Isle of Man, the best of pilots, weather-wise, and able to transform himself as he pleased. The Cóir Anmann adds that the Britons and the men of Erin deemed him god of the sea. 305 That position is plainly seen in many tales, e.g. in the magnificent passage of The Voyage of Bran, where he suddenly sweeps into sight, riding in a chariot across the waves from the Land of Promise; or in the tale of Cúchulainn's Sickness, where his wife Fand sees him, "the horseman of the crested sea," coming across the waves. In the Agallamh na Senorach he appears as a cavalier breasting the waves. "For the space of nine waves he would be submerged in the sea, but would rise on the crest of the tenth without wetting chest or breast." 306 In one archaic tale he is identified with a great sea wave which swept away Tuag, while the waves are sometimes called "the son of Lir's horses"—a name still current in Ireland, or, again, "the locks of Manannan's wife." 307 His position as god of the sea may have given rise to the belief that he was ruler of the oversea Elysium, and, later, of the other-world as a magical domain coterminous with this earth. He is still remembered in the Isle of Man, which may owe its name to him, and which, like many another island, was regarded by the Goidels as the island Elysium under its name of Isle of Falga. He is also the Manawyddan of Welsh story.

Manannan appears in the Cúchulainn and Fionn cycles, usually as a ruler of the Other-world. His wife Fand was Cúchulainn's mistress, Diarmaid was his pupil in fairyland, and Cormac was his guest there. Even in Christian times surviving pagan beliefs caused legend to be busy with his name. King Fiachna was fighting the Scots and in great danger, when a stranger appeared to his wife and announced that he would save her husband's life if she would consent to abandon herself to him. She reluctantly agreed, and the child of the amour was the seventh-century King Mongan, of whom the annalist says, "every one knows that his real father was Manannan." 308 Mongan was also believed to be a rebirth of Fionn. Manannan is still remembered in folk-tradition, and in the Isle of Man, where his grave is to be seen, some of his ritual survived until lately, bundles of rushes being placed for him on midsummer eve on two hills. 309 Barintus, who steers Arthur to the fortunate isles, and S. Barri, who crossed the sea on horseback, may have been legendary forms of a local sea-god akin to Manannan, or of Manannan himself. 310 His steed was Enbarr, "water foam or hair," and Manannan was "the horseman of the manéd sea." "Barintus," perhaps connected with barr find, "white-topped," would thus be a surname of the god who rode on Enbarr, the foaming wave, or who was himself the wave, while his mythic sea-riding was transferred to the legend of S. Barri, if such a person ever existed.

Various magical possessions were ascribed to Manannan—his armour and sword, the one making the wearer invulnerable, the other terrifying all who beheld it; his horse and canoe; his swine, which came to life again when killed; his magic cloak; his cup which broke when a lie was spoken; his tablecloth, which, when waved, produced food. Many of these are found everywhere in Märchen, and there is nothing peculiarly Celtic in them. We need not, therefore, with the mythologists, see in his armour the vapoury clouds or in his sword lightning or the sun's rays. But their magical nature as well as the fact that so much wizardry is attributed to Manannan, points to a copious mythology clustering round the god, now for ever lost.

The parentage of Lug is differently stated, but that account which makes him son of Cian and of Ethne, daughter of Balor, is best attested. 311 Folk-tradition still recalls the relation of Lug and Balor. Balor, a robber living in Tory Island, had a daughter whose son was to kill her father. He therefore shut her up in an inaccessible place, but in revenge for Balor's stealing MacIneely's cow, the latter gained access to her, with the result that Ethne bore three sons, whom Balor cast into the sea. One of them, Lug, was recovered by MacIneely and fostered by his brother Gavida. Balor now slew MacIneely, but was himself slain by Lug, who pierced his single eye with a red-hot iron. 312 In another version, Kian takes MacIneely's place and is aided by Manannan, in accordance with older legends. 313 But Lug's birth-story has been influenced in these tales by the Märchen formula of the girl hidden away because it has been foretold that she will have a son who will slay her father.

Lug is associated with Manannan, from whose land he comes to assist the Tuatha Déa against the Fomorians. His appearance was that of the sun, and by this brilliant warrior's prowess the hosts were utterly defeated. 314 This version, found in The Children of Tuirenn, differs from the account in the story of Mag-tured. Here Lug arrives at the gates of Tara and offers his services as a craftsman. Each offer is refused, until he proclaims himself "the man of each and every art," or samildánach, "possessing many arts." Nuada resigns his throne to him for thirteen days, and Lug passes in review the various craftsmen (i.e. the gods), and though they try to prevent such a marvellous person risking himself in fight, he escapes, heads the warriors, and sings his war-song. Balor, the evil-eyed, he slays with a sling-stone, and his death decided the day against the Fomorians. In this account Lug samildánach is a patron of the divine patrons of crafts; in other words, he is superior to a whole group of gods. He was also inventor of draughts, ball-play, and horsemanship. But, as M. D'Arbois shows, samildánach is the equivalent of "inventor of all arts," applied by Cæsar to the Gallo-Roman Mercury, who is thus an equivalent of Lug. 315 This is attested on other grounds. As Lug's name appears in Irish Louth (Lug-magh) and in British Lugu-vallum, near Hadrian's Wall, so in Gaul the names Lugudunum (Lyons), Lugudiacus, and Lugselva ("devoted to Lugus") show that a god Lugus was worshipped there. A Gaulish feast of Lugus in August—the month of Lug's festival in Ireland—was perhaps superseded by one in honour of Augustus. No dedication to Lugus has yet been found, but images of and inscriptions to Mercury abound at Lugudunum Convenarum. 316 As there were three Brigits, so there may have been several forms of Lugus, and two dedications to the Lugoves have been found in Spain and Switzerland, one of them inscribed by the shoemakers of Uxama. 317 Thus the Lugoves may have been multiplied forms of Lugus or Lugovos, "a hero," the meaning given to "Lug" by O'Davoren. 318 Shoe-making was not one of the arts professed by Lug, but Professor Rh[^y]s recalls the fact that the Welsh Lleu, whom he equates with Lug, disguised himself as a shoemaker. 319 Lugus, besides being a mighty hero, was a great Celtic culture-god, superior to all other culture divinities.

The euhemerists assigned a definite date to Lug's death, but side by side with this the memory of his divinity prevailed, and he appears as the father and helper of Cúchulainn, who was possibly a rebirth of the god. 320 His high position appears in the fact that the Gaulish assembly at Lugudunum was held in his honour, like the festival of Lugnasad in Ireland. Craftsmen brought their wares to sell at this festival of the god of crafts, while it may also have been a harvest festival. 321 Whether it was a strictly solar feast is doubtful, though Professor Rh[^y]s and others insist that Lug is a sun-god. The name of the Welsh Lleu, "light," is equated with Lug, and the same meaning assigned to the latter. 322 This equation has been contested and is doubtful, Lugus probably meaning "hero." 323 Still the sun-like traits ascribed to Lug before Mag-tured suggest that he was a sun-god, and solar gods elsewhere, e.g. the Polynesian Maui, are culture-gods as well. But it should be remembered that Lug is not associated with the true solar festivals of Beltane and Midsummer.

While our knowledge of the Tuatha Dé Danann is based upon a series of mythic tales and other records, that of the gods of the continental Celts, apart from a few notices in classical authors and elsewhere, comes from inscriptions. But as far as can be judged, though the names of the two groups seldom coincide, their functions must have been much alike, and their origins certainly the same. The Tuatha Dé Danann were nature divinities of growth, light, agriculture—their symbols and possessions suggesting fertility, e.g. the cauldron. They were divinities of culture and crafts, and of war. There must have been many other gods in Ireland than those described here, while some of those may not have been worshipped all over Ireland. Generally speaking, there were many local gods in Gaul with similar functions but different names, and this may have been true of Ireland. Perhaps the different names given to Dagda, Manannan, and others were simply names of similar local gods, one of whom became prominent, and attracted to himself the names of the others. So, too, the identity of Danu and Brigit might be explained, or the fact that there were three Brigits. We read also in the texts of the god of Connaught, or of Ulster, and these were apparently regional divinities, or of "the god of Druidism" — perhaps a god worshipped specially by Druids. 324 The remote origin of some of these divinities may be sought in the primitive cult of the Earth personified as a fertile being, and in that of vegetation and corn-spirits, and the vague spirits of nature in all its aspects. Some of these still continued to be worshipped when the greater gods had been evolved. Though animal worship was not lacking in Ireland, divinities who are anthropomorphic forms of earlier animal-gods are less in evidence than on the Continent. The divinities of culture, crafts, and war, and of departments of nature, must have slowly assumed the definite personality assigned them in Irish religion. But, doubtless, they already possessed that before the Goidels reached Ireland. Strictly speaking, the underground domain assigned later to the Tuatha Dé Danann belongs only to such of them as were associated with fertility. But in course of time most of the group, as underground dwellers, were connected with growth and increase. These could be blighted by their enemies, or they themselves could withhold them when their worshippers offended them. 325

Irish mythology points to the early pre-eminence of goddesses. As agriculture and many of the arts were first in the hands of women, goddesses of fertility and culture preceded gods, and still held their place when gods were evolved. Even war-goddesses are prominent in Ireland. Celtic gods and heroes are often called after their mothers, not their fathers, and women loom largely in the tales of Irish colonisation, while in many legends they play a most important part. Goddesses give their name to divine groups, and, even where gods are prominent, their actions are free, their personalities still clearly defined. The supremacy of the divine women of Irish tradition is once more seen in the fact that they themselves woo and win heroes; while their capacity for love, their passion, their eternal youthfulness and beauty are suggestive of their early character as goddesses of ever-springing fertility. 326

This supremacy of goddesses is explained by Professor Rh[^y]s as non-Celtic, as borrowed by the Celts from the aborigines. 327 But it is too deeply impressed on the fabric of Celtic tradition to be other than native, and we have no reason to suppose that the Celts had not passed through a stage in which such a state of things was normal. Their innate conservatism caused them to preserve it more than other races who had long outgrown such a state of things.

Footnote 199: HL 89; Stokes, RC xii. 129. D'Arbois, ii. 125, explains it as "Folk of the god whose mother is called Danu."

Footnote 200: RC xii. 77. The usual Irish word for "god" is dia; other names are Fiadu, Art, Dess.

Footnote 201: See Joyce, SII. i. 252, 262; PN i. 183.

Footnote 202: LL 245b.

Footnote 203: LL 11.

Footnote 204: LL 127. The mounds were the sepulchres of the euhemerised gods.

Footnote 205: Book of Fermoy, fifteenth century.

Footnote 206: LL 11b.

Footnote 207: IT i. 14, 774; Stokes, TL i. 99, 314, 319. Síd is a fairy hill, the hill itself or the dwelling within it. Hence those who dwell in it are Aes or Fir síde, "men of the mound," or síde, fairy folk. The primitive form is probably sêdos, from sêd, "abode" or "seat"; cf. Greek [Greek: edos] "a temple." Thurneysen suggests a connection with a word equivalent to Lat. sidus, "constellation," or "dwelling of the gods."

Footnote 208: Joyce, SH i. 252; O'Curry, MS. Mat. 505.

Footnote 209: "Vision of Oengus," RC iii. 344; IT i. 197 f.

Footnote 210: Windisch, Ir. Gram. 118; O'Curry, MC ii. 71; infra.

Footnote 211: Windisch, Ir. Gram. 118, § 6; IT iii. 407; RC xvi. 139.

Footnote 212: Shore, JAI xx. 9.

Footnote 213: Rh[^y]s, HL 203 f. Pennocrucium occurs in the Itinerary of Antoninus.

Footnote 214: Keating, 434.

Footnote 215: Joyce, SH i. 252.

Footnote 216: In Scandinavia the dead were called elves, and lived feasting in their barrows or in hills. These became the seat of ancestral cults. The word "elf" also means any divine spirit, later a fairy. "Elf" and síde may thus, like the "elf-howe" and rrrthe síd or mound, have a parallel history. See Vigfusson-Powell, Corpus Poet. Boreale, i. 413 f.

Footnote 217: Tuan MacCairill (LU 166) calls the Tuatha Déa, "dée ocus andée," and gives the meaning as "poets and husbandmen." This phrase, with the same meaning, is used in "Cóir Anmann" (IT iii. 355), but there we find that it occurred in a pagan formula of blessing—"The blessing of gods and not-gods be on thee." But the writer goes on to say—"These were their gods, the magicians, and their non-gods, the husbandmen." This may refer to the position of priest-kings and magicians as gods. Rh[^y]s compares Sanskrit deva and adeva (HL 581). Cf. the phrase in a Welsh poem (Skene, i. 313), "Teulu Oeth et Anoeth," translated by Rh[^y]s as "Household of Power and Not-Power" (CFL ii. 620), but the meaning is obscure. See Loth, i. 197.

Footnote 218: LL 10b.

Footnote 219: Cormac, 4. Stokes (US 12) derives Anu from (p)an, "to nourish"; cf. Lat. panis.

Footnote 220: Leicester County Folk-lore, 4. The Cóir Anmann says that Anu was worshipped as a goddess of plenty (IT iii. 289).

Footnote 221: Rh[^y]s, Trans. 3rd Inter. Cong. Hist. of Rel. ii. 213. See Grimm, Teut. Myth. 251 ff., and infra.

Footnote 222: Rh[^y]s, ibid. ii. 213. He finds her name in the place-name Bononia and its derivatives.

Footnote 223: Cormac, 23.

Footnote 224: Cæsar, vi. 17; Holder, s.v.; Stokes, TIG 33.

Footnote 225: Girald. Cambr. Top. Hib. ii. 34 f. Vengeance followed upon rash intrusion. For the breath tabu see Frazer, Early Hist. of the Kingship, 224.

Footnote 226: Joyce, SH i. 335.

Footnote 227: supra.

Footnote 228: Martin, 119; Campbell, Witchcraft, 248.

Footnote 229: Frazer, op. cit. 225.

Footnote 230: Joyce, PN i. 195; O'Grady, ii. 198; Wood-Martin, i. 366; supra.

Footnote 231: Fitzgerald, RC iv. 190. Aine has no connection with Anu, nor is she a moon-goddess, as is sometimes supposed.

Footnote 232: RC iv. 189.

Footnote 233: Keating, 318; IT iii. 305; RC xiii. 435.

Footnote 234: O'Grady, ii. 197.

Footnote 235: RC xii. 109, xxii. 295; Cormac, 87; Stokes, TIG xxxiii.

Footnote 236: Holder, i. 341; CIL vii. 1292; Cæsar, ii. 23.

Footnote 237: LL 11b; Cormac, s.v. Neit; RC iv. 36; Arch. Rev. i. 231; Holder, ii. 714, 738.

Footnote 238: Stokes, TIG, LL 11a.

Footnote 239: Rh[^y]s, HL 43; Stokes, RC xii. 128.

Footnote 240: RC xii. 91, 110.

Footnote 242: Petrie, Tara, 147; Stokes, US 175; Meyer, Cath Finntrága, Oxford, 1885, 76 f.; RC xvi. 56, 163, xxi. 396.

Footnote 243: CIL vii. 507; Stokes, US 211.

Footnote 244: RC i. 41, xii. 84.

Footnote 245: RC xxi. 157, 315; Miss Hull, 247. A baobh (a common Gaelic name for "witch") appears to Oscar and prophesies his death in a Fionn ballad (Campbell, The Fians, 33). In Brittany the "night-washers," once water-fairies, are now regarded as revenants (Le Braz, i. 52).

Footnote 246: Joyce, SH i. 261; Miss Hull, 186; Meyer, Cath Finntraga, 6, 13; IT i. 131, 871.

Footnote 247: LL 10a.

Footnote 248: LL 10a, 30b, 187c.

Footnote 249: RC xxvi. 13; LL 187c.

Footnote 250: Cf. the personification of the three strains of Dagda's harp (Leahy, ii. 205).

Footnote 251: infra.

Footnote 252: D'Arbois, ii. 372.

Footnote 253: RC xii. 77, 83.

Footnote 254: LL 11; Atlantis, London, 1858-70, iv. 159.

Footnote 255: O'Donovan, Grammar, Dublin, 1845, xlvii.

Footnote 256: RC xii. 77.

Footnote 257: Lucian, Herakles.

Footnote 258: RC xii. 89. The name is found in Gaulish Gobannicnos, and in Welsh Abergavenny.

Footnote 259: IT i. 56; Zimmer, Glossæ Hibernicæ, 1881, 270.

Footnote 260: Atlantis, 1860, iii. 389.

Footnote 261: RC xii. 89.

Footnote 262: LL lla.

Footnote 263: RC xii. 93.

Footnote 264: Connac, 56, and Cóir Anmann (IT iii. 357) divide the name as día-na-cecht and explain it as "god of the powers."

Footnote 265: RC xii. 67. For similar stories of plants springing from graves, see my Childhood of Fiction, 115.

Footnote 266: RC xii, 89, 95.

Footnote 267: RC vi. 369; Cormac, 23.

Footnote 268: Cormac, 47, 144; IT iii. 355, 357.

Footnote 269: IT iii. 355; D'Arbois, i. 202.

Footnote 270: LL 246a.

Footnote 271: Irish MSS. Series, i. 46; D'Arbois, ii. 276. In a MS. edited by Dr. Stirn, Oengus was Dagda's son by Elemar's wife, the amour taking place in her husband's absence. This incident is a parallel to the birth-stories of Mongan and Arthur, and has also the Fatherless Child theme, since Oengus goes in tears to Mider because he has been taunted with having no father or mother. In the same MS. it is the Dagda who instructs Oengus how to obtain Elemar's síd. See RC xxvii. 332, xxviii. 330.

Footnote 272: LL 245b.

Footnote 273: IT iii. 355.

Footnote 274: O'Donovan, Battle of Mag-Rath, Dublin, 1842, 50; LL 246a.

Footnote 275: D'Arbois, v. 427, 448.

Footnote 276: The former is Rh[^y]s's interpretation (HL 201) connecting Cruaich with crúach, "a heap"; the latter is that of D'Arbois (ii. 106), deriving Cruaich from cru, "blood." The idea of the image being bent or crooked may have been due to the fact that it long stood ready to topple over, as a result of S. Patrick's miracle. , infra.

Footnote 277: Vallancey, in Coll. de Rebus Hib. 1786, iv. 495.

Footnote 278: LL 213b. D'Arbois thinks Cromm was a Fomorian, the equivalent of Taranis (ii. 62). But he is worshipped by Gaels. Crin, "withered," probably refers to the idol's position after S. Patrick's miracle, no longer upright but bent like an old man. Dr. Hyde, Lit. Hist. of Ireland, 87, with exaggerated patriotism, thinks the sacrificial details are copied by a Christian scribe from the Old Testament, and are no part of the old ritual.

Footnote 279: RC xvi. 35, 163.

Footnote 280: Fitzgerald, RL iv. 175.

Footnote 281: RC xxvi. 19.

Footnote 282: Annals of the Four Masters, A.M. 3450.

Footnote 283: RC xii. 83, 85; Hyde, op. cit. 288.

Footnote 284: LU 94.

Footnote 285: RC xii. 65. Elsewhere three supreme "ignorances" are ascribed to Oengus (RL xxvi. 31).

Footnote 286: RC iii. 342.

Footnote 287: LL 11c; LU 129; IT i. 130. Cf. the glass house, placed between sky and moon, to which Tristan conducts the queen. Bedier, Tristan et Iseut, 252. In a fragmentary version of the story Oengus is Etain's wooer, but Mider is preferred by her father, and marries her. In the latter half of the story, Oengus does not appear (see p. , infra). Mr. Nutt (RC xxvii. 339) suggests that Oengus, not Mider, was the real hero of the story, but that its Christian redactors gave Mider his place in the second part. The fragments are edited by Stirn (ZCP vol. v.).

Footnote 288: HL 146.

Footnote 289: See my Childhood of Fiction, 114, 153. The tale has some unique features, as it alone among Western Märchen and saga variants of the "True Bride" describes the malicious woman as the wife of Mider. In other words, the story implies polygamy, rarely found in European folk-tales.

Footnote 290: O'Grady, TOS iii.

Footnote 291: RC i. 41.

Footnote 292: O'Curry, MC i. 71.

Footnote 293: LL 117a. infra.

Footnote 294: Cumont, RC xxvi. 47; D'Arbois, RC xxvii. 127, notes the difficulty of explaining the change of e to i in the names.

Footnote 295: HL 121.

Footnote 296: See Crooke, Folk-Lore, viii. 341. Cf. Herod, ii. 131.

Footnote 297: Loth, i. 269.

Footnote 298: HL 563.

Footnote 299: Train, Isle of Man, Douglas, 1845, ii. 118; Grimm, Teut. Myth. ii. ch. 24; Frazer, GB 2 ii. 99 f.

Footnote 300: Bathurst, Roman Antiquities at Lydney Park, 1879; Holder, s.v. "Nodons."

Footnote 301: See Rh[^y]s, HL 122; Cook, Folk-Lore, xvii. 30.

Footnote 302: Stokes, US 194-195; Rh[^y]s, HL, 128, IT i. 712.

Footnote 303: Loth, ii. 235, 296. infra.

Footnote 304: Joyce, OCR.

Footnote 305: For these four Manannans see Cormac 114, RC xxiv. 270, IT iii. 357.

Footnote 306: O'Grady, ii.

Footnote 307: Bodley Dindsenchas, No. 10, RC xii. 105; Joyce, SH i. 259; Otia Merseiana, ii. "Song of the Sea."

Footnote 308: LU 133.

Footnote 309: Moore, 6.

Footnote 310: Geoffrey, Vita Merlini, 37; Rees, 435. Other saintly legends are derived from myths, e.g. that of S. Barri in his boat meeting S. Scuithne walking on the sea. Scuithne maintains he is walking on a field, and plucks a flower to prove it, while Barri confutes him by pulling a salmon out of the sea. This resembles an episode in the meeting of Bran and Manannan (Stokes, Félire, xxxix.; Nutt-Meyer, i. 39). Saints are often said to assist men just as the gods did. Columcille and Brigit appeared over the hosts of Erin assisting and encouraging them (RC xxiv. 40).

Footnote 311: RC xii. 59.

Footnote 312: Folk-Lore Journal, v. 66; Rh[^y]s, HL 314.

Footnote 313: Larminie, "Kian, son of Kontje."

Footnote 314: Joyce, OCR 37.

Footnote 315: D'Arbois, vi. 116, Les Celtes, 39, RC xii. 75, 101, 127, xvi. 77. Is the defaced inscription at Geitershof, Deo M ... Sam ... (Holder, ii. 1335), a dedication to Mercury Samildánach? An echo of Lug's story is found in the Life of S. Herve, who found a devil in his monastery in the form of a man who said he was rrra good carpenter, mason, locksmith, etc., but who could not make the sign of the cross. Albert le Grand, Saints de la Bretagne, 49, RC vii. 231.

Footnote 316: Holder, s.v.; D'Arbois, Les Celtes, 44, RC vii. 400.

Footnote 317: Holder, s.v. "Lugus."

Footnote 318: Stokes, TIG 103. Gaidoz contests the identification of the Lugoves and of Lug with Mercury, and to him the Lugoves are grouped divinities like the Matres (RC vi. 489).

Footnote 319: HL 425.

Footnote 320: infra.

Footnote 321: infra.

Footnote 322: HL 409.

Footnote 323: See Loth, RC x. 490.

Footnote 324: Leahy, i. 138, ii. 50, 52, LU 124b.

Footnote 325: LL 215a supra.

Footnote 326: See, further, infra.

Footnote 327: The Welsh People, 61. Professor Rh[^y]s admits that the theory of borrowing "cannot easily be proved."

CHAPTER VI
THE GODS OF THE BRYTHONS

Our knowledge of the gods of the Brythons, i.e. as far as Wales is concerned, is derived, apart from inscriptions, from the Mabinogion, which, though found in a fourteenth century MS., was composed much earlier, and contains elements from a remote past. Besides this, the Triads, probably of twelfth-century origin, the Taliesin, and other poems, though obscure and artificial, the work of many a "confused bard drivelling" (to cite the words of one of them), preserve echoes of the old mythology. 328 Some of the gods may lurk behind the personages of Geoffrey of Monmouth's Historia Britonum and of the Arthurian cycle, though here great caution is required. The divinities have become heroes and heroines, kings and princesses, and if some of the episodes are based on ancient myths, they are treated in a romantic spirit. Other episodes are mere Märchen formulæ. Like the wreckage of some rich galleon, the débris of the old mythology has been used to construct a new fabric, and the old divinities have even less of the god-like traits of the personages of the Irish texts.

Some of the personages bear similar names to the Irish divinities, and in some cases there is a certain similarity of incidents to those of the Irish tales. 329 Are, then, the gods dimly revealed in Welsh literature as much Goidelic as Brythonic? Analysing the incidents of the Mabinogion, Professor Anwyl has shown that they have an entirely local character, and are mainly associated with the districts of Dyfed and Gwent, of Anglesey, and of Gwynedd, of which Pryderi, Branwen, and Gwydion are respectively the heroic characters. 330 These are the districts where a strong Goidelic element prevailed, whether these Goidels were the original inhabitants of Britain, driven there by Brythons, 331 or tribes who had settled there from Ireland, 332 or perhaps a mixture of both. In any case they had been conquered by Brythons and had become Brythonic in speech from the fifth century onwards. On account of this Goidelic element, it has been claimed that the personages of the Mabinogion are purely Goidelic. But examination proves that only a few are directly parallel in name with Irish divinities, and while here there are fundamental likenesses, the incidents with Irish parallels may be due to mere superficial borrowings, to that interchange of Märchen and mythical données which has everywhere occurred. Many incidents have no Irish parallels, and most of the characters are entirely different in name from Irish divinities. Hence any theory which would account for the likenesses, must also account for the differences, and must explain why, if the Mabinogion is due to Irish Goidels, there should have been few or no borrowings in Welsh literature from the popular Cúchulainn and Ossianic sagas, 333 and why, at a time when Brythonic elements were uppermost, such care should have been taken to preserve Goidelic myths. If the tales emanated from native Welsh Goidels, the explanation might be that they, the kindred of the Irish Goidels, must have had a certain community with them in divine names and myths, while others of their gods, more local in character, would differ in name. Or if they are Brythonic, the likenesses might be accounted for by an early community in myth and cult among the common ancestors of Brythons and Goidels. 334 But as the date of the composition of the Mabinogion is comparatively late, at a time when Brythons had overrun these Goidelic districts, more probably the tales contain a mingling of Goidelic (Irish or Welsh) and Brythonic divinities, though some of these may be survivals of the common Celtic heritage. 335 Celtic divinities were mainly of a local, tribal character. Hence some would be local Goidelic divinities, others, classed with these, local Brythonic divinities. This would explain the absence of divinities and heroes of other local Brythonic groups, e.g. Arthur, from the Mabinogion. But with the growing importance of these, they attracted to their legend the folk of the Mabinogion and other tales. These are associated with Arthur in Kulhwych, and the Dôn group mingles with that of Taliesin in the Taliesin poems. 336 Hence Welsh literature, as far as concerns the old religion, may be regarded as including both local Goidelic and Brythonic divinities, of whom the more purely Brythonic are Arthur, Gwynn, Taliesin, etc. 337 They are regarded as kings and queens, or as fairies, or they have magical powers. They are mortal and die, and the place of their burial is pointed out, or existing tumuli are associated with them, All this is parallel to the history of the Tuatha Dé Danann, and shows how the same process of degradation had been at work in Wales as in Ireland.

The story of the Llyr group is told in the Mabinogion of Branwen and of Manawyddan. They are associated with the Pwyll group, and apparently opposed to that of Dôn. Branwen is married to Matholwych, king of Ireland, but is ill-treated by him on account of the insults of the mischievous Evnissyen, in spite of the fact that Bran had atoned for the insult by many gifts, including that of a cauldron of regeneration. Now he crosses with an army to Ireland, where Evnissyen throws Branwen's child, to whom the kingdom is given, on the fire. A fight ensues; the dead Irish warriors are resuscitated in the cauldron, but Evnissyen, at the cost of his life, destroys it. Bran is slain, and by his directions his head is cut off and carried first to Harlech, then to Gwales, where it will entertain its bearers for eighty years. At the end of that time it is to be taken to London and buried. Branwen, departing with the bearers, dies of a broken heart at Anglesey, and meanwhile Caswallyn, son of Beli, seizes the kingdom. 338 Two of the bearers of the head are Manawyddan and Pryderi, whose fortunes we follow in the Mabinogi of the former. Pryderi gives his mother Rhiannon to Manawyddan as his wife, along with some land which by magic art is made barren. After following different crafts, they are led by a boar to a strange castle, where Rhiannon and Pryderi disappear along with the building. Manawyddan, with Pryderi's wife Kieva, set out as shoemakers, but are forced to abandon this craft on account of the envy of the craftsmen. Finally, we learn how Manawyddan overcame the enchanter Llwyt, who, because of an insult offered by Pryderi's father to his friend Gwawl, had made Rhiannon and Pryderi disappear. They are now restored, and Llwyt seeks no further revenge.

The story of Branwen is similar to a tale of which there are variants in Teutonic and Scandinavian sagas, but the resemblance is closer to the latter. 339 Possibly a similar story with their respective divinities or heroes for its characters existed among Celts, Teutons, and Norsemen, but more likely it was borrowed from Norsemen who occupied both sides of the Irish Sea in the ninth and tenth century, and then naturalised by furnishing it with Celtic characters. But into this framework many native elements were set, and we may therefore scrutinise the story for Celtic mythical elements utilised by its redactor, who probably did not strip its Celtic personages of their earlier divine attributes. In the two Mabinogi these personages are Llyr, his sons Bran and Manawyddan, his daughter Branwen, their half-brothers Nissyen and Evnissyen, sons of Llyr's wife Penardim, daughter of Beli, by a previous marriage with Eurosswyd.

Llyr is the equivalent of the Irish Ler, the sea-god, but two other Llyrs, probably duplicates of himself, are known to Welsh story—Llyr Marini, and the Llyr, father of Cordelia, of the chroniclers. 340 He is constantly confused with Lludd Llawereint, e.g. both are described as one of three notable prisoners of Britain, and both are called fathers of Cordelia or Creiddylad. 341 Perhaps the two were once identical, for Manannan is sometimes called son of Alloid (= Lludd), in Irish texts, as well as son of Ler. 342 But the confusion may be accidental, nor is it certain that Nodons or Lludd was a sea-god. Llyr's prison was that of Eurosswyd, 343 whose wife he may have abducted and hence suffered imprisonment. In the Black Book of Caermarthen Bran is called son of Y Werydd or "Ocean," according to M. Loth's interpretation of the name, which would thus point to Llyr's position as a sea-god. But this is contested by Professor Rh[^y]s who makes Ywerit wife of Llyr, the name being in his view a form of the Welsh word for Ireland. In Geoffrey and the chroniclers Llyr becomes a king of Britain whose history and that of his daughters was immortalised by Shakespeare. Geoffrey also refers to Llyr's burial in a vault built in honour of Janus. 344 On this Professor Rh[^y]s builds a theory that Llyr was a form of the Celtic Dis with two faces and ruler of a world of darkness. 345 But there is no evidence that the Celtic Dispater was lord of a gloomy underworld, and it is best to regard Llyr as a sea-divinity.

Manawyddan is not god-like in these tales in the sense in which the majestic Manannan of Irish story is, though elsewhere we learn that "deep was his counsel." 346 Though not a magician, he baffles one of the great wizards of Welsh story, and he is also a master craftsman, who instructs Pryderi in the arts of shoe-making, shield-making, and saddlery. In this he is akin to Manannan, the teacher of Diarmaid. Incidents of his career are reflected in the Triads, and his union with Rhiannon may point to an old myth in which they were from the first a divine pair, parents of Pryderi. This would give point to his deliverance of Pryderi and Rhiannon from the hostile magician. 347 Rhiannon resembles the Irish Elysium goddesses, and Manawyddan, like Manannan, is lord of Elysium in a Taliesin poem. 348 He is a craftsman and follows agriculture, perhaps a reminiscence of the old belief that fertility and culture come from the god's land. Manawyddan, like other divinities, was drawn into the Arthurian cycle, and is one of those who capture the famous boar, the Twrch Trwyth. 349

Bran, or Bendigeit Vran ("Bran the Blessed"), probably an old pagan title which appropriately enough denotes one who figured later in Christian hagiology, is so huge that no house or ship can hold him. Hence he wades over to Ireland, and as he draws near is thought to be a mountain. This may be an archaic method of expressing his divinity—a gigantic non-natural man like some of the Tuatha Déa and Ossianic heroes. But Bran also appears as the Urdawl Ben, or "Noble Head," which makes time pass to its bearers like a dream, and when buried protects the land from invasion. Both as a giant squatting on a rock and as a head, Bran is equated by Professor Rh[^y]s with Cernunnos, the squatting god, represented also as a head, and also with the Welsh Urien whose attribute was a raven, the supposed meaning of Bran's name. 350 He further equates him with Uthr Ben, "Wonderful Head," the superior bard, harper and piper of a Taliesin poem. 351 Urien, Bran, and Uthr are three forms of a god worshipped by bards, and a "dark" divinity, whose wading over to Ireland signifies crossing to Hades, of which he, like Yama, who first crossed the rapid waters to the land of death, is the ruler. 352 But Bran is not a "dark" god in the sense implied here. Cernunnos is god of a happy underworld, and there is nothing dark or evil in him or in Bran and his congeners. Professor Rh[^y]s's "dark" divinities are sometimes, in his view, "light" gods, but they cannot be both. The Celtic lords of the dead had no "dark" character, and as gods of fertility they were, so to speak, in league with the sun-god, the slayer of Bran, according to Professor Rh[^y]s's ingenious theory. And although to distracted Irish secretaries Ireland may be Hades, its introduction into this Mabinogi merely points to the interpretation of a mythico-historic connection between Wales and Ireland. Thus if Bran is Cernunnos, this is because he is a lord of the underworld of fertility, the counterpart of which is the distant Elysium, to which Bran seems rather to belong. Thus, in presence of his head, time passes as a dream in feasting and joy. This is a true Elysian note, and the tabued door of the story is also suggestive of the tabus of Elysium, which when broken rob men of happiness. 353 As to the power of the head in protecting the land, this points to actual custom and belief regarding the relics of the dead and the power of divine images or sculptured heads. The god Bran has become a king and law-giver in the Mabinogion and the Triads, 355 while Geoffrey of Monmouth describes how Belinus and Brennus, in the Welsh version Beli and Bran, dispute the crown of Britain, are reconciled, and finally conquer Gaul and Rome. 356 The mythic Bran is confused with Brennus, leader of the Gauls against Rome in 390 B.C., and Belinus may be the god Belenos, as well as Beli, father of Lludd and Caswallawn. But Bran also figures as a Christian missionary. He is described as hostage at Rome for his son Caradawc, returning thence as preacher of Christianity to the Cymry—a legend arising out of a misunderstanding of his epithet "Blessed" and a confusing of his son with the historic Caractacus. 357 Hence Bran's family is spoken of as one of the three saintly families of Prydein, and he is ancestor of many saints. 358

Branwen, "White Bosom," daughter of a sea-god, may be a sea-goddess, "Venus of the northern sea," 359 unless with Mr. Nutt we connect her with the cauldron described in her legend, 360 symbol of an orgiastic cult, and regard her as a goddess of fertility. But the connection is not clear in the story, though in some earlier myth the cauldron may have been her property. As Brangwaine, she reappears in romance, giving a love-potion to Tristram—perhaps a reminiscence of her former functions as a goddess of love, or earlier of fertility. In the Mabinogion she is buried in Anglesey at Ynys Bronwen, where a cairn with bones discovered in 1813 was held to be the grave and remains of Branwen. 361

The children of Dôn, the equivalent of Danu, and probably like her, a goddess of fertility, are Gwydion, Gilvæthwy, Amæthon, Govannon, and Arianrhod, with her sons, Dylan and Llew. 362 These correspond, therefore, in part to the Tuatha Déa, though the only members of the group who bear names similar to the Irish gods are Govannon (= Goibniu) and possibly Llew (= Lug). Gwydion as a culture-god corresponds to Ogma. In the Triads Beli is called father of Arianrhod, 363 and assuming that this Arianrhod is identical with the daughter of Dôn, Professor Rh[^y]s regards Beli as husband of Dôn. But the identification is far from certain, and the theory built upon it that Beli is one with the Irish Bile, and that both are lords of a dark underworld, has already been found precarious. 364 In later belief Dôn was associated with the stars, the constellation Cassiopeia being called her court. She is described as "wise" in a Taliesin poem. 365

This group of divinities is met with mainly in the Mabinogi of Math, which turns upon Gilvæthwy's illicit love of Math's "foot-holder" Goewin. To assist him in his amour, Gwydion, by a magical trick, procures for Math from the court of Pryderi certain swine sent him by Arawn, king of Annwfn. In the battle which follows when the trick is discovered, Gwydion slays Pryderi by enchantment. Math now discovers that Gilvæthwy has seduced Goewin, and transforms him and Gwydion successively into deer, swine, and wolves. Restored to human form, Gwydion proposes that Arianrhod should be Math's foot-holder, but Math by a magic test discovers that she is not a virgin. She bears two sons, Dylan, fostered by Math, and another whom Gwydion nurtures and for whom he afterwards by a trick obtains a name from Arianrhod, who had sworn never to name him. The name is Llew Llaw Gyffes, "Lion of the Sure Hand." By magic, Math and Gwydion form a wife for Llew out of flowers. She is called Blodeuwedd, and later, at the instigation of a lover, Gronw, she discovers how Llew can be killed. Gronw attacks and wounds him, and he flies off as an eagle. Gwydion seeks for Llew, discovers him, and retransforms him to human shape. Then he changes Blodeuwedd into an owl, and slays Gronw. 366 Several independent tales have gone to the formation of this Mabinogi, but we are concerned here merely with the light it may throw on the divine characters who figure in it.

Math or Math Hen, "the Ancient," 367 is probably an old divinity of Gwyned, of which he is called lord. He is a king and a magician, pre-eminent in wizardry, which he teaches to Gwydion, and in a Triad he is called one of the great men of magic and metamorphosis of Britain. 368 More important are his traits of goodness to the suffering, and justice with no trace of vengeance to the wrong-doer. Whether these are derived from his character as a god or from the Celtic kingly ideal, it is impossible to say, though the former is by no means unlikely. Possibly his supreme magical powers make him the equivalent of the Irish "god of Druidism," but this is uncertain, since all gods were more or less dowered with these.

Gwydion's magical powers are abundantly illustrated in the tale. At Pryderi's court he changes fungus into horses and dogs, and afterwards slays Pryderi by power of enchantments; he produces a fleet by magic before Arianrhod's castle; with Math's help he forms Blodeuwedd out of flowers; he gives Llew his natural shape when he finds him as a wasted eagle on a tree, his flesh and the worms breeding in it dropping from him; he transforms the faithless Blodeuwedd into an owl. Some of these and other deeds are referred to in the Taliesin poems, while Taliesin describes himself as enchanted by Gwydion. 369 In the Triads he is one of the three great astrologers of Prydein, and this emphasis laid on his powers of divination is significant when it is considered that his name may be derived from a root vet, giving words meaning "saying" or "poetry," while cognate words are Irish fáith, "a prophet" or "poet," German wuth, "rage," and the name of Odinn. 370 The name is suggestive of the ecstasy of inspiration producing prophetic and poetic utterance. In the Mabinogion he is a mighty bard, and in a poem, he, under the name of Gweir, is imprisoned in the Other-world, and there becomes a bard, thus receiving inspiration from the gods' land. 371 He is the ideal fáith — diviner, prophet, and poet, and thus the god of those professing these arts. Strabo describes how the Celtic vates (fáith) was also a philosopher, and this character is given in a poem to Seon (probably = Gwydion), whose artists are poets and magicians. 372 But he is also a culture-god, bringing swine to men from the gods' land. For though Pryderi is described as a mortal who has himself received the swine from Annwfn (Elysium), there is no doubt that he himself was a lord of Annwfn, and it was probably on account of Gwydion's theft from Annwfn that he, as Gweir, was imprisoned there "through the messenger of Pwyll and Pryderi." 373 A raid is here made directly on the god's land for the benefit of men, and it is unsuccessful, but in the Mabinogi a different version of the raid is told. Perhaps Gwydion also brought kine from Annwfn, since he is called one of the three herds of Britain, 374 while he himself may once have been an animal god, then an anthropomorphic deity associated with animals. Thus in the Mabinogi, when Gwydion flees with the swine, he rests each night at a place one of the syllables of which is Moch, "swine" — an ætiological myth explaining why places which were once sites of the cult of a swine-god, afterwards worshipped as Gwydion, were so called.

Gwydion has also a tricky, fraudulent character in the Mabinogi, and although "in his life there was counsel," yet he had a "vicious muse." 375 It is also implied that he is lover of his sister Arianrhod and father of Dylan and Llew — the mythic reflections of a time when such unions, perhaps only in royal houses, were permissible. Instances occur in Irish tales, and Arthur was also his sister's lover. 376 In later belief Gwydion was associated with the stars; and the Milky Way was called Caer Gwydion. Across it he had chased the faithless Blodeuwedd. 377 Professor Rh[^y]s equates him with Odinn, and regards both as representing an older Celto-Teutonic hero, though many of the alleged similarities in their respective mythologies are not too obvious. 378

Amæthon the good is described in Kulhwych as the only husbandman who could till or dress a certain piece of land, though Kulhwych will not be able to force him or to make him follow him. 379 This, together with the name Amæthon, from Cymric amæth, "labourer" or "ploughman," throws some light on his functions. 380 He was a god associated with agriculture, either as one who made waste places fruitful, or possibly as an anthropomorphic corn divinity. But elsewhere his taking a roebuck and a whelp, and in a Triad, a lapwing from Arawn, king of Annwfn, led to the battle of Godeu, in which he fought Arawn, aided by Gwydion, who vanquished one of Arawn's warriors, Bran, by discovering his name. 381 Amæthon, who brings useful animals from the gods' land, plays the same part as Gwydion, bringer of the swine. The dog and deer are frequent representatives of the corn-spirit, of which Amæthon may have been an anthropomorphic form, or they, with the lapwing, may have been earlier worshipful animals, associated with Amæthon as his symbols, while later myth told how he had procured them from Annwfn.

The divine functions of Llew Llaw Gyffes are hardly apparent in the Mabinogi. The incident of Blodeuwedd's unfaithfulness is simply that of the Märchen formula of the treacherous wife who discovers the secret of her husband's life, and thus puts him at her lover's mercy. 382 But since Llew is not slain, but changes to eagle form, this unusual ending may mean that he was once a bird divinity, the eagle later becoming his symbol. Some myth must have told of his death, or he was afterwards regarded as a mortal who died, for a poem mentions his tomb, and adds, "he was a man who never gave justice to any one." Dr. Skene suggests that truth, not justice, is here meant, and finds in this a reference to Llew's disguises. 383 Professor Rh[^y]s, for reasons not held convincing by M. Loth, holds that Llew, "lion," was a misapprehension for his true name Lleu, interpreted by him "light." 384 This meaning he also gives to Lug, equating Lug and Llew, and regarding both as sun-gods. He also equates Llaw Gyffes, "steady or strong hand," with Lug's epithet Lám fada, "long hand," suggesting that gyffes may have meant "long," although it was Llew's steadiness of hand in shooting which earned him the title. 385 Again, Llew's rapid growth need not make him the sun, for this was a privilege of many heroes who had no connection with the sun. Llew's unfortunate matrimonial affairs are also regarded as a sun myth. Blodeuwedd is a dawn goddess dividing her love between the sun-god and the prince of darkness. Llew as the sun is overcome by the latter, but is restored by the culture-hero Gwydion, who slays the dark rival. The transformation of Blodeuwedd into an owl means that the Dawn has become the Dusk. 386 As we have seen, all this is a Märchen formula with no mythical significance. Evidence of the precariousness of such an interpretation is furnished from the similar interpretation of the story of Curoi's wife, Blathnat, whose lover Cúchulainn slew Curoi. 387 Here a supposed sun-god is the treacherous villain who kills a dark divinity, husband of a dawn goddess.

If Llew is a sun-god, the equivalent of Lug, it is curious that he is never connected with the August festival in Wales which corresponds to Lugnasad in Ireland. There may be some support to the theory which makes him a sun-god in a Triad where he is one of the three ruddroawc who cause a year's sterility wherever they set their feet, though in this Arthur excels them, for he causes seven years' sterility! 388 Does this point to the scorching of vegetation by the summer sun? The mythologists have not made use of this incident. On the whole the evidence for Llew as a sun-god is not convincing. The strongest reason for identifying him with Lug rests on the fact that both have uncles who are smiths and have similar names—Govannon and Gavida (Goibniu). Like Amæthon, Govannon, the artificer or smith (gôf, "smith"), is mentioned in Kulhwych as one whose help must be gained to wait at the end of the furrows to cleanse the iron of the plough. 389 Here he is brought into connection with the plough, but the myth to which the words refer is lost. A Taliesin poem associates him with Math—"I have been with artificers, with the old Math and with Govannon," and refers to his Caer or castle. 390

Arianrhod, "silver wheel," has a twofold character. She pretends to be a virgin, and disclaims all knowledge of her son Llew, yet she is mistress of Gwydion. In the Triads she appears as one of the three blessed (or white) ladies of Britain. 391 Perhaps these two aspects of her character may point to a divergence between religion and mythology, the cult of a virgin goddess of whom myth told discreditable things. More likely she was an old Earth-goddess, at once a virgin and a fruitful mother, like Artemis, the virgin goddess, yet neither chaste nor fair, or like a Babylonian goddess addressed as at once "mother, wife, and maid." Arianrhod, "beauty famed beyond summer's dawn," is mentioned in a Taliesin poem, and she was later associated with the constellation Corona Borealis. 392 Possibly her real name was forgotten, and that of Arianrhod derived from a place-name, "Caer Arianrhod," associated with her. The interpretation which makes her a dawn goddess, mother of light, Lleu, and darkness, Dylan, is far from obvious. 393 Dylan, after his baptism, rushed into the sea, the nature of which became his. No wave ever broke under him; he swam like a fish; and hence was called Dylan Eil Ton or "son of the wave." Govannon, his uncle, slew him, an incident interpreted as the defeat of darkness, which "hies away to lurk in the sea." Dylan, however, has no dark traits and is described as a blonde. The waves lament his death, and, as they dash against the shore, seek to avenge it. His grave is "where the wave makes a sullen sound," but popular belief identifies him with the waves, and their noise as they press into the Conway is his dying groan. Not only is he Eil Ton, "son of the wave," but also Eil Mor, "son of the sea." 394 He is thus a local sea-god, and like Manannan identified with the waves, and yet separate from them, since they mourn his death. The Mabinogi gives us the débris of myths explaining how an anthropomorphic sea-god was connected with the goddess Arianrhod and slain by a god Govannon.

Another Mabinogion group is that of Pwyll, prince of Dyved, his wife Rhiannon, and their son Pryderi. 395 Pwyll agrees with Arawn, king of Annwfn (Elysium), to reign over his kingdom for a year. At the end of that time he slays Arawn's rival Havgan. Arawn sends him gifts, and Pwyll is now known as Pen or Head of Annwfn, a title showing that he was once a god, belonging to the gods' land, later identified with the Christian Hades. Pwyll now agrees with Rhiannon, 396 who appears mysteriously on a magic hillock, and whom he captures, to rid her of an unwelcome suitor Gwawl. He imprisons him in a magical bag, and Rhiannon weds Pwyll. The story thus resolves itself into the formula of the Fairy Bride, but it paves the way for the vengeance taken on Pryderi and Rhiannon by Gwawl's friend Llwyt. Rhiannon has a son who is stolen as soon as born. She is accused of slaying him and is degraded, but Teyrnon recovers the child from its superhuman robber and calls him Gwri. As he grows up, Teyrnon notices his resemblance to Pwyll, and takes him to his court. Rhiannon is reinstated, and because she cries that her anguish (pryderi) is gone, the boy is now called Pryderi. Here, again, we have Märchen incidents, which also appear in the Fionn saga. 397

Though there is little that is mythological here, it is evident that Pwyll is a god and Rhiannon a goddess, whose early importance, like that of other Celtic goddesses, appears from her name, a corruption of Rigantona, "great queen." Elsewhere we hear of her magic birds whose song charmed Bran's companions for seven years, and of her marriage to Manawyddan—an old myth in which Manawyddan may have been Pryderi's father, while possibly in some other myth Pryderi may have been child of Rigantona and Teyrnon (=Tigernonos, "king"). 398 We may postulate an old Rhiannon saga, fragments of which are to be found in the Mabinogi, and there may have been more than one goddess called Rigantona, later fused into one. But in the tales she is merely a queen of old romance.

Pryderi, as has been seen, was despoiled of his swine by Gwydion. They were the gift of Arawn, but in the Triads they seem to have been brought from Annwfn by Pwyll, while Pryderi acted as swineherd. 399 Both Pwyll and Pryderi are thus connected with those myths which told of the bringing of domestic animals from the gods' land. But since they are certainly gods, associated with the gods' land, this is perhaps the result of misunderstanding. A poem speaks of the magic cauldron of Pen Annwfn, i.e. Pwyll, and this points to a myth explaining his connection with Annwfn in a different way from the account in the Mabinogi. The poem also tells how Gweir was imprisoned in Caer Sidi (=Annwfn) "through the messenger of Pwyll and Pryderi." 400 They are thus lords of Annwfn, whose swine Gweir (Gwydion) tries to steal. Elsewhere Caer Sidi is associated with Manawyddan and Pryderi, perhaps a reference to their connection as father and son. 401 Thus Pryderi and Pwyll belong to the bright Elysium, and may once have been gods of fertility associated with the under-earth region, which was by no means a world of darkness. Whatever be the meaning of the death of Pryderi at the hands of Gwydion, it is connected with later references to his grave. 402

A fourth group is that of Beli and his sons, referred to in the Mabinogi of Branwen, where one of them, Caswallawn, usurps the throne, and thus makes Manawyddan, like MacGregor, landless. In the Dream of Maxen, the sons of Beli are Lludd, Caswallawn, Nynnyaw, and Llevelys. 403 Geoffrey calls Beli Heli, and speaks of an earlier king Belinus, at enmity with his brother Brennius. 404 But probably Beli or Heli and Belinus are one and the same, and both represent the earlier god Belenos. Caswellawn becomes Cassivellaunus, opponent of Cæsar, but in the Mabinogi he is hostile to the race of Llyr, and this may be connected with whatever underlies Geoffrey's account of the hostility of Belinus and Brennius (=Bran, son of Llyr), perhaps, like the enmity of the race of D[^o]n to Pryderi, a reminiscence of the strife of rival tribes or of Goidel and Brython. 405 As has been seen, the evidence for regarding Beli as D[^o]n's consort or the equivalent of Bile is slender. Nor, if he is Belenos, the equivalent of Apollo, is he in any sense a "dark" god. He is regarded as a victorious champion, preserver of his "honey isle" and of the stability of his kingdom, in a Taliesin poem and in the Triads. 406

The personality of Casswallawn is lost in that of the historic Cassivellaunus, but in a reference to him in the Triads where, with Caradawc and Gweirydd, he bears the title "war king," we may see a glimpse of his divine character, that of a god of war, invisibly leading on armies to battle, and as such embodied in great chiefs who bore his name. 407 Nynnyaw appears in Geoffrey's pages as Nennius, who dies of wounds inflicted by Cæsar, to the great grief of Cassivellaunus. 408

The theory that Lludd Llaw Ereint or Lodens Lamargentios represents Nodens (Nuada) L[=a]margentios, the change being the result of alliteration, has been contested, 409 while if the Welsh Lludd and Nudd were identical it is strange that they should have become distinct personalities, Gwyn, son of Nudd, being the lover of Creiddylad, daughter of Lludd, 410 unless in some earlier myth their love was that of brother and sister. Lludd is also confused or is identical with Llyr, just as the Irish Ler is with Alloid. He is probably the son of Beli who, in the tale of Lludd and Llevelys, by the advice of Llevelys rids his country of three plagues. 411 These are, first, the Coranians who hear every whisper, and whom he destroys by throwing over them water in which certain insects given him by Levelys have been bruised. The second is a shriek on May-eve which makes land and water barren, and is caused by a dragon which attacks the dragon of the land. These Lludd captures and imprisons at Dinas Emreis, where they afterwards cause trouble to Vortigern at the building of his castle. The third is that of the disappearance of a year's supply of food by a magician, who lulls every one to sleep and who is captured by Lludd. Though the Coranians appear in the Triads as a hostile tribe, 412 they may have been a supernatural folk, since their name is perhaps derived from còr, "dwarf," and they are now regarded as mischievous fairies. 413 They may thus be analogous to the Fomorians, and their story, like that of the dragon and the magician who produce blight and loss of food, may be based on older myth or ritual embodying the belief in powers hostile to fertility, though it is not clear why those powers should be most active on May-day. But this may be a misunderstanding, and the dragons are overcome on May-eve. The references in the tale to Lludd's generosity and liberality in giving food may reflect his function as a god of growth, but, like other euhemerised gods, he is also called a mighty warrior, and is said to have rebuilt the walls of Caer Ludd (London), his name still surviving in "Ludgate Hill," where he was buried. 414 This legend doubtless points to some ancient cult of Lludd at this spot.

Nudd already discussed under his title Nodons, is less prominent than his son Gwyn, whose fight with Gwthur we have explained as a mythic explanation of ritual combats for the increase of fertility. He also appears as a hunter and as a great warrior, 415 "the hope of armies," and thus he may be a god of fertility who became a god of war and the chase. But legend associated him with Annwfn, and regarded him, like the Tuatha Déa, as a king of fairyland. 416 In the legend of S. Collen, the saint tells two men, whom he overhears speaking of Gwyn and the fairies, that these are demons. "Thou shalt receive a reproof from Gwyn," said one of them, and soon after Collen was summoned to meet the king of Annwfn on Glastonbury Tor. He climbed the hill with a flask of holy water, and saw on its top a splendid castle, with crowds of beautiful and youthful folk, while the air resounded with music. He was brought to Gwyn, who politely offered him food, but "I will not eat of the leaves of the tree," cried the saint; and when he was asked to admire the dresses of the crowd, all he would say was that the red signified burning, the blue coldness. Then he threw the holy water over them, and nothing was left but the bare hillside. 417 Though Gwyn's court on Glastonbury is a local Celtic Elysium, which was actually located there, the story marks the hostility of the Church to the cult of Gwyn, perhaps practised on hilltops, and this is further seen in the belief that he hunts souls of the wicked and is connected with Annwfn in its later sense of hell. But a mediant view is found in Kulhwych, where it is said of him that he restrains the demons of hell lest they should destroy the people of this world. In the Triads he is, like other gods, a great magician and astrologer. 418

Another group, unknown to the Mabinogion, save that Taliesin is one of the bearers of Bran's head, is found in the Book of Taliesin and in the late story of Taliesin. These, like the Arthur cycle, often refer to personages of the Mabinogion; hence we gather that local groups of gods, originally distinct, were later mingled in story, the references in the poems reflecting this mingling. Late as is the Hanes Taliesin or story of Taliesin, and expressed as much of it is in a Märchen formula, it is based on old myths about Cerridwen and Taliesin of which its compiler made use, following an old tradition already stereotyped in one of the poems in the Märchen formula of the Transformation Combat. 419 But the mythical fragments are also mingled with traditions regarding the sixth century poet Taliesin. The older saga was perhaps developed in a district south of the Dyfi estuary. 420 In Lake Tegid dwell Tegid Voel, Cerridwen, and their children—the fair maiden Creirwy, Morvran, and the ugly Avagddu. To give Avagddu knowledge, his mother prepares a cauldron of inspiration from which three drops of inspiration will be produced. These fall on the finger of Gwion, whom she set to stir it. He put the finger in his mouth, and thus acquired the inspiration. He fled, and Cerridwen pursued, the rest of the story being accommodated to the Transformation Combat formula. Finally, Cerridwen as a hen swallows Gwion as a grain of wheat, and bears him as a child, whom she throws into the sea. Elphin, who rescues him, calls him Taliesin, and brings him up as a bard. 421

The water-world of Tegid is a submarine Elysium with the customary cauldron of inspiration, regeneration, and fertility, like the cauldron associated with a water-world in the Mabinogion. "Shall not my chair be defended from the cauldron of Cerridwen," runs a line in a Taliesin poem, while another speaks of her chair, which was probably in Elysium like that of Taliesin himself in Caer Sidi. 422 Further references to her connection with poetry show that she may have been worshipped by bards, her cauldron being the source of their inspiration. 423 Her anger at Gwion may point to some form of the Celtic myth of the theft of the elements of culture from the gods' land. But the cauldron was first of all associated with a fertility cult, 424 and Cerridwen must therefore once have been a goddess of fertility, who, like Brigit, was later worshipped by bards. She may also have been a corn-goddess, since she is called a goddess of grain, and tradition associates the pig—a common embodiment of the corn-spirit—with her. 425 If the tradition is correct, this would be an instance, like that of Demeter and the pig, of an animal embodiment of the corn-spirit being connected with a later anthropomorphic corn-goddess.

Taliesin was probably an old god of poetic inspiration confused with the sixth century poet of the same name, perhaps because this boastful poet identified himself or was identified by other bards with the gods. He speaks of his "splendid chair, inspiration of fluent and urgent song" in Caer Sidi or Elysium, and, speaking in the god's name or identifying himself with him, describes his presence with Llew, Bran, Gwydion, and others, as well as his creation and his enchantment before he became immortal. 426 He was present with Arthur when a cauldron was stolen from Aunwfn, and basing his verses on the mythic transformations and rebirths of the gods, recounts in highly inflated language his own numerous forms and rebirths. 427 His claims resemble those of the Shaman who has the entree of the spirit-world and can transform himself at will. Taliesin's rebirth is connected with his acquiring of inspiration. These incidents appear separately in the story of Fionn, who acquired his inspiration by an accident, and was also said to have been reborn as Mongan. They are myths common to various branches of the Celtic people, and applied in different combinations to outstanding gods or heroes. 428 The Taliesin poems show that there may have been two gods or two mythic aspects of one god, later combined together. He is the son of the goddess and dwells in the divine land, but he is also a culture-hero stealing from the divine land. Perhaps the myths reflect the encroachment of the cult of a god on that of a goddess, his worshippers regarding him as her son, her worshippers reflecting their hostility to the new god in a myth of her enmity to him. Finally, the legend of the rescue of Taliesin the poet from the waves became a myth of the divine outcast child rescued by Elphin, and proving himself a bard when normal infants are merely babbling.

The occasional and obscure references to the other members of this group throw little light on their functions, save that Morvran, "sea-crow," is described in Kulhwych as so ugly and terrible that no one would strike him at the battle of Camlan. He may have been a war-god, like the scald-crow goddesses of Ireland, and he is also spoken of in the Triads as an "obstructor of slaughter" or "support of battle." 429

Ingenuity and speculation have busied themselves with trying to prove that the personages of the Arthurian cycle are the old gods of the Brythons, and the incidents of the romances fragments of the old mythology. While some of these personages—those already present in genuinely old Welsh tales and poems or in Geoffrey's History—are reminiscent of the old gods, the romantic presentment of them in the cycle itself is so largely imaginative, that nothing certain can be gained from it for the understanding of the old mythology, much less the old religion. Incidents which are the common stock of real life as well as of romance are interpreted mythologically, and it is never quite obvious why the slaying of one hero by another should signify the conquest of a dark divinity by a solar hero, or why the capture of a heroine by one knight when she is beloved of another, should make her a dawn-goddess sharing her favours, now with the sun-god, now with a "dark" divinity. Or, even granting the truth of this method, what light does it throw on Celtic religion?

We may postulate a local Arthur saga fusing an old Brythonic god with the historic sixth century Arthur. From this or from Geoffrey's handling of it sprang the great romantic cycle. In the ninth century Nennius Arthur is the historic war-chief, possibly Count of Britain, but in the reference to his hunting the Porcus Troit (the Twrch Trwyth) the mythic Arthur momentarily appears. 430 Geoffrey's Arthur differs from the later Arthur of romance, and he may have partially rationalised the saga, which was either of recent formation or else local and obscure, since there is no reference to Arthur in the Mabinogion—a fact which shows that "in the legends of Gwynedd and Dyfedd he had no place whatever," 431 and also that Arthur the god or mythic hero was also purely local. In Geoffrey Arthur is the fruit of Igerna's amour with Uther, to whom Merlin has given her husband's shape. Arthur conquers many hosts as well as giants, and his court is the resort of all valorous persons. But he is at last wounded by his wife's seducer, and carried to the Isle of Avallon to be cured of his wounds, and nothing more is ever heard of him. 432 Some of these incidents occur also in the stories of Fionn and Mongan, and those of the mysterious begetting of a wonder child and his final disappearance into fairyland are local forms of a tale common to all branches of the Celts. 433 This was fitted to the history of the local god or hero Arthur, giving rise to the local saga, to which was afterwards added events from the life of the historic Arthur. This complex saga must then have acquired a wider fame long before the romantic cycle took its place, as is suggested by the purely Welsh tales of Kulhwych and the Dream of Rhonabwy, in the former of which the personages (gods) of the Mabinogion figure in Arthur's train, though he is far from being the Arthur of the romances. Sporadic references to Arthur occur also in Welsh literature, and to the earlier saga belongs the Arthur who spoils Elysium of its cauldron in a Taliesin poem. 434 In the Triads there is a mingling of the historic, the saga, and the later romance Arthur, but probably as a result of the growing popularity of the saga Arthur he is added to many Triads as a more remarkable person than the three whom they describe. 435 Arthurian place-names over the Brythonic area are more probably the result of the popularity of the saga than that of the later romantic cycle, a parallel instance being found in the extent of Ossianic place-names over the Goidelic area as a result of the spread of the Fionn saga.

The character of the romance Arthur—the flower of knighthood and a great warrior—and the blending of the historic war-leader Arthur with the mythic Arthur, suggest that the latter was the ideal hero of certain Brythonic groups, as Fionn and Cúchulainn of certain Goidelic groups. He may have been the object of a cult as these heroes perhaps were, or he may have been a god more and more idealised as a hero. If the earlier form of his name was Artor, "a ploughman," but perhaps with a wider significance, and having an equivalent in Artaius, a Gaulish god equated with Mercury, 436 he may have been a god of agriculture who became a war-god. But he was also regarded as a culture-hero, stealing a cauldron and also swine from the gods' land, the last incident euhemerised into the tale of an unsuccessful theft from March, son of Meirchion, 437 while, like other culture-heroes, he is a bard. To his story was easily fitted that of the wonder-child, who, having finally disappeared into Elysium (later located at Glastonbury), would reappear one day, like Fionn, as the Saviour of his people. The local Arthur finally attained a fame far exceeding that of any Brythonic god or hero.

Merlin, or Myrddin, appears in the romances as a great magician who is finally overcome by the Lady of the Lake, and is in Geoffrey son of a mysterious invisible personage who visits a woman, and, finally taking human shape, begets Merlin. As a son who never had a father he is chosen as the foundation sacrifice for Vortigern's tower by his magicians, but he confutes them and shows why the tower can never be built, namely, because of the dragons in the pool beneath it. Then follow his prophecies regarding the dragons and the future of the country, and the story of his removal of the Giant's Dance, or Stonehenge, from Ireland to its present site—an ætiological myth explaining the origin of the great stone circle. His description of how the giants used the water with which they washed the stones for the cure of sickness or wounds, probably points to some ritual for healing in connection with these megaliths. Finally, we hear of his transformation of the lovelorn Uther and of his confidant Ulfin, as well as of himself. 438 Here he appears as little more than an ideal magician, possibly an old god, like the Irish "god of Druidism," to whose legend had been attached a story of supernatural conception. Professor Rh[^y]s regards him as a Celtic Zeus or as the sun, because late legends tell of his disappearance in a glass house into the sea. The glass house is the expanse of light travelling with the sun (Merlin), while the Lady of the Lake who comes daily to solace Merlin in his enchanted prison is a dawn-goddess. Stonehenge was probably a temple of this Celtic Zeus "whose late legendary self we have in Merlin." 439 Such late romantic episodes and an ætiological myth can hardly be regarded as affording safe basis for these views, and their mythological interpretation is more than doubtful. The sun is never prisoner of the dawn as Merlin is of Viviane. Merlin and his glass house disappear for ever, but the sun reappears every morning. Even the most poetic mythology must conform in some degree to actual phenomena, but this cannot be said of the systems of mythological interpretation. If Merlin belongs to the pagan period at all, he was probably an ideal magician or god of magicians, prominent, perhaps, in the Arthur saga as in the later romances, and credited with a mysterious origin and an equally mysterious ending, the latter described in many different ways.

The boastful Kei of the romances appears already in Kulhwych, while in Geoffrey he is Arthur's seneschal. 440 Nobler traits are his in later Welsh poetry; he is a mighty warrior, fighting even against a hundred, though his powers as a toper are also great. Here, too, his death is lamented. 441 He may thus have been a god of war, and his battle-fury may be poetically described in a curious passage referring to him in Kulhwych: "His breath lasted nine days and nine nights under water. He could remain without sleep for the same period. No physician could heal a wound inflicted by his sword. When he pleased he could make himself as tall as the tallest tree in the wood. And when it rained hardest, whatever he carried remained dry above and below his hand to the distance of a handbreadth, so great was his natural heat. When it was coldest he was as glowing fuel to his companions." 442 This almost exactly resembles Cúchulainn's aspect in his battle-fury. In a curious poem Gwenhyvar (Guinevere) extols his prowess as a warrior above that of Arthur, and in Kulhwych and elsewhere there is enmity between the two. 443 This may point to Kei's having been a god of tribes hostile to those of whom Arthur was hero.

Mabon, one of Arthur's heroes in Kulhwych and the Dream of Rhonabwy, whose name, from mab (map), means "a youth," may be one with the god Maponos equated with Apollo in Britain and Gaul, perhaps as a god of healing springs. 444 His mother's name, Modron, is a local form of Matrona, a river-goddess and probably one of the mother-goddesses as her name implies. In the Triads Mabon is one of the three eminent prisoners of Prydein. To obtain his help in hunting the magic boar his prison must be found, and this is done by animals, in accordance with a Märchen formula, while the words spoken by them show the immense duration of his imprisonment—perhaps a hint of his immortality. 445 But he was also said to have died and been buried at Nantlle, 446 which, like Gloucester, the place of his prison, may have been a site of his widely extended cult. 447

Taken as a whole the various gods and heroes of the Brythons, so far as they are known to us, just as they resemble the Irish divinities in having been later regarded as mortals, magicians, and fairies, so they resemble them in their functions, dimly as these are perceived. They are associated with Elysium, they are lords of fertility and growth, of the sea, of the arts of culture and of war. The prominent position of certain goddesses may point to what has already been discovered of them in Gaul and Ireland—their pre-eminence and independence. But, like the divinities of Gaul and Ireland, those of Wales were mainly local in character, and only in a few cases attained a wider popularity and cult.

Certain British gods mentioned on inscriptions may be identified with some of those just considered—Nodons with Nudd or Lludd, Belenos with Belinus or Beli, Maponos with Mabon, Taranos (in continental inscriptions only), with a Taran mentioned in Kulhwych. 448 Others are referred to in classical writings—Andrasta, a goddess of victory, to whom Boudicca prayed; 449 Sul, a goddess of hot springs, equated with Minerva at Bath. 450 Inscriptions also mention Epona, the horse-goddess; Brigantia, perhaps a form of Brigit; Belisama (the Mersey in Ptolemy), 451 a goddess in Gaulish inscriptions. Others refer to the group goddesses, the Matres. Some gods are equated with Mars—Camulos, known also on the Continent and perhaps the same as Cumal, father of Fionn; Belatucadros, "comely in slaughter"; Cocidius, Corotiacus, Barrex, and Totatis (perhaps Lucan's Teutates). Others are equated with Apollo in his character as a god of healing—Anextiomarus, Grannos (at Musselburgh and in many continental inscriptions), Arvalus, Mogons, etc. Most of these and many others found on isolated inscriptions were probably local in character, though some, occurring also on the Continent, had attained a wider popularity. 452 But some of the inscriptions referring to the latter may be due to Gaulish soldiers quartered in Britain.

COMPARATIVE TABLE OF DIVINITIES WITH SIMILAR NAMES IN IRELAND, BRITAIN, AND GAUL.

Italics denote names found in Inscriptions.

IRELAND.	BRITAIN.	GAUL.
	Anextiomarus	Anextiomarus
Anu	Anna (?)	Anoniredi, "chariot of Anu"
Badb		Bodua
	Beli, *Belinus*	Belenos
	Belisama	Belisama
Brigit	Brigantia	Brigindu
Bron	Bran	Brennus (?)
Buanann		Buanu
Cumal	Camulos	Camulos
Danu	Dôn	
	Epona	Epona
Goibniu	Govannon	
	Grannos	Grannos
Ler	Llyr	
Lug	Llew or Lleu (?)	*Lugus*, Lugores
	Mabon, Maponos	Maponos
Manannan	Manawyddan	
	Matres	Matres
Mider		Medros (?)
	Modron	Matrona (?)
Nemon		Nemetona
Nét		Neton
Nuada	Nodons, Nudd Hael, Llûdd (?)	
Ogma		Ogmíos
	Silvanus	Silvanus
	Taran	Taranis
	Totatis, Tutatis	*Teutates*

Footnote 328: The text of the Mabinogion has been edited by Rh[^y]s and Evans, 1887, and it has been translated into English by Lady Guest, and more critically, into French, by Loth. Many of the Triads will be found in Loth's second volume. For the poetry see Skene, Four Ancient Books of Wales.

Footnote 329: These incidents are found mainly in the story of Branwen, e.g. those of the cauldron, a frequent accessory in Irish tales; the regeneration of the warriors, also found in the story of Mag-tured, though no cauldron is used; the red-hot house, occurring also in Mesca Ulad; the description of Bran paralleled by that of MacCecht.

Footnote 330: Anwyl, ZCP i. 277, ii. 124, iii. 122.

Footnote 331: Bp. of S. Davids, Vestiges of the Gael in Gwynned, 1851; Rh[^y]s, TSC 1894-1895, 21.

Footnote 332: Skene, i. 45; Meyer, TSC 1895-1896, 55.

Footnote 333: Cf. John, The Mabinogion, 1901, 19. Curoi appears as Kubert, and Conchobar as Knychur in Kulhwych (Loth, i. 202). A poem of Taliesin has for subject the death of Corroi, son of Dayry (Curoi mac Daire), Skene, i. 254.

Footnote 334: Loth, RC x. 356; John, op. cit. 19; Nutt, Arch. Rev. i. 331.

Footnote 335: The giant Ysppadden in Kulhwych resembles Balor, but has no evil eye.

Footnote 336: Anwyl, ZCP ii. 127-128, "The merging of the two legends [of Dôn and Taliesin] may have arisen through the fusion of Penllyn with Ardudwy and Arvon."

Footnote 337: Professor Rh[^y]s thinks that the Llyr family may be pre-Celtic, TSC 1894-1895, 29 f.; CFL 552.

Footnote 338: Loth, i. 97 f.; Lady Guest, iii. 143 f.

Footnote 339: See Nutt, Folk-lore Record, v. 1 f.

Footnote 340: Loth, i. 298, ii. 243-244; Geoffrey, Hist. Brit. ii. 11.

Footnote 341: Loth, i. 224, 265, ii. 215, 244; Geoff. ii. 11.

Footnote 342: Skene, i. 81; Rh[^y]s, Academy, Jan. 7, 1882.

Footnote 343: Triads, Loth, ii. 293; Nutt, Folk-lore Record, v. 9.

Footnote 344: Hist. Brit. ii. 11-14.

Footnote 345: AL 131.

Footnote 346: Skene, i. 262.

Footnote 347: See Nutt-Meyer, ii. 17.

Footnote 348: Skene, i. 276.

Footnote 349: Loth, i. 208, 280; see also i. 197, ii. 245, 294.

Footnote 350: See Skene i. 355. The raven is rather the bird of prey come to devour Urien than his "attribute."

Footnote 351: Skene, i. 298.

Footnote 352: For these theories see Rh[^y]s, HL 90f.; AL ch. 11; CFL 552.

Footnote 353: See Ch. XXIV.

Footnote 355: Loth, i. 65, ii. 285.

Footnote 356: Hist. Brit. iii. 1f. Geoffrey says that Billingsgate was called after Belinus, and that his ashes were preserved in the gate, a tradition recalling some connection of the god with the gate.

Footnote 357: An early Caradawc saga may have become mingled with the story of Caractacus.

Footnote 358: Rees, 77.

Footnote 359: So Elton, 291.

Footnote 360: Folk-lore Record, v. 29.

Footnote 361: Lady Guest, iii. 134.

Footnote 362: Dôn is sometimes held to be male, but she is distinctly called sister of Math (Loth, i. 134), and as the equivalent of Danu she must be female.

Footnote 363: Loth, ii. 209.

Footnote 364: supra, and Rh[^y]s, HL 90f.

Footnote 365: Lady Guest, iii. 255; Skene, i. 297, 350.

Footnote 366: For this Mabinogi see Loth, i. 117f.; Guest, iii. 189f.

Footnote 367: Skene, i. 286.

Footnote 368: Loth, ii. 229, 257; and for other references to Math, Skene, i. 281, 269, 299.

Footnote 369: Skene, i. 296, 281.

Footnote 370: Loth, ii. 297; Rh[^y]s, HL 276.

Footnote 371: Skene, i. 264.

Footnote 372: Rh[^y]s, HL 270. Skene, i. 430, 537, gives a different meaning to seon.

Footnote 373: Skene, i. 264.

Footnote 374: Loth, ii. 296.

Footnote 375: Skene, i. 299, 531.

Footnote 376: infra.

Footnote 377: Guest, iii. 255; Morris, Celtic Remains, 231.

Footnote 378: HL 283 f. See also Grimm, Teut. Myth. i. 131.

Footnote 379: Loth, i. 240.

Footnote 380: Stokes, US 34.

Footnote 381: Myvyrian Archæol. i. 168; Skene, i. 275, 278 f.; Loth, ii. 259.

Footnote 382: See my Childhood of Fiction, 127. Llew's vulnerability does not depend on the discovery of his separable soul, as is usual. The earliest form of this Märchen is the Egyptian story of the rrrTwo Brothers, and that of Samson and Delilah is another old form of it.

Footnote 383: Skene, i. 314, ii. 342.

Footnote 384: HL 408; RC x. 490.

Footnote 385: HL 237, 319, 398, 408.

Footnote 386: HL 384.

Footnote 387: HL 474, 424.

Footnote 388: Loth, ii. 231.

Footnote 389: Loth, i. 240.

Footnote 390: Skene, i, 286-287.

Footnote 391: Loth, ii. 263.

Footnote 392: Skene, ii. 159; Rh[^y]s, HL 157; Guest, iii. 255.

Footnote 393: Rh[^y]s, HL 161, 566.

Footnote 394: Skene, i. 282, 288, 310, 543, ii. 145; Loth, i. 135; Rh[^y]s, HL 387.

Footnote 395: Loth, i. 27 f.; Guest, iii. 7 f.

Footnote 396: Rhiannon is daughter of Heveidd Hen or "the Ancient," probably an old divinity.

Footnote 397: In the Mabinogi and in Fionn tales a mysterious hand snatches away newly-born children. Cf. ZCP i. 153.

Footnote 398: Anwyl, ZCP i. 288.

Footnote 399: Loth, ii. 247.

Footnote 400: Skene, i. 264.

Footnote 401: Ibid. i. 276.

Footnote 402: Ibid. i. 310.

Footnote 403: Loth, i. 166.

Footnote 404: Hist. Brit. ii. 11, iii. 1, 20, iv. 3.

Footnote 405: Cf. Anwyl, ZCP i. 287.

Footnote 406: Skene, i. 431; Loth, ii. 278. Some phrases seem to connect Beli with the sea—the waves are his cattle, the brine his liquor.

Footnote 407: Loth, ii. 209, 249, 260, 283.

Footnote 408: Geoffrey, Brit. Hist. iv. 3. 4.

Footnote 409: Rh[^y]s, HL 125 f.; Loth, i. 265; MacBain, CM ix. 66.

Footnote 410: See Loth, i. 269; and Skene, i. 293.

Footnote 411: Loth, i. 173 f.

Footnote 412: Loth, ii. 256, 274.

Footnote 413: Rh[^y]s, HL 606. Cf. the Breton fairies, the Korr and Korrigan.

Footnote 414: Geoffrey, iii. 20.

Footnote 415: Loth, i. 253-254; Skene, i. 293.

Footnote 416: Guest, iii. 323.

Footnote 417: Ibid. 325.

Footnote 418: Loth, i. 253, ii. 297.

Footnote 419: infra.; Skene, i. 532.

Footnote 420: Anwyl, ZCP i. 293.

Footnote 421: Guest, iii. 356 f.

Footnote 422: Skene, i. 275, 296.

Footnote 423: Ibid. i. 498, 500.

Footnote 424: infra.

Footnote 425: Mon. Hist. Brit. i. 698, ii.; Thomas, Revue de l'hist. des Religions, xxxviii. 339.

Footnote 426: Skene, i. 263, 274-276, 278, 281-282, 286-287. His "chair" bestows immortal youth and freedom from sickness.

Footnote 427: Skene, i. 264, 376 f., 309, 532. infra.

Footnote 428: infra. Fionn and Taliesin are examples of the Märchen formula of a hero expelled and brought back to honour, Nutt-Meyer, ii. 88.

Footnote 429: Loth, i. 209, ii. 238; Skene, ii. 459.

Footnote 430: Nennius, ch. 50, 79.

Footnote 431: Anwyl, ZCP i. 293.

Footnote 432: Geoffrey, viii. 9-xi. 3.

Footnote 433: Nutt-Meyer, ii. 22 f.

Footnote 434: infra.

Footnote 435: Loth, ii. 232, 245.

Footnote 436: Rh[^y]s, AL, 39 f. Others derive the name from arto-s, "bear." MacBain, 357.

Footnote 437: Loth. ii. 247; Skene, ii. 459.

Footnote 438: Geoffrey, vi. 17-19, vii. viii. 1, 10-12, 19. In a poem (Skene, i. 478), Myrddin is called "the man who speaks from the grave" — a conception familiar to the Celts, who thought of the dead as living on in the grave.infra.

Footnote 439: Rh[^y]s, HL, 154 f., 158-159, 194.

Footnote 440: Geoffrey, ix. 12, etc.

Footnote 441: Skene, ii. 51.

Footnote 442: Loth. i. 225; cf. p. 131, infra. From this description Elton supposes Kei to have been a god of fire.

Footnote 443: Myv. Arch. i. 175; Loth, i. 269. Rh[^y]s, AL 59, thinks Merlin may have been Guinevere's ravisher.

Footnote 444: Holder, i. 414.

Footnote 445: Loth i. 250, 260 f., 280, ii. 215, 244.

Footnote 446: Skene, i. 363, ii. 406; Myv. Arch. i. 78.

Footnote 447: Hu Gadarn is mentioned in the Triads as a leader of the Cymry from the east and their teacher in ploughing. He divided them into clans, and invented music and song. The monster avanc was drawn by him from the lake which had burst and caused the flood (, infra). Perhaps Hu is an old culture-god of some tribes, but the Triads referring to him are of late date (Loth, ii. 271, 289, 290-291, 298-299). For the ridiculous Neo-Druidic speculations based on Hu, see Davies, Celtic Researches and Mythology and Rites of the Druids.

Gurgiunt, son of Belinus, in Geoffrey, iii. 11, may be the French legendary Gargantua, perhaps an old god. See the works of Sébillot and Gaidoz on Gargantua.

Footnote 448: Loth, i. 270.

Footnote 449: Dio Cassius, lxii. 6.

Footnote 450: Solinus, xxii. 10. See p. 2, supra.

Footnote 451: Ptol. ii. 3. 2.

Footnote 452: For all these see Holder, s.v.

CHAPTER VII
THE CÚCHULAINN CYCLE

The events of the Cúchulainn cycle are supposed to date from the beginning of the Christian era—King Conchobar's death synchronising with the crucifixion. But though some personages who are mentioned in the Annals figure in the tales, on the whole they deal with persons who never existed. They belong to a world of romance and myth, and embody the ideals of Celtic paganism, modified by Christian influences and those of classical tales and romantic sagas of other regions, mainly Scandinavian. The present form of the tales as they exist in the Book of the Dun Cow and the Book of Leinster must have been given them in the seventh or eighth century, but they embody materials of a far older date. At an early time the saga may have had a more or less definite form, but new tales were being constantly added to it, and some of the longer tales are composed of incidents which once had no connection with each other.

Cúchulainn is the central figure of the cycle, and its central episode is that of the Táin bó Cuailgne, or "Cattle Spoil of Cooley." Other personages are Conchobar and Dechtire, Ailill and Medb, Fergus, Conall Cernach, Cúroi, Deirdre, and the sons of Usnach. Some of these are of divine descent, some are perhaps euhemerised divinities; Conchobar is called día talmaide, "a terrestrial god," and Dechtire a goddess. The cycle opens with the birth of Conchobar, son of Cathbad and of Nessa, daughter of one of the Tuatha Dé Danann, though in an older rescension of the tale he is Nessa's son by the god Lug. During Conchobar's reign over Ulster Cúchulainn was born. He was son of Dechtire, either by Sualtaim, or by her brother Conchobar, or by the god Lug, of whom he may also be a reincarnation. 453 Like other heroes of saga, he possesses great strength and skill at a tender age, and, setting out for Conchobar's court, overpowers the king's "boy corps," and then becomes their chief. His next adventure is the slaying of the watch-dog of Culann the smith, and his appeasing the anger of its owner by offering to act as his watch-dog. Cathbad now announced that his name would henceforth be Cú Chulainn, "Culann's hound." 454 At the mature age of seven he obtained Conchobar's spears, sword, shield, and chariot, and with these he overcame three mighty champions, returning in the distortion of his "battle-fury" to Emania. To prevent mischief from his rage, the women went forth naked to meet him. He modestly covered his eyes, for it was one of his geasa not to look on a woman's breast. Thus taken unawares, he was plunged into three successive vats of cold water until his natural appearance was restored to him, although the water boiled and hissed from his heat. 455

As Cúchulainn grew up, his strength, skill, wisdom, and beauty were unsurpassed. All women fell in love with him, and to forestall a series of bonnes fortunes, the men of Ulster sought a wife for him. But the hero's heart was set on Emer, daughter of Forgall, whom he wooed in a strange language which none but she could understand. At last she consented to be his wife if he would slay a number of warriors. Forgall was opposed to the match, and with a view to Cúchulainn's destruction suggested that he should go to Donall in Alba to increase his skill, and to Scathach if he would excel all other warriors. He agreed, provided that Forgall would give him whatever he asked for on his return. Arrived in Alba, he refused the love of Donall's daughter, Dornolla, who swore to be avenged. Thence he went to Scathach, overcoming all the dangers of the way, leaping in safety the gulf surrounding her island, after essaying in vain to cross a narrow, swinging bridge. From Scathach he learned supreme skill in arms, and overcame her Amazonian rival Aife. He begat a son by Aife, and instructed her to call him Conla, to give him his father's ring, to send him to seek Cúchulainn, and to forbid him to reveal his name. In the sequel, Cúchulainn, unaware that Conla was his son, slew him in single combat, too late discovering his identity from the ring which he wore. This is the well-known saga formula of Sohrab and Rustum, of Theseus and Hippolytus. On his return from Scathach's isle Cúchulainn destroyed Forgall's rath with many of its inmates, including Forgall, and carried off Emer. To the ten years which followed, during which he was the great champion of Ulster, belong many tales in which he figures prominently. One of these is The Debility of the Ultonians. This was caused by Macha, who, during her pregnancy, was forced to run a race with Conchobar's horses. She outran them, but gave birth immediately to twins, and, in her pangs, cursed the men of Ulster, with a curse that, in time of oppression, they would be overcome with the weakness of childbirth. From this Cúchulainn was exempt, for he was not of Ulster, but a son of Lug. 456 Various attempts have been made to explain this "debility." It may be a myth explaining a Celtic use of the "couvade," though no example of a simultaneous tribal couvade is known, unless we have here an instance of Westermarck's "human pairing season in primitive times," with its consequent simultaneous birth-period for women and couvade for men. 457 Others, with less likelihood, explain it as a period of tabu, with cessation from work and warfare, at a funeral or festival. 458 In any case Macha's curse is a myth explanatory of the origin of some existing custom, the duration of which is much exaggerated by the narrator. To this period belong also the tale of Cúchulainn's visit to Elysium, and others to be referred to later. Another story describes his attack upon Morrigan because she would neither yield up the cows which she was driving away nor tell her true name — an instance of the well-known name tabu. Morrigan took the form of a bird, and was then recognised by Cúchulainn, who poured scorn upon her, while she promised to oppose him during the fight of the Táin in the forms of an eel, a wolf, and a cow, all of which he vowed to destroy. 459 Like many others in the saga, this story is introductory to the main episode of the Táin. To this we now turn.

Medb had been wife of Conchobar, but, leaving him, had married in succession two chiefs called Ailill, the second of whom had a bull, Findbennach, the White-horned, which she resolved to match by one in every way its equal. Having been refused the Brown Bull of Cuailgne, she summoned all her forces to invade Ulster. The moment was inauspicious for Ulster, for all its men were suffering from their "debility." Cúchulainn, therefore, went out to encounter the host, and forced Medb to agree that a succession of her warriors should engage him in single combat. Among these was his old friend Ferdia, and nothing is so touching as his reluctance to fight him or so pathetic as his grief when Ferdia falls. The reluctance is primarily due to the tie of blood-brotherhood existing between them. Finally, the Ulstermen rose in force and defeated Medb, but not before she had already captured the bull and sent it into her own land. There it was fought by the Findbennach and slew it, rushing back to Ulster with the mangled body on its horns. But in its frenzy a rock seemed to be another bull, which it charged; its brains were dashed out, and it fell dead.

The Morrigan had warned the bull of the approach of Medb's army, and she had also appeared in the form of a beautiful woman to Cúchulainn offering him her love, only to be repulsed. Hence she turned against him, and described how she would oppose him as an eel, a wolf, and a red heifer — an incident which is probably a variant of that already described. 460 In each of these shapes she was conquered and wounded by the hero, and knowing that none whom he hurt could be healed save by himself, she appeared to him as an old crone milking a cow. At each draught of the milk which he received from her he blessed her with "the blessing of gods and not-gods," and so her wounds were healed. 461 For this, at a later time, she tried to ward off his death, but unsuccessfully. During the progress of the Táin, one of Cúchulainn's "fairy kinsmen," namely, Lug, who announced himself as his father, appeared to aid him, while others of the Tuatha Déa threw "herbs of healing" into the streams in which his wounds were washed. 462

During the Táin, Cúchulainn slaughtered the wizard Calatin and his daughters. But Calatin's wife bore three posthumous sons and three daughters, and through their means the hero was at last slain. Everything was done to keep him back from the host which now advanced against Ulster, but finally one of Calatin's daughters took the form of Niamh and bade him go forth. As he passed to the fight, Calatin's daughters persuaded him to eat the flesh of a dog—a fatal deed, for it was one of his geasa never to eat dog's flesh. So it was that in the fight he was slain by Lugaid, 463 and his soul appeared to the thrice fifty queens who had loved him, chanting a mystic song of the coming of Christ and the day of doom—an interesting example of a phantasm coincidental with death. 464 This and other Christian touches show that the Christian redactors of the saga felt tenderly towards the old pagan hero. This is even more marked in the story in which he appears to King Loegaire and S. Patrick, begging the former to believe in God and the saint, and praying Patrick to "bring me with thy faithful ones unto the land of the living." 465 A similar Christianising appears in the story of Conchobar's death, the result of his mad frenzy on hearing from his Druid that an earthquake is the result of the shameful crucifixion of Christ. 466

In the saga, Cúchulainn appears as the ideal Celtic warrior, but, like other ideal warriors, he is a "magnified, non-natural man," many of his deeds being merely exaggerations of those common among barbaric folk. Even his "distortion" or battle frenzy is but a magnifying of the wild frenzy of all wild fighters. To the person of this ideal warrior, some of whose traits may have been derived from traditional stories of actual heroes, Märchen and saga episodes attached themselves. Of every ideal hero, Celtic, Greek, Babylonian, or Polynesian, certain things are told—his phenomenal strength as a child; his victory over enormous forces; his visits to the Other-world; his amours with a goddess; his divine descent. These belong to the common stock of folk-tale episodes, and accumulate round every great name. Hence, save in the colouring given to them or the use made of them by any race, they do not afford a key to the mythic character of the hero. Such deeds are ascribed to Cúchulainn, as they doubtless were to the ideal heroes of the "undivided Aryans," but though parallels may be found between him and the Greek Heracles, they might just as easily be found in non-Aryan regions, e.g. in Polynesia. Thus the parallels between Cúchulainn and Heracles throw little light on the personality of the former, though here and there in such parallels we observe a peculiarly Celtic touch. Thus, while the Greek hero rescues Hesione from a dragon, it is from three Fomorians that Cúchulainn rescues Devorgilla, namely, from beings to whom actual human sacrifice was paid. Thus a Märchen formula of world-wide existence has been moulded by Celtic religious belief and ritual practice. 467

It was inevitable that the "mythological school" should regard Cúchulainn as a solar hero. Thus "he reaches his full development at an unusually early age," as the sun does, 468 but also as do many other heroes of saga and Märchen who are not solar. The three colours of Cúchulainn's hair, dark near the skin, red in the middle, golden near the top, are claimed to be a description of the sun's rays, or of the three parts into which the Celts divided the day. 469 Elsewhere his tresses are yellow, like Prince Charlie's in fact and in song, yet he was not a solar hero. Again, the seven pupils of his eyes perhaps "referred to the days of the week." 470 Blindness befell all women who loved him, a reference to the difficulty of gazing at the sun. 471 This is prosaic! The blindness was a compliment paid to Cúchulainn the blind, by women who made themselves blind while talking to him, just as Conall Cernach's mistresses squinted as he did. 472 Cúchulainn's blindness arose from his habit of sinking one eye into his head and protruding the other — a well-known solar trait! His "distortion," during which, besides this "blindness," blood shot upwards from his head and formed a magic mist, and his anger caused showers of sparks to mount above him, points to dawn or sunset, 473 though the setting sun would rather suggest a hero sinking calmly to rest than a mad giant setting out to slaughter friend and foe. The "distortion," as already pointed out, is the exaggerated description of the mad warrior rage, just as the fear which produced death to those who saw him brandish his weapons, was also produced by Maori warrior methods. 474 Lug, who may be a sun-god, has no such "distortion." The cooling of the hero in three vats, the waters of which boil over, and his emergence from them pinky red in colour, symbolise the sun sinking into the waters and reappearing at dawn. 475 Might it not describe in an exaggerated way the refreshing bath taken by frenzied warriors, the water being supposed to grow warm from the heat of their bodies? 476 One of the hero's geasa was not to see Manannan's horses, the waves; which, being interpreted, means that the sun is near its death as it approaches the sea. Yet Lug, a sun-god, rides the steed Enbarr, a personification of the waves, while Cúchulainn himself often crossed the sea, and also lived with the sea-god's wife, Fand, without coming to grief. Again, the magic horses which he drives, black and grey in colour, are "symbols of day and night," 477 though it is not obvious why a grey horse should symbolise day, which is not always grey even in the isles of the west. Unlike a solar hero, too, Cúchulainn is most active in winter, and rests for a brief space from slaughtering at midday — the time of the sun's greatest activity both in summer and winter.

Another theory is that every visit of the hero to a strange land signifies a descent to Hades, suggested by the sun sinking in the west. Scathach's island may be Hades, but it is more probably Elysium with some traits borrowed from the Christian idea of hell. But Emer's land, also visited by Cúchulainn, suggests neither Hades nor Elysium. Emer calls herself ingen rig richis garta, translated by Professor Rh[^y]s as "daughter of the coal-faced king," i.e. she is daughter of darkness. Hence she is a dawn-maiden and becomes the sun-hero's wife. 478 There is nothing in the story to corroborate this theory, apart from the fact that it is not clear, even to the hypothetical primitive mind, why dawn and sun should be a divine pair. Emer's words probably mean that she is "daughter of a king" and "a flame of hospitality" (richis garta.) 479 Cúchulainn, in visiting her, went from west to east, contrary to the apparent course of the sun. The extravagance of the solar theory is further seen in the hypothesis that because Cúchulainn has other wives, the sun-god made love to as many dawn-maidens as there are days in the year, 480 like the king in Louys' romance with his 366 wives, one for each day of the year, leap-year included.

Further examples of the solar theory need not be cited. It is enough to see in Cúchulainn the ideal warrior, whose traits are bombastic and obscure exaggerations of actual custom and warfare, or are borrowed from folk-tale motifs not exclusively Celtic. Possibly he may have been a war-god, since he is associated with Badb 481 and also with Morrigan. But he has also some traits of a culture hero. He claims superiority in wisdom, in law, in politics, in the art of the Filid, and in Druidism, while he brings various things from the world of the gods 482 . In any case the Celts paid divine honours to heroes, living or dead, 483 and Cúchulainn, god or ideal hero, may have been the subject of a cult. This lends point to the theory of M. D'Arbois that Cúchulainn and Conall Cernach are the equivalents of Castor and Pollux, the Dioscuri, said by Diodorus to be worshipped among the Celts near the Ocean. 484 Cúchulainn, like Pollux, was son of a god, and was nursed, according to some accounts, by Findchoém, mother of Conall, 485 just as Leda was mother of Castor as well as of Pollux. But, on the other hand, Cúchulainn, unlike Pollux, was mortal. M. D'Arbois then identifies the two pairs of heroes with certain figures on an altar at Cluny. These are Castor and Pollux; Cernunnos and Smertullos. He equates Castor with Cernunnos, and Pollux with Smertullos. Smertullos is Cúchulainn, and the name is explained from an incident in the Táin, in which the hero, reproached for his youth, puts on a false beard before attacking Morrigan in her form as an eel. This is expressed by smérthain, "to attach", and is thus connected with and gave rise to the name Smertullos. On the altar Smertullos is attacking an eel or serpent. Hence Pollux is Smertullos-Cúchulainn. 486 Again, the name Cernunnos signifies "the horned one," from cernu, "horn," a word found in Conall's epithet Cernach. But this was not given him because he was horned, but because of the angular shape of his head, the angle (cern) being the result of a blow. 487 The epithet may mean "victorious." 488 On the whole, the theory is more ingenious than convincing, and we have no proof that the figures of Castor and Pollux on the altar were duplicates of the Celtic pair. Cernunnos was an underworld god, and Conall has no trace of such a character.

M. D'Arbois also traces the saga in Gaul in the fact that on the menhir of Kervadel Mercury is figured with a child, Mercury, in his opinion, being Lug, and the child Cúchulainn. 489 On another altar are depicted (1) a woodman, Esus, cutting down a tree, and (2) a bull on which are perched three birds—Tarvos Trigaranos. The two subjects, as M. Reinach points out, are combined on another altar at Trèves, on which a woodman is cutting down a tree in which are perched three birds, while a bull's head appears in the branches. 490 These represent, according to M. D'Arbois, incidents of the Táin—the cutting down of trees by Cúchulainn and placing them in the way of his enemies, and the warning of the bull by Morrigan in the bird form which she shared with her sisters Badb and Macha. 491 Why, then, is Cúchulainn called Esus? "Esus" comes from a root which gives words meaning "rapid motion," "anger," "strength"—all shown by the hero. 492 The altars were found in the land of the Belgic Treveri, and some Belgic tribes may have passed into Britain and Ireland carrying the Esus-Cúchulainn legend there in the second century B.C., e.g. the Setantii, dwelling by the Mersey, and bearing a name similar to that of the hero in his childhood—Setanta (Setantios) as well as the Menapii and Brigantes, located in Ireland by Ptolemy. 493 In other words, the divine Esus, with his surname Smertullos, was called in Ireland Setanta, after the Setantii, and at a later date, Cúchulainn. The princely name Donnotaurus resembles Dond tarb, the "Brown Bull" of the saga, and also suggests its presence in Gaul, while the name [Greek: dêiotaros], perhaps the equivalent of De[^u]iotaruos, "Divine Bull," is found in Galatia. 494 Thus the main elements of the saga may have been known to the continental Celts before it was localised in Ireland, 495 and, it may be added, if it was brought there by Gallo-British tribes, this might account for the greater popularity of the native, possibly pre-Celtic, Fionn saga among the folk, as well as for the finer literary quality of the Cúchulainn saga. But the identification of Esus with Cúchulainn rests on slight grounds; the names Esus and Smertullos are not found in Ireland, and the Gaulish Esus, worshipped with human sacrifice, has little affinity with the hero, unless his deeds of slaughter are reminiscent of such rites. It is possible, however, that the episode of the Táin came from a myth explaining ritual acts. This myth may have been the subject of the bas-reliefs, carried to Ireland, and there worked into the saga.

The folk-versions of the saga, though resembling the literary versions, are less elaborate and generally wilder, and perhaps represent its primitive form. 496 The greatest differences are found in versions of the Táin and of Cúchulainn's death, which, separate in the saga, are parts of one folk-tale, the death occurring during the fighting over the bull. The bull is his property, and Medb sends Garbh mac Stairn to take it from him. He pretends to be a child, goes to bed, and tricks Garbh, who goes off to get the bull. Cúchulainn arrives before him and personates the herdsman. Each seizes a horn, and the bull is torn in two. 497 Does this represent the primitive form of the Táin, and, further, were the bull and Cúchulainn once one and the same—a bull, the incarnation of a god or vegetation spirit, being later made anthropomorphic—a hero-god whose property or symbol was a bull? Instances of this process are not unknown among the Celts. 498 In India, Indra was a bull and a divine youth, in Greece there was the bull-Dionysos, and among the Celts the name of the divine bull was borne by kings. 499 In the saga Morrigan is friendly to the bull, but fights for Medb; but she is now friendly, now hostile to Cúchulainn, finally, however, trying to avert his doom. If he had once been the bull, her friendliness would not be quite forgotten, once he became human and separate from the bull. When she first met Cúchulainn she had a cow on whom the Brown Bull was to beget a calf, and she told the hero that "So long as the calf which is in this cow's body is a yearling, it is up to that time that thou art in life; and it is this that will lead to the Táin." 500 This suggests that the hero was to die in the battle, but it shows that the Brown Bull's calf is bound up his life. The Bull was a reincarnation of a divine swineherd, and if, as in the case of Cúchulainn, "his rebirth could only be of himself," 501 the calf was simply a duplicate of the bull, and, as it was bound up with the hero's life, bull and hero may well have been one. The life or soul was in the calf, and, as in all such cases, the owner of the soul and that in which it is hidden are practically identical. Cúchulainn's "distortion" might then be explained as representing the bull's fury in fight, and the folk-tales would be popular forms of an old myth explaining ritual in which a bull, the incarnation of a tree or vegetation spirit, was slain, and the sacred tree cut down and consumed, as in Celtic agricultural ritual. This would be the myth represented on the bas-reliefs, and in the ritual the bull would be slain, rent, and eaten by his worshippers. Why, then, should Cúchulainn rend the bull? In the later stages of such rites the animal was slain, not so much as a divine incarnation as a sacrifice to the god once incarnated in him. And when a god was thus separated from his animal form, myths often arose telling how he himself had slain the animal.

502 In the case of Cúchulainn and the bull, the god represented by the bull became separate from it, became anthropomorphic, and in that form was associated with or actually was the hero Cúchulainn. Bull sacrifices were common among the Celts with whom the bull had been a divine animal. 503 Possibly a further echo of this myth and ritual is to be found in the folk-belief that S. Martin was cut up and eaten in the form of an ox — the god incarnate in the animal being associated with a saint. 504 Thus the literary versions of the Táin, departing from the hypothetical primitive versions, kept the bull as the central figure, but introduced a rival bull, and described its death differently, while both bulls are said to be reincarnations of divine swine-herds. 505 The idea of a fight for a bull is borrowed from actual custom, and thus the old form of the story was further distorted.

The Cúchulainn saga is more coherent than the Fionn saga, because it possesses one central incident. The "canon" of the saga was closed at an early date, while that of Fionn has practically never been closed, mainly because it has been more a saga of the folk than that of Cúchulainn. In some respects the two may have been rivals, for if the Cúchulainn saga was introduced by conquerors from Britain or Gaul, it would not be looked on with favour by the folk. Or if it is the saga of Ulster as opposed to that of Leinster, rivalry would again ensue. The Fionn saga lives more in the hearts of the people, though it sometimes borrows from the other. This borrowing, however, is less than some critics, e.g. Zimmer, maintain. Many of the likenesses are the result of the fact that wherever a hero exists a common stock of incidents becomes his. Hence there is much similarity in all sagas wherever found.

Footnote 453: IT i. 134; Nutt-Meyer, ii. 38 f.; Windisch, Táin, 342; L. Duvau, "La Legende de la Conception de Cúchulainn," RC ix. 1 f.

Footnote 454: Windisch, Táin, 118 f. For a similar reason Finnchad was called Cú Cerca, "the hound of Cerc" (IT iii. 377).

Footnote 455: For the boyish exploits, see Windisch, Táin, 106 f.

Footnote 456: RC vii. 225; Windisch, Táin, 20. Macha is a granddaughter of Ler, but elsewhere she is called Mider's daughter (RC xvi. 46).

Footnote 457: Rh[^y]s, CFL ii. 654; Westermarck, Hist. of Human Marriage, ch. 2.

Footnote 458: Miss Hull, Folk-Lore, xii. 60, citing instances from Jevons, Hist. of Religion, 65.

Footnote 459: Windisch, IT ii. 239.

Footnote 460: Windisch, 184, 312, 330; cf. IT iii. 355; Miss Hull, 164 f.; Rh[^y]s, HL 468.

Footnote 461: LL 119a; RC iii. 175.

Footnote 462: Windisch, 342.

Footnote 463: RC iii. 175 f.

Footnote 464: Ibid. 185.

Footnote 465: Crowe, Jour. Kilkenny Arch. Soc. 1870-1871, 371 f.

Footnote 466: LL 79a; O'Curry, MS. Mat, 640.

Footnote 467: LL 125a. See my Childhood of fiction, ch. 14.

Footnote 468: Miss Hull, lxxvi.

Footnote 469: "Da Derga's Hostel," RC xxii. 283; Rh[^y]s, HL 438.

Footnote 470: LL 68a; Rh[^y]s, 437; Ingcel the one-eyed has also many pupils (RC xxii. 58).

Footnote 471: Miss Hull, lxiii.

Footnote 472: RC viii. 49.

Footnote 473: LL 77b; Miss Hull, lxii.

Footnote 474: Other Celtic heroes undergo this distortion, which resembles the Scandinavian warrior rage followed by languor, as in the case of Cúchulainn.

Footnote 475: Miss Hull, p. lxvi.

Footnote 476: Irish saints, standing neck deep in freezing water, made it hot.

Footnote 477: IT i. 268; D'Arbois, v. 103; Miss Hull, lxvi.

Footnote 478: HL 448.

Footnote 479: See Meyer, RC xi. 435; Windisch, IT i. 589, 740. Though richis means "charcoal," it is also glossed "flame," hence it could only be glowing charcoal, without any idea of darkness.

Footnote 480: HL 458.

Footnote 481: IT i. 107.

Footnote 482: Arch. Rev. i. 1 f.; IT i. 213; infra.

Footnote 483: infra.

Footnote 484: Diod. Siculus, iv. 56.

Footnote 485: IT iii. 393.

Footnote 486: Les Celtes, 58 f. Formerly M. D'Arbois identified Smertullos with Lug, ii. 217; Holder, i. 46, 262. For the incident of the beard, see Windisch, Táin, 308.

Footnote 487: IT iii. 395.

Footnote 488: IT i. 420.

Footnote 489: RC xxvii. 319 f.

Footnote 490: RC xviii. 256.

Footnote 491: Les Celtes, 63; RC xix. 246.

Footnote 492: D'Arbois, RC xx. 89.

Footnote 493: D'Arbois, RC xxvii. 321; Les Celtes, 65.

Footnote 494: Les Celtes, 49; Cæsar, vi. 14.

Footnote 495: In contradiction to this, M. D'Arbois elsewhere thinks that Druids from Britain may have taught the Cúchulainn legend in Gaul (RC xxvii. 319).

Footnote 496: See versions in Book of the Dean of Lismore; CM xiii.; Campbell, The Fians, 6 f.

Footnote 497: CM xiii. 327, 514. The same story is told of Fionn, ibid. 512. See also ballad versions in Campbell, LF 3 f.

Footnote 498: infra.

Footnote 499: A Galatian king was called Brogitaros, probably a form of Brogitaruos, "bull of the province," a title borne by Conchobar, tarb in chóicid (IT i. 72). This with the epithets applied to heroes in the Triads, "bull-phantom," "prince bull of combat" (Loth, ii. 232, 243), may be an appellative denoting great strength.

Footnote 500: IT ii. 241 f.; D'Arbois, Les Druides, 168.

Footnote 501: Miss Hull, 58.

Footnote 502: infra.

Footnote 503: infra.

Footnote 504: Fitzgerald, RC vi. 254.

Footnote 505: infra.

CHAPTER VIII THE FIONN SAGA

The most prominent characters in the Fionn saga, after the death of Fionn's father Cumal, are Fionn, his son Oisin, his grandson Oscar, his nephew Diarmaid with his ball-seire, or "beauty-spot," which no woman could resist; Fergus famed for wisdom and eloquence; Caoilte mac Ronan, the swift; Conan, the comic character of the saga; Goll mac Morna, the slayer of Cumal, but later the devoted friend of Fionn, besides a host of less important personages. Their doings, like those of the heroes of saga and epos everywhere, are mainly hunting, fighting, and love-making. They embody much of the Celtic character—vivacity, valour, kindness, tenderness, as well as boastfulness and fiery temper. Though dating from pagan times, the saga throws little light upon pagan beliefs, but reveals much concerning the manners of the period. Here, as always in early Celtdom, woman is more than a mere chattel, and occupies a comparatively high place. The various parts of the saga, like those of the Finnish Kalevala, always existed separately, never as one complete epos, though always bearing a certain relation to each other. Lonnrot, in Finland, was able, by adding a few connecting links of his own, to give unity to the Kalevala, and had MacPherson been content to do this for the Fionn saga, instead of inventing, transforming, and serving up the whole in the manner of the sentimental eighteenth century, what a boon would he have conferred on Celtic literature. The various parts of the saga belong to different centuries and come from different authors, all, however, imbued with the spirit of the Fionn tradition.

A date cannot be given to the beginnings of the saga, and additions have been made to it even down to the eighteenth century, Michael Comyn's poem of Oisin in Tir na n-Og being as genuine a part of it as any of the earlier pieces. Its contents are in part written, but much more oral. Much of it is in prose, and there is a large poetic literature of the ballad kind, as well as Märchen of the universal stock made purely Celtic, with Fionn and the rest of the heroic band as protagonists. The saga embodies Celtic ideals and hopes; it was the literature of the Celtic folk on which was spent all the riches of the Celtic imagination; a world of dream and fancy into which they could enter at all times and disport themselves. Yet, in spite of its immense variety, the saga preserves a certain unity, and it is provided with a definite framework, recounting the origin of the heroes, the great events in which they were concerned, their deaths or final appearances, and the breaking up of the Fionn band.

The historic view of the Fians is taken by the annalists, by Keating, O'Curry, Dr. Joyce, and Dr. Douglas Hyde. 506 According to this view, they were a species of militia maintained by the Irish kings for the support of the throne and the defence of the country. From Samhain to Beltane they were quartered on the people, and from Beltane to Samhain they lived by hunting. How far the people welcomed this billeting, we are not told. Their method of cooking the game which they hunted was one well known to all primitive peoples. Holes were dug in the ground; in them red-hot stones were placed, and on the stones was laid venison wrapped in sedge. All was then covered over, and in due time the meat was done to a turn. Meanwhile the heroes engaged in an elaborate toilette before sitting down to eat. Their beds were composed of alternate layers of brushwood, moss, and rushes. The Fians were divided into Catha of three thousand men, each with its commander, and officers to each hundred, each fifty, and each nine, a system not unlike that of the ancient Peruvians. Each candidate for admission to the band had to undergo the most trying ordeals, rivalling in severity those of the American Indians, and not improbably genuine though exaggerated reminiscences of actual tests of endurance and agility. Once admitted he had to observe certain geasa or "tabus," e.g. not to choose his wife for her dowry like other Celts, but solely for her good manners, not to offer violence to a woman, not to flee when attacked before less than nine warriors, and the like.

All this may represent some genuine tradition with respect to a warrior band, with many exaggerations in details and numbers. Some of its outstanding heroes may have had names derived from or corresponding to those of the heroes of an existing saga. But as time went on they became as unhistorical as their ideal prototypes; round their names crystallised floating myths and tales; things which had been told of the saga heroes were told of them; their names were given to the personages of existing folk-tales. This might explain the great divergence between the "historical" and the romantic aspects of the saga as it now exists. Yet we cannot fail to see that what is claimed as historical is full of exaggeration, and, in spite of the pleading of Dr. Hyde and other patriots, little historic fact can be found in it. Even if this exists, it is the least important part of the saga. What is important is that part—nine-tenths of the whole—which "is not true because it cannot be true." It belongs to the region of the supernatural and the unreal. But personages, nine-tenths of whose actions belong to this region, must bear the same character themselves, and for that reason are all the more interesting, especially when we remember that the Celts firmly believed in them and in their exploits. A Fionn myth arose as all myths do, increasing as time went on, and the historical nucleus, if it ever existed, was swamped and lost. Throughout the saga the Fians are more than mere mortals, even in those very parts which are claimed as historical. They are giants; their story "bristles with the supernatural"; they are the ideal figures of Celtic legend throwing their gigantic shadows upon the dim and misty background of the past. We must therefore be content to assume that whether personages called Fionn, Oisin, Diarmaid, or Conan, ever existed, what we know of them now is purely mythical.

Bearing in mind that they are the cherished heroes of popular fancy in Ireland and the Scottish Highlands, we have now to inquire whether they were Celtic in origin. We have seen that the Celts were a conquering people in Ireland, bringing with them their own religion and mythology, their own sagas and tales reflected now in the mythological and Cúchulainn cycles, which found a local habitation in Ireland. Cúchulainn was the hero of a saga which flourished more among the aristocratic and lettered classes than among the folk, and there are few popular tales about him. But it is among the folk that the Fionn saga has always been popular, and for every peasant who could tell a story of Cúchulainn a thousand could tell one of Fionn. Conquerors often adopt beliefs, traditions, and customs of the aboriginal folk, after hostilities have ceased, and if the pre-Celtic people had a popular hero and a saga concerning him, it is possible that in time it was accepted by the Celts or by the lower classes among them. But in the process it must have been completely Celticised, like the aborigines themselves; to its heroes were given Celtic names, or they may have been associated with existing Celtic personages like Cumal, and the whole saga was in time adapted to the conceptions and legendary history of the Celts. Thus we might account for the fact that it has so largely remained without admixture with the mythological and Cúchulainn cycles, though its heroes are brought into relation with the older gods. Thus also we might account for its popularity as compared with the Cúchulainn saga among the peasantry in whose veins must flow so much of the aboriginal blood both in Ireland and the Highlands. In other words, it was the saga of a non-Celtic people occupying both Ireland and Scotland. If Celts from Western Europe occupied the west of Scotland at an early date, they may have been so few in number that their own saga or sagas died out. Or if the Celtic occupation of the West Highlands originated first from Ireland, the Irish may have been unable to impose their Cúchulainn saga there, or if they themselves had already adopted the Fionn saga and found it again in the Highlands, they would but be the more attached to what was already localised there. This would cut the ground from the theory that the Fionn saga was brought to Scotland from Ireland, and it would account for its popularity in the Highlands, as well as for the fact that many Fionn stories are attached to Highland as well as to Irish localities, while many place-names in both countries have a Fian origin. Finally, the theory would explain the existence of so many Märchen about Fionn and his men, so few about Cúchulainn.

Returning to the theory of the historic aspect of the Fians, it should be noted that, while, when seen through the eyes of the annalists, the saga belongs to a definite historical period, when viewed by itself it belongs to a mythic age, and though the Fians are regarded as champions of Ireland, their foes are usually of a supernatural kind, and they themselves move in a magic atmosphere. They are also brought into connection with the unhistoric Tuatha Dé Danann; they fight with them or for them; they have amours with or wed their women; and some of the gods even become members of the Fian band. Diarmaid was the darling of the gods Oengus and Manannan, and in his direst straits was assisted by the former. In all this we are in the wonderland of myth, not the terra firma of history. There is a certain resemblance between the Cúchulainn and Fionn sagas, but no more than that which obtains between all sagas everywhere. Both contain similar incidents, but these are the stock episodes of universal saga belief, fitted to the personages of individual sagas. Hence we need not suppose with Professor Windisch that the mythic incidents of the Fionn saga are derived from the Cúchulainn cycle.

The personages against whom Fionn and his men fight show the mythic nature of the saga. As champions of Leinster they fight the men of Ulster and Connaught, but they also war against oversea invaders—the Lochlanners. While Lochlann may mean any land beyond the sea, like the Welsh Llychlyn it probably meant "the fabulous land beneath the lakes or the waves of the sea," or simply the abode of hostile, supernatural beings. Lochlanners would thus be counterparts of the Fomorians, and the conflicts of the Fians with them would reflect old myths. But with the Norse invasions, the Norsemen became the true Lochlanners, against whom Fionn and his men fight as Charlemagne fought Muhammadans—a sheer impossibility. Professor Zimmer, however, supposes that the Fionn saga took shape during the Norse occupation from the ninth century onwards. Fionn is half Norse, half Irish, and equivalent to Caittil Find, who commanded the apostate Irish in the ninth century, while Oisin and Oscar are the Norse Asvin and Asgeirr. But it is difficult to understand why one who was half a Norseman should become the chosen hero of the Celts in the very age in which Norsemen were their bitter enemies, and why Fionn, if of Norse origin, fights against Lochlanners, i.e. Norsemen. It may also be inquired why the borrowing should have affected the saga only, not the myths of the gods. No other Celtic scholar has given the slightest support to this brilliant but audacious theory. On the other hand, if the saga has Norse affinities, and if it is, in origin, pre-Celtic, these may be sought in an earlier connection of Ireland with Scandinavia in the early Bronze Age. Ireland had a flourishing civilisation then, and exported beautiful gold ornaments to Scandinavia, where they are still found in Bronze Age deposits. 507 This flourishing civilisation was overwhelmed by the invasion of the Celtic barbarians. But if the Scandinavians borrowed gold and artistic decorations from Ireland, and if the Fionn saga or part of it was already in existence, why should they not have borrowed some of its incidents, or why, on the other hand, should not some episodes have found their way from the north to Ireland? We should also consider, however, that similar incidents may have been evolved in both countries on similar lines and quite independently.

The various contents of the saga can only be alluded to in the briefest manner. Fionn's birth-story belongs to the well-known "Expulsion and Return" formula, applied to so many heroes of saga and folk-tale, but highly elaborated in his case at the hands of the annalists. Thus his father Cumal, uncle of Conn the Hundred Fighter, 122-157 A.D., wished to wed Muirne, daughter of Conn's chief druid, Tadg. Tadg refused, knowing that through this marriage he would lose his ancestral seat. Cumal seized Muirne and married her, and the king, on Tadg's appeal, sent an army against him. Cumal was slain; Muirne fled to his sister, and gave birth to Demni, afterwards known as Fionn. Perhaps in accordance with old matriarchal usage, Fionn's descent through his mother is emphasised, while he is related to the ancient gods, Tadg being son of Nuada. This at once points to the mythical aspect of the saga. Cumal may be identical with the god Camulos. In a short time, Fionn, now a marauder and an outlaw, appeared at Conn's Court, and that same night slew one of the Tuatha Déa, who came yearly and destroyed the palace. For this he received his rightful heritage — the leadership of the Fians, formerly commanded by Cumal. 508 Another incident of Fionn's youth tells how he obtained his "thumb of knowledge." The eating of certain "salmon of knowledge" was believed to give inspiration, an idea perhaps derived from earlier totemistic beliefs. The bard Finnéces, having caught one of the coveted salmon, set his pupil Fionn to cook it, forbidding him to taste it. But as he was turning the fish Fionn burnt his thumb and thrust it into his mouth, thus receiving the gift of inspiration. Hereafter he had only to suck his thumb in order to obtain secret information. 509 In another story the inspiration is already in his thumb, as Samson's strength was in his hair, but the power is also partly in his tooth, under which, after ritual preparation, he has to place his thumb and chew it. 510

Fionn had many wives and sweethearts, one of them, Saar, being mother of Oisin. Saar was turned into a fawn by a Druid, and fled from Fionn's house. Long after he found a beast-child in the forest and recognised him as his son. He nourished him until his beast nature disappeared, and called him Oisin, "little fawn." Round this birth legend many stories sprang up—a sure sign of its popularity. 511 Oisin's fame as a poet far excelled that of Fionn, and he became the ideal bard of the Gaels.

By far the most passionate and tragic story of the saga is that of Diarmaid and Grainne, to whom Fionn was betrothed. Grainne put geasa upon Diarmaid to elope with her, and these he could not break. They fled, and for many days were pursued by Fionn, who at last overtook them, but was forced by the Fians to pardon the beloved hero. Meanwhile Fionn waited for his revenge. Knowing that it was one of Diarmaid's geasa never to hunt a wild boar, he invited him to the chase of the boar of Gulban. Diarmaid slew it, and Fionn then bade him measure its length with his foot. A bristle pierced his heel, and he fell down in agony, beseeching Fionn to bring him water in his hand, for if he did this he would heal him. In spite of repeated appeals, Fionn, after bringing the water, let it drip from his hands. Diarmaid's brave soul passed away, and on Fionn's character this dire blot was fixed for ever. 512

Other tales relate how several of the Fians were spirited away to the Land beyond the Seas, how they were rescued, how Diarmaid went to Land under Waves, and how Fionn and his men were entrapped in a Fairy Palace. Of greater importance are those which tell the end of the Fian band. This, according to the annalists, was the result of their exactions and demands. Fionn was told by his wife, a wise woman, never to drink out of a horn, but coming one day thirsty to a well, he forgot this tabu, and so brought the end near. He encountered the sons of Uirgrenn, whom he had slain, and in the fight with them he fell. 513 Soon after were fought several battles, culminating in that of Gabhra in which all but a few Fians perished. Among the survivors were Oisin and Caoilte, who lingered on until the coming of S. Patrick. Caoilte remained on earth, but Oisin, whose mother was of the síd folk, went to fairyland for a time, ultimately returning and joining S. Patrick's company. 514 But a different version is given in the eighteenth century poem of Michael Comyn, undoubtedly based on popular tales. Oisin met the Queen of Tir na n-Og and went with her to fairyland, where time passed as a dream until one day he stood on a stone against which she had warned him. He saw his native land and was filled with home-sickness. The queen tried to dissuade him, but in vain. Then she gave him a horse, warning him not to set foot on Irish soil. He came to Ireland; and found it all changed. Some puny people were trying in vain to raise a great stone, and begged the huge stranger to help them. He sprang from his horse and flung the stone from its resting-place. But when he turned, his horse was gone, and he had become a decrepit old man. Soon after he met S. Patrick and related the tale to him.

Of most of the tales preserved in twelfth to fifteenth century MSS. it may be said that in essence they come down to us from a remote antiquity, like stars pulsing their clear light out of the hidden depths of space. Many of them exist as folk-tales, often wild and weird in form, while some folk-tales have no literary parallels. Some are Märchen with members of the Fian band as heroes, and of these there are many European parallels. But it is not unlikely that, as in the case of the Cúchulainn cycle, the folk versions may be truer to the original forms of the saga than the rounded and polished literary versions. Whatever the Fians were in origin—gods, mythic heroes, or actual personages—it is probable that a short Heldensage was formed in early times. This slowly expanded, new tales were added, and existing Märchen formulæ were freely made use of by making their heroes the heroes of the saga. Then came the time when many of the tales were written down, while later they were adapted to a scheme of Irish history, the heroes becoming warriors of a definite historic period, or perhaps connected with such warriors. But these heroes belonged to a timeless world, whose margins are "the shore of old romance," and it was as if they, who were not for an age but for all time, scorned to become the puppets of the page of history.

The earliest evidence of the attitude of the ecclesiastical world to these heroes is found in the Agallamh na Senorach, or "Colloquy of the Ancients." 515 This may have been composed in the thirteenth century, and its author knew scores of Fionn legends. Making use of the tradition that Caoilte and Oisin had met S. Patrick, he makes Caoilte relate many of the tales, usually in connection with some place-name of Fian origin. The saint and his followers are amazed at the huge stature of the Fians, but Patrick asperges them with holy water, and hosts of demons flee from them. At each tale which Caoilte tells, the saint says, "Success and benediction, Caoilte. All this is to us a recreation of spirit and of mind, were it only not a destruction of devotion and a dereliction of prayer." But presently his guardian angel appears, and bids him not only listen to the tales but cause them to be written down. He and his attendant clerics now lend a willing ear to the recital and encourage the narrator with their applause. Finally, baptism is administered to Caoilte and his men, and by Patrick's intercessions Caoilte's relations and Fionn himself are brought out of hell. In this work the representatives of paganism are shown to be on terms of friendliness with the representatives of Christianity.

But in Highland ballads collected in the sixteenth century by the Dean of Lismore, as well as in Irish ballads found in MSS. dating from the seventeenth century onwards, the saint is a sour and intolerant cleric, and the Fians are equally intolerant and blasphemous pagans. There is no attempt at compromise; the saint rejoices that the Fian band are in hell, and Oisin throws contempt on the God of the shaven priests. But sometimes this contempt is mingled with humour and pathos. Were the heroes of Oisin's band now alive, scant work would be made of the monks' bells, books, and psalm-singing. It is true that the saint gives the weary old man hospitality, but Oisin's eyes are blinded with tears as he thinks of the departed glories of the Fians, and his ears are tormented "by jangling bells, droning psalms, and howling clerics." These ballads probably represent one main aspect of the attitude of the Church to Celtic paganism. How, then, did the more generous Colloquy come into being? We must note first that some of the ballads have a milder tone. Oisin is urged to accept the faith, and he prays for salvation. Probably these represent the beginning of a reaction in favour of the old heroes, dating from a time when the faith was well established. There was no danger of a pagan revival, and, provided the Fians were Christianised, it might be legitimate to represent them as heroic and noble. The Colloquy would represent the high-water mark of this reaction among the lettered classes, for among the folk, to judge by popular tales, the Fians had never been regarded in other than a favourable light. The Colloquy re-established the dignity of the Fian band in the eyes of official Christianity. They are baptized or released from hell, and in their own nature they are virtuous and follow lofty ideals. "Who or what was it that maintained you in life?" asks Patrick. And Caoilte gives the noble reply, "Truth that was in our hearts, and strength in our arms, and fulfilment in our tongues." Patrick says of Fionn: "He was a king, a seer, a poet, a lord with a manifold and great train; our magician, our knowledgeable one, our soothsayer; all whatsoever he said was sweet with him. Excessive, perchance, as ye deem my testimony of Fionn, although ye hold that which I say to be overstrained, nevertheless, and by the King that is above me, he was three times better still." Not only so, but Caoilte maintains that Fionn and his men were aware of the existence of the true God. They possessed the anima naturaliter Christiana. The growing appreciation of a wider outlook on life, and possibly acquaintance with the romances of chivalry, made the composition of the Colloquy possible, but, again, it may represent a more generous conception of paganism existing from the time of the first encounter of Christianity with it in Ireland.

The strife of creeds in Ireland, the old order changing, giving place to new, had evidently impressed itself on the minds of Celtic poets and romancers. It suggested itself to them as providing an excellent "situation"; hence we constantly hear of the meeting of gods, demigods, or heroes with the saints of the new era. Frequently they bow before the Cross, they are baptized and receive the Christian verity, as in the Colloquy and in some documents of the Cúchulainn cycle. Probably no other European folk-literature so takes advantage of just this situation, this meeting of creeds, one old and ready to vanish away, the other with all the buoyant freshness of youth.

Was MacPherson's a genuine Celtic epic unearthed by him and by no one else? No mortal eye save his has ever seen the original, but no one who knows anything of the contents of the saga can deny that much of his work is based on materials collected by him. He knew some of the tales and ballads current among the folk, possibly also some of the Irish MS. versions. He saw that there was a certain unity among them, and he saw that it was possible to make it more evident still. He fitted the floating incidents into an epic framework, adding, inventing, altering, and moulding the whole into an English style of his own. Later he seems to have translated the whole into Gaelic. He gave his version to the world, and found himself famous, but he gave it as the genuine translation of a genuine Celtic epic. Here was his craft; here he was the "charlatan of genius." His genius lay in producing an epic which people were willing to read, and in making them believe it to be not his work but that of the Celtic heroic age. Any one can write an epic, but few can write one which thousands will read, which men like Chateaubriand, Goethe, Napoleon, Byron, and Coleridge will admire and love, and which will, as it were, crystallise the aspirations of an age weary with classical formalism. MacPherson introduced his readers to a new world of heroic deeds, romantic adventure, deathless love, exquisite sentiments sentimentally expressed. He changed the rough warriors and beautiful but somewhat unabashed heroines of the saga into sentimental personages, who suited the taste of an age poised between the bewigged and powdered formalism of the eighteenth century, and the outburst of new ideals which was to follow. His Ossian is a cross between Pope's Homer and Byron's Childe Harold. His heroes and heroines are not on their native heath, and are uncertain whether to mince and strut with Pope or to follow nature with Rousseau's noble savages and Saint Pierre's Paul and Virginia. The time has gone when it was heresy to cast doubt upon the genuineness of MacPherson's epic, but if any one is still doubtful, let him read it and then turn to the existing versions, ballads, and tales. He will find himself in a totally different atmosphere, and will recognise in the latter the true epic note—the warrior's rage and the warrior's generosity, dire cruelty yet infinite tenderness, wild lust yet also true love, a world of magic supernaturalism, but an exact copy of things as they were in that far-off age. The barbarism of the time is in these old tales—deeds which make one shiver, customs regarding the relations of the sexes now found only among savages, social and domestic arrangements which are somewhat lurid and disgusting. And yet, withal, the note of bravery, of passion, of authentic life is there; we are held in the grip of genuine manhood and womanhood. MacPherson gives a picture of the Ossianic age as he conceived it, an age of Celtic history that "never was on sea or land." Even his ghosts are un-Celtic, misty and unsubstantial phantasms, unlike the embodied revenants of the saga which are in agreement with the Celtic belief that the soul assumed a body in the other world. MacPherson makes Fionn invariably successful, but in the saga tales he is often defeated. He mingles the Cúchulainn and Ossianic cycles, but these, save in a few casual instances, are quite distinct in the old literature. Yet had not his poem been so great as it is, though so un-Celtic, it could not have influenced all European literature. But those who care for genuine Celtic literature, the product of a people who loved nature, romance, doughty deeds, the beauty of the world, the music of the sea and the birds, the mountains, valour in men, beauty in women, will find all these in the saga, whether in its literary or its popular forms. And through it all sounds the undertone of Celtic pathos and melancholy, the distant echo

"Of old unhappy, far-off things

And battles long ago."

Footnote 506: See Joyce, OCR 447.

Footnote 507: Montelius, Les Temps Préhistoriques, 57, 151; Reinach, RC xxi. 8.

Footnote 508: The popular versions of this early part of the saga differ much in detail, but follow the main outlines in much the same way. See Curtin, HTI 204; Campbell, LF 33 f.; WHT iii. 348.

Footnote 509: In a widespread group of tales supernatural knowledge is obtained by eating part of some animal, usually a certain snake. In many of these tales the food is eaten by another person than he who obtained it, as in the case of Fionn. Cf. the Welsh story of Gwion, p. 116, and the Scandinavian of Sigurd, and other parallels in Miss Cox, Cinderella, 496; Frazer, Arch. Rev. i. 172 f. The story is thus a folk-tale formula applied to Fionn, doubtless because it harmonised with Celtic or pre-Celtic totemistic ideas. But it is based on ancient ideas regarding the supernatural knowledge possessed by reptiles or fish, and among American Indians, Maoris, Solomon Islanders, and others there are figured representations of a man holding such an animal, its tongue being attached to his tongue. He is a shaman, and American Indians believe that his inspiration comes from the tongue of a mysterious river otter, caught by him. See Dall, Bureau of Ethnol. 3rd report; and Miss Buckland, Jour. Anth. Inst. xxii. 29.

Footnote 510: TOS iv.; O'Curry, MS. Mat. 396; Joyce, OCR 194, 339.

Footnote 511: For ballad versions see Campbell, LF 198.

Footnote 512: Numerous ballad versions are given in Campbell LF 152 f. The tale is localised in various parts of Ireland and the Highlands, many dolmens in Ireland being known as Diarmaid and Grainne's beds.

Footnote 513: For an account differing from this annalistic version, see ZCP i. 465.

Footnote 514: O'Grady, ii. 102. This, on the whole, agrees with the Highland ballad version, LF 198.

Footnote 515: IT iv.; O'Grady, Silva Gad. text and translation.

CHAPTER IX
GODS AND MEN

Though man usually makes his gods in his own image, they are unlike as well as like him. Intermediate between them and man are ideal heroes whose parentage is partly divine, and who may themselves have been gods. One mark of the Celtic gods is their great stature. No house could contain Bran, and certain divine people of Elysium who appeared to Fionn had rings "as thick as a three-ox goad." 516 Even the Fians are giants, and the skull of one of them could contain several men. The gods have also the attribute of invisibility, and are only seen by those to whom they wish to disclose themselves, or they have the power of concealing themselves in a magic mist. When they appear to mortals it is usually in mortal guise, sometimes in the form of a particular person, but they can also transform themselves into animal shapes, often that of birds. The animal names of certain divinities show that they had once been animals pure and simple, but when they became anthropomorphic, myths would arise telling how they had appeared to men in these animal shapes. This, in part, accounts for these transformation myths. The gods are also immortal, though in myth we hear of their deaths. The Tuatha Dé Danann are "unfading," their "duration is perennial." 517 This immortality is sometimes an inherent quality; sometimes it is the result of eating immortal food—Manannan's swine, Goibniu's feast of age and his immortal ale, or the apples of Elysium. The stories telling of the deaths of the gods in the annalists may be based on old myths in which they were said to die, these myths being connected with ritual acts in which the human representatives of gods were slain. Such rites were an inherent part of Celtic religion. Elsewhere the ritual of gods like Osiris or Adonis, based on their functions as gods of vegetation, was connected with elaborate myths telling of their death and revival. Something akin to this may have occurred among the Celts.

The divinities often united with mortals. Goddesses sought the love of heroes who were then sometimes numbered among the gods, and gods had amours with the daughters of men. 518 Frequently the heroes of the sagas are children of a god or goddess and a mortal, 519 and this divine parentage was firmly believed in by the Celts, since personal names formed of a divine name and -genos or -gnatos, "born of," "son of," are found in inscriptions over the whole Celtic area, or in Celtic documents—Boduogenos, Camulognata, etc. Those who first bore these names were believed to be of divine descent on one side. Spirits of nature or the elements of nature personified might also be parents of mortals, as a name like Morgen, from Morigenos, "Son of the Sea," and many others suggest. For this and for other reasons the gods frequently interfere in human affairs, assisting their children or their favourites. Or, again, they seek the aid of mortals or of the heroes of the sagas in their conflicts or in time of distress, as when Morrigan besought healing from Cúchulainn.

As in the case of early Greek and Roman kings, Celtic kings who bore divine names were probably believed to be representatives or incarnations of gods. Perhaps this explains why a chief of the Boii called himself a god and was revered after his death, and why the Gauls so readily accepted the divinity of Augustus. Irish kings bear divine names, and of these Nuada occurs frequently, one king, Irél Fáith, being identified with Nuada Airgetlam, while in one text nuadat is glossed in ríg, "of the king," as if Nuada had come to be a title meaning "king." Welsh kings bear the name Nudd (Nodons), and both the actual and the mythic leader Brennus took their name from the god Bran. King Conchobar is called día talmaide, "a terrestrial god." If kings were thought to be god-men like the Pharaohs, this might account for the frequency of tales about divine fatherhood or reincarnation, while it would also explain the numerous geasa which Irish kings must observe, unlike ordinary mortals. Prosperity was connected with their observance, though this prosperity was later thought to depend on the king's goodness. The nature of the prosperity—mild seasons, abundant crops, fruit, fish, and cattle—shows that the king was associated with fertility, like the gods of growth. 520 Hence they had probably been once regarded as incarnations of such gods. Wherever divine kings are found, fertility is bound up with them and with the due observance of their tabus. To prevent misfortune to the land, they are slain before they grow old and weak, and their vigour passes on to their successors. Their death benefits their people. 521 But frequently the king might reign as long as he could hold his own against all comers, or, again, a slave or criminal was for a time treated as a mock king, and slain as the divine king's substitute. Scattered hints in Irish literature and in folk survivals show that some such course as this had been pursued by the Celts with regard to their divine kings, as it was also elsewhere. 522 It is not impossible that some at least of the Druids stood in a similar relation to the gods. Kings and priests were probably at first not differentiated. In Galatia twelve "tetrarchs" met annually with three hundred assistants at Drunemeton as the great national council. 523 This council at a consecrated place (nemeton), its likeness to the annual Druidic gathering in Gaul, and the possibility that Dru- has some connection with the name "Druid," point to a religious as well as political aspect of this council. The "tetrarchs" may have been a kind of priest-kings; they had the kingly prerogative of acting as judges as had the Druids of Gaul. The wife of one of them was a priestess, 524 the office being hereditary in her family, and it may have been necessary that her husband should also be a priest. One tetrarch, Deiotarus, "divine bull," was skilled in augury, and the priest-kingship of Pessinus was conferred on certain Celts in the second century B.C., as if the double office were already a Celtic institution. 525 Mythic Celtic kings consulted the gods without any priestly intervention, and Queen Boudicca had priestly functions. 526 Without giving these hints undue emphasis, we may suppose that the differentiation of the two offices would not be simultaneous over the Celtic area. But when it did take effect priests would probably lay claim to the prerogatives of the priest-king as incarnate god. Kings were not likely to give these up, and where they retained them priests would be content with seeing that the tabus and ritual and the slaying of the mock king were duly observed. Irish kings were perhaps still regarded as gods, though certain Druids may have been divine priests, since they called themselves creators of the universe, and both continental and Irish Druids claimed superiority to kings. Further, the name [Greek: semnotheoi], applied along with the name "Druids" to Celtic priests, though its meaning is obscure, points to divine pretensions on their part. 527

The incarnate god was probably representative of a god or spirit of earth, growth, or vegetation, represented also by a tree. A symbolic branch of such a tree was borne by kings, and perhaps by Druids, who used oak branches in their rites. 528 King and tree would be connected, the king's life being bound up with that of the tree, and perhaps at one time both perished together. But as kings were represented by a substitute, so the sacred tree, regarded as too sacred to be cut down, may also have had its succedaneum. The Irish bile or sacred tree, connected with the kings, must not be touched by any impious hand, and it was sacrilege to cut it down. 529 Probably before cutting down the tree a branch or something growing upon it, e.g. mistletoe, had to be cut, or the king's symbolic branch secured before he could be slain. This may explain Pliny's account of the mistletoe rite. The mistletoe or branch was the soul of the tree, and also contained the life of the divine representative. It must be plucked before the tree could be cut down or the victim slain. Hypothetical as this may be, Pliny's account is incomplete, or he is relating something of which all the details were not known to him. The rite must have had some other purpose than that of the magico-medical use of the mistletoe which he describes, and though he says nothing of cutting down the tree or slaying a human victim, it is not unlikely that, as human sacrifice had been prohibited in his time, the oxen which were slain during the rite took the place of the latter. Later romantic tales suggest that, before slaying some personage, the mythico-romantic survivor of a divine priest or king, a branch carried by him had to be captured by his assailant, or plucked from the tree which he defended. 530 These may point to an old belief in tree and king as divine representatives, and to a ritual like that associated with the Priest of Nemi. The divine tree became the mystic tree of Elysium, with gold and silver branches and marvellous fruits. Armed with such a branch, the gift of one of its people, mortals might penetrate unhindered to the divine land. Perhaps they may be regarded as romantic forms of the old divine kings with the branch of the divine tree.

If in early times the spirit of vegetation was feminine, her representative would be a woman, probably slain at recurring festivals by the female worshippers. This would explain the slaying of one of their number at a festival by Namnite women. But when male spirits or gods superseded goddesses, the divine priest-king would take the place of the female representative. On the other hand, just as the goddess became the consort of the god, a female representative would continue as the divine bride in the ritual of the sacred marriage, the May Queen of later folk-custom. Sporadically, too, conservatism would retain female cults with female divine incarnations, as is seen by the presence of the May Queen alone in certain folk-survivals, and by many Celtic rituals from which men were excluded. 531

Footnote 516: O'Grady, ii. 228.

Footnote 517: Ibid. ii. 203. Cf. Cæsar, vi. 14, "the immortal gods" of Gaul.

Footnote 518: Cf. Ch. XXIV.; O'Grady, ii. 110, 172; Nutt-Meyer, i. 42.

Footnote 519: Leahy, ii. 6.

Footnote 520: IT iii. 203; Trip. Life, 507; Annals of the Four Masters, A.D. 14; RC xxii. 28, 168. Chiefs as well as kings probably influenced fertility. A curious survival of this is found in the belief that herrings abounded in Dunvegan Loch when MacLeod arrived at his castle there, and in the desire of the people in Skye during the potato famine that his fairy banner should be waved.

Footnote 521: An echo of this may underlie the words attributed to King Ailill, "If I am slain, it will be the redemption of many" (O'Grady, ii. 416).

Footnote 522: See Frazer, Kingship; Cook, Folk-Lore, 1906, "The European Sky-God." Mr. Cook gives ample evidence for the existence of Celtic incarnate gods. With his main conclusions I agree, though some of his inferences seem far-fetched. The divine king was, in his view, a sky-god; he was more likely to have been the representative of a god or spirit of growth or vegetation.

Footnote 523: Strabo, xii. 5. 2.

Footnote 524: Plutarch, de Virt. Mul. 20.

Footnote 525: Cicero, de Div. i. 15, ii. 36; Strabo, xii. 5. 3; Stachelin, Gesch. der Kleinasiat. Galater.

Footnote 526: Livy, v. 34; Dio Cass. lxii. 6.

Footnote 527: Ancient Laws of Ireland, i. 22; Diog. Laert. i. proem 1;infra.

Footnote 528: Pliny, xvi. 95.

Footnote 529: infra.

Footnote 530: Cf. the tales of Gawain and the Green Knight with his holly bough, and of Gawain's attempting to pluck the bough of a tree guarded by Gramoplanz (Weston, Legend of Sir Gawain, 22, 86). Cf. also the tale of Diarmaid's attacking the defender of a tree to obtain its fruit, and the subsequent slaughter of each man who attacks the hero hidden in its branches (TOS vol. iii.). Cf. Cook, Folk-Lore, xvii. 441.

Footnote 531: See Chap. XVIII.

CHAPTER X
THE CULT OF THE DEAD

The custom of burying grave-goods with the dead, or slaying wife or slaves on the tomb, does not necessarily point to a cult of the dead, yet when such practices survive over a long period they assume the form of a cult. These customs flourished among the Celts, and, taken in connection with the reverence for the sepulchres of the dead, they point to a worship of ancestral spirits as well as of great departed heroes. Heads of the slain were offered to the "strong shades"—the ghosts of tribal heroes whose praises were sung by bards. 532 When such heads were placed on houses, they may have been devoted to the family ghosts. The honour in which mythic or real heroes were held may point to an actual cult, the hero being worshipped when dead, while he still continued his guardianship of the tribe. We know also that the tomb of King Cottius in the Alps was a sacred place, that Irish kings were often inaugurated on ancestral burial cairns, and that Irish gods were associated with barrows of the dead. 533

The cult of the dead culminated at the family hearth, around which the dead were even buried, as among the Aeduii; this latter custom may have been general. 534 In any case the belief in the presence of ancestral ghosts around the hearth was widespread, as existing superstitions show. In Brittany the dead seek warmth at the hearth by night, and a feast is spread for them on All Souls' eve, or crumbs are left for them after a family gathering. 535 But generally the family ghost has become a brownie, lutin, or pooka, haunting the hearth and doing the household work. 536 Fairy corresponds in all respects to old ancestral ghost, and the one has succeeded to the place of the other, while the fairy is even said to be the ghost of a dead person. 537 Certain archæological remains have also a connection with this ancient cult. Among Celtic remains in Gaul are found andirons of clay, ornamented with a ram's head. M. Dechelette sees in this "the symbol of sacrifice offered to the souls of ancestors on the altar of the hearth." 538 The ram was already associated as a sacrificial animal with the cult of fire on the hearth, and by an easy transition it was connected with the cult of the dead there. It is found as an emblem on ancient tombs, and the domestic Lar was purified by the immolation of a ram. 539 Figurines of a ram have been found in Gaulish tombs, and it is associated with the god of the underworld. 540 The ram of the andirons was thus a permanent representative of the victim offered in the cult of the dead. A mutilated inscription on one of them may stand for Laribus augustis, and certain markings on others may represent the garlands twined round the victim. 541 Serpents with rams' heads occur on the monuments of the underworld god. The serpent was a chthonian god or the emblem of such a god, and it may have been thought appropriate to give it the head of an animal associated with the cult of the dead.

The dead were also fed at the grave or in the house. Thus cups were placed in the recess of a well in the churchyard of Kilranelagh by those interring a child under five, and the ghost of the child was supposed to supply the other spirits with water from these cups. 542 In Ireland, after a death, food is placed out for the spirits, or, at a burial, nuts are placed in the coffin. 543 In some parts of France, milk is poured out on the grave, and both in Brittany and in Scotland the dead are supposed to partake of the funeral feast. 544 These are survivals from pagan times and correspond to the rites in use among those who still worship ancestors. In Celtic districts a cairn or a cross is placed over the spot where a violent or accidental death has occurred, the purpose being to appease the ghost, and a stone is often added to the cairn by all passers-by. 545

Festivals were held in Ireland on the anniversaries of the death of kings or chiefs, and these were also utilised for purposes of trade, pleasure, or politics. They sometimes occurred on the great festivals, e.g. Lugnasad and Samhain, and were occasionally held at the great burial-places. 546 Thus the gathering at Taillti on Lugnasad was said to have been founded by Lug in memory of his foster-mother, Tailtiu, and the Leinstermen met at Carman on the same day to commemorate King Garman, or in a variant account, a woman called Carman. She and her sons had tried to blight the corn of the Tuatha Dé Danann, but the sons were driven off and she died of grief, begging that a fair should always be held in her name, and promising abundance of milk, fruit, and fish for its observance. 547 These may be ætiological myths explaining the origin of these festivals on the analogy of funeral festivals, but more likely, since Lugnasad was a harvest festival, they are connected with the custom of slaying a representative of the corn-spirit. The festival would become a commemoration of all such victims, but when the custom itself had ceased it would be associated with one particular personage, the corn-goddess regarded as a mortal.

This would be the case where the victim was a woman, but where a male was slain, the analogy of the slaying of the divine king or his succedaneum would lead to the festivals being regarded as commemorative of a king, e.g. Garman. This agrees with the statement that observance of the festival produced plenty; non-observance, dearth. The victims were slain to obtain plenty, and the festival would also commemorate those who had died for this good cause, while it would also appease their ghosts should these be angry at their violent deaths. Certain of the dead were thus commemorated at Lugnasad, a festival of fertility. Both the corn-spirit or divinity slain in the reaping of the corn, and the human victims, were appeased by its observance. 548 The legend of Carman makes her hostile to the corn—a curious way of regarding a corn-goddess. But we have already seen that gods of fertility were sometimes thought of as causing blight, and in folk-belief the corn-spirit is occasionally believed to be dangerous. Such inversions occur wherever revolutions in religion take place.

The great commemoration of the dead was held on Samhain eve, a festival intended to aid the dying powers of vegetation, whose life, however, was still manifested in evergreen shrubs, in the mistletoe, in the sheaf of corn from last harvest—the abode of the corn-spirit. 549 Probably, also, human representatives of the vegetation or corn-spirit were slain, and this may have suggested the belief in the presence of their ghosts at this festival. Or the festival being held at the time of the death of vegetation, the dead would naturally be commemorated then. Or, as in Scandinavia, they may have been held to have an influence on fertility, as an extension of the belief that certain slain persons represented spirits of fertility, or because trees and plants growing on the barrows of the dead were thought to be tenanted by their spirits. 550 In Scandinavia, the dead were associated with female spirits or fylgjur, identified with the disir, a kind of earth-goddesses, living in hollow hills. 551 The nearest Celtic analogy to these is the Matres, goddesses of fertility. Bede says that Christmas eve was called Modranicht, "Mothers' Night," 552 and as many of the rites of Samhain were transferred to Yule, the former date of Modranicht may have been Samhain, just as the Scandinavian Disablot, held in November, was a festival of the disir and of the dead. 553 It has been seen that the Celtic Earth-god was lord of the dead, and that he probably took the place of an Earth-goddess or goddesses, to whom the Matres certainly correspond. Hence the connection of the dead with female Earth-spirits would be explained. Mother Earth had received the dead before her place was taken by the Celtic Dispater. Hence the time of Earth's decay was the season when the dead, her children, would be commemorated. Whatever be the reason, Celts, Teutons, and others have commemorated the dead at the beginning of winter, which was the beginning of a new year, while a similar festival of the dead at New Year is held in many other lands.

Both in Ireland and in Brittany, on November eve food is laid out for the dead who come to visit the houses and to warm themselves at the fire in the stillness of the night, and in Brittany a huge log burns on the hearth. We have here returned to the cult of the dead at the hearth. 554 Possibly the Yule log was once a log burned on the hearth — the place of the family ghosts — at Samhain, when new fire was kindled in each house. On it libations were poured, which would then have been meant for the dead. The Yule log and the log of the Breton peasants would thus be the domestic aspect of the fire ritual, which had its public aspect in the Samhain bonfires.

All this has been in part affected by the Christian feast of All Souls. Dr. Frazer thinks that the feast of All Saints (November 1st) was intended to take the place of the pagan cult of the dead. As it failed to do this, All Souls, a festival of all the dead, was added on November 2nd. 555 To some extent, but not entirely, it has neutralised the pagan rites, for the old ideas connected with Samhain still survive here and there. It is also to be noted that in some cases the friendly aspect of the dead has been lost sight of, and, like the síd-folk, they are popularly connected with evil powers which are in the ascendant on Samhain eve.

Footnote 532: Silius Italicus, v. 652; Lucan, i. 447. Cf. p. 241, infra.

Footnote 533: Ammian. Marcell. xv. 10. 7; Joyce, SH i. 45.

Footnote 534: Bulliot, Fouilles du Mont Beuvray, Autun, 1899, i. 76, 396.

Footnote 535: Le Braz, ii. 67; Sauvé, Folk-lore des Hautes Vosges, 295; Bérenger-Féraud, Superstitions et Survivances, i. 11.

Footnote 536: Hearn, Aryan Household, 43 f.; Bérenger-Féraud, i. 33; Rev. des Trad. i. 142; Carmichael, ii. 329; Cosquin, Trad. Pop. de la Lorraine, i. 82.

Footnote 537: Kennedy, 126. The mischievous brownie who overturns furniture and smashes crockery is an exact reproduction of the Poltergeist.

Footnote 538: Dechelette, Rev. Arch. xxxiii, (1898), 63, 245, 252.

Footnote 539: Cicero, De Leg. ii. 22.

Footnote 540: Dechelette, 256; Reinach, BF 189.

Footnote 541: Dechelette, 257-258. In another instance the ram is marked with crosses like those engraved on images of the underworld god with the hammer.

Footnote 542: Kennedy, 187.

Footnote 543: Lady Wilde, 118; Curtin, Tales, 54.

Footnote 544: Le Braz, i. 229; Gregor, 21; Cambry, Voyage dans le Finistère, i. 229.

Footnote 545: Le Braz, ii. 47; Folk-Lore, iv. 357; MacCulloch, Misty Isle of Skye, 254; Sébillot, i. 235-236.

Footnote 546: Names of places associated with the great festivals are also those of the chief pagan cemeteries, Tara, Carman, Taillti, etc. (O'Curry, MC ii. 523).

Footnote 547: Rennes Dindsenchas, RC xv. 313-314.

Footnote 548: Cf. Frazer, Adonis, 134.

Footnote 549: Cf. Chambers, Mediæval Stage, i. 250, 253.

Footnote 550: See Vigfusson-Powell, Corpus Poet. Boreale, i. 405, 419. Perhaps for a similar reason a cult of the dead may have occurred at the Midsummer festival.

Footnote 551: Miss Faraday, Folk-Lore, xvii. 398 f.

Footnote 552: Bede, de Temp. Rat. c. xv.

Footnote 553: Vigfusson-Powell, i. 419.

Footnote 554: Curtin, Tales, 157; Haddon, Folk-Lore, iv. 359; Le Braz, ii. 115 et passim.

Footnote 555: Frazer, Adonis, 253 f.

CHAPTER XI
PRIMITIVE NATURE WORSHIP

In early thought everything was a person, in the loose meaning then possessed by personality, and many such "persons" were worshipped— earth, sun, moon, sea, wind, etc. This led later to more complete personification, and the sun or earth divinity or spirit was more or less separated from the sun or earth themselves. Some Celtic divinities were thus evolved, but there still continued a veneration of the objects of nature in themselves, as well as a cult of nature spirits or secondary divinities who peopled every part of nature. "Nor will I call out upon the mountains, fountains, or hills, or upon the rivers, which are now subservient to the use of man, but once were an abomination and destruction to them, and to which the blind people paid divine honours," cries Gildas. 556 This was the true cult of the folk, the "blind people," even when the greater gods were organised, and it has survived with modifications in out-of-the-way places, in spite of the coming of Christianity.

S. Kentigern rebuked the Cambrians for worshipping the elements, which God made for man's use. 557 The question of the daughters of Loegaire also throws much light on Celtic nature worship. "Has your god sons or daughters?... Have many fostered his sons? Are his daughters dear and beautiful to men? Is he in heaven or on earth, in the sea, in the rivers, in the mountains, in the valleys?" 558 The words suggest a belief in divine beings filling heaven, earth, sea, air, hills, glens, lochs, and rivers, and following human customs. A naïve faith, full of beauty and poetry, even if it had its dark and grim aspects! These powers or personalities had been invoked from time immemorial, but the invocations were soon stereotyped into definite formulas. Such a formula is put into the mouth of Amairgen, the poet of the Milesians, when they were about to invade Erin, and it may have been a magical invocation of the powers of nature at the beginning of an undertaking or in times of danger:

"I invoke the land of Ireland!

Shining, shining sea!

Fertile, fertile mountain!

Wooded vale!

Abundant river, abundant in waters!

Fish abounding lake!

Fish abounding sea!

Fertile earth!

Irruption of fish! Fish there!

Bird under wave! Great fish!

Crab hole! Irruption of fish!

Fish abounding sea!" 559

A similar formula was spoken after the destruction of Da Derga's Hostel by MacCecht on his finding water. He bathed in it and sang—

"Cold fountain! Surface of strand ...

Sea of lake, water of Gara, stream of river;

High spring well; cold fountain!" 560

The goddess Morrigan, after the defeat of the Fomorians, invokes the powers of nature and proclaims the victory to "the royal mountains of Ireland, to its chief waters, and its river mouths." 561 It was also customary to take oaths by the elements—heaven, earth, sun, fire, moon, sea, land, day, night, etc., and these punished the breaker of the oath. 562 Even the gods exacted such an oath of each other. Bres swore by sun, moon, sea, and land, to fulfil the engagement imposed on him by Lug. 563 The formulæ survived into Christian times, and the faithful were forbidden to call the sun and moon gods or to swear by them, while in Breton folk-custom at the present day oaths by sun, moon, or earth, followed by punishment of the oath-breaker by the moon, are still in use. 564 These oaths had originated in a time when the elements themselves were thought to be divine, and similar adjurations were used by Greeks and Scandinavians.

While the greater objects of nature were worshipped for themselves alone, the Celts also peopled the earth with spirits, benevolent or malevolent, of rocks, hills, dales, forests, lakes, and streams, 565 and while greater divinities of growth had been evolved, they still believed in lesser spirits of vegetation, of the corn, and of fertility, connected, however, with these gods. Some of these still survive as fairies seen in meadows, woodlands, or streams, or as demoniac beings haunting lonely places. And even now, in French folk-belief, sun, moon, winds, etc., are regarded as actual personages. Sun and moon are husband and wife; the winds have wives; they are addressed by personal names and reverenced. 566 Some spirits may already have had a demoniac aspect in pagan times. The Tuatha Déa conjured up meisi, "spectral bodies that rise from the ground," against the Milesians, and at their service were malignant sprites—urtrochta, and "forms, spectres, and great queens" called guidemain (false demons). The Druids also sent forth mischievous spirits called siabra. In the Táin there are references to bocânachs, banânaichs, and geniti-glinni, "goblins, eldritch beings, and glen-folk." 567 These are twice called Tuatha Dé Danann, and this suggests that they were nature-spirits akin to the greater gods. 568 The geniti-glinni would be spirits haunting glen and valley. They are friendly to Cúchulainn in the Táin, but in the Feast of Bricriu he and other heroes fight and destroy them. 569 In modern Irish belief they are demons of the air, perhaps fallen angels. 570

Much of this is probably pre-Celtic as well as Celtic, but it held its ground because it was dear to the Celts themselves. They upheld the aboriginal cults resembling those which, in the lands whence they came, had been native and local with themselves. Such cults are as old as the world, and when Christianity expelled the worship of the greater gods, younger in growth, the ancient nature worship, dowered with immortal youth,

"bowed low before the blast

In patient deep disdain,"

to rise again in vigour. Preachers, councils, and laws inveighed against it. The old rites continued to be practised, or survived under a Christian dress and colouring. They are found in Breton villages, in Highland glens, in Welsh and Cornish valleys, in Irish townships, and only the spread of school-board education, with its materialism and uninviting common sense, is forcing them at last to yield.

The denunciations of these cults throw some light upon them. Offerings at trees, stones, fountains, and cross-roads, the lighting of fires or candles there, and vows or incantations addressed to them, are forbidden, as is also the worship of trees, groves, stones, rivers, and wells. The sun and moon are not to be called lords. Wizardry, and divination, and the leapings and dancings, songs and choruses of the pagans, i.e. their orgiastic cults, are not to be practised. Tempest-raisers are not to ply their diabolical craft. 571 These denunciations, of course, were not without their effect, and legend told how the spirits of nature were heard bewailing the power of the Christian saints, their mournful cries echoing in wooded hollows, secluded valleys, and shores of lake and river. 572 Their power, though limited, was not annihilated, but the secrecy in which the old cults often continued to be practised gave them a darker colour. They were identified with the works of the devil, and the spirits of paganism with dark and grisly demons. 573

This culminated in the mediæval witch persecutions, for witchcraft was in part the old paganism in a new guise. Yet even that did not annihilate superstition, which still lives and flourishes among the folk, though the actual worship of nature-spirits has now disappeared.

Perhaps the most important object in nature to the early Celts as to most primitive folk was the moon. The phases of the moon were apparent before men observed the solstices and equinoxes, and they formed an easy method of measuring time. The Celtic year was at first lunar—Pliny speaks of the Celtic method of counting the beginning of months and years by the moon—and night was supposed to precede day. 574 The festivals of growth began, not at sunrise, but on the previous evening with the rising of the moon, and the name La Lunade is still given to the Midsummer festival in parts of France. 575 At Vallon de la Suille a wood on the slope where the festival is held is called Bois de la Lune; and in Ireland, where the festival begins on the previous evening, in the district where an ascent of Cnoc Aine is made, the position of the moon must be observed. A similar combination of sun and moon cults is found in an inscription at Lausanne—To the genius of the sun and moon. 576

Possibly sun festivals took the place of those of the moon. Traces of the connection of the moon with agriculture occur in different regions, the connection being established through the primitive law of sympathetic magic. The moon waxes and wanes, therefore it must affect all processes of growth or decay. Dr. Frazer has cited many instances of this belief, and has shown that the moon had a priority to the sun in worship, e.g. in Egypt and Babylon. 577 Sowing is done with a waxing moon, so that, through sympathy, there may be a large increase. But harvesting, cutting timber, etc., should be done with a waning moon, because moisture being caused by a waxing moon, it was necessary to avoid cutting such things as would spoil by moisture at that time. Similar beliefs are found among the Celts. Mistletoe and other magical plants were culled with a waxing moon, probably because their power would thus be greater. Dr. Johnson noted the fact that the Highlanders sowed their seed with a waxing moon, in the expectation of a better harvest. For similar occult reasons, it is thought in Brittany that conception during a waxing moon produces a male child, during a waning moon a female, while accouchements at the latter time are dangerous. Sheep and cows should be killed at the new moon, else their flesh will shrink, but peats should be cut in the last quarter, otherwise they will remain moist and give out "a power of smoke." 578

These ideas take us back to a time when it was held that the moon was not merely the measurer of time, but had powerful effects on the processes of growth and decay. Artemis and Diana, moon-goddesses, had power over all growing things, and as some Celtic goddesses were equated with Diana, they may have been connected with the moon, more especially as Gallo-Roman images of Diana have the head adorned with a crescent moon. In some cases festivals of the moon remained intact, as among the Celtiberians and other peoples to the north of them, who at the time of full moon celebrated the festival of a nameless god, dancing all night before the doors of their houses. 579 The nameless god may have been the moon, worshipped at the time of her intensest light. Moonlight dances round a great stone, with singing, on the first day of the year, occurred in the Highlands in the eighteenth century. 580 Other survivals of cult are seen in the practices of bowing or baring the head at new moon, or addressing it with words of adoration or supplication. In Ireland, Camden found the custom at new moon of saying the Lord's Prayer with the addition of the words, "Leave us whole and sound as Thou hast found us." Similar customs exist in Brittany, where girls pray to the moon to grant them dreams of their future husbands. 581 Like other races, the Celts thought that eclipses were caused by a monster attacking the moon, while it could be driven off with cries and shouts. In 218 B.C. the Celtic allies of Attalus were frightened by an eclipse, and much later Christian legislation forbade the people to assemble at an eclipse and shout, Vince, Luna! 582 Such a practice was observed in Ireland in the seventeenth century. At an earlier time, Irish poets addressed sun and moon as divinities, and they were represented on altars even in Christian times. 583

While the Celts believed in sea-gods—Manannan, Morgen, Dylan—the sea itself was still personified and regarded as divine. It was thought to be a hostile being, and high tides were met by Celtic warriors, who advanced against them with sword and spear, often perishing in the rushing waters rather than retreat. The ancients regarded this as bravado. M. Jullian sees in it a sacrifice by voluntary suicide; M. D'Arbois, a tranquil waiting for death and the introduction to another life. 584 But the passages give the sense of an actual attack on the waves—living things which men might terrify, and perhaps with this was combined the belief that no one could die during a rising tide. Similarly French fishermen threaten to cut a fog in two with a knife, while the legend of S. Lunaire tells how he threw a knife at a fog, thus causing its disappearance. 585 Fighting the waves is also referred to in Irish texts. Thus Tuirbe Trágmar would "hurl a cast of his axe in the face of the flood-tide, so that he forbade the sea, which then would not come over the axe." Cúchulainn, in one of his fits of anger, fought the waves for seven days, and Fionn fought and conquered the Muireartach, a personification of the wild western sea. 586 On the French coast fishermen throw harpoons at certain harmful waves called the Three Witch Waves, thus drawing their blood and causing them to subside. 587 In some cases human victims may have been offered to the rising waters, since certain tales speak of a child set floating on the waves, and this, repeated every seven years, kept them in their place. 588

The sea had also its beneficent aspects. The shore was "a place of revelation of science," and the sea sympathised with human griefs. At the Battle of Ventry "the sea chattered, telling the losses, and the waves raised a heavy, woeful great moan in wailing them." 589 In other cases in Ireland, by a spell put on the waves, or by the intuitive knowledge of the listener, it was revealed that they were wailing for a death or describing some distant event. 590 In the beautiful song sung by the wife of Cael, "the wave wails against the shore for his death," and in Welsh myth the waves bewailed the death of Dylan, "son of the wave," and were eager to avenge it. The noise of the waves rushing into the vale of Conwy were his dying groans. 591 In Ireland the roaring of the sea was thought to be prophetic of a king's death or the coming of important news; and there, too, certain great waves were celebrated in story—Clidna's, Tuaithe's, and Rudhraidhe's. 592 Nine waves, or the ninth wave, partly because of the sacred nature of the number nine, partly because of the beneficent character of the waves, had a great importance. They formed a barrier against invasion, danger, or pestilence, or they had a healing effect. 593

The wind was also regarded as a living being whose power was to be dreaded. It punished King Loegaire for breaking his oath. But it was also personified as a god Vintius, equated with Pollux and worshipped by Celtic sailors, or with Mars, the war-god who, in his destructive aspect, was perhaps regarded as the nearest analogue to a god of stormy winds. 594 Druids and Celtic priestesses claimed the power of controlling the winds, as did wizards and witches in later days. This they did, according to Christian writers, by the aid of demons, perhaps the old divinities of the air. Bishop Agobard describes how the tempestarii raised tempests which destroyed the fruits of the earth, and drew "aerial ships" from Magonia, whither the ships carried these fruits. 595 Magonia may be the upper air ruled over by a sky god Magounos or Mogounos, equated with Apollo. 596 The winds may have been his servants, ruled also by earthly magicians. Like Yahweh, as conceived by Hebrew poets, he "bringeth the winds out of his treasures," and "maketh lightnings with rain."

Footnote 556: Gildas ii. 4.

Footnote 557: Jocelyn, Vila Kentig. c. xxxii.

Footnote 558: Trip. Life, 315.

Footnote 559: LL 12b. The translation is from D'Arbois, ii. 250 f; cf. O'Curry, MC ii. 190.

Footnote 560: RC xxii. 400.

Footnote 561: RC xii. 109.

Footnote 562: Petrie, Tara, 34; RC vi. 168; LU 118.

Footnote 563: Joyce, OCR 50.

Footnote 564: D'Achery, Spicelegium, v. 216; Sébillot, i. 16 f., 56, 211.

Footnote 565: Gregory of Tours, Hist. ii. 10, speaks of the current belief in the divinity of waters, birds, and beasts.

Footnote 566: Sébillot, i. 9, 35, 75, 247, etc.

Footnote 567: Joyce, SH ii. 273; Cormac, 87; Stokes, TIG xxxiii., RC xv. 307.

Footnote 568: Miss Hull, 170, 187, 193; IT i. 214; Leahy, i. 126.

Footnote 569: IT i. 287.

Footnote 570: Henderson, Irish Texts, ii. 210.

Footnote 571: Capit. Karoli Magni, i. 62; Leges Luitprand. ii. 38; Canon 23, 2nd Coun. of Arles, Hefele, Councils, iii. 471; D'Achery, v. 215. Some of these attacks were made against Teutonic superstitions, but similar superstitions existed among the Celts.

Footnote 572: See Grimm, Teut. Myth. ii. 498.

Footnote 573: A more tolerant note is heard, e.g., in an Irish text which says that the spirits which appeared of old were divine ministrants not demoniacal, while angels helped the ancients because they followed natural truth. "Cormac's Sword," IT iii. 220-221. Cf. p. 152 , supra.

Footnote 574: Cæsar, vi. 18; Pliny xxii. 14. Pliny speaks of culling mistletoe on the sixth day of the moon, which is to them the beginning of months and years (sexta luna, quae principia, etc.). This seems to make the sixth, not the first, day of the moon that from which the calculation was made. But the meaning is that mistletoe was culled on the sixth day of the moon, and that the moon was that by which months and years were measured. Luna, not sexta luna, is in apposition with quae. Traces of the method of counting by nights or by the moon survive locally in France, and the usage is frequent in Irish and Welsh literature. See my article "Calendar" (Celtic) in Hastings' Encyclop. of Religion and Ethics, iii. 78 f.

Footnote 575: Delocke, "La Procession dite La Lunade," RC ix. 425.

Footnote 576: Monnier, 174, 222; Fitzgerald, RC iv. 189.

Footnote 577: Frazer, Golden Bough 2, ii. 154 f.

Footnote 578: Pliny, xvi. 45; Johnson, Journey, 183; Ramsay, Scotland in the Eighteenth Century, ii. 449; Sébillot, i. 41 f.; MacCulloch, Misty Isle of Skye, 236. In Brittany it is thought that girls may conceive by the moon's power (RC iii. 452).

Footnote 579: Strabo, iii. 4. 16.

Footnote 580: Brand, s.v. "New Year's Day."

Footnote 581: Chambers, Popular Rhymes, 35; Sébillot, i. 46, 57 f.

Footnote 582: Polybius, v. 78; Vita S. Eligii, ii. 15.

Footnote 583: Osborne, Advice to his Son (1656), 79; RC xx. 419, 428.

Footnote 584: Aristotle, Nic. Eth. iii. 77; Eud. Eth. iii. 1. 25; Stobæus, vii. 40; Ælian, xii. 22; Jullian, 54; D'Arbois, vi. 218.

Footnote 585: Sébillot, i. 119. The custom of throwing something at a "fairy eddy," i.e. a dust storm, is well known on Celtic ground and elsewhere.

Footnote 586: Folk-Lore, iv. 488; Curtin, HTI 324; Campbell, The Fians, 158. Fian warriors attacked the sea when told it was laughing at them.

Footnote 587: Mélusine, ii. 200.

Footnote 588: Sébillot, ii. 170.

Footnote 589: Meyer, Cath. Finntraga, 40.

Footnote 590: RC xvi. 9; LB 32b, 55.

Footnote 591: Meyer, op. cit. 55; Skene, i. 282, 288, 543; Rh[^y]s, HL 387.

Footnote 592: Meyer, 51; Joyce, PN i. 195, ii. 257; RC xv. 438.

Footnote 593: 55, supra; IT i. 838, iii. 207; RC ii. 201, ix. 118.

Footnote 594: Holder, s.v. "Vintius."

Footnote 595: Agobard, i. 146.

Footnote 596: See Stokes, RC vi. 267.

CHAPTER XII
RIVER AND WELL WORSHIP

Among the Celts the testimony of contemporary witnesses, inscriptions, votive offerings, and survivals, shows the importance of the cult of waters and of water divinities. Mr. Gomme argues that Celtic water-worship was derived from the pre-Celtic aborigines, 597 but if so, the Celts must have had a peculiar aptitude for it, since they were so enthusiastic in its observance. What probably happened was that the Celts, already worshippers of the waters, freely adopted local cults of water wherever they came. Some rivers or river-goddesses in Celtic regions seem to posses pre-Celtic names. 598

Treasures were flung into a sacred lake near Toulouse to cause a pestilence to cease. Caepion, who afterwards fished up this treasure, fell soon after in battle—a punishment for cupidity, and aurum Tolosanum now became an expression for goods dishonestly acquired. 599 A yearly festival, lasting three days, took place at Lake Gévaudan. Garments, food, and wax were thrown into the waters, and animals were sacrificed. On the fourth day, it is said, there never failed to spring up a tempest of rain, thunder, and lightning—a strange reward for this worship of the lake. 600 S. Columba routed the spirits of a Scottish fountain which was worshipped as a god, and the well now became sacred, perhaps to the saint himself, who washed in it and blessed it so that it cured diseases. 601

On inscriptions a river name is prefixed by some divine epithet—dea, augusta, and the worshipper records his gratitude for benefits received from the divinity or the river itself. Bormanus, Bormo or Borvo, Danuvius (the Danube), and Luxovius are found on inscriptions as names of river or fountain gods, but goddesses are more numerous—Acionna, Aventia, Bormana, Brixia, Carpundia, Clutoida, Divona, Sirona, Ura—well-nymphs; and Icauna (the Yonne), Matrona, and Sequana (the Seine)—river-goddesses. 602 No inscription to the goddess of a lake has yet been found. Some personal names like Dubrogenos (son of the Dubron), Enigenus (son of the Aenus), and the belief of Virdumarus that one of his ancestors was the Rhine, 603 point to the idea that river-divinities might have amours with mortals and beget progeny called by their names. In Ireland, Conchobar was so named from the river whence his mother Nessa drew water, perhaps because he was a child of the river-god. 604

The name of the water-divinity was sometimes given to the place of his or her cult, or to the towns which sprang up on the banks of rivers — the divinity thus becoming a tutelary god. Many towns (e.g. Divonne or Dyonne, etc.) have names derived from a common Celtic river name Deuona, "divine." This name in various forms is found all over the Celtic area, 605 and there is little doubt that the Celts, in their onward progress, named river after river by the name of the same divinity, believing that each new river was a part of his or her kingdom. The name was probably first an appellative, then a personal name, the divine river becoming a divinity. Deus Nemausus occurs on votive tablets at Nimes, the name Nemausus being that of the clear and abundant spring there whence flowed the river of the same name. A similar name occurs in other regions — Nemesa, a tributary of the Moselle; Nemh, the source of the Tara and the former name of the Blackwater; and Nimis, a Spanish river mentioned by Appian. Another group includes the Matrona (Marne), the Moder, the Madder, the Maronne and Maronna, and others, probably derived from a word signifying "mother." 606 The mother-river was that which watered a whole region, just as in the Hindu sacred books the waters are mothers, sources of fertility. The Celtic mother-rivers were probably goddesses, akin to the Matres, givers of plenty and fertility. In Gaul, Sirona, a river-goddess, is represented like the Matres. She was associated with Grannos, perhaps as his mother, and Professor Rh[^y]s equates the pair with the Welsh Modron and Mabon; Modron is probably connected with Matrona. 607 In any case the Celts regarded rivers as bestowers of life, health, and plenty, and offered them rich gifts and sacrifices. 608

Gods like Grannos, Borvo, and others, equated with Apollo, presided over healing springs, and they are usually associated with goddesses, as their husbands or sons. But as the goddesses are more numerous, and as most Celtic river names are feminine, female divinities of rivers and springs doubtless had the earlier and foremost place, especially as their cult was connected with fertility. The gods, fewer in number, were all equated with Apollo, but the goddesses were not merged by the Romans into the personality of one goddess, since they themselves had their groups of river-goddesses, Nymphs and Naiads. Before the Roman conquest the cult of water-divinities, friends of mankind, must have formed a large part of the popular religion of Gaul, and their names may be counted by hundreds. Thermal springs had also their genii, and they were appropriated by the Romans, so that the local gods now shared their healing powers with Apollo, Æsculapius, and the Nymphs. Thus every spring, every woodland brook, every river in glen or valley, the roaring cataract, and the lake were haunted by divine beings, mainly thought of as beautiful females with whom the Matres were undoubtedly associated. There they revealed themselves to their worshippers, and when paganism had passed away, they remained as fées or fairies haunting spring, or well, or river. 609 Scores of fairy wells still exist, and by them mediæval knights had many a fabled amour with those beautiful beings still seen by the "ignorant" but romantic peasant.

Sanctuaries were erected at these springs by grateful worshippers, and at some of them festivals were held, or they were the resort of pilgrims. As sources of fertility they had a place in the ritual of the great festivals, and sacred wells were visited on Midsummer day, when also the river-gods claimed their human victims. Some of the goddesses were represented by statues or busts in Gallo-Roman times, if not earlier, and other images of them which have been found were of the nature of ex votos, presented by worshippers in gratitude for the goddess's healing gifts. Money, ingots of gold or silver, and models of limbs or other parts of the body which had been or were desired to be healed, were also presented. Gregory of Tours says of the Gauls that they "represent in wood or bronze the members in which they suffer, and whose healing they desire, and place them in a temple." 610 Contact of the model with the divinity brought healing to the actual limbs on the principle of sympathetic magic. Many such models have been discovered. Thus in the shrine of Dea Sequana was found a vase with over a hundred; another contained over eight hundred. Inscriptions were engraved on plaques which were fastened to the walls of temples, or placed in springs. 611 Leaden tablets with inscriptions were placed in springs by those who desired healing or when the waters were low, and on some the actual waters are hardly discriminated from the divinities. The latter are asked to heal or flow or swell—words which apply more to the waters than to them, while the tablets, with their frank animism, also show that, in some cases, there were many elemental spirits of a well, only some of whom were rising to the rank of a goddess. They are called collectively Niskas—the Nixies of later tradition, but some have personal names—Lerano, Dibona, Dea—showing that they were tending to become separate divine personalities. The Peisgi are also appealed to, perhaps the later Piskies, unless the word is a corrupt form of a Celtic peiskos, or the Latin piscus, "fish." 612 This is unlikely, as fish could not exist in a warm sulphurous spring, though the Celts believed in the sacred fish of wells or streams. The fairies now associated with wells or with a water-world beneath them, are usually nameless, and only in a few cases have a definite name. They, like the older spirits of the wells, have generally a beneficent character. 613 Thus in the fountains of Logres dwelt damsels who fed the wayfarer with meat and bread, until grievous wrong was done them, when they disappeared and the land became waste. 614 Occasionally, however, they have a more malevolent character. 615

The spirit of the waters was often embodied in an animal, usually a fish. Even now in Brittany the fairy dweller in a spring has the form of an eel, while in the seventeenth century Highland wells contained fish so sacred that no one dared to catch them. 616 In Wales S. Cybi's well contained a huge eel in whose virtues the villagers believed, and terror prevailed when any one dared to take it from the water. Two sacred fish still exist in a holy well at Nant Peris, and are replaced by others when they die, the dead fish being buried. 617 This latter act, solemnly performed, is a true sign of the divine or sacred character of the animal. Many wells with sacred fish exist in Ireland, and the fish have usually some supernatural quality — they never alter in size, they become invisible, or they take the form of beautiful women. 618 Any one destroying such fish was regarded as a sacrilegious person, and sometimes a hostile tribe killed and ate the sacred fish of a district invaded by them, just as Egyptians of one nome insulted those of another by killing their sacred animals. 619 In old Irish beliefs the salmon was the fish of knowledge. Thus whoever ate the salmon of Connla's well was dowered with the wisdom which had come to them through eating nuts from the hazels of knowledge around the well. In this case the sacred fish was eaten, but probably by certain persons only — those who had the right to do so. Sinend, who went to seek inspiration from the well, probably by eating one of its salmon, was overwhelmed by its waters. The legend of the salmon is perhaps based on old ritual practices of the occasional eating of a divine animal. In other cases, legends of a miraculous supply of fish from sacred wells are perhaps later Christian traditions of former pagan beliefs or customs concerning magical methods of increasing a sacred or totem animal species, like those used in Central Australia and New Guinea. 620 The frog is sometimes the sacred animal, and this recalls the Märchen of the Frog Bridegroom living in a well, who insisted on marrying the girl who drew its waters. Though this tale is not peculiar to the Celts, it is not improbable that the divine animal guardian of a well may have become the hero of a folk-tale, especially as such wells were sometimes tabu to women. 621 A fly was the guardian spirit of S. Michael's well in Banffshire. Auguries regarding health were drawn from its movements, and it was believed that the fly, when it grew old, transmigrated into another. 622

Such beliefs were not peculiarly Celtic. They are found in all European folk-lore, and they are still alive among savages — the animal being itself divine or the personification of a divinity. A huge sacred eel was worshipped by the Fijians; in North America and elsewhere there were serpent guardians of the waters; and the Semites worshipped the fish of sacred wells as incarnations or symbols of a god.

Later Celtic folk-belief associated monstrous and malevolent beings with rivers and lakes. These may be the older divinities to whom a demoniac form has been given, but even in pagan times such monstrous beings may have been believed in, or they may be survivals of the more primitive monstrous guardians of the waters. The last were dragons or serpents, conventional forms of the reptiles which once dwelt in watery places, attacking all who came near. This old idea certainly survived in Irish and Highland belief, for the Fians conquered huge dragons or serpents in lochs, or saints chained them to the bottom of the waters. Hence the common place-name of Loch na piast, "Loch of the Monster." In other tales they emerge and devour the impious or feast on the dead. 623 The Dracs of French superstition—river monsters who assume human form and drag down victims to the depths, where they devour them—resemble these.

The Each Uisge, or "Water-horse," a horse with staring eyes, webbed feet, and a slimy coat, is still dreaded. He assumes different forms and lures the unwary to destruction, or he makes love in human shape to women, some of whom discover his true nature by seeing a piece of water-weed in his hair, and only escape with difficulty. Such a water-horse was forced to drag the chariot of S. Fechin of Fore, and under his influence became "gentler than any other horse." 624 Many Highland lochs are still haunted by this dreaded being, and he is also known in Ireland and France, where, however, he has more of a tricky and less of a demoniac nature. 625 His horse form is perhaps connected with the similar form ascribed to Celtic water-divinities. Manannan's horses were the waves, and he was invariably associated with a horse. Epona, the horse-goddess, was perhaps originally goddess of a spring, and, like the Matres, she is sometimes connected with the waters. 626 Horses were also sacrificed to river-divinities. 627 But the beneficent water-divinities in their horse form have undergone a curious distortion, perhaps as the result of later Christian influences. The name of one branch of the Fomorians, the Goborchinn, means the "Horse-headed," and one of their kings was Eochaid Echchenn, or "Horse-head." 628 Whether these have any connection with the water-horse is uncertain.

The foaming waters may have suggested another animal personification, since the name of the Boyne in Ptolemy, [Greek: bououinda], is derived from a primitive bóu-s, "ox," and vindo-s, "white," in Irish bó find, "white cow." 629 But it is not certain that this or the Celtic cult of the bull was connected with the belief in the Tarbh Uisge, or "Water-bull," which had no ears and could assume other shapes. It dwells in lochs and is generally friendly to man, occasionally emerging to mate with ordinary cows. In the

Isle of Man the Tarroo Ushtey, however, begets monsters. 630 These Celtic water-monsters have a curious resemblance to the Australian Bunyip.

The Uruisg, often confused with the brownie, haunts lonely places and waterfalls, and, according to his mood, helps or harms the wayfarer. His appearance is that of a man with shaggy hair and beard. 631 In Wales the afanc is a water-monster, though the word first meant "dwarf," then "water-dwarf," of whom many kinds existed. They correspond to the Irish water-dwarfs, the Luchorpáin, descended with the Fomorians and Goborchinn from Ham. 632

In other cases the old water beings have a more pleasing form, like the syrens and other fairy beings who haunt French rivers, or the mermaids of Irish estuaries. 633 In Celtic France and Britain lake fairies are connected with a water-world like that of Elysium tales, the region of earlier divinities. 634 They unite with mortals, who, as in the Swan-maiden tales, lose their fairy brides through breaking a tabu. In many Welsh tales the bride is obtained by throwing bread and cheese on the waters, when she appears with an old man who has all the strength of youth. He presents his daughter and a number of fairy animals to the mortal. When she disappears into the waters after the breaking of the tabu, the lake is sometimes drained in order to recover her; the father then appears and threatens to submerge the whole district. Father and daughters are earlier lake divinities, and in the bread and cheese we may see a relic of the offerings to these. 635

Human sacrifice to water-divinities is suggested by the belief that water-monsters devour human beings, and by the tradition that a river claims its toll of victims every year. In popular rhymes the annual character of the sacrifice is hinted at, and Welsh legend tells of a voice heard once a year from rivers or lakes, crying, "The hour is come, but the man is not." 636 Here there is the trace of an abandoned custom of sacrifice and of the traditional idea of the anger of the divinity at being neglected. Such spirits or gods, like the water-monsters, would be ever on the watch to capture those who trespassed on their domain. In some cases the victim is supposed to be claimed on Midsummer eve, the time of the sacrifice in the pagan period. 637 The spirits of wells had also a harmful aspect to those, at least, who showed irreverence in approaching them. This is seen in legends about the danger of looking rashly into a well or neglecting to cover it, or in the belief that one must not look back after visiting the well. Spirits of wells were also besought to do harm to enemies.

Legends telling of the danger of removing or altering a well, or of the well moving elsewhere because a woman washed her hands in it, point to old tabus concerning wells. Boand, wife of Nechtain, went to the fairy well which he and his cup-bearers alone might visit, and when she showed her contempt for it, the waters rose and destroyed her. They now flow as the river Boyne. Sinend met with a similar fate for intruding on Connla's well, in this case the pursuing waters became the Shannon. 638 These are variants of a story which might be used to explain the origin of any river, but the legends suggest that certain wells were tabu to women because certain branches of knowledge, taught by the well, must be reserved for men. 639 The legends said in effect, "See what came of women obtruding beyond their proper sphere." Savage "mysteries" are usually tabu to women, who also exclude men from their sacred rites. On the other hand, as all tribal lore was once in the hands of the wise woman, such tabus and legends may have arisen when men began to claim such lore. In other legends women are connected with wells, as the guardians who must keep them locked up save when water was drawn. When the woman neglected to replace the cover, the waters burst forth, overwhelming her, and formed a loch. 640 The woman is the priestess of the well who, neglecting part of its ritual, is punished. Even in recent times we find sacred wells in charge of a woman who instructs the visitors in the due ritual to be performed. 641 If such legends and survivals thus point to former Celtic priestesses of wells, these are paralleled by the Norse Horgabrudar, guardians of wells, now elves living in the waters. 642 That such legends are based on the ritual of well-worship is suggested by Boand's walking three times widdershins round the well, instead of the customary deiseil. The due ritual must be observed, and the stories are a warning against its neglect.

In spite of twenty centuries of Christianity and the anathemas of saints and councils, the old pagan practices at healing wells have survived — a striking instance of human conservatism. S. Patrick found the pagans of his day worshipping a well called Slán, "health-giving," and offering sacrifices to it, 643 and the Irish peasant to-day has no doubt that there is something divine about his holy wells. The Celts brought the belief in the divinity of springs and wells with them, but would naturally adopt local cults wherever they found them. Afterwards the Church placed the old pagan wells under the protection of saints, but part of the ritual often remained unchanged. Hence many wells have been venerated for ages by different races and through changes in religion and polity. Thus at the thermal springs of Vicarello offerings have been found which show that their cult has continued from the Stone Age, through the Bronze Age, to the days of Roman civilisation, and so into modern times; nor is this a solitary instance. 644 But it serves to show that all races, high and low, preserve the great outlines of primitive nature religion unchanged. In all probability the ritual of the healing wells has also remained in great part unaltered, and wherever it is found it follows the same general type. The patient perambulated the well three times deiseil or sun-wise, taking care not to utter a word. Then he knelt at the well and prayed to the divinity for his healing. In modern times the saint, but occasionally the well itself, is prayed to. 645 Then he drank of the waters, bathed in them, or laved his limbs or sores, probably attended by the priestess of the well. Having paid her dues, he made an offering to the divinity of the well, and affixed the bandage or part of his clothing to the well or a tree near by, that through it he might be in continuous rapport with the healing influences. Ritual formulæ probably accompanied these acts, but otherwise no word was spoken, and the patient must not look back on leaving the well. Special times, Beltane, Midsummer, or August 1st, were favourable for such visits, 646 and where a patient was too ill to present himself at the well, another might perform the ritual for him. 647

The rag or clothing hung on the tree seems to connect the spirit of the tree with that of the well, and tree and well are often found together. But sometimes it is thrown into the well, just as the Gaulish villagers of S. Gregory's day threw offerings of cloth and wool into a sacred lake. 648 The rag is even now regarded in the light of an offering, and such offerings, varying from valuable articles of clothing to mere rags, are still hung on sacred trees by the folk. It thus probably has always had a sacrificial aspect in the ritual of the well, but as magic and religion constantly blend, it had also its magical aspect. The rag, once in contact with the patient, transferred his disease to the tree, or, being still subtly connected with him, through it the healing properties passed over to him.

The offering thrown into the well—a pin, coin, etc., may also have this double aspect. The sore is often pricked or rubbed with the pin as if to transfer the disease to the well, and if picked up by another person, the disease may pass to him. This is also true of the coin. 649 But other examples show the sacrificial nature of the pin or other trifle, which is probably symbolic or a survival of a more costly offering. In some cases it is thought that those who do not leave it at the well from which they have drunk will die of thirst, and where a coin is offered it is often supposed to disappear, being taken by the spirit of the well. 650 The coin has clearly the nature of an offering, and sometimes it must be of gold or silver, while the antiquity of the custom on Celtic ground is seen by the classical descriptions of the coins glittering in the pool of Clitumnus and of the "gold of Toulouse" hid in sacred tanks. 651 It is also an old and widespread belief that all water belongs to some divine or monstrous guardian, who will not part with any of it without a quid pro quo. In many cases the two rites of rag and pin are not both used, and this may show that originally they had the same purpose—magical or sacrificial, or perhaps both. Other sacrifices were also made—an animal, food, or an ex voto, the last occurring even in late survivals as at S. Thenew's

Well, Glasgow, where even in the eighteenth century tin cut to represent the diseased member was placed on the tree, or at S. Winifred's Well in Wales, where crutches were left.

Certain waters had the power of ejecting the demon of madness. Besides drinking, the patient was thrown into the waters, the shock being intended to drive the demon away, as elsewhere demons are exorcised by flagellation or beating. The divinity of the waters aided the process, and an offering was usually made to him. In other cases the sacred waters were supposed to ward off disease from the district or from those who drank of them. Or, again, they had the power of conferring fertility. Women made pilgrimages to wells, drank or bathed in the waters, implored the spirit or saint to grant them offspring, and made a due offering. 652 Spirit or saint, by a transfer of his power, produced fruitfulness, but the idea was in harmony with the recognised power of water to purify, strengthen, and heal. Women, for a similar reason, drank or washed in the waters or wore some articles dipped in them, in order to have an easy delivery or abundance of milk. 653

The waters also gave oracles, their method of flowing, the amount of water in the well, the appearance or non-appearance of bubbles at the surface when an offering was thrown in, the sinking or floating of various articles, all indicating whether a cure was likely to occur, whether fortune or misfortune awaited the inquirer, or, in the case of girls, whether their lovers would be faithful. The movements of the animal guardian of the well were also ominous to the visitor. 654 Rivers or river divinities were also appealed to. In cases of suspected fidelity the Celts dwelling by the Rhine placed the newly-born child in a shield on the waters. If it floated the mother was innocent; if it sank it was allowed to drown, and she was put to death. 655 Girls whose purity was suspected were similarly tested, and S. Gregory of Tours tells how a woman accused of adultery was proved by being thrown into the Saône. 656 The mediæval witch ordeal by water is connected with this custom, which is, however, widespread. 657

The malevolent aspect of the spirit of the well is seen in the "cursing wells" of which it was thought that when some article inscribed with an enemy's name was thrown into them with the accompaniment of a curse, the spirit of the well would cause his death. In some cases the curse was inscribed on a leaden tablet thrown into the waters, just as, in other cases, a prayer for the offerer's benefit was engraved on it. Or, again, objects over which a charm had been said were placed in a well that the victim who drew water might be injured. An excellent instance of a cursing-well is that of Fynnon Elian in Denbigh, which must once have had a guardian priestess, for in 1815 an old woman who had charge of it presided at the ceremony. She wrote the name of the victim in a book, receiving a gift at the same time.

A pin was dropped into the well in the name of the victim, and through it and through knowledge of his name, the spirit of the well acted upon him to his hurt. 658 Obviously rites like these, in which magic and religion mingle, are not purely Celtic, but it is of interest to note their existence in Celtic lands and among Celtic folk.

Footnote 597: Ethnol. in Folklore, 104 f.

Footnote 598: D'Arbois, PH ii. 132, 169; Dottin, 240.

Footnote 599: Justin, xxxii. 3; Strabo, iv. 1. 13.

Footnote 600: S. Gregory, In Glor. Conf. ch. 2. Perhaps the feast and offerings were intended to cause rain in time of drought. infra.

Footnote 601: Adamman, Vita Colum. ii. 10.

Footnote 602: See Holder, s.v.

Footnote 603: D'Arbois, RC x. 168, xiv. 377; CIL xii. 33; Propertius, iv. 10. 41.

Footnote 604: infra.

Footnote 605: Cf. Ptolemy's [Greek: Dêouana] and [Greek: Dêouna] (ii. 3. 19, 11. 29); the Scots and English Dee; the Divy in Wales; Dêve, Dive, and Divette in France; Devon in England; Deva in Spain (Ptolemy's [Greek: Dêoua], ii. 6. 8). The Shannon is surnamed even in the seventh century "the goddess" (Trip. Life, 313).

Footnote 606: Holder, s.v.; D'Arbois, PH ii. 119, thinks Matrona is Ligurian. But it seems to have strong Celtic affinities.

Footnote 607: Rh[^y]s, HL 27-29, RC iv. 137.

Footnote 608: On the whole subject see Pictet, "Quelques noms celtiques de rivières," RC ii. 1 f. Orosius, v. 15. 6, describes the sacrifices of gold, silver, and horses, made to the Rhône.

Footnote 609: Maury, 18. By extension of this belief any divinity might appear by the haunted spring. S. Patrick and his synod of bishops at an Irish well were supposed to be síd or gods (p. 64, supra.) By a fairy well Jeanne d'Arc had her first vision.

Footnote 610: Greg. Tours, Vita Patr. c. 6.

Footnote 611: See Reinach, Catal. Sommaire, 23, 115; Baudot, Rapport sur les fouilles faits aux sources de la Seine, ii. 120; RC ii. 26.

Footnote 612: For these tablets see Nicolson, Keltic Studies, 131 f.; Jullian, RC 1898.

Footnote 613: Sébillot, ii. 195.

Footnote 614: Prologue to Chrestien's Conte du Graal.

Footnote 615: Sébillot, ii. 202 f.

Footnote 616: Ibid. 196-197; Martin, 140-141; Dalyell, 411.

Footnote 617: Rh[^y]s, CFL i. 366; Folk-Lore, viii. 281. If the fish appeared when an invalid drank of the well, this was a good omen. For the custom of burying sacred animals, see Herod, ii. 74; Ælian, xiii. 26.

Footnote 618: Gomme, Ethnol. in Folklore, 92.

Footnote 619: Trip. Life, 113; Tigernach, Annals, A.D. 1061.

Footnote 620: Mackinley, 184.

Footnote 621: Burne, Shropshire Folk-Lore, 416; Campbell, WHT ii. 145.

Footnote 622: Old Stat. Account, xii. 465.

Footnote 623: S. Patrick, when he cleared Ireland of serpents, dealt in this way with the worst specimens. S. Columba quelled a monster which terrified the dwellers by the Ness. Joyce, PN i. 197; Adamnan, Vita Columb. ii. 28; Kennedy, 12, 82, 246; RC iv. 172, 186.

Footnote 624: RC xii. 347.

Footnote 625: For the water-horse, see Campbell, WHT iv. 307; Macdongall, 294; Campbell, Superstitions, 203; and for the Manx Glashtyn, a kind of water-horse, see Rh[^y]s, CFL i. 285. For French cognates, see Bérenger-Féraud, Superstitions et Survivances, i. 349 f.

Footnote 626: Reinach, CMR i. 63.

Footnote 627: Orosius, v. 15. 6.

Footnote 628: LU 2a. Of Eochaid is told a variant of the Midas story — the discovery of his horse's ears. This is also told of Labraid Lore (RC ii. 98; Kennedy, 256) and of King Marc'h in Brittany and in Wales (Le Braz, ii. 96; Rh[^y]s,

CFL 233). Other variants are found in non-Celtic regions, so the story has no mythological significance on Celtic ground.

Footnote 629: Ptol. ii. 2. 7.

Footnote 630: Campbell, WHT iv. 300 f.; Rh[^y]s, CFL i. 284; Waldron, Isle of Man, 147.

Footnote 631: Macdougall, 296; Campbell, Superstitions, 195. For the Uruisg as Brownie, see WHT ii. 9; Graham, Scenery of Perthshire, 19.

Footnote 632: Rh[^y]s, CFL ii. 431, 469, HL, 592; Book of Taliesin, vii. 135.

Footnote 633: Sébillot, ii. 340; LL 165; IT i. 699.

Footnote 634: Sébillot, ii. 409.

Footnote 635: See Pughe, The Physicians of Myddfai, 1861 (these were descendants of a water-fairy); Rh[^y]s, Y Cymmrodor, iv. 164; Hartland, Arch. Rev. i. 202. Such water-gods with lovely daughters are known in most mythologies—the Greek Nereus and the Nereids, the Slavonic Water-king, and the Japanese god Ocean-Possessor (Ralston, Songs of the Russian People, 148; Chamberlain, Ko-ji-ki, 120). Manannan had nine daughters (Wood-Martin, i. 135).

Footnote 636: Sébillot, ii. 338, 344; Rh[^y]s, CFL i. 243; Henderson, Folk-Lore of the N. Counties, 262. Cf. the rhymes, "L'Arguenon veut chaque année son poisson," the "fish" being a human victim, and

"Blood-thirsty Dee

Each year needs three,

But bonny Don,

She needs none."

Footnote 637: Sébillot, ii. 339.

Footnote 638: Rendes Dindsenchas, RC xv. 315, 457. Other instances of punishment following misuse of a well are given in Sébillot, ii. 192; Rees, 520, 523. An Irish lake no longer healed after a hunter swam his mangy hounds through it (Joyce, PN ii. 90). A similar legend occurs with the Votiaks, one of whose sacred lakes was removed to its present position because a woman washed dirty clothes in it (L'Anthropologie, xv. 107).

Footnote 639: Rh[^y]s, CFL i. 392.

Footnote 640: Girald. Cambr. Itin. Hib. ii. 9; Joyce, OCR 97; Kennedy, 281; O'Grady, i. 233; Skene, ii. 59; Campbell, WHT ii. 147. The waters often submerge a town, now seen below the waves—the town of Is in Armorica (Le Braz, i. p. xxxix), or the towers under Lough Neagh. In some Welsh instances a man is the culprit (Rh[^y]s, CFL i. 379). In the case of Lough Neagh the keeper of the well was Liban, who lived on in the waters as a mermaid. Later she was caught and received the baptismal name of Muirghenn, "sea-birth." Here the myth of a water-goddess, said to have been baptized, is attached to the legend of the careless guardian of a spring, with whom she is identified (O'Grady, ii. 184, 265).

Footnote 641: Roberts, Cambrian Pop. Antiq. 246; Hunt, Popular Romances, 291; New Stat. Account, x. 313.

Footnote 642: Thorpe, Northern Myth. ii. 78.

Footnote 643: Joyce, PN ii. 84. Slán occurs in many names of wells. Well-worship is denounced in the canons of the Fourth Council of Arles.

Footnote 644: Cartailhac, L'Age de Pierre, 74; Bulliot et Thiollier, Mission de S. Martin, 60.

Footnote 645: Sébillot, ii. 284.

Footnote 646: Dalyell, 79-80; Sébillot, ii. 282, 374; infra.

Footnote 647: I have compiled this account of the ritual from notices of the modern usages in various works. See, e.g., Moore, Folk-Lore, v. 212; Mackinley, passim; Hope, Holy Wells; Rh[^y]s, CFL; Sébillot, 175 f.; Dixon, Gairloch, 150 f.

Footnote 648: Brand, ii. 68; Greg. In Glor. Conf. c. 2.

Footnote 649: Sébillot, ii. 293, 296; Folk-Lore, iv. 55.

Footnote 650: Mackinley, 194; Sébillot, ii. 296.

Footnote 651: Folk-Lore, iii. 67; Athenæum, 1893, 415; Pliny, Ep. viii. 8; Strabo, iv. 287; Diod. Sic. v. 9.

Footnote 652: Walker, Proc. Soc. Ant. Scot. vol. v.; Sébillot, ii. 232. In some early Irish instances a worm swallowed with the waters by a woman causes pregnancy. , infra.

Footnote 653: Sébillot, ii. 235-236.

Footnote 654: See Le Braz, i. 61; Folk-Lore, v. 214; Rh[^y]s, CFL i. 364; Dalyell, 506-507; Scott, Minstrelsy, Introd. xliii; Martin, 7; Sébillot, ii. 242 f.; RC ii. 486.

Footnote 655: Jullian, Ep. to Maximin, 16. The practice may have been connected with that noted by Aristotle, of plunging the newly-born into a river, to strengthen it, as he says (Pol. vii. 15. 2), rrrbut more probably as a baptismal or purificatory rite. , infra.

Footnote 656: Lefevre, Les Gaulois, 109; Michelet, Origines du droit français, 268.

Footnote 657: See examples of its use in Post, Grundriss der Ethnol. Jurisprudenz, ii. 459 f.

Footnote 658: Roberts, Cambrian Popular Antiquities, 246.

CHAPTER XIII
TREE AND PLANT WORSHIP

The Celts had their own cult of trees, but they adopted local cults—Ligurian, Iberian, and others. The Fagus Deus (the divine beech), the Sex arbor or Sex arbores of Pyrenean inscriptions, and an anonymous god represented by a conifer on an altar at Toulouse, probably point to local Ligurian tree cults continued by the Celts into Roman times. 659 Forests were also personified or ruled by a single goddess, like Dea Arduinna of the Ardennes and Dea Abnoba of the Black Forest. 660 But more primitive ideas prevailed, like that which assigned a whole class of tree-divinities to a forest, e.g. the Fatæ Dervones, spirits of the oak-woods of Northern Italy. 661 Groups of trees like Sex arbores were venerated, perhaps for their height, isolation, or some other peculiarity.

The Celts made their sacred places in dark groves, the trees being hung with offerings or with the heads of victims. Human sacrifices were hung or impaled on trees, e.g. by the warriors of Boudicca. 662 These, like the offerings still placed by the folk on sacred trees, were attached to them because the trees were the abode of spirits or divinities who in many cases had power over vegetation.

Pliny said of the Celts: "They esteem nothing more sacred than the mistletoe and the tree on which it grows. But apart from this they choose oak-woods for their sacred groves, and perform no sacred rite without using oak branches." 663 Maximus of Tyre also speaks of the Celtic (? German) image of Zeus as a lofty oak, and an old Irish glossary gives daur, "oak," as an early Irish name for "god," and glosses it by dia, "god." 664 The sacred need-fire may have been obtained by friction from oak-wood, and it is because of the old sacredness of the oak that a piece of its wood is still used as a talisman in Brittany. 665 Other Aryan folk besides the Celts regarded the oak as the symbol of a high god, of the sun or the sky, 666 but probably this was not its earliest significance. Oak forests were once more extensive over Europe than they are now, and the old tradition that men once lived on acorns has been shown to be well-founded by the witness of archæological finds, e.g. in Northern Italy. 667 A people living in an oak region and subsisting in part on acorns might easily take the oak as a representative of the spirit of vegetation or growth. It was long-lived, its foliage was a protection, it supplied food, its wood was used as fuel, and it was thus clearly the friend of man. For these reasons, and because it was the most abiding and living thing men knew, it became the embodiment of the spirits of life and growth. Folk-lore survivals show that the spirit of vegetation in the shape of his representative was annually slain while yet in full vigour, that his life might benefit all things and be passed on undiminished to his successor. 668 Hence the oak or a human being representing the spirit of vegetation, or both together, were burned in the Midsummer fires. How, then, did the oak come to symbolise a god equated with Zeus. Though the equation may be worthless, it is possible that the connection lay in the fact that Zeus and Juppiter had agricultural functions, or that, when the equation was made, the earlier spirit of vegetation had become a divinity with functions resembling those of Zeus. The fires were kindled to recruit the sun's life; they were fed with oak-wood, and in them an oak or a human victim representing the spirit embodied in the oak was burned. Hence it may have been thought that the sun was strengthened by the fire residing in the sacred oak; it was thus "the original storehouse or reservoir of the fire which was from time to time drawn out to feed the sun." 669 The oak thus became the symbol of a bright god also connected with growth. But, to judge by folk survivals, the older conception still remained potent, and tree or human victim affected for good all vegetable growth as well as man's life, while at the same time the fire strengthened the sun.

Dr. Evans argues that "the original holy object within the central triliths of Stonehenge was a sacred tree," an oak, image of the Celtic Zeus. The tree and the stones, once associated with ancestor worship, had become symbols of "a more celestial Spirit or Spirits than those of departed human beings." 670 But Stonehenge has now been proved to have been in existence before the arrival of the Celts, hence such a cult must have been pre-Celtic, though it may quite well have been adopted by the Celts. Whether this hypothetical cult was practised by a tribe, a group of tribes, or by the whole people, must remain obscure, and, indeed, it may well be questioned whether Stonehenge was ever more than the scene of some ancestral rites.

Other trees—the yew, the cypress, the alder, and the ash, were venerated, to judge by what Lucan relates of the sacred grove at Marseilles. The Irish Druids attributed special virtues to the hazel, rowan, and yew, the wood of which was used in magical ceremonies described in Irish texts. 671 Fires of rowan were lit by the Druids of rival armies, and incantations said over them in order to discomfit the opposing host, 672 and the wood of all these trees is still believed to be efficacious against fairies and witches.

The Irish bile was a sacred tree, of great age, growing over a holy well or fort. Five of them are described in the Dindsenchas, and one was an oak, which not only yielded acorns, but nuts and apples. 673 The mythic trees of Elysium had the same varied fruitage, and the reason in both cases is perhaps the fact that when the cultivated apple took the place of acorns and nuts as a food staple, words signifying "nut" or "acorn" were transferred to the apple. A myth of trees on which all these fruits grew might then easily arise. Another Irish bile was a yew described in a poem as "a firm strong god," while such phrases in this poem as "word-pure man," "judgment of origin," "spell of knowledge," may have some reference to the custom of writing divinations in ogham on rods of yew. The other bile were ash-trees, and from one of them the Fir Bile, "men of the tree," were named—perhaps a totem-clan. 674 The lives of kings and chiefs appear to have been connected with these trees, probably as representatives of the spirit of vegetation embodied in the tree, and under their shadow they were inaugurated. But as a substitute for the king was slain, so doubtless these pre-eminent sacred trees were too sacred, too much charged with supernatural force, to be cut down and burned, and the yearly ritual would be performed with another tree. But in time of feud one tribe gloried in destroying the bile of another; and even in the tenth century, when the bile maighe Adair was destroyed by Maelocohlen the act was regarded with horror. "But, O reader, this deed did not pass unpunished." 675 Of another bile, that of Borrisokane, it was said that any house in which a fragment of it was burned would itself be destroyed by fire. 676

Tribal and personal names point to belief in descent from tree gods or spirits and perhaps to totemism. The Eburones were the yew-tree tribe (eburos); the Bituriges perhaps had the mistletoe for their symbol, and their surname Vivisci implies that they were called "Mistletoe men." 677 If bile (tree) is connected with the name Bile, that of the ancestor of the Milesians, this may point to some myth of descent from a sacred tree, as in the case of the Fir Bile, or "men of the tree." 678 Other names like Guidgen (Viduo-genos, "son of the tree"), Dergen (Dervo-genos, "son of the oak"), Guerngen (Verno-genos, "son of the alder"), imply filiation to a tree. Though these names became conventional, they express what had once been a living belief. Names borrowed directly from trees are also found—-Eburos or Ebur, "yew," Derua or Deruacus, "oak," etc.

The veneration of trees growing beside burial mounds or megalithic monuments was probably a pre-Celtic cult continued by the Celts. The tree embodied the ghost of the person buried under it, but such a ghost could then hardly be differentiated from a tree spirit or divinity. Even now in Celtic districts extreme veneration exists for trees growing in cemeteries and in other places. It is dangerous to cut them down or to pluck a leaf or branch from them, while in Breton churchyards the yew is thought to spread a root to the mouth of each corpse. 679 The story of the grave of Cyperissa, daughter of a Celtic king in the Danube region, from which first sprang the "mournful cypress," 680 is connected with universal legends of trees growing from the graves of lovers until their branches intertwine. These embody the belief that the spirit of the dead is in the tree, which was thus in all likelihood the object of a cult. Instances of these legends occur in Celtic story. Yew-stakes driven through the bodies of Naisi and Deirdre to keep them apart, became yew-trees the tops of which embraced over Armagh Cathedral. A yew sprang from the grave of Bailé Mac Buain, and an apple-tree from that of his lover Aillinn, and the top of each had the form of their heads. 681 The identification of tree and ghost is here complete.

The elder, rowan, and thorn are still planted round houses to keep off witches, or sprigs of rowan are placed over doorways—a survival from the time when they were believed to be tenanted by a beneficent spirit hostile to evil influences. In Ireland and the Isle of Man the thorn is thought to be the resort of fairies, and they, like the woodland fairies or "wood men" are probably representatives of the older tree spirits and gods of groves and forests. 682

Tree-worship was rooted in the oldest nature worship, and the Church had the utmost difficulty in suppressing it. Councils fulminated against the cult of trees, against offerings to them or the placing of lights before them and before wells or stones, and against the belief that certain trees were too sacred to be cut down or burned. Heavy fines were levied against those who practised these rites, yet still they continued. 683 Amator, Bishop of Auxerre, tried to stop the worship of a large pear-tree standing in the centre of the town and on which the semi-Christian inhabitants hung animals' heads with much ribaldry. At last S. Germanus destroyed it, but at the risk of his life. S. Martin of Tours was allowed to destroy a temple, but the people would not permit him to attack a much venerated pine-tree which stood beside it—an excellent example of the way in which the more official paganism fell before Christianity, while the older religion of the soil, from which it sprang, could not be entirely eradicated. 684 The Church often effected a compromise. Images of the gods affixed to trees were replaced by those of the Virgin, but with curious results. Legends arose telling how the faithful had been led to such trees and there discovered the image of the Madonna miraculously placed among the branches. 685 These are analogous to the legends of the discovery of images of the Virgin in the earth, such images being really those of the Matres.

Representations of sacred trees are occasionally met with on coins, altars, and ex votos. 686 If the interpretation be correct which sees a representation of part of the Cúchulainn legend on the Paris and Trèves altars, the trees figured there would not necessarily be sacred. But otherwise they may depict sacred trees.

We now turn to Pliny's account of the mistletoe rite. The Druids held nothing more sacred than this plant and the tree on which it grew, probably an oak. Of it groves were formed, while branches of the oak were used in all religious rites. Everything growing on the oak had been sent from heaven, and the presence of the mistletoe showed that God had selected the tree for especial favour. Rare as it was, when found the mistletoe was the object of a careful ritual. On the sixth day of the moon it was culled. Preparations for a sacrifice and feast were made beneath the tree, and two white bulls whose horns had never been bound were brought there. A Druid, clad in white, ascended the tree and cut the mistletoe with a golden sickle. As it fell it was caught in a white cloth; the bulls were then sacrificed, and prayer was made that God would make His gift prosperous to those on whom He had bestowed it. The mistletoe was called "the universal healer," and a potion made from it caused barren animals to be fruitful. It was also a remedy against all poisons. 687 We can hardly believe that such an elaborate ritual merely led up to the medico-magical use of the mistletoe. Possibly, of course, the rite was an attenuated survival of something which had once been more important, but it is more likely that Pliny gives only a few picturesque details and passes by the rationale of the ritual. He does not tell us who the "God" of whom he speaks was, perhaps the sun-god or the god of vegetation. As to the "gift," it was probably in his mind the mistletoe, but it may quite well have meant the gift of growth in field and fold. The tree was perhaps cut down and burned; the oxen may have been incarnations of a god of vegetation, as the tree also may have been. We need not here repeat the meaning which has been given to the ritual, 688 but it may be added that if this meaning is correct, the rite probably took place at the time of the Midsummer festival, a festival of growth and fertility. Mistletoe is still gathered on Midsummer eve and used as an antidote to poisons or for the cure of wounds. Its Druidic name is still preserved in Celtic speech in words signifying "all-healer," while it is also called sùgh an daraich, "sap of the oak," and Druidh lus, "Druid's weed." 689

Pliny describes other Celtic herbs of grace. Selago was culled without use of iron after a sacrifice of bread and wine—probably to the spirit of the plant. The person gathering it wore a white robe, and went with unshod feet after washing them. According to the Druids, Selago preserved one from accident, and its smoke when burned healed maladies of the eye. 690

Samolus was placed in drinking troughs as a remedy against disease in cattle. It was culled by a person fasting, with the left hand; it must be wholly uprooted, and the gatherer must not look behind him. 691 Vervain was gathered at sunrise after a sacrifice to the earth as an expiation—perhaps because its surface was about to be disturbed. When it was rubbed on the body all wishes were gratified; it dispelled fevers and other maladies; it was an antidote against serpents; and it conciliated hearts. A branch of the dried herb used to asperge a banquet-hall made the guests more convivial 692

The ritual used in gathering these plants—silence, various tabus, ritual purity, sacrifice—is found wherever plants are culled whose virtue lies in this that they are possessed by a spirit. Other plants are still used as charms by modern Celtic peasants, and, in some cases, the ritual of gathering them resembles that described by Pliny. 693 In Irish sagas plants have magical powers. "Fairy herbs" placed in a bath restored beauty to women bathing therein. 694 During the Táin Cúchulainn's wounds were healed with "balsams and healing herbs of fairy potency," and Diancecht used similar herbs to restore the dead at the battle of Mag-tured. 695

Footnote 659: Sacaze, Inscr. des Pyren. 255; Hirschfeld, Sitzungsberichte (Berlin, 1896), 448.

Footnote 660: CIL vi. 46; CIR 1654, 1683.

Footnote 661: D'Arbois, Les Celtes, 52.

Footnote 662: Lucan, Phar. Usener's ed., 32; Orosius, v. 16. 6; Dio Cass. lxii. 6.

Footnote 663: Pliny, xvi. 44. The Scholiast on Lucan says that the Druids divined with acorns (Usener, 33).

Footnote 664: Max. Tyr. Diss. viii. 8; Stokes, RC i. 259.

Footnote 665: Le Braz, ii. 18.

Footnote 666: Mr. Chadwick (Jour. Anth. Inst. xxx. 26) connects this high god with thunder, and regards the Celtic Zeus (Taranis, in his opinion) as a thunder-god. The oak was associated with this god because his worshippers dwelt under oaks.

Footnote 667: Helbig, Die Italiker in der Poebene, 16 f.

Footnote 668: Mannhardt, Baumkultus; Frazer, Golden Bough 2 iii. 198.

Footnote 669: Frazer, loc. cit.

Footnote 670: Evans, Arch. Rev. i. 327 f.

Footnote 671: Joyce, SH i. 236.

Footnote 672: O'Curry, MC i. 213.

Footnote 673: LL 199b; Rennes Dindsenchas, RC xv. 420.

Footnote 674: RC xv. 455, xvi. 279; Hennessey, Chron. Scot. 76.

Footnote 675: Keating, 556; Joyce, PN i. 499.

Footnote 676: Wood-Martin, ii. 159.

Footnote 677: D'Arbois, Les Celtes, 51; Jullian, 41.

Footnote 678: Cook, Folk-Lore, xvii. 60.

Footnote 679: See Sébillot, i. 293; Le Braz, i. 259; Folk-Lore Journal, v. 218; Folk-Lore Record, 1882.

Footnote 680: Val. Probus, Comm. in Georgica, ii. 84.

Footnote 681: Miss Hull, 53; O'Ourry, MS. Mat. 465. Writing tablets, made from each of the trees when they were cut down, sprang together and could not be separated.

Footnote 682: Stat. Account, iii. 27; Moore, 151; Sébillot, i. 262, 270.

Footnote 683: Dom Martin, i. 124; Vita S. Eligii, ii. 16.

Footnote 684: Acta Sanct. (Bolland.), July 31; Sulp. Sever. Vita S. Mart. 457.

Footnote 685: Grimm, Teut. Myth. 76; Maury, 13, 299. The story of beautiful women found in trees may be connected with the custom of placing images in trees, or with the belief that a goddess might be seen emerging from the tree in which she dwelt.

Footnote 686: De la Tour, Atlas des Monnaies Gaul, 260, 286; Reinach, Catal. Sommaire, 29.

Footnote 687: Pliny, HN xvi. 44.

Footnote 688: supra.

Footnote 689: See Cameron, Gaelic Names of Plants, 45. In Gregoire de Rostren, Dict. françois-celt. 1732, mistletoe is translated by dour-dero, "oak-water," and is said to be good for several evils.

Footnote 690: Pliny, xxiv. 11.

Footnote 691: Ibid.

Footnote 692: Ibid. xxv. 9.

Footnote 693: See Carmichael, Carmina Gadelica; De Nore, Coutumes ... des Provinces de France, 150 f.; Sauvé, RC vi. 67, CM ix. 331.

Footnote 694: O'Grady, ii. 126.

Footnote 695: Miss Hull, 172; supra.

CHAPTER XIV
ANIMAL WORSHIP

Animal worship pure and simple had declined among the Celts of historic times, and animals were now regarded mainly as symbols or attributes of divinities. The older cult had been connected with the pastoral stage in which the animals were divine, or with the agricultural stage in which they represented the corn-spirit, and perhaps with totemism. We shall study here (1) traces of the older animal cults; (2) the transformation of animal gods into symbols; and (3) traces of totemism.

1.

The presence of a bull with three cranes (Tarvos Trigaranos) on the Paris altar, along with the gods Esus, Juppiter, and Vulcan, suggests that it was a divine animal, or the subject of a divine myth. As has been seen, this bull may be the bull of the Táin bó Cuailgne. Both it and its opponent were reincarnations of the swine-herds of two gods. In the Irish sagas reincarnation is only attributed to gods or heroes, and this may point to the divinity of the bulls. We have seen that this and another altar may depict some myth in which the bull was the incarnation of a tree or vegetation spirit. The divine nature of the bull is attested by its presence on Gaulish coins as a religious symbol, and by images of the animal with three horns—an obvious symbol of divinity. 696 On such an image in bronze the Cimbri, Celticised Germans, swore. The images are pre-Roman, since they are found at Hallstadt and La Tène. Personal names like Donnotaurus (the equivalent of the Donn Taruos of the Táin) or Deiotaros ("divine bull"), show that men were called after the divine animal. 697 Similarly many place-names in which the word taruos occurs, in Northern Italy, the Pyrenees, Scotland, Ireland, and elsewhere, suggest that the places bearing these names were sites of a bull cult or that some myth, like that elaborated in the Táin, had been there localised. 698 But, as possibly in the case of Cúchulainn and the bull, the animal tended to become the symbol of a god, a tendency perhaps aided by the spread of Mithraism with its symbolic bull. A god Medros leaning on a bull is represented at Haguenau, possibly a form of Mider or of Meduris, a surname of Toutatis, unless Medros is simply Mithras.

699 Echoes of the cult of the bull or cow are heard in Irish tales of these animals brought from the síd, or of magic bulls or of cows which produced enormous supplies of milk, or in saintly legends of oxen leading a saint to the site of his future church. 700 These legends are also told of the swine, 701 and they perhaps arose when a Christian church took the place of the site of a local animal cult, legend fusing the old and the new cult by making the once divine animal point out the site of the church. A late relic of a bull cult may be found in the carnival procession of the Boeuf Gras at Paris.

A cult of a swine-god Moccus has been referred to. The boar was a divine symbol on standards, coins, and altars, and many bronze images of the animal have been found. These were temple treasures, and in one case the boar is three-horned. 702 But it was becoming the symbol of a goddess, as is seen by the altars on which it accompanies a goddess, perhaps of fertility, and by a bronze image of a goddess seated on a boar. The altars occur in Britain, of which the animal may be the emblem—the "Caledonian monster" of Claudian's poem. 703 The Galatian Celts abstained from eating the swine, and there has always been a prejudice against its flesh in the Highlands. This has a totemic appearance. 704 But the swine is esteemed in Ireland, and in the texts monstrous swine are the staple article of famous feasts. 705 These may have been legendary forms of old swine-gods, the feasts recalling sacrificial feasts on their flesh. Magic swine were also the immortal food of the gods. But the boar was tabu to certain persons, e.g. Diarmaid, though whether this is the attenuated memory of a clan totem restriction is uncertain. In Welsh story the swine comes from Elysium—a myth explaining the origin of its domestication, while domestication certainly implies an earlier cult of the animal. When animals come to be domesticated, the old cult restrictions, e.g. against eating them, usually pass away. For this reason, perhaps, the Gauls, who worshipped an anthropomorphic swine-god, trafficked in the animal and may have eaten it. 706 Welsh story also tells of the magic boar, the Twrch Trwyth, hunted by Arthur, possibly a folk-tale reminiscence of a boar divinity. 707 Place-names also point to a cult of the swine, and a recollection of its divinity may underlie the numerous Irish tales of magical swine. 708 The magic swine which issued from the cave of Cruachan and destroyed the young crops are suggestive of the theriomorphic corn-spirit in its occasional destructive aspect. 709 Bones of the swine, sometimes cremated, have been found in Celtic graves in Britain and at Hallstadt, and in one case the animal was buried alone in a tumulus at Hallstadt, just as sacred animals were buried in Egypt, Greece, and elsewhere. 710 When the animal was buried with the dead, it may have been as a sacrifice to the ghost or to the god of the underworld.

The divinity of the serpent is proved by the occurrence of a horned serpent with twelve Roman gods on a Gallo-Roman altar. 711 In other cases a horned or ram's-headed serpent appears as the attribute of a god, and we have seen that the ram's-headed serpent may be a fusion of the serpent as a chthonian animal with the ram, sacrificed to the dead. In Greece Dionysus had the form both of a bull and a horned serpent, the horn being perhaps derived from the bull symbol. M. Reinach claims that the primitive elements of the Orphic myth of the Thracian Dionysos-Zagreus—divine serpents producing an egg whence came the horned snake Zagreus, occur in dislocated form in Gaul. There enlacing serpents were believed to produce a magic egg, and there a horned serpent was worshipped, but was not connected with the egg. But they may once have been connected, and if so, there may be a common foundation both for the Greek and the Celtic conceptions in a Celtic element in Thrace. 712 The resemblances, however, may be mere coincidences, and horned serpents are known in other mythologies—the horn being perhaps a symbol of divinity. The horned serpent sometimes accompanies a god who has horns, possibly Cernunnos, the underworld god, in accordance with the chthonian character of the serpent. 713 In the Cùchulainn cycle Loeg on his visit to the Other-world saw two-headed serpents—perhaps a further hint of this aspect of the animal. 714

In all these instances of animal cults examples of the tendency to make the divine animal anthropomorphic have been seen. We have now to consider some instances of the complete anthropomorphic process.

2.

An old bear cult gave place to the cult of a bear goddess and probably of a god. At Berne—an old Celtic place-name meaning "bear"—was found a bronze group of a goddess holding a patera with fruit, and a bear approaching her as if to be fed. The inscription runs, Deae Artioni Licinia Sabinilla. 715 A local bear-cult had once existed at Berne, and is still recalled in the presence of the famous bears there, but the divine bear had given place to a goddess whose name and symbol were ursine. From an old Celtic Artos, fem. Arta, "bear," were derived various divine names. Of these Dea Artio(n) means "bear goddess," and Artaios, equated with Mercury, is perhaps a bear god. 716 Another bear goddess, Andarta, was honoured at Die (Drôme), the word perhaps meaning "strong bear"—And- being an augmentive. 717 Numerous place-names derived from Artos perhaps witness to a widespread cult of the bear, and the word also occurs in Welsh, and Irish personal names—Arthmael, Arthbiu, and possibly Arthur, and the numerous Arts of Irish texts. Descent from the divine bear is also signified in names like Welsh Arthgen, Irish Artigan, from Artigenos, "son of the bear." Another Celtic name for "bear" was the Gaulish matu, Irish math, found in

Matugenos, "son of the bear," and in MacMahon, which is a corrupt form of Mac-math-ghamhain, "son of the bear's son," or "of the bear." 718

Similarly a cult of the stag seems to have given place to that of a god with stag's horns, represented on many bas-reliefs, and probably connected with the underworld. 719 The stag, as a grain-eater, may have been regarded as the embodiment of the corn-spirit, and then associated with the under-earth region whence the corn sprang, by one of those inversions of thought so common in the stage of transition from animal gods to gods with animal symbols. The elk may have been worshipped in Ireland, and a three antlered stag is the subject of a story in the Fionn saga. 720 Its third antler, like the third horn of bull or boar, may be a sign of divinity.

The horse had also been worshipped, but a goddess Epona (Gaul. epo-s, "horse"), protectress of horses and asses, took its place, and had a far-spread cult. She rides a horse or mare with its foal, or is seated among horses, or feeds horses. A representation of a mare suckling a foal—a design analogous to those in which Epona feeds foals—shows that her primitive equine nature had not been forgotten. 721 The Gauls were horse-rearers, and Epona was the goddess of the craft; but, as in other cases, a cult of the horse must have preceded its domestication, and its flesh may not have been eaten, or, if so, only sacramentally. 722 Finally, the divine horse became the anthropomorphic horse-goddess. Her images were placed in stables, and several inscriptions and statuettes have been found in such buildings or in cavalry barracks. 723 The remains of the cult have been found in the Danube and Rhine valleys, in Eastern Gaul, and in Northern Italy, all Celtic regions, but it was carried everywhere by Roman cavalry recruited from the Celtic tribes. 724 Epona is associated with, and often has, the symbols of the Matres, and one inscription reads Eponabus, as if there were a group of goddesses called Epona. 725 A goddess who promoted the fertility of mares would easily be associated with goddesses of fertility. Epona may also have been confused with a river-goddess conceived of as a spirited steed. Water-spirits took that shape, and the Matres were also river-goddesses.

A statuette of a horse, with a dedication to a god Rudiobus, otherwise unknown, may have been carried processionally, while a mule has a dedication to Segomo, equated elsewhere with Mars. A mule god Mullo, also equated with Mars, is mentioned on several inscriptions. 726 The connection with Mars may have been found in the fact that the October horse was sacrificed to him for fertility, while the horse was probably associated with fertility among the Celts. The horse was sacrificed both by Celts and Teutons at the Midsummer festival, undoubtedly as a divine animal. Traces of the Celtic custom survive in local legends, and may be interpreted in the fuller light of the Teutonic accounts. In Ireland a man wearing a horse's head rushed through the fire, and was supposed to represent all cattle; in other words, he was a surrogate for them. The legend of Each Labra, a horse which lived in a mound and issued from it every Midsummer eve to give oracles for the coming year, is probably connected with the Midsummer sacrifice of the horse. 727 Among the Teutons the horse was a divine sacrificial animal, and was also sacred to Freyr, the god of fertility, while in Teutonic survivals a horse's head was placed in the Midsummer fire. 728 The horse was sporadically the representative of the corn-spirit, and at Rome the October horse was sacrificed in that capacity and for fertility. 729 Among the Celts, the horse sacrificed at Midsummer may have represented the vegetation-spirit and benefited all domestic animals—the old rite surviving in an attenuated form, as described above.

Perhaps the goddess Damona was an animal divinity, if her name is derived from damatos, "sheep," cognate to Welsh dafad, "sheep," and Gaelic damh, "ox." Other divine animals, as has been seen, were associated with the waters, and the use of beasts and birds in divination doubtless points to their divine character. A cult of bird-gods may lurk behind the divine name Bran, "raven," and the reference to the magic birds of Rhiannon in the Triads.

3.

Animal worship is connected with totemism, and certain things point to its existence among the Celts, or to the existence of conditions out of which totemism was elsewhere developed. These are descent from animals, animal tabus, the sacramental eating of an animal, and exogamy.

(1) Descent from animals.—Celtic names implying descent from animals or plants are of two classes, clan and personal names. If the latter are totemistic, they must be derived from the former, since totemism is an affair of the clan, while the so-called "personal totem," exemplified by the American Indian manitou, is the guardian but never the ancestor of a man. Some clan names have already been referred to. Others are the Bibroci of south-east Britain, probably a beaver clan (bebros), and the Eburones, a yew-tree clan (eburos). 730 Irish clans bore animal names: some groups were called "calves," others "griffins," others "red deer," and a plant name is seen in Fir Bile, "men of the tree." 731 Such clan totemism perhaps underlies the stories of the "descendants of the wolf" at Ossory, who became wolves for a time as the result of a saintly curse. Other instances of lycanthropy were associated with certain families. 732 The belief in lycanthropy might easily attach itself to existing wolf-clans, the transformation being then explained as the result of a curse. The stories of Cormac mac Art, suckled by a she-wolf, of Lughaid mac Con, "son of a wolf-dog," suckled by that animal, and of Oisin, whose mother was a fawn, and who would not eat venison,

are perhaps totemistic, while to totemism or to a cult of animals may be ascribed what early travellers in Ireland say of the people taking wolves as god-fathers and praying to them to do them no ill. 733 In Wales bands of warriors at the battle of Cattraeth are described in Oneurin's Gododin as dogs, wolves, bears, and ravens, while Owein's band of ravens which fought against Arthur, may have been a raven clan, later misunderstood as actual ravens. 734 Certain groups of Dalriad Scots bore animal names—Cinel Gabran, "Little goat clan," and Cinel Loarn, "Fox clan." Possibly the custom of denoting Highland clans by animal or plant badges may be connected with a belief in descent from plants or animals. On many coins an animal is represented on horseback, perhaps leading a clan, as birds led the Celts to the Danube area, and these may depict myths telling how the clan totem animal led the clan to its present territory. 735 Such myths may survive in legends relating how an animal led a saint to the site of his church. 736 Celtic warriors wore helmets with horns, and Irish story speaks of men with cat, dog, or goat heads. 737 These may have been men wearing a head-gear formed of the skin or head of the clan totem, hence remembered at a later time as monstrous beings, while the horned helmets would be related to the same custom. Solinus describes the Britons as wearing animal skins before going into battle. 738 Were these skins of totem animals under whose protection they thus placed themselves? The "forms of beasts, birds, and fishes" which the Cruithne or Picts tattooed on their bodies may have been totem marks, while the painting of their bodies with woad among the southern Britons may have been of the same character, though Cæsar's words hardly denote this. Certain marks on faces figured on Gaulish coins seem to be tattoo marks. 739

It is not impossible that an early wolf-totem may have been associated, because of the animal's nocturnal wanderings in forests, with the underworld whence, according to Celtic belief, men sprang and whither they returned, and whence all vegetation came forth. The Gallo-Roman Silvanus, probably an underworld god, wears a wolf-skin, and may thus be a wolf-god. There were various types of underworld gods, and this wolf-type—perhaps a local wolf-totem ancestor assimilated to a local "Dispater"—may have been the god of a clan who imposed its mythic wolf origin on other clans. Some Celtic bronzes show a wolf swallowing a man who offers no resistance, probably because he is dead. The wolf is much bigger than the man, and hence may be a god. 740 These bronzes would thus represent a belief setting forth the return of men to their totem ancestor after death, or to the underworld god connected with the totem ancestor, by saying that he devoured the dead, like certain Polynesian divinities and the Greek Eurynomos.

In many individual names the first part is the name of an animal or plant, the second is usually genos, "born from," or "son of," e.g. Artigenos, Matugenos, "son of the bear" (artos, matu-); Urogenos, occurring as Urogenertos, "he who has the strength of the son of the urus"; Brannogenos, "son of the raven"; Cunogenos, "son of the dog." 741 These names may be derived from clan totem names, but they date back to a time when animals, trees, and men were on a common footing, and the possibility of human descent from a tree or an animal was believed in. Professor Rh[^y]s has argued from the frequency of personal names in Ireland, like Cúrói, "Hound of Rói," Cú Corb, "Corb's Hound," Mac Con, "Hound's Son," and Maelchon, "Hound's Slave," that there existed a dog totem or god, not of the Celts, but of a pre-Celtic race. 742 This assumes that totemism was non-Celtic, an assumption based on preconceived notions of what Celtic institutions ought to have been. The names, it should be observed, are personal, not clan names.

(2) Animal tabus. — Besides the dislike of swine's flesh already noted among certain Celtic groups, the killing and eating of the hare, hen, and goose were forbidden among the Britons. Cæsar says they bred these animals for amusement, but this reason assigned by him is drawn from his knowledge of the breeding of rare animals by rich Romans as a pastime, since he had no knowledge of the breeding of sacred animals which were not eaten — a common totemic or animal cult custom. 743 The hare was used for divination by Boudicca, 744 doubtless as a sacred animal, and it has been found that a sacred character still attaches to these animals in Wales. A cock or hen was ceremonially killed and eaten on Shrove Tuesday, either as a former totemic animal, or, less likely, as a representative of the corn-spirit. The hare is not killed in certain districts, but occasionally it is ceremonially hunted and slain annually, while at yearly fairs the goose is sold exclusively and eaten. 745 Elsewhere, e.g. in Devon, a ram or lamb is ceremonially slain and eaten, the eating being believed to confer luck. 746 The ill-luck supposed to follow the killing of certain animals may also be reminiscent of totemic tabus. Fish were not eaten by the Pictish Meatæ and Caledonii, and a dislike of eating certain fresh-water fish was observed among certain eighteenth century Highlanders. 747 It has been already seen that certain fish living in sacred wells were tabu, and were believed to give oracles. Heron's flesh was disliked in Ireland, and it was considered unlucky to kill a swan in the Hebrides. 748 Fatal results following upon the killing or eating of an animal with which the eater was connected by name or descent are found in the Irish sagas. Conaire was son of a woman and a bird which could take human shape, and it was forbidden to him to hunt birds. On one occasion he did so, and for this as well as the breaking of other tabus, he

lost his life. 749 It was tabu to Cúchulainn, "the hound of Culann," to eat dog's flesh, and, having been persuaded to do this, his strength went from him, and he perished. Diarmaid, having been forbidden to hunt a boar with which his life was connected, was induced by Fionn to break this tabu, and in consequence he lost his life by one of the boar's bristles entering his foot, or (in a variant) by the boar's killing him. Another instance is found in a tale of certain men transformed to badgers. They were slain by Cormac, and brought to his father Tadg to eat. Tadg unaccountably loathed them, because they were transformed men and his cousins. 750 In this tale, which may contain the débris of totemic usage, the loathing arises from the fact that the badgers are men—a common form of myths explanatory of misunderstood totemic customs, but the old idea of the relation between a man and his totem is not lost sight of. The other tales may also be reminiscent of a clan totem tabu, later centred in a mythic hero. Perhaps the belief in lucky or unlucky animals, or in omens drawn from their appearance, may be based on old totem beliefs or in beliefs in the divinity of the animals.

(3) Sacramental eating of an animal.—The custom of "hunting the wren," found over the whole Celtic area, is connected with animal worship and may be totemistic in origin. In spite of its small size, the wren was known as the king of birds, and in the Isle of Man it was hunted and killed on Christmas or S. Stephen's day. The bird was carried in procession from door to door, to the accompaniment of a chant, and was then solemnly buried, dirges being sung. In some cases a feather was left at each house and carefully treasured, and there are traces of a custom of boiling and eating the bird. 751 In Ireland, the hunt and procession were followed by a feast, the materials of which were collected from house to house, and a similar usage obtained in France, where the youth who killed the bird was called "king." 752 In most of these districts it was considered unlucky or dangerous to kill the bird at any other time, yet it might be ceremonially killed once a year, the dead animal conferred luck, and was solemnly eaten or buried with signs of mourning. Similar customs with animals which are actually worshipped are found elsewhere, 753 and they lend support to the idea that the Celts regarded the wren as a divine animal, or perhaps a totem animal, that it was necessary to slay it ritually, and to carry it round the houses of the community to obtain its divine influence, to eat it sacramentally or to bury it. Probably like customs were followed in the case of other animals, 754 and these may have given rise to such stories as that of the eating of MacDatho's wonderful boar, as well as to myths which regarded certain animals, e.g. the swine, as the immortal food of the gods. Other examples of ritual survivals of such sacramental eating have already been noted, and

it is not improbable that the eating of a sacred pastoral animal occurred at Samhain.

(4) Exogamy.—Exogamy and the counting of descent through the mother are closely connected with totemism, and some traces of both are found among the Celts. Among the Picts, who were, perhaps, a Celtic group of the Brythonic stock, these customs survived in the royal house. The kingship passed to a brother of the king by the same mother, or to a sister's son, while the king's father was never king and was frequently a "foreigner." Similar rules of succession prevailed in early Aryan royal houses—Greek and Roman,—and may, as Dr. Stokes thought, have existed at Tara in Ireland, while in a Fian tale of Oisin he marries the daughter of the king of Tír na n-Og, and succeeds him as king partly for that reason, and partly because he had beaten him in the annual race for the kingship. 755 Such an athletic contest for the kingship was known in early Greece, and this tale may support the theory of the Celtic priest-kingship, the holder of the office retaining it as long as he was not defeated or slain. Traces of succession through a sister's son are found in the Mabinogion, and Livy describes how the mythic Celtic king Ambicatus sent not his own but his sister's sons to found new kingdoms. 756 Irish and Welsh divine and heroic groups are named after the mother, not the father—the children of Danu and of Dôn, and the men of Domnu. Anu is mother of the gods, Buanann of heroes. The eponymous ancestor of the Scots is a woman, Scota, and the earliest colonisers of Ireland are women, not men. In the sagas gods and heroes have frequently a matronymic, and the father's name is omitted—Lug mac Ethnend, Conchobar mac Nessa, Indech, son of De Domnann, Corpre, son of Etain, and others. Perhaps parallel to this is the custom of calling men after their wives—e.g. the son of Fergus is Fer Tlachtga, Tlachtga's husband. 757 In the sagas, females (goddesses and heroines) have a high place accorded to them, and frequently choose their own lovers or husbands—customs suggestive of the matriarchate. Thus what was once a general practice was later confined to the royal house or told of divine or heroic personages. Possibly certain cases of incest may really be exaggerated accounts of misunderstood unions once permissible by totemic law. Cæsar speaks of British polyandry, brothers, sons, and fathers sharing a wife in common. 758 Strabo speaks of Irish unions with mothers and sisters, perhaps referring not to actual practice but to reports of saga tales of incest. 759 Dio Cassius speaks of community of wives among the Caledonians and Meatæ, and Jerome says much the same of the Scoti and Atecotti. 760 These notices, with the exception of Cæsar's, are vague, yet they refer to marriage customs different from those known to their reporters. In Irish sagas incest legends circle round the descendants of Etain—fathers unite with daughters, a son

with his mother, a woman has a son by her three brothers (just as Ecne was son of Brian, Iuchar, and Iucharba), and is also mother of Crimthan by that son. 761 Brother and sister unions occur both in Irish and Welsh story. 762

In these cases incest with a mother cannot be explained by totemic usage, but the cases may be distorted reminiscences of what might occur under totemism, namely, a son taking the wives of his father other than his own mother, when those were of a different totem from his own. Under totemism, brothers and sisters by different mothers having different totems, might possibly unite, and such unions are found in many mythologies. Later, when totemism passed away, the unions, regarded with horror, would be supposed to take place between children by the same mother. According to totem law, a father might unite with his daughter, since she was of her mother's totem, but in practice this was frowned upon. Polygamy also may co-exist with totemism, and of course involves the counting of descent through the mother as a rule. If, as is suggested by the "debility" of the Ultonians, and by other evidence, the couvade was a Celtic institution, this would also point to the existence of the matriarchate with the Celts. To explain all this as pre-Aryan, or to say that the classical notices refer to non-Aryan tribes and that the evidence in the Irish sagas only shows that the Celts had been influenced by the customs of aboriginal tribes among whom they lived, 763 is to neglect the fact that the customs are closely bound up with Celtic life, while it leaves unexplained the influence of such customs upon a people whose own customs, according to this theory, were so totally different. The evidence, taken as a whole, points to the existence of totemism among the early Celts, or, at all events, of the elements which elsewhere compose it.

Celtic animal worship dates back to the primitive hunting and pastoral period, when men worshipped the animals which they hunted or reared. They may have apologised to the animal hunted and slain — a form of worship, or, where animals were not hunted or were reared and worshipped, one of them may have been slain annually and eaten to obtain its divine power. Care was taken to preserve certain sacred animals which were not hunted, and this led to domestication, the abstinence of earlier generations leading to an increased food supply at a later time, when domesticated animals were freely slain. But the earlier sacramental slaying of such animals survived in the religious aspect of their slaughter at the beginning of winter. 764 The cult of animals was also connected with totemic usage, though at a later stage this cult was replaced by that of anthropomorphic divinities, with the older divine animals as their symbols, sacrificial victims, and the like. This evolution now led to the removal of restrictions upon slaying and eating the animals. On the other hand, the more primitive animal cults may have remained here and there. Animal cults were, perhaps, largely confined to men. With the rise of agriculture mainly as an art in the hands of women, and the consequent cult of the Earth-mother, of fertility and corn-spirits probably regarded as female, the sacramental eating of the divine animal may have led to the slaying and eating of a human or animal victim supposed to embody such a spirit. Later the two cults were bound to coalesce, and the divine animal and the animal embodiment of the vegetation spirit would not be differentiated. On the other hand, when men began to take part in women's fertility cults, the fact that such spirits were female or were perhaps coming to be regarded as goddesses, may have led men to envisage certain of the anthropomorphic animal divinities as goddesses, since some of these, e.g. Epona and Damona, are female. But with the increasing participation of men in agriculture, the spirits or goddesses of fertility would tend to become male, or the consorts or mothers of gods of fertility, though the earlier aspect was never lost sight of, witness the Corn-Mother. The evolution of divine priest-kings would cause them to take the place of the earlier priestesses of these cults, one of whom may have been the divine victim. Yet in local survivals certain cults were still confined to women, and still had their priestesses. 765

>**Footnote 696:** Reinach, BF 66, 244. The bull and three cranes may be a rebus on the name of the bull, Tarvos Trikarenos, "the three-headed," or perhaps Trikeras, "three-horned."
>
>**Footnote 697:** Plutarch, Marius, 23; Cæsar, vii. 65; D'Arbois, Les Celtes, 49.
>
>**Footnote 698:** Holder, s.v. Tarba, Tarouanna, Tarvisium, etc.; D'Arbois, Les Druides, 155; S. Greg. In Glor. Conf. 48.
>
>**Footnote 699:** CIL xiii. 6017; RC xxv. 47; Holder, ii. 528.
>
>**Footnote 700:** Leahy, ii. 105 f.; Curtin, MFI 264, 318; Joyce, PN i. 174; Rees, 453. Cf. Ailred, Life of S. Ninian, c. 8.
>
>**Footnote 701:** Jocelyn, Vita S. Kentig. c. 24; Rees, 293, 323.
>
>**Footnote 702:** Tacitus, Germ. xlv.; Blanchet, i. 162, 165; Reinach, BF 255 f., CMR i. 168; Bertrand, Arch. Celt. 419.
>
>**Footnote 703:** Pennant, Tour in Scotland, 268; Reinach, RC xxii. 158, CMR i. 67.
>
>**Footnote 704:** Pausan, vii. 17, 18; Johnson, Journey, 136.
>
>**Footnote 705:** Joyce, SH ii. 127; IT i. 99, 256 (Bricriu's feast and the tale of Macdatho's swine).

Footnote 706: Strabo, iv. 4. 3, says these swine attacked strangers. Varro, de Re Rustica, ii. 4, admires their vast size. Cf. Polyb. ii. 4.

Footnote 707: The hunt is first mentioned in Nennius, c. 79, and then appears as a full-blown folk-tale in Kulhwych, Loth, i. 185 f. Here the boar is a transformed prince.

Footnote 708: I have already suggested, p. 106, supra, that the places where Gwydion halted with the swine of Elysium were sites of a swine-cult.

Footnote 709: RC xiii. 451. Cf. also TOS vi. "The Enchanted Pigs of Oengus," and Campbell, LF 53.

Footnote 710: L'Anthropologie, vi. 584; Greenwell, British Barrows, 274, 283, 454; Arch. Rev. ii. 120.

Footnote 711: Rev. Arch. 1897, 313.

Footnote 712: Reinach, "Zagreus le serpent cornu," Rev. Arch. xxxv. 210.

Footnote 713: Reinach, BF 185; Bertrand, 316.

Footnote 714: "Cúchulainn's Sick-bed," D'Arbois, v. 202.

Footnote 715: See Reinach, CMR i. 57.

Footnote 716: CIL xiii. 5160, xii. 2199. Rh[^y]s, however, derives Artaios from ar, "ploughed land," and equates the god with Mercurius Cultor.

Footnote 717: CIL xii. 1556-1558; D'Arbois, RC x. 165.

Footnote 718: For all these place and personal names, see Holder and D'Arbois, op. cit. Les Celtes, 47 f., Les Druides, 157 f.

Footnote 719: supra; Reinach, CMR i. 72, Rev. Arch. ii. 123.

Footnote 720: O'Grady, ii. 123.

Footnote 721: Epona is fully discussed by Reinach in his Epona, 1895, and in articles (illustrated) in Rev. Arch. vols. 26, 33, 35, 40, etc. See also ii. [1898], 190.

Footnote 722: Reinach suggests that this may explain why Vercingetorix, in view of siege by the Romans, sent away his horses. They were too sacred to be eaten. Cæsar, vii. 71; Reinach, RC xxvii. 1 f.

Footnote 723: Juvenal, viii. 154; Apul. Metam. iii. 27; Min. Felix, Octav. xxvii. 7.

Footnote 724: For the inscriptions, see Holder, s.v. "Epona."

Footnote 725: CIL iii. 7904.

Footnote 726: CIL xiii. 3071; Reinach, BF 253, CMR i. 64, Répert. de la Stat. ii. 745; Holder, ii. 651-652.

Footnote 727: Granger, Worship of the Romans, 113; Kennedy, 135.

Footnote 728: Grimm, Teut. Myth. 49, 619, 657, 661-664.

Footnote 729: Frazer, Golden Bough 2, ii. 281, 315.

Footnote 730: Cæsar, v. 21, 27. Possibly the Dea Bibracte of the Aeduans was a beaver goddess.

Footnote 731: O'Curry, MC ii. 207; Elton, 298.

Footnote 732: Girald. Cambr. Top. Hib. ii. 19, RC ii. 202; Folk-Lore, v. 310; IT iii. 376.

Footnote 733: O'Grady, ii. 286, 538; Campbell, The Fians, 78; Thiers, Traité des Superstitions, ii. 86.

Footnote 734: Lady Guest, ii. 409 f.

Footnote 735: Blanchet, i. 166, 295, 326, 390.

Footnote 736: supra.

Footnote 737: Diod. Sic. v. 30; IT iii. 385; RC xxvi. 139; Rh[^y]s, HL 593.

Footnote 738: Man. Hist. Brit. p. x.

Footnote 739: Herodian, iii. 14, 8; Duald MacFirbis in Irish Nennius, p. vii; Cæsar, v. 10; ZCP iii. 331.

Footnote 740: See Reinach, "Les Carnassiers androphages dans l'art gallo-romain," CMR i. 279.

Footnote 741: See Holder, s.v.

Footnote 742: Rh[^y]s, CB 4 267.

Footnote 743: Cæsar, v. 12.

Footnote 744: Dio Cassius, lxii. 2.

Footnote 745: See a valuable paper by N.W. Thomas, "Survivance du Culte des Animaux dans le Pays de Galles," in Rev. de l'Hist. des Religions, xxxviii. 295 f., and a similar paper by Gomme, Arch. Rev. 1889, 217 f. Both writers seem to regard these cults as pre-Celtic.

Footnote 746: Gomme, Ethnol. in Folklore, 30, Village Community, 113.

Footnote 747: Dio Cass. lxxii. 21; Logan, Scottish Gael, ii. 12.

Footnote 748: Joyce, SH ii. 529; Martin, 71.

Footnote 749: RC xxii. 20, 24, 390-1.

Footnote 750: IT iii. 385.

Footnote 751: Waldron, Isle of Man, 49; Train, Account of the Isle of Man, ii. 124.

Footnote 752: Vallancey, Coll. de Reb. Hib. iv. No. 13; Clément, Fétes, 466. For English customs, see Henderson, Folklore of the Northern Counties, 125.

Footnote 753: Frazer, Golden Bough 2, ii. 380, 441, 446.

Footnote 754: For other Welsh instances of the danger of killing certain birds, see Thomas, op. cit. xxxviii. 306.

Footnote 755: Frazer, Kingship, 261; Stokes, RC xvi. 418; Larminie, Myths and Folk-tales, 327.

Footnote 756: See Rh[^y]s, Welsh People, 44; Livy, v. 34.

Footnote 757: Cf. IT iii. 407, 409.

Footnote 758: Cæsar, v. 14.

Footnote 759: Strabo, iv. 5. 4.

Footnote 760: Dio Cass. lxxvi. 12; Jerome, Adv. Jovin. ii. 7. Giraldus has much to say of incest in Wales, probably actual breaches of moral law among a barbarous people (Descr. Wales, ii. 6).

Footnote 761: RC xii. 235, 238, xv. 291, xvi. 149; LL 23a, 124b. In various Irish texts a child is said to have three fathers — probably a reminiscence of polyandry. supra, and RC xxiii. 333.

Footnote 762: IT i. 136; Loth, i. 134 f.; Rh[^y]s, HL 308.

Footnote 763: Zimmer, "Matriarchy among the Picts," in Henderson, Leadbhar nan Gleann.

Footnote 764: infra.

Footnote 765: infra.

CHAPTER XV
COSMOGONY

Whether the early Celts regarded Heaven and Earth as husband and wife is uncertain. Such a conception is world-wide, and myth frequently explains in different ways the reason of the separation of the two. Among the Polynesians the children of heaven and earth—the winds, forests, and seas personified—angry at being crushed between their parents in darkness, rose up and separated them. This is in effect the Greek myth of Uranus, or Heaven, and Gæa, or Earth, divorced by their son Kronos, just as in Hindu myth Dyaus, or Sky, and Prithivi, or Earth, were separated by Indra. Uranus in Greece gave place to Zeus, and, in India, Dyaus became subordinate to Indra. Thus the primitive Heaven personified recedes, and his place is taken by a more individualised god. But generally Mother Earth remains a constant quantity. Earth was nearer man and was more unchanging than the inconstant sky, while as the producer of the fruits of the earth, she was regarded as the source of all things, and frequently remained as an important divinity when a crowd of other divinities became prominent. This is especially true of agricultural peoples, who propitiate Earth with sacrifice, worship her with orgiastic rites, or assist her processes by magic. With advancing civilisation such a goddess is still remembered as the friend of man, and, as in the Eleusinia, is represented sorrowing and rejoicing like man himself. Or where a higher religion ousts the older one, the ritual is still retained among the folk, though its meaning may be forgotten.

The Celts may thus have possessed the Heaven and Earth myth, but all trace of it has perished. There are, however, remnants of myths showing how the sky is supported by trees, a mountain, or by pillars. A high mountain near the sources of the Rhone was called "the column of the sun," and was so lofty as to hide the sun from the people of the south. 766 It may have been regarded as supporting the sky, while the sun moved round it. In an old Irish hymn and its gloss, Brigit and Patrick are compared to the two pillars of the world, probably alluding to some old myth of sky or earth resting on pillars. 767 Traces of this also exist in folk-belief, as in the accounts of islands resting on four pillars, or as in the legend of the church of Kernitou which rests on four pillars on a congealed sea and which will be submerged when the sea liquefies—a combination of the cosmogonic myth with that of a great inundation. 768 In some mythologies a bridge or ladder connects heaven and earth. There may be a survival of some such myth in an Irish poem which speaks of the drochet bethad, or "bridge of life," or in the drochaid na flaitheanas, or "bridge of heaven," of Hebridean folk-lore. 769

Those gods who were connected with the sky may have been held to dwell there or on the mountain supporting it. Others, like the Celtic Dispater, dwelt underground. Some were connected with mounds and hills, or were supposed to have taken up their abode in them. Others, again, dwelt in a distant region, the Celtic Elysium, which, once the Celts reached the sea, became a far-off island. Those divinities worshipped in groves were believed to dwell there and to manifest themselves at midday or midnight, while such objects of nature as rivers, wells, and trees were held to be the abode of gods or spirits. Thus it is doubtful whether the Celts ever thought of their gods as dwelling in one Olympus. The Tuatha Dé Danann are said to have come from heaven, but this may be the mere assertion of some scribe who knew not what to make of this group of beings.

In Celtic belief men were not so much created by gods as descended from them. "All the Gauls assert that they are descended from Dispater, and this, they say, has been handed down to them by the Druids." 770 Dispater was a Celtic underworld god of fertility, and the statement probably presupposes a myth, like that found among many primitive peoples, telling how men once lived underground and thence came to the surface of the earth. But it also points to their descent from the god of the underworld. Thither the dead returned to him who was ancestor of the living as well as lord of the dead. 771 On the other hand, if the earth had originally been thought of as a female, she as Earth-mother would be ancestress of men. But her place in the myth would easily be taken by the Earth or Under-earth god, perhaps regarded as her son or her consort. In other cases, clans, families, or individuals often traced their descent to gods or divine animals or plants. Classical writers occasionally speak of the origin of branches of the Celtic race from eponymous founders, perhaps from their knowledge of existing Celtic myths. 772 Ammianus Marcellinus also reports a Druidic tradition to the effect that some Gauls were indigenous, some had come from distant islands, and others from beyond the Rhine. 773 But this is not so much a myth of origins, as an explanation of the presence of different peoples in Gaul—the aborigines, the Celtæ, and the Belgic Gauls. M. D'Arbois assumes that "distant islands" means the Celtic Elysium, which he regards as the land of the dead, 774 but the phrase is probably no more than a distorted reminiscence of the far-off lands whence early groups of Celts had reached Gaul.

Of the creation of the world no complete myth has survived, though from a gloss to the Senchus Mór we learn that the Druids, like the Br[=a]hmans, boasted that they had made sun, moon, earth, and sea—a boast in keeping with their supposed powers over the elements. 775 Certain folk-beliefs, regarding the origin of different parts of nature, bear a close resemblance to primitive cosmogonic myths, and they may be taken as disjecta membra of similar myths held by the Celts and perhaps taught by the Druids. Thus sea, rivers, or springs arose from the micturition of a giant, fairy, or saint, or from their sweat or blood. Islands are rocks cast by giants, and mountains are the material thrown up by them as they were working on the earth. Wells sprang up from the blood of a martyr or from the touch of a saint's or a fairy's staff. 776 The sea originated from a magic cask given by God to a woman. The spigot, when opened, could not be closed again, and the cask never ceased running until the waters covered the earth—a tale with savage parallels. 777 In all these cases, giant, saint, or fairy has doubtless taken the place of a god, since the stories have a very primitive facies. The giant is frequently Gargantua, probably himself once a divinity. Other references in Irish texts point to the common cosmogonic myth of the earth having gradually assumed its present form. Thus many new lakes and plains are said to have been formed in Ireland during the time of Partholan and Nemed, the plains being apparently built up out of existing materials. 778 In some cases the formation of a lake was the result of digging the grave of some personage after whom the lake was then named. 779 Here we come upon the familiar idea of the danger of encroaching on the domain of a deity, e.g. that of the Earth-god, by digging the earth, with the consequent punishment by a flood. The same conception is found in Celtic stories of a lake or river formed from the overflowing of a sacred well through human carelessness or curiosity, which led to the anger of the divinity of the well. 780 Or, again, a town or castle is submerged on account of the wickedness of its inhabitants, the waters being produced by the curse of God or a saint (replacing a pagan god) and forming a lake. 781 These may be regarded as forms of a Celtic deluge-myth, which in one case, that of the Welsh story of the ship of Nevyd, which saved Dwyvan and Dwyfach and a pair of all kinds of animals when Lake Llion overflowed, has apparently borrowed from the Biblical story. 782 In other cases lakes are formed from the tears of a god, e.g. Manannan, whose tears at the death of his son formed three lochs in Erin. 783 Apollonius reports that the waters of Eridanus originated from the tears of Apollo when driven from heaven by his father. 784 This story, which he says is Celtic, has been clothed by him in a Greek form, and the god in question may have been Belenos, equated with Apollo. Sometimes the formation of streams was ascribed to great hail-storms—an evident mythic rendering of the damage done by actual spates, while the Irish myths of "illimitable sea-bursts," of which three particular instances are often mentioned, were doubtless the result of the experience of tidal waves.

Although no complete account of the end of all things, like that of the Scandinavian Ragnarok, has survived, scattered hints tell of its former existence. Strabo says that the Druids taught that "fire and water must one day prevail"—an evident belief in some final cataclysm. 785 This is also hinted at in the words of certain Gauls to Alexander, telling him that what they feared most of all was the fall of the heavens upon their heads. 786 In other words, they feared what would be the signal of the end of all things. On Irish ground the words of Conchobar may refer to this. He announced that he would rescue the captives and spoil taken by Medb, unless the heavens fell, and the earth burst open, and the sea engulphed all things. 787 Such a myth mingled with Christian beliefs may underlie the prophecy of Badb after Mag-tured regarding the evils to come and the end of the world, and that of Fercertne in the Colloquy of the Two Sages. 788 Both have a curious resemblance to the Sybil's prophecy of doom in the Voluspa. If the gods themselves were involved in such a catastrophe, it would not be surprising, since in some aspects their immortality depended on their eating and drinking immortal food and drink. 789

Footnote 766: Avienus, Ora Maritima, 644 f.

Footnote 767: IT i. 25; Gaidoz, ZCP i. 27.

Footnote 768: Annales de Bretagne, x. 414.

Footnote 769: IT i. 50, cf. 184; Folk-Lore, vi. 170.

Footnote 770: Cæsar, vi. 18.

Footnote 771: infra.

Footnote 772: Diod. Sic. v. 24; Appian, Illyrica, 2.

Footnote 773: Amm. Marcel, xv. 9.

Footnote 774: D'Arbois, ii. 262, xii. 220.

Footnote 775: Antient Laws of Ireland, i. 23. In one MS. Adam is said to have been created thus—his body of earth, his blood of the sea, his face of the sun, his breath of the wind, etc. This is also found in a Frisian tale (Vigfusson-Powell, Corpus Poet. Bor. i. 479), and both stories present an inversion of well-known myths about the creation of the universe from the members of a giant.

Footnote 776: Sébillot, i. 213 f., ii. 6, 7, 72, 97, 176, 327-328. Cf. RC xv. 482, xvi. 152.

Footnote 777: Sébillot, ii. 6.

Footnote 778: LL 56; Keating, 117, 123.

Footnote 779: RC xv. 429, xvi. 277.

Footnote 780: supra.

Footnote 781: Sébillot, ii. 41 f., 391, 397; infra.

Footnote 782: Triads in Loth, ii. 280, 299; Rh[^y]s, HL 583, 663.

Footnote 783: RC xvi. 50, 146.

Footnote 784: Apoll. iv. 609 f.

Footnote 785: Strabo, iv. 4. 4.

Footnote 786: Arrian, Anab. i. 4. 7; Strabo, vii. 3. 8. Cf. Jullian, 85.

Footnote 787: LL 94; Miss Hull, 205.

Footnote 788: RC xii. 111, xxvi. 33.

Footnote 789: A possible survival of a world-serpent myth may be found in "Da Derga's Hostel" (RC xxii. 54), where we hear of Leviathan that surrounds the globe and strikes with his tail to overwhelm the world. But this may be a reflection of Norse myths of the Midgard serpent, sometimes equated with Leviathan.

CHAPTER XVI
SACRIFICE, PRAYER, AND DIVINATION

The Semites are often considered the worst offenders in the matter of human sacrifice, but in this, according to classical evidence, they were closely rivalled by the Celts of Gaul. They offered human victims on the principle of a life for a life, or to propitiate the gods, or in order to divine the future from the entrails of the victim. We shall examine the Celtic custom of human sacrifice from these points of view first.

Cæsar says that those afflicted with disease or engaged in battle or danger offer human victims or vow to do so, because unless man's life be given for man's life, the divinity of the gods cannot be appeased. 790 The theory appears to have been that the gods sent disease or ills when they desired a human life, but that any life would do; hence one in danger might escape by offering another in his stead. In some cases the victims may have been offered to disease demons or diseases personified, such as Celtic imagination still believes in, 791 rather than to gods, or, again, they may have been offered to native gods of healing. Coming danger could also be averted on the same principle, and though the victims were usually slaves, in times of great peril wives and children were sacrificed. 792 After a defeat, which showed that the gods were still implacable, the wounded and feeble were slain, or a great leader would offer himself. 793 Or in such a case the Celts would turn their weapons against themselves, making of suicide a kind of sacrifice, hoping to bring victory to the survivors. 794

The idea of the victim being offered on the principle of a life for a life is illustrated by a custom at Marseilles in time of pestilence. One of the poorer classes offered himself to be kept at the public expense for some time. He was then led in procession, clad in sacred boughs, and solemnly cursed, and prayer was made that on him might fall the evils of the community. Then he was cast headlong down. Here the victim stood for the lives of the city and was a kind of scape-victim, like those at the Thargelia. 795

Human victims were also offered by way of thanksgiving after victory, and vows were often made before a battle, promising these as well as part of the spoil. For this reason the Celts would never ransom their captives, but offered them in sacrifice, animals captured being immolated along with them. 796 The method of sacrifice was slaughter by sword or spear, hanging, impaling, dismembering, and drowning. Some gods were propitiated by one particular mode of sacrifice—Taranis by burning, Teutates by suffocation, Esus (perhaps a tree-god) by hanging on a tree. Drowning meant devoting the victim to water-divinities. 797

Other propitiatory sacrifices took place at intervals, and had a general or tribal character, the victims being criminals or slaves or even members of the tribe. The sacrificial pile had the rude outline of a human form, the limbs of osier, enclosing human as well as some animal victims, who perished by fire. Diodorus says that the victims were malefactors who had been kept in prison for five years, and that some of them were impaled. 798 This need not mean that the holocausts were quinquennial, for they may have been offered yearly, at Midsummer, to judge by the ritual of modern survivals. 799 The victims perished in that element by which the sun-god chiefly manifested himself, and by the sacrifice his powers were augmented, and thus growth and fertility were promoted. These holocausts were probably extensions of an earlier slaying of a victim representing the spirit of vegetation, though their value in aiding fertility would be still in evidence. This is suggested by Strabo's words that the greater the number of murders the greater would be the fertility of the land, probably meaning that there would then be more criminals as sacrificial victims. 800 Varro also speaks of human sacrifice to a god equated with Saturn, offered because of all seeds the human race is the best, i.e. human victims are most productive of fertility. 801 Thus, looked at in one way, the later rite was a propitiatory sacrifice, in another it was an act of magico-religious ritual springing from the old rite of the divine victim. But from both points of view the intention was the same—the promotion of fertility in field and fold.

Divination with the bodies of human victims is attested by Tacitus, who says that "the Druids consult the gods in the palpitating entrails of men," and by Strabo, who describes the striking down of the victim by the sword and the predicting of the future from his convulsive movements. 802 To this we shall return.

Human sacrifice in Gaul was put down by the Romans, who were amazed at its extent, Suetonius summing up the whole religion in a phrase— druidarum religionem diræ immanitatis. 803 By the year 40 A.D. it had ceased, though victims were offered symbolically, the Druids pretending to strike them and drawing a little blood from them. 804 Only the pressure of a higher civilisation forced the so-called philosophic Druids to abandon their revolting customs. Among the Celts of Britain human sacrifice still prevailed in 77 A.D. 805 Dio Cassius describes the refinements of cruelty practised on female victims (prisoners of war) in honour of the goddess Andrasta—their breasts cut off and placed over their mouths, and a stake driven through their bodies, which were then hung in the sacred grove. 806 Tacitus speaks of the altars in Mona (Anglesey) laved with human blood. As to the Irish Celts, patriotic writers have refused to believe them guilty of such practices, 807 but there is no a priori reason which need set them apart from other races on the same level of civilisation in this custom. The Irish texts no doubt exaggerate the number of the victims, but they certainly attest the existence of the practice. From the Dindsenchas, which describes many archaic usages, we learn that "the firstlings of every issue and the chief scions of every clan" were offered to Cromm Cruaich—a sacrifice of the first-born,—and that at one festival the prostrations of the worshippers were so violent that three-fourths of them perished, not improbably an exaggerated memory of orgiastic rites. 808 Dr. Joyce thinks that these notices are as incredible as the mythic tales in the Dindsenchas. Yet the tales were doubtless quite credible to the pagan Irish, and the ritual notices are certainly founded on fact. Dr. Joyce admits the existence of foundation sacrifices in Ireland, and it is difficult to understand why human victims may not have been offered on other occasions also.

The purpose of the sacrifice, namely, fertility, is indicated in the poetical version of the cult of Cromm—

"Milk and corn

They would ask from him speedily,

In return for one-third of their healthy issue." 809

The Nemedian sacrifice to the Fomorians is said to have been two-thirds of their children and of the year's supply of corn and milk 810 —an obvious misunderstanding, the victims really being offered to obtain corn and milk. The numbers are exaggerated, 811 but there can be no doubt as to the nature of the sacrifice—the offering of an agricultural folk to the divinities who helped or retarded growth. Possibly part of the flesh of the victims, at one time identified with the god, was buried in the fields or mixed with the seed-corn, in order to promote fertility. The blood was sprinkled on the image of the god. Such practices were as obnoxious to Christian missionaries as they had been to the Roman Government, and we learn that S. Patrick preached against "the slaying of yoke oxen and milch cows and the burning of the first-born progeny" at the Fair of Taillte. 812 As has been seen, the Irish version of the Perseus and Andromeda story, in which the victim is offered not to a dragon, but to the Fomorians, may have received this form from actual ritual in which human victims were sacrificed to the Fomorians. 813 In a Japanese version of the same story the maiden is offered to the sea-gods. Another tale suggests the offering of human victims to remove blight. In this case the land suffers from blight because the adulteress Becuma, married to the king of Erin, has pretended to be a virgin. The Druids announced that the remedy was to slay the son of an undefiled couple and sprinkle the doorposts and the land with his blood. Such a youth was found, but at his mother's request a two-bellied cow, in which two birds were found, was offered in his stead. 814 In another instance in the Dindsenchas, hostages, including the son of a captive prince, are offered to remove plagues—an equivalent to the custom of the Gauls. 815

Human sacrifices were also offered when the foundation of a new building was laid. Such sacrifices are universal, and are offered to propitiate the Earth spirits or to provide a ghostly guardian for the building. A Celtic legend attaches such a sacrifice to the founding of the monastery at Iona. S. Oran agrees to adopt S. Columba's advice "to go under the clay of this island to hallow it," and as a reward he goes straight to heaven. 816 The legend is a semi-Christian form of the memory of an old pagan custom, and it is attached to Oran probably because he was the first to be buried in the island. In another version, nothing is said of the sacrifice. The two saints are disputing about the other world, and Oran agrees to go for three days into the grave to settle the point at issue. At the end of that time the grave is opened, and the triumphant Oran announces that heaven and hell are not such as they are alleged to be. Shocked at his latitudinarian sentiments, Columba ordered earth to be piled over him, lest he cause a scandal to the faith, and Oran was accordingly buried alive. 817 In a Welsh instance, Vortigern's castle cannot be built, for the stones disappear as soon as they are laid. Wise men, probably Druids, order the sacrifice of a child born without a father, and the sprinkling of the site with his blood. 818 "Groaning hostages" were placed under a fort in Ireland, and the foundation of the palace of Emain Macha was also laid with a human victim. 819 Many similar legends are connected with buildings all over the Celtic area, and prove the popularity of the pagan custom. The sacrifice of human victims on the funeral pile will be discussed in a later chapter.

Of all these varieties of human sacrifice, those offered for fertility, probably at Beltane or Midsummer, were the most important. Their propitiatory nature is of later origin, and their real intention was to strengthen the divinity by whom the processes of growth were directed. Still earlier, one victim represented the divinity, slain that his life might be revived in vigour. The earth was sprinkled with his blood and fed with his flesh in order to fertilise it, and possibly the worshippers partook sacramentally of the flesh. Propitiatory holocausts of human victims had taken the place of the slain representative of a god, but their value in promoting fertility was not forgotten. The sacramental aspect of the rite is perhaps to be found in Pliny's words regarding "the slaying of a human being as a most religious act and eating the flesh as a wholesome remedy" among the Britons. 820 This may merely refer to "medicinal cannibalism," such as still survives in Italy, but the passage rather suggests sacramental cannibalism, the eating of part of a divine victim, such as existed in Mexico and elsewhere. Other acts of cannibalism are referred to by classical writers. Diodorus says the Irish ate their enemies, and Pausanias describes the eating the flesh and drinking the blood of children among the Galatian Celts. Drinking out of a skull the blood of slain (sacrificial) enemies is mentioned by Ammianus and Livy, and Solinus describes the Irish custom of bathing the face in the blood of the slain and drinking it. 821 In some of these cases the intention may simply have been to obtain the dead enemy's strength, but where a sacrificial victim was concerned, the intention probably went further than this. The blood of dead relatives was also drunk in order to obtain their virtues, or to be brought into closer rapport with them. 822 This is analogous to the custom of blood brotherhood, which also existed among the Celts and continued as a survival in the Western Isles until a late date. 823

One group of Celtic human sacrifices was thus connected with primitive agricultural ritual, but the warlike energies of the Celts extended the practice. Victims were easily obtained, and offered to the gods of war. Yet even these sacrifices preserved some trace of the older rite, in which the victim represented a divinity or spirit.

Head-hunting, described in classical writings and in Irish texts, had also a sacrificial aspect. The heads of enemies were hung at the saddle-bow or fixed on spears, as the conquerors returned home with songs of victory. 824 This gruesome picture often recurs in the texts. Thus, after the death of Cúchulainn, Conall Cernach returned to Emer with the heads of his slayers strung on a withy. He placed each on a stake and told Emer the name of the owner. A Celtic oppidum or a king's palace must have been as gruesome as a Dayak or Solomon Island village. Everywhere were stakes crowned with heads, and the walls of houses were adorned with them. Poseidonius tells how he sickened at such a sight, but gradually became more accustomed to it. 825 A room in the palace was sometimes a store for such heads, or they were preserved in cedar-wood oil or in coffers. They were proudly shown to strangers as a record of conquest, but they could not be sold for their weight in gold. 826 After a battle a pile of heads was made and the number of the slain was counted, and at annual festivals warriors produced the tongues of enemies as a record of their prowess. 827

These customs had a religious aspect. In cutting off a head the Celt saluted the gods, and the head was offered to them or to ancestral spirits, and sometimes kept in grove or temple. 828 The name given to the heads of the slain in Ireland, the "mast of Macha," shows that they were dedicated to her, just as skulls found under an altar had been devoted to the Celtic Mars. 829 Probably, as among Dayaks, American Indians, and others, possession of a head was a guarantee that the ghost of its owner would be subservient to its Celtic possessor, either in this world or in the next, since they are sometimes found buried in graves along with the dead. 830 Or, suspended in temples, they became an actual and symbolical offering of the life of their owners, if, as is probable, the life or soul was thought to be in the head. Hence, too, the custom of drinking from the skull of the slain had the intention of transferring his powers directly to the drinker. 831 Milk drunk from the skull of Conall Cernach restored to enfeebled warriors their pristine strength, 832 and a folk-survival in the Highlands—that of drinking from the skull of a suicide (here taking the place of the slain enemy) in order to restore health—shows the same idea at work. All these practices had thus one end, that of the transference of spirit force—to the gods, to the victor who suspended the head from his house, and to all who drank from the skull. Represented in bas-relief on houses or carved on dagger-handles, the head may still have been thought to possess talismanic properties, giving power to house or weapon. Possibly this cult of human heads may have given rise to the idea of a divine head like those figured on Gaulish images, or described, e.g., in the story of Bran. His head preserved the land from invasion, until Arthur disinterred it, 833 the story being based on the belief that heads or bodies of great warriors still had a powerful influence. 834 The representation of the head of a god, like his whole image, would be thought to possess the same preservative power.

A possible survival of the sacrifice of the aged may be found in a Breton custom of applying a heavy club to the head of old persons to lighten their death agonies, the clubs having been formerly used to kill them. They are kept in chapels, and are regarded with awe. 835

Animal victims were also frequently offered. The Galatian Celts made a yearly sacrifice to their Artemis of a sheep, goat, or calf, purchased with money laid by for each animal caught in the chase. Their dogs were feasted and crowned with flowers. 836 Further details of this ritual are unfortunately lacking. Animals captured in war were sacrificed to the war-gods by the Gauls, or to a river-god, as when the horses of the defeated host were thrown into the Rhine by the Gaulish conquerors of Mallius. 837 We have seen that the white oxen sacrificed at the mistletoe ritual may once have been representatives of the vegetation-spirit, which also animated the oak and the mistletoe. Among the insular Celts animal sacrifices are scarcely mentioned in the texts, probably through suppression by later scribes, but the lives of Irish saints contain a few notices of the custom, e.g. that of S. Patrick, which describes the gathering of princes, chiefs, and Druids at Tara to sacrifice victims to idols. 838 In Ireland the peasantry still kill a sheep or heifer for S. Martin on his festival, and ill-luck is thought to follow the non-observance of the rite. 839 Similar sacrifices on saints' days in Scotland and Wales occurred in Christian times. 840 An excellent instance is that of the sacrifice of bulls at Gairloch for the cure of lunatics on S. Maelrubha's day (August 25th). Libations of milk were also poured out on the hills, ruined chapels were perambulated, wells and stones worshipped, and divination practised. These rites, occurring in the seventeenth century, were condemned by the Presbytery of Dingwall, but with little effect, and some of them still survive. 841 In all these cases the saint has succeeded to the ritual of an earlier god. Mr. Cook surmises that S. Maelrubha was the successor of a divine king connected with an oak and sacred well, the god or spirit of which was incarnate in him. These divine kings may at one time have been slain, or a bull, similarly incarnating the god or spirit, may have been killed as a surrogate. This slaying was at a later time regarded as a sacrifice and connected with the cure of madness. 842 The rite would thus be on a parallel with the slaying of the oxen at the mistletoe gathering, as already interpreted. Eilean Maree (Maelrubha), where the tree and well still exist, was once known as Eilean mo righ ("the island of my king"), or Eilean a Mhor Righ ("of the great king"), the king having been worshipped as a god. This piece of corroborative evidence was given by the oldest inhabitant to Sir Arthur Mitchell. 843 The people also spoke of the god Mourie.

Other survivals of animal sacrifice are found in cases of cattle-plague, as in Morayshire sixty years ago, in Wales, Devon, and the Isle of Man. The victim was burned and its ashes sprinkled on the herd, or it was thrown into the sea or over a precipice. 844 Perhaps it was both a propitiatory sacrifice and a scape-animal, carrying away the disease, though the rite may be connected with the former slaying of a divine animal whose death benefited all the cattle of the district. In the Hebrides the spirits of earth and air were propitiated every quarter by throwing outside the door a cock, hen, duck, or cat, which was supposed to be seized by them. If the rite was neglected, misfortune was sure to follow. The animal carried away evils from the house, and was also a propitiatory sacrifice.

The blood of victims was sprinkled on altars, images, and trees, or, as among the Boii, it was placed in a skull adorned with gold. 845 Other libations are known mainly from folk-survivals. Thus Breton fishermen salute reefs and jutting promontories, say prayers, and pour a glass of wine or throw a biscuit or an old garment into the sea. 846 In the Hebrides a curious rite was performed on Maundy Thursday. After midnight a man walked into the sea, and poured ale or gruel on the waters, at the same time singing:

> "O God of the sea,
>
> Put weed in the drawing wave,
>
> To enrich the ground,
>
> To shower on us food."

Those on shore took up the strain in chorus. 847 Thus the rite was described by one who took part in it a century ago, but Martin, writing in the seventeenth century, gives other details. The cup of ale was offered with the words, "Shony, I give you this cup of ale, hoping that you will be so kind as to send plenty of seaweed for enriching our ground for the ensuing year." All then went in silence to the church and remained there for a time, after which they indulged in an orgy out-of-doors. This orgiastic rite may once have included the intercourse of the sexes—a powerful charm for fertility. "Shony" was some old sea-god, and another divinity of the sea, Brianniul, was sometimes invoked for the same purpose. 848 Until recently milk was poured on "Gruagach stones" in the Hebrides, as an offering to the Gruagach, a brownie who watched over herds, and who had taken the place of a god. 849

PRAYER

Prayer accompanied most rites, and probably consisted of traditional formulæ, on the exact recital of which depended their value. The Druids invoked a god during the mistletoe rite, and at a Galatian sacrifice, offered to bring birds to destroy grasshoppers, prayer was made to the birds themselves. 850 In Mona, at the Roman invasion, the Druids raised their arms and uttered prayers for deliverance, at the same time cursing the invaders, and Boudicca invoked the protection of the goddess Andrasta in a similar manner. 851 Chants were sung by the "priestesses" of Sena to raise storms, and they were also sung by warriors both before and after a battle, to the accompaniment of a measured dance and the clashing of arms. 852 These warrior chants were composed by bards, and probably included invocations of the war-gods and the recital of famous deeds. They may also have been of the nature of spells ensuring the help of the gods, like the war-cries uttered by a whole army to the sound of trumpets. 853 These consisted of the name of a god, of a tribe or clan, or of some well-known phrase. As the recital of a divine name is often supposed to force the god to help, these cries had thus a magical aspect, while they also struck terror into the foe. 854 Warriors also advanced dancing to the fray, and they are depicted on coins dancing on horseback or before a sword, which was worshipped by the Celts. 855 The Celtiberian festival at the full moon consisted entirely of dancing. The dance is a primitive method of expressing religious emotion, and where it imitates certain actions, it is intended by magical influence to crown the actions themselves with success. It is thus a kind of acted prayer with magical results.

DIVINATION

A special class of diviners existed among the Celts, but the Druids practised divination, as did also the unofficial layman. Classical writers speak of the Celts as of all nations the most devoted to, and the most experienced in, the science of divination. Divination with a human victim is described by Diodorus. Libations were poured over him, and he was then slain, auguries being drawn from the method of his fall, the movements of his limbs, and the flowing of his blood. Divination with the entrails was used in Galatia, Gaul, and Britain. 856 Beasts and birds also provided omens. The course taken by a hare let loose gave an omen of success to the Britons, and in Ireland divination was used with a sacrificial animal. 857 Among birds the crow was pre-eminent, and two crows are represented speaking into the ears of a man on a bas-relief at Compiègne. The Celts believed that the crow had shown where towns should be founded, or had furnished a remedy against poison, and it was also an arbiter of disputes. 858 Artemidorus describes how, at a certain place, there were two crows. Persons having a dispute set out two heaps of sweetmeats, one for each disputant. The birds swooped down upon them, eating one and dispersing the other. He whose heap had been scattered won the case. 859 Birds were believed to have guided the migrating Celts, and their flight furnished auguries, because, as Deiotaurus gravely said, birds never lie. Divination by the voices of birds was used by the Irish Druids. 860

Omens were drawn from the direction of the smoke and flames of sacred fires and from the condition of the clouds. 861 Wands of yew were carried by Druids—"the wand of Druidism" of many folk-tales—and were used perhaps as divining-rods. Ogams were also engraved on rods of yews, and from these Druids divined hidden things. By this means the Druid Dalan discovered where Etain had been hidden by the god Mider. The method used may have been that of drawing one of the rods by lot and then divining from the marks upon it. A similar method was used to discover the route to be taken by invaders, the result being supposed to depend on divine interposition. 862 The knowledge of astronomy ascribed by Cæsar to the Druids was probably of a simple kind, and much mixed with astrology, and though it furnished the data for computing a simple calendar, its use was largely magical. 863 Irish diviners forecast the time to build a house by the stars, and the date at which S. Columba's education should begin, was similarly discovered. 864

The Imbas Forosnai, "illumination between the hands," was used by the Filé to discover hidden things. He chewed a piece of raw flesh and placed it as an offering to the images of the gods whom he desired to help him. If enlightenment did not come by the next day, he pronounced incantations on his palms, which he then placed on his cheeks before falling asleep. The revelation followed in a dream, or sometimes after awaking. 865 Perhaps the animal whose flesh was eaten was a sacred one. Another method was that of the Teinm Laegha. The Filé made a verse and repeated it over some person or thing regarding which he sought information, or he placed his staff on the person's body and so obtained what he sought. The rite was also preceded by sacrifice; hence S. Patrick prohibited both it and the Imbas Forosnai. 866 Another incantation, the Cétnad, was sung through the fist to discover the track of stolen cattle or of the thief. If this did not bring enlightenment, the Filé went to sleep and obtained the knowledge through a dream. 867 Another Cétnad for obtaining information regarding length of life was addressed to the seven daughters of the sea. Perhaps the incantation was repeated mechanically until the seer fell into a kind of trance. Divination by dreams was also used by the continental Celts. 868

Other methods resemble "trance-utterance." "A great obnubilation was conjured up for the bard so that he slept a heavy sleep, and things magic-begotten were shewn to him to enunciate," apparently in his sleep. This was called "illumination by rhymes," and a similar method was used in Wales. When consulted, the seer roared violently until he was beside himself, and out of his ravings the desired information was gathered. When aroused from this ecstatic condition, he had no remembrance of what he had uttered. Giraldus reports this, and thinks, with the modern spiritualist, that the utterance was caused by spirits. 869 The resemblance to modern trance-utterance and to similar methods used by savages is remarkable, and psychological science sees in it the promptings of the subliminal self in sleep.

The taghairm of the Highlanders was a survival from pagan times. The seer was usually bound in a cow's hide—the animal, it may be conjectured, having been sacrificed in earlier times. He was left in a desolate place, and while he slept spirits were supposed to inspire his dreams. 870 Clothing in the skin of a sacrificial animal, by which the person thus clothed is brought into contact with it and hence with the divinity to which it is offered, or with the divine animal itself where the victim is so regarded, is a widespread custom. Hence, in this Celtic usage, contact with divinity through the hide would be expected to produce enlightenment. For a like reason the Irish sacrificed a sheep for the recovery of the sick, and clothed the patient in its skin. 871 Binding the limbs of the seer is also a widespread custom, perhaps to restrain his convulsions or to concentrate the psychic force.

Both among the continental and Irish Celts those who sought hidden knowledge slept on graves, hoping to be inspired by the spirits of the dead. 872 Legend told how, the full version of the Táin having been lost, Murgan the Filé sang an incantation over the grave of Fergus mac Roig. A cloud hid him for three days, and during that time the dead man appeared and recited the saga to him.

In Ireland and the Highlands, divination by looking into the shoulder-blade of a sheep was used to discover future events or things happening at a distance, a survival from pagan times. 873 The scholiast on Lucan describes the Druidic method of chewing acorns and then prophesying, just as, in Ireland, eating nuts from the sacred hazels round Connla's well gave inspiration. 874 The "priestesses" of Sena and the "Druidesses" of the third century had the gift of prophecy, and it was also ascribed freely to the Filid, the Druids, and to Christian saints. Druids are said to have prophesied the coming of S. Patrick, and similar prophecies are put in the mouths of Fionn and others, just as Montezuma's priests foretold the coming of the Spaniards. 875 The word used for such prophecies—baile, means "ecstasy," and it suggests that the prophet worked himself into a frenzy and then fell into a trance, in which he uttered his forecast. Prophecies were also made at the birth of a child, describing its future career. 876 Careful attention was given to the utterances of Druidic prophets, e.g. Medb's warriors postponed their expedition for fifteen days, because the Druids told them they would not succeed if they set out sooner. 877

Mythical personages or divinities are said in the Irish texts to have stood on one leg, with one arm extended, and one eye closed, when uttering prophecies or incantations, and this was doubtless an attitude used by the seer. 878 A similar method is known elsewhere, and it may have been intended to produce greater force. From this attitude may have originated myths of beings with one arm, one leg, and one eye, like some Fomorians or the Fachan whose weird picture Campbell of Islay drew from verbal descriptions. 879

Early Celtic saints occasionally describe lapses into heathenism in Ireland, not characterised by "idolatry," but by wizardry, dealing in charms, and fidlanna, perhaps a kind of divination with pieces of wood. 880 But it is much more likely that these had never really been abandoned. They belong to the primitive element of religion and magic which people cling to long after they have given up "idolatry."

Footnote 790: Cæsar, vi. 16.

Footnote 791: Rh[^y]s, CB 4 68.

Footnote 792: Justin, xxvi. 2; Pomp. Mela, iii. 2.

Footnote 793: Diod. Sic. xxii. 9.

Footnote 794: See Jullian, 53.

Footnote 795: Servius on Æneid, iii. 57.

Footnote 796: Cæsar, vi. 16; Livy, xxxviii. 47; Diod. Sic. v. 32, xxxi. 13; Athenæus, iv. 51; Dio Cass., lxii. 7.

Footnote 797: Diod. Sic, xxxiv. 13; Strabo, iv. 4; Orosius, v. 16; Schol. on Lucan, Usener's ed. 32.

Footnote 798: Cæsar, vi. 16; Strabo, iv. 4; Diod. Sic. v. 32; Livy, xxxviii. 47.

Footnote 799: Mannhardt, Baumkultus, 529 f.

Footnote 800: Strabo, ibid. 4. 4.

Footnote 801: S. Aug. de Civ. Dei, vii. 19.

Footnote 802: Tac. Ann. xiv. 30; Strabo, iv. 4. 4.

Footnote 803: Suet. Claud. 25.

Footnote 804: Pomp. Mela, iii. 2. 18.

Footnote 805: Pliny, HN xxx. 4. 13.

Footnote 806: Dio. Cass. lxii. 6.

Footnote 807: O'Curry, MC ii. 222; Joyce, SH i. ch. 9.

Footnote 808: RC xvi. 35.

Footnote 809: LL 213b.

Footnote 810: supra.

Footnote 811: See, however, accounts of reckless child sacrifices in Ellis, Polynesian Researches, i. 252, and Westermarck, Moral Ideas, i. 397.

Footnote 812: O'Curry, MC Intro, dcxli.

Footnote 813: LU 126a. A folk-version is given by Larminie, West Irish Folk-Tales, 139.

Footnote 814: Book of Fermoy, 89a.

Footnote 815: O'Curry, MC Intro. dcxl, ii. 222.

Footnote 816: Adamnan, Vita S. Col. Reeve's ed. 288.

Footnote 817: Carmichael, Carmina Gadelica, ii. 317.

Footnote 818: Nennius, Hist. Brit. 40.

Footnote 819: Stokes, TIG xli.; O'Curry, MC ii. 9.

Footnote 820: Pliny, HN xxx. 1. The feeding of Ethni, daughter of Crimthann, on human flesh that she might sooner attain maturity may be an instance of "medicinal cannibalism" (IT iii. 363). The eating of parents among the Irish, described by Strabo (iv. 5), was an example of "honorific cannibalism." See my article "Cannibalism" in Hastings' Encycl. of Rel. and Ethics, iii, 194.

Footnote 821: Diod. Sic. vi. 12; Paus. x. 22. 3; Amm. Marc. xxvii. 4; Livy, xxiii. 24; Solin. xxii. 3.

Footnote 822: This custom continued in Ireland until Spenser's time.

Footnote 823: Leahy, i. 158; Giraldus, Top. Hib. iii. 22; Martin, 109.

Footnote 824: Sil. Ital. iv. 213; Diod. Sic. xiv. 115; Livy, x. 26; Strabo, iv. 4. 5; Miss Hull, 92.

Footnote 825: Diod. Sic. v. 29; Strabo, iv. 4. 5.

Footnote 826: D'Arbois, v. 11; Diod. Sic. v. 29; Strabo, loc. cit.

Footnote 827: Annals of the Four Masters, 864; IT i. 205.

Footnote 828: Sil. Ital. iv. 215, v. 652; Lucan, Phar. i. 447; Livy, xxiii. 24.

Footnote 829: supra; CIL xii. 1077. A dim memory of head-taking survived in the seventeenth century in Eigg, where headless skeletons were found, of which the islanders said that an enemy had cut off their heads (Martin, 277).

Footnote 830: Belloguet, Ethnol. Gaul. iii. 100.

Footnote 831: Sil. Ital. xiii. 482; Livy, xxiii. 24; Florus, i. 39.

Footnote 832: ZCP i. 106.

Footnote 833: Loth, i. 90 f., ii. 218-219. Sometimes the weapons of a great warrior had the same effect. The bows of Gwerthevyr were hidden in different parts of Prydein and preserved the land from Saxon invasion, until Gwrtheyrn, for love of a woman, dug them up (Loth, ii. 218-219).

Footnote 834: infra. In Ireland, the brain of an enemy was taken from the head, mixed with lime, and made into a ball. This was allowed to harden, and was then placed in the tribal armoury as a trophy.

Footnote 835: L'Anthropologie, xii. 206, 711. Cf. the English tradition of the "Holy Mawle," said to have been used for the same purpose. Thorns, Anecdotes and Traditions, 84.

Footnote 836: Arrian, Cyneg. xxxiii.

Footnote 837: Cæsar, vi. 17; Orosius, v. 16. 6.

Footnote 838: D'Arbois, i. 155.

Footnote 839: Curtin, Tales of the Fairies, 72; Folk-Lore, vii. 178-179.

Footnote 840: Mitchell, Past in the Present, 275.

Footnote 841: Mitchell, op. cit. 271 f.

Footnote 842: Cook, Folk-Lore, xvii. 332.

Footnote 843: Mitchell, loc. cit. 147. The corruption of "Maelrubha" to "Maree" may have been aided by confusing the name with mo or mhor righ.

Footnote 844: Mitchell, loc. cit.; Moore, 92, 145; Rh[^y]s, CFL i. 305; Worth, Hist. of Devonshire, 339; Dalyell, passim.

Footnote 845: Livy, xxiii. 24.

Footnote 846: Sébillot, ii. 166-167; L'Anthrop. xv. 729.

Footnote 847: Carmichael, Carm. Gad. i. 163.

Footnote 848: Martin, 28. A scribe called "Sonid," which might be the equivalent of "Shony," is mentioned in the Stowe missal (Folk-Lore, 1895).

Footnote 849: Campbell, Superstitions, 184 f; Waifs and Strays of Celtic Trad. ii. 455.

Footnote 850: Aelian, xvii. 19.

Footnote 851: Tacitus, Ann. xiv. 30; Dio Cass. lxii. 6.

Footnote 852: Appian, Celtica, 8; Livy, xxi. 28, xxxviii. 17, x. 26.

Footnote 853: Livy, v. 38, vii. 23; Polybius, ii. 29. Cf. Watteville, Le cri de guerre chez les differents peuples, Paris, 1889.

Footnote 854: Livy, v. 38.

Footnote 855: Appian, vi. 53; Muret et Chabouillet, Catalogue des monnaies gauloises, 6033 f., 6941 f.

Footnote 856: Diod. v. 31; Justin, xxvi. 2, 4; Cicero, de Div. ii. 36, 76; Tac. Ann. xiv. 30; Strabo, iii. 3. 6.

Footnote 857: Dio Cass. lxii. 6.

Footnote 858: Reinach, Catal. Sommaire, 31; Pseudo-Plutarch, de Fluviis, vi. 4; Mirab. Auscult. 86.

Footnote 859: Strabo, iv. 4. 6.

Footnote 860: Justin, xxiv, 4; Cicero, de Div. i. 15. 26. (Cf. the two magic crows which announced the coming of Cúchulainn to the other rrrworld (D'Arbois, v. 203); Irish Nennius, 145; O'Curry, MC ii. 224; cf. for a Welsh instance, Skene, i. 433.)

Footnote 861: Joyce, SH i. 229; O'Curry, MC ii. 224, MS Mat. 284.

Footnote 862: IT i. 129; Livy, v. 34; Loth, RC xvi. 314. The Irish for consulting a lot is crann-chur, "the act of casting wood."

Footnote 863: Cæsar, vi. 14.

Footnote 864: O'Curry, MC ii. 46, 224; Stokes, Three Irish Homilies, 103.

Footnote 865: Cormac, 94. Fionn's divination by chewing his thumb is called Imbas Forosnai (RC xxv. 347).

Footnote 866: Antient Laws of Ireland, i. 45.

Footnote 867: Hyde, Lit. Hist. of Ireland, 241.

Footnote 868: Justin, xliii. 5.

Footnote 869: O'Grady, ii. 362; Giraldus, Descr. Camb. i. 11.

Footnote 870: Pennant, Tour in Scotland, i. 311; Martin, 111.

Footnote 871: Richardson, Folly of Pilgrimages, 70.

Footnote 872: Tertullian, de Anima, 57; Coll. de Reb. Hib. iii. 334.

Footnote 873: Campbell, Superstitions, 263; Curtin, Tales, 84.

Footnote 874: Lucan, ed. Usener, 33.

Footnote 875: See examples in O'Curry, MS Mat. 383 f.

Footnote 876: Miss Hull, 19, 20, 23.

Footnote 877: LU 55.

Footnote 878: RC xii. 98, xxi. 156, xxii. 61.

Footnote 879: RC xv. 432; Annals of the Four Masters, A.M. 2530; Campbell, WHT iv. 298.

Footnote 880: See "Adamnan's Second Vision." RC xii. 441.

CHAPTER XVII
TABU

The Irish geis, pl. geasa, which may be rendered by Tabu, had two senses. It meant something which must not be done for fear of disastrous consequences, and also an obligation to do something commanded by another.

As a tabu the geis had a large place in Irish life, and was probably known to other branches of the Celts. 881 It followed the general course of tabu wherever found. Sometimes it was imposed before birth, or it was hereditary, or connected with totemism. Legends, however, often arose giving a different explanation to geasa, long after the customs in which they originated had been forgotten. It was one of Diarmaid's geasa not to hunt the boar of Ben Gulban, and this was probably totemic in origin. But legend told how his father killed a child, the corpse being changed into a boar by the child's father, who said its span of life would be the same as Diarmaid's, and that he would be slain by it. Oengus put geasa on Diarmaid not to hunt it, but at Fionn's desire he broke these, and was killed. 882 Other geasa—those of Cúchulainn not to eat dog's flesh, and of Conaire never to chase birds—also point to totemism.

In some cases geasa were based on ideas of right and wrong, honour or dishonour, or were intended to cause avoidance of unlucky days. Others are unintelligible to us. The largest number of geasa concerned kings and chiefs, and are described, along with their corresponding privileges, in the Book of Rights. Some of the geasa of the king of Connaught were not to go to an assembly of women at Leaghair, not to sit in autumn on the sepulchral mound of the wife of Maine, not to go in a grey-speckled garment on a grey-speckled horse to the heath of Cruachan, and the like. 883 The meaning of these is obscure, but other examples are more obvious and show that all alike corresponded to the tabus applying to kings in primitive societies, who are often magicians, priests, or even divine representatives. On them the welfare of the tribe and the making of rain or sunshine, and the processes of growth depend. They must therefore be careful of their actions, and hence they are hedged about with tabus which, however unmeaning, have a direct connection with their powers. Out of such conceptions the Irish kingly geasa arose. Their observance made the earth fruitful, produced abundance and prosperity, and kept both the king and his land from misfortune. In later times these were supposed to be dependent on the "goodness" or the reverse of the king, but this was a departure from the older idea, which is clearly stated in the Book of Rights. 884 The kings were divinities on whom depended fruitfulness and plenty, and who must therefore submit to obey their geasa. Some of their prerogatives seem also to be connected with this state of things. Thus they might eat of certain foods or go to certain places on particular days. 885 In primitive societies kings and priests often prohibit ordinary mortals from eating things which they desire for themselves by making them tabu, and in other cases the fruits of the earth can only be eaten after king or priest has partaken of them ceremonially. This may have been the case in Ireland. The privilege relating to places may have meant that these were sacred and only to be entered by the king at certain times and in his sacred capacity.

As a reflection from this state of things, the heroes of the sagas, Cúchulainn and Fionn, had numerous geasa applicable to themselves, some of them religious, some magical, others based on primitive ideas of honour, others perhaps the invention of the narrators. 886

Geasa, whether in the sense of tabus or of obligations, could be imposed by any one, and must be obeyed, for disobedience produced disastrous effects. Probably the obligation was framed as an incantation or spell, and the power of the spell being fully believed in, obedience would follow as a matter of course. 887 Examples of such geasa are numerous in Irish literature. Cúchulainn's father-in-law put geasa on him that he should know no rest until he found out the cause of the exile of the sons of Doel. And Grainne put geasa on Diarmaid that he should elope with her, and this he did, though the act was repugnant to him.

Among savages the punishment which is supposed to follow tabu-breaking is often produced through auto-suggestion when a tabu has been unconsciously infringed and this has afterwards been discovered. Fear produces the result which is feared. The result is believed, however, to be the working of divine vengeance. In the case of Irish geasa, destruction and death usually followed their infringement, as in the case of Diarmaid and Cúchulainn. But the best instance is found in the tale of The Destruction of Da Derga's Hostel, in which the síd-folk avenge themselves for Eochaid's action by causing the destruction of his descendant Conaire, who is forced to break his geasa. These are first minutely detailed; then it is shown how, almost in spite of himself, Conaire was led on to break them, and how, in the sequel, his tragic death occurred. 888 Viewed in this light as the working of divine vengeance to a remote descendant of the offender by forcing him to break his tabus, the story is one of the most terrible in the whole range of Irish literature.

Footnote 881: The religious interdictions mentioned by Cæsar (vi. 13) may be regarded as tabus, while the spoils of war placed in a consecrated place (vi. 18), and certain animals among the Britons (v. 12), were clearly under tabu.

Footnote 882: Joyce, OCR 332 f.

Footnote 883: Book of Rights, ed. O'Donovan, 5.

Footnote 884: Book of Rights, 7.

Footnote 885: Ibid. 3 f.

Footnote 886: LL 107; O'Grady, ii. 175.

Footnote 887: In Highland tales geasa is translated "spells."

Footnote 888: RC xxii. 27 f. The story of Da Choca's Hostel has for its subject the destruction of Cormac through breaking his geasa (RC xxi. 149 f.).

CHAPTER XVIII
FESTIVALS

The Celtic year was not at first regulated by the solstices and equinoxes, but by some method connected with agriculture or with the seasons. Later, the year was a lunar one, and there is some evidence of attempts at synchronising solar and lunar time. But time was mainly measured by the moon, while in all calculations night preceded day. 889 Thus oidhche Samhain was the night preceding Samhain (November 1st), not the following night. The usage survives in our "sennight" and "fortnight." In early times the year had two, possibly three divisions, marking periods in pastoral or agricultural life, but it was afterwards divided into four periods, while the year began with the winter division, opening at Samhain. A twofold, subdivided into a fourfold division is found in Irish texts, 890 and may be tabulated as follows:—

A. Geimredh (winter half)
  1st quarter, Geimredh, beginning with the festival of Samhain, November 1st.
  2nd quarter, Earrach, beginning February 1st (sometimes called Oimelc).

B. Samradh (summer half)
  3rd quarter, Samradh, beginning with the festival of Beltane, May 1st (called also Cét-soman or Cét-samain, 1st day of Samono-s; cf. Welsh Cyntefyn).
  4th quarter, Foghamar, beginning with the festival of Lugnasadh, August 1st (sometimes called Brontroghain).

These divisions began with festivals, and clear traces of three of them occur over the whole Celtic area, but the fourth has now been merged in S. Brigit's day. Beltane and Samhain marked the beginning of the two great divisions, and were perhaps at first movable festivals, according as the signs of summer or winter appeared earlier or later. With the adoption of the Roman calendar some of the festivals were displaced, e.g. in Gaul, where the Calends of January took the place of Samhain, the ritual being also transferred.

None of the four festivals is connected with the times of equinox and solstice. This points to the fact that originally the Celtic year was independent of these. But Midsummer day was also observed not only by the Celts, but by most European folk, the ritual resembling that of Beltane. It has been held, and an old tradition in Ireland gives some support to the theory, that under Christian influences the old pagan feast of Beltane was merged in that of S. John Baptist on Midsummer day. 891 But, though there are Christian elements in the Midsummer ritual, denoting a desire to bring it under Church influence, the pagan elements in folk-custom are strongly marked, and the festival is deeply rooted in an earlier paganism all over Europe. Without much acquaintance with astronomy, men must have noted the period of the sun's longest course from early times, and it would probably be observed ritually. The festivals of Beltane and Midsummer may have arisen independently, and entered into competition with each other. Or Beltane may have been an early pastoral festival marking the beginning of summer when the herds went out to pasture, and Midsummer a more purely agricultural festival. And since their ritual aspect and purpose as seen in folk-custom are similar, they may eventually have borrowed each from the other. Or they may be later separate fixed dates of an earlier movable summer festival. For our purpose we may here consider them as twin halves of such a festival. Where Midsummer was already observed, the influence of the Roman calendar would confirm that observance. The festivals of the Christian year also affected the older observances. Some of the ritual was transferred to saints' days within the range of the pagan festival days, thus the Samhain ritual is found observed on S. Martin's day. In other cases, holy days took the place of the old festivals—All Saints' and All Souls' that of Samhain, S. Brigit's day that of February 1st, S. John Baptist's day that of Midsummer, Lammas that of Lugnasad, and some attempt was made to hallow, if not to oust, the older ritual.

The Celtic festivals being primarily connected with agricultural and pastoral life, we find in their ritual survivals traces not only of a religious but of a magical view of things, of acts designed to assist the powers of life and growth. The proof of this will be found in a detailed examination of the surviving customs connected with them.

SAMHAIN

Samhain, 892 beginning the Celtic year, was an important social and religious occasion. The powers of blight were beginning their ascendancy, yet the future triumph of the powers of growth was not forgotten. Probably Samhain had gathered up into itself other feasts occurring earlier or later. Thus it bears traces of being a harvest festival, the ritual of the earlier harvest feast being transferred to the winter feast, as the Celts found themselves in lands where harvest is not gathered before late autumn. The harvest rites may, however, have been associated with threshing rather than ingathering. Samhain also contains in its ritual some of the old pastoral cults, while as a New Year feast its ritual is in great part that of all festivals of beginnings.

New fire was brought into each house at Samhain from the sacred bonfire, 893 itself probably kindled from the need-fire by the friction of pieces of wood. This preserved its purity, the purity necessary to a festival of beginnings. 894 The putting away of the old fires was probably connected with various rites for the expulsion of evils, which usually occur among many peoples at the New Year festival. By that process of dislocation which scattered the Samhain ritual over a wider period and gave some of it to Christmas, the kindling of the Yule log may have been originally connected with this festival.

Divination and forecasting the fate of the inquirer for the coming year also took place. Sometimes these were connected with the bonfire, stones placed in it showing by their appearance the fortune or misfortune awaiting their owners. 895 Others, like those described by Burns in his "Hallowe'en," were unconnected with the bonfire and were of an erotic nature. 896

The slaughter of animals for winter consumption which took place at Samhain, or, as now, at Martinmas, though connected with economic reasons, had a distinctly religious aspect, as it had among the Teutons. In recent times in Ireland one of the animals was offered to S. Martin, who may have taken the place of a god, and ill-luck followed the non-observance of the custom. 897 The slaughter was followed by general feasting. This later slaughter may be traced back to the pastoral stage, in which the animals were regarded as divine, and one was slain annually and eaten sacramentally. Or, if the slaughter was more general, the animals would be propitiated. But when the animals ceased to be worshipped, the slaughter would certainly be more general, though still preserving traces of its original character. The pastoral sacrament may also have been connected with the slaying and eating of an animal representing the corn-spirit at harvest time. In one legend S. Martin is associated with the animal slain at Martinmas, and is said to have been cut up and eaten in the form of an ox, 898 as if a former divine animal had become an anthropomorphic divinity, the latter being merged in the personality of a Christian saint.

Other rites, connected with the Calends of January as a result of dislocation, point also in this direction. In Gaul and Germany riotous processions took place with men dressed in the heads and skins of animals. 899 This rite is said by Tille to have been introduced from Italy, but it is more likely to have been a native custom. 900 As the people ate the flesh of the slain animals sacramentally, so they clothed themselves in the skins to promote further contact with their divinity. Perambulating the township sunwise dressed in the skin of a cow took place until recently in the Hebrides at New Year, in order to keep off misfortune, a piece of the hide being burned and the smoke inhaled by each person and animal in the township. 901 Similar customs have been found in other Celtic districts, and these animal disguises can hardly be separated from the sacramental slaughter at Samhain. 902

Evils having been or being about to be cast off in the New Year ritual, a few more added to the number can make little difference. Hence among primitive peoples New Year is often characterised by orgiastic rites. These took place at the Calends in Gaul, and were denounced by councils and preachers. 903 In Ireland the merriment at Samhain is often mentioned in the texts, 904 and similar orgiastic rites lurk behind the Hallowe'en customs in Scotland and in the licence still permitted to youths in the quietest townships of the West Highlands at Samhain eve.

Samhain, as has been seen, was also a festival of the dead, whose ghosts were fed at this time. 905

As the powers of growth were in danger and in eclipse in winter, men thought it necessary to assist them. As a magical aid the Samhain bonfire was chief, and it is still lit in the Highlands. Brands were carried round, and from it the new fire was lit in each house. In North Wales people jumped through the fire, and when it was extinct, rushed away to escape the "black sow" who would take the hindmost. 906 The bonfire represented the sun, and was intended to strengthen it. But representing the sun, it had all the sun's force, hence those who jumped through it were strengthened and purified. The Welsh reference to the hindmost and to the black sow may point to a former human sacrifice, perhaps of any one who stumbled in jumping through the fire. Keating speaks of a Druidic sacrifice in the bonfire, whether of man or beast is not specified. 907 Probably the victim, like the scapegoat, was laden with the accumulated evils of the year, as in similar New Year customs elsewhere. Later belief regarded the sacrifice, if sacrifice there was, as offered to the powers of evil — the black sow, unless this animal is a reminiscence of the corn-spirit in its harmful aspect. Earlier powers, whether of growth or of blight, came to be associated with Samhain as demoniac beings — the "malignant bird flocks" which blighted crops and killed animals, the samhanach which steals children, and Mongfind the banshee, to whom "women and the rabble" make petitions on Samhain eve. 908 Witches, evil-intentioned fairies, and the dead were particularly active then.

Though the sacrificial victim had come to be regarded as an offering to the powers of blight, he may once have represented a divinity of growth or, in earlier times, the corn-spirit. Such a victim was slain at harvest, and harvest is often late in northern Celtic regions, while the slaying was sometimes connected not with the harvest field, but with the later threshing. This would bring it near the Samhain festival. The slaying of the corn-spirit was derived from the earlier slaying of a tree or vegetation-spirit embodied in a tree and also in a human or animal victim. The corn-spirit was embodied in the last sheaf cut as well as in an animal or human being. 909 This human victim may have been regarded as a king, since in late popular custom a mock king is chosen at winter festivals. 910 In other cases the effigy of a saint is hung up and carried round the different houses, part of the dress being left at each. The saint has probably succeeded to the traditional ritual of the divine victim. 911 The primitive period in which the corn-spirit was regarded as female, with a woman as her human representative, is also recalled in folk-custom. The last sheaf is called the Maiden or the Mother, while, as in Northamptonshire, girls choose a queen on S. Catharine's day, November 26th, and in some Christmas pageants "Yule's wife," as well as Yule, is present, corresponding to the May queen of the summer festival. 912 Men also masqueraded as women at the Calends. The dates of these survivals may be explained by that dislocation of the Samhain festival already pointed out. This view of the Samhain human sacrifices is supported by the Irish offerings to the Fomorians—gods of growth, later regarded as gods of blight, and to Cromm Cruaich, in both cases at Samhain. 913 With the evolution of religious thought, the slain victim came to be regarded as an offering to evil powers.

This aspect of Samhain, as a festival to promote and assist festivity, is further seen in the belief in the increased activity of fairies at that time. In Ireland, fairies are connected with the Tuatha Dé Danann, the divinities of growth, and in many folk-tales they are associated with agricultural processes. The use of evergreens at Christmas is perhaps also connected with the carrying of them round the fields in older times, as an evidence that the life of nature was not extinct. 914

Samhain may thus be regarded as, in origin, an old pastoral and agricultural festival, which in time came to be looked upon as affording assistance to the powers of growth in their conflict with the powers of blight. Perhaps some myth describing this combat may lurk behind the story of the battle of Mag-tured fought on Samhain between the Tuatha Dé Danann and the Fomorians. While the powers of blight are triumphant in winter, the Tuatha Déa are represented as the victors, though they suffer loss and death. Perhaps this enshrines the belief in the continual triumph of life and growth over blight and decay, or it may arise from the fact that Samhain was both a time of rejoicing for the ingathered harvest, and of wailing for the coming supremacy of winter and the reign of the powers of blight.

BELTANE

In Cormac's Glossary and other texts, "Beltane" is derived from bel-tene, "a goodly fire," or from bel-dine, because newly-born (dine) cattle were offered to Bel, an idol-god. 915 The latter is followed by those who believe in a Celtic Belus, connected with Baal. No such god is known, however, and the god Belenos is in no way connected with the Semitic divinity. M. D'Arbois assumes an unknown god of death, Beltene (from beltu, "to die"), whose festival Beltane was. 916 But Beltane was a festival of life, of the sun shining in his strength. Dr. Stokes gives a more acceptable explanation of the word. Its primitive form was belo-te[p]niâ, from belo-s, "clear," "shining," the root of the names Belenos and Belisama, and te[p]nos, "fire." Thus the word would mean something like "bright fire," perhaps the sun or the bonfire, or both. 917

The folk-survivals of the Beltane and Midsummer festivals show that both were intended to promote fertility.

One of the chief ritual acts at Beltane was the kindling of bonfires, often on hills. The house-fires in the district were often extinguished, the bonfire being lit by friction from a rotating wheel—the German "need-fire." 918 The fire kept off disease and evil, hence cattle were driven through it, or, according to Cormac, between two fires lit by Druids, in order to keep them in health during the year. 919 Sometimes the fire was lit beneath a sacred tree, or a pole covered with greenery was surrounded by the fuel, or a tree was burned in the fire. 920 These trees survive in the Maypole of later custom, and they represented the vegetation-spirit, to whom also the worshippers assimilated themselves by dressing in leaves. They danced sunwise round the fire or ran through the fields with blazing branches or wisps of straw, imitating the course of the sun, and thus benefiting the fields. 921 For the same reason the tree itself was probably borne through the fields. Houses were decked with boughs and thus protected by the spirit of vegetation. 922

An animal representing the spirit of vegetation may have been slain. In late survivals of Beltane at Dublin, a horse's skull and bones were thrown into the fire, 923 the attenuated form of an earlier sacrifice or slaying of a divine victim, by whom strength was transferred to all the animals which passed through the fire. In some cases a human victim may have been slain. This is suggested by customs surviving in Perthshire in the eighteenth century, when a cake was broken up and distributed, and the person who received a certain blackened portion was called the "Beltane carline" or "devoted." A pretence was made of throwing him into the fire, or he had to leap three times through it, and during the festival he was spoken of as "dead." 924 Martin says that malefactors were burned in the fire, 925 and though he cites no authority, this agrees with the Celtic use of criminals as victims. Perhaps the victim was at one time a human representative of the vegetation-spirit.

Beltane cakes or bannocks, perhaps made of the grain of the sacred last sheaf from the previous harvest, and therefore sacramental in character, were also used in different ways in folk-survivals. They were rolled down a slope—a magical imitative act, symbolising and aiding the course of the sun. The cake had also a divinatory character. If it broke on reaching the foot of the slope this indicated the approaching death of its owner. In another custom in Perthshire, part of a cake was thrown over the shoulder with the words, "This I give to thee, preserve thou my horses; this to thee, preserve thou my sheep; this to thee, O fox, preserve thou my lambs; this to thee, O hooded crow; this to thee, O eagle." Here there is an appeal to beneficial and noxious powers, whether this was the original intention of the rite. 926 But if the cakes were made of the last sheaf, they were probably at one time eaten sacramentally, their sacrificial use emerging later.

The bonfire was a sun-charm, representing and assisting the sun. Rain-charms were also used at Beltane. Sacred wells were visited and the ceremony performed with their waters, these perhaps being sprinkled over the tree or the fields to promote a copious rainfall for the benefit of vegetation. The use of such rites at Beltane and at other festivals may have given rise to the belief that wells were especially efficacious then for purposes of healing. The custom of rolling in the grass to benefit by May dew was probably connected with magical rites in which moisture played an important part. 927

The idea that the powers of growth had successfully combated those of blight may have been ritually represented. This is suggested by the mimic combats of Summer and Winter at this time, to which reference has already been made. Again, the May king and queen represent earlier personages who were regarded as embodying the spirits of vegetation and fertility at this festival, and whose marriage or union magically assisted growth and fertility, as in numerous examples of this ritual marriage elsewhere. 928 It may be assumed that a considerable amount of sexual licence also took place with the same magical purpose. Sacred marriage and festival orgy were an appeal to the forces of nature to complete their beneficial work, as well as a magical aid to them in that work. Analogy leads to the supposition that the king of the May was originally a priest-king, the incarnation of the spirit of vegetation. He or his surrogate was slain, while his bodily force was unabated, in order that it might be passed on undiminished to his successor. But the persistent place given to the May queen rather than to the king suggests the earlier prominence of women and of female spirits of fertility or of a great Mother-goddess in such rites. It is also significant that in the Perthshire ritual the man chosen was still called the Beltane carlane or cailleach ("old woman"). And if, as Professor Pearson maintains, witch orgies are survivals of old sex-festivals, then the popular belief in the activity of witches on Beltane eve, also shows that the festival had once been mainly one in which women took part. Such orgies often took place on hills which had been the sites of a cult in former times. 929

MIDSUMMER

The ritual of the Midsummer festival did not materially differ from that of Beltane, and as folk-survivals show, it was practised not only by the Celts, but by many other European peoples. It was, in fact, a primitive nature festival such as would readily be observed by all under similar psychic conditions and in like surroundings. A bonfire was again the central rite of this festival, the communal nature of which is seen in the fact that all must contribute materials to it. In local survivals, mayor and priest, representing the earlier local chief and priest, were present, while a service in church preceded the procession to the scene of the bonfire. Dancing sunwise round the fire to the accompaniment of songs which probably took the place of hymns or tunes in honour of the Sun-god, commonly occurred, and by imitating the sun's action, may have been intended to make it more powerful. The livelier the dance the better would be the harvest. 930 As the fire represented the sun, it possessed the purifying and invigorating powers of the sun; hence leaping through the fire preserved from disease, brought prosperity, or removed barrenness. Hence also cattle were driven through the fire. But if any one stumbled as he leaped, ill-luck was supposed to follow him. He was devoted to the fadets or spirits, 931 and perhaps, like the "devoted" Beltane victim, he may formerly have been sacrificed. Animal sacrifices are certainly found in many survivals, the victims being often placed in osier baskets and thrown into the fire. In other districts great human effigies of osier were carried in procession and burned. 932

The connection of such sacrifices with the periodical slaying of a representative of the vegetation-spirit has been maintained by Mannhardt and Dr. Frazer. 933 As has been seen, periodic sacrifices for the fertility of the land are mentioned by Cæsar, Strabo, and Diodorus, human victims and animals being enclosed in an osier image and burned. 934 These images survive in the osier effigies just referred to, while they may also be connected with the custom of decking the human representatives of the spirit of vegetation in greenery. The holocausts may be regarded as extensions of the earlier custom of slaying one victim, the incarnation of a vegetation-spirit. This slaying was gradually regarded as sacrificial, but as the beneficial effect of the sacrifice on growth was still believed in, it would naturally be thought that still better effects would be produced if many victims were offered. The victims were burned in a fire representing the sun, and vegetation was thus doubly benefited, by the victims and by the sun-god.

The oldest conception of the vegetation-spirit was that of a tree-spirit which had power over rain, sunshine, and every species of fruitfulness. For this reason a tree had a prominent place both in the Beltane and Midsummer feasts. It was carried in procession, imparting its benefits to each house or field. Branches of it were attached to each house for the same purpose. It was then burned, or it was set up to procure benefits to vegetation during the year and burned at the next Midsummer festival. 935 The sacred tree was probably an oak, and, as has been seen, the mistletoe rite probably took place on Midsummer eve, as a preliminary to cutting down the sacred tree and in order to secure the life or soul of the tree, which must first be secured before the tree could be cut down. The life of the tree was in the mistletoe, still alive in winter when the tree itself seemed to be dead. Such beliefs as this concerning the detachable soul or life survive in Märchen, and are still alive among savages. 936

Folk-survivals show that a human or an animal representative of the vegetation-spirit, brought into connection with the tree, was also slain or burned along with the tree. 937 Thus the cutting of the mistletoe would be regarded as a preliminary to the slaying of the human victim, who, like the tree, was the representative of the spirit of vegetation.

The bonfire representing the sun, and the victims, like the tree, representing the spirit of vegetation, it is obvious why the fire had healing and fertilising powers, and why its ashes and the ashes or the flesh of the victims possessed the same powers. Brands from the fire were carried through the fields or villages, as the tree had been, or placed on the fields or in houses, where they were carefully preserved for a year. All this aided growth and prosperity, just as the smoke of the fire, drifting over the fields, produced fertility. Ashes from the fire, and probably the calcined bones or even the flesh of the victims, were scattered on the fields or preserved and mixed with the seed corn. Again, part of the flesh may have been eaten sacramentally, since, as has been seen, Pliny refers to the belief of the Celts in the eating of human flesh as most wholesome.

In the Stone Age, as with many savages, a circle typified the sun, and as soon as the wheel was invented its rolling motion at once suggested that of the sun. In the Edda the sun is "the beautiful, the shining wheel," and similar expressions occur in the Vedas. Among the Celts the wheel of the sun was a favourite piece of symbolism, and this is seen in various customs at the Midsummer festival. A burning wheel was rolled down a slope or trundled through the fields, or burning brands were whirled round so as to give the impression of a fiery wheel. The intention was primarily to imitate the course of the sun through the heavens, and so, on the principle of imitative magic, to strengthen it. But also, as the wheel was rolled through the fields, so it was hoped that the direct beneficial action of the sun upon them would follow. Similar rites might be performed not only at Midsummer, but at other times, to procure blessing or to ward off evil, e.g. carrying fire round houses or fields or cattle or round a child deiseil or sunwise, 938 and, by a further extension of thought, the blazing wheel, or the remains of the burning brands thrown to the winds, had also the effect of carrying off accumulated evils. 939

Beltane and Midsummer thus appear as twin halves of a spring or early summer festival, the intention of which was to promote fertility and health. This was done by slaying the spirit of vegetation in his representative — tree, animal, or man. His death quickened the energies of earth and man. The fire also magically assisted the course of the sun. Survival of the ancient rites are or were recently found in all Celtic regions, and have been constantly combated by the Church. But though they were continued, their true meaning was forgotten, and they were mainly performed for luck or out of sheer conservatism. Sometimes a Christian aspect was given to them, e.g. by connecting the fires with S. John, or by associating the rites with the service of the Church, or by the clergy being present at them. But their true nature was still evident as acts of pagan worship and magic which no veneer of Christianity could ever quite conceal. 940

LUGNASAD

The 1st of August, coming midway between Beltane and Samhain, was an important festival among the Celts. In Christian times the day became Lammas, but its name still survives in Irish as Lugnasad, in Gaelic as Lunasdal or Lunasduinn, and in Manx as Laa Luanys, and it is still observed as a fair or feast in many districts. Formerly assemblies at convenient centres were held on this day, not only for religious purposes, but for commerce and pleasure, both of these being of course saturated with religion. "All Ireland" met at Taillti, just as "all Gaul" met at Lugudunum, "Lug's town," or Lyons, in honour of Augustus, though the feast there had formerly been in honour of the god Lugus. 941 The festival was here Romanised, as it was also in Britain, where its name appears as Goel-aoust, Gul-austus, and Gwyl Awst, now the "August feast," but formerly the "feast of Augustus," the name having replaced one corresponding to Lugnasad. 942

Cormac explains the name Lugnasad as a festival of Lugh mac Ethlenn, celebrated by him in the beginning of autumn, and the Rennes Dindsenchas accounts for its origin by saying that Lug's foster-mother, Tailtiu, having died on the Calends of August, he directed an assembly for lamentation to be held annually on that day at her tomb. 943 Lug is thus the founder of his own festival, for that it was his, and not Tailtiu's, is clear from the fact that his name is attached to it. As Lammas was a Christian harvest thanksgiving, so also was Lugnasad a pagan harvest feast, part of the ritual of which passed over to Samhain. The people made glad before the sun-god—Lug perhaps having that character—who had assisted them in the growth of the things on which their lives depended. Marriages were also arranged at this feast, probably because men had now more leisure and more means for entering upon matrimony. Possibly promiscuous love-making also occurred as a result of the festival gladness, agricultural districts being still notoriously immoral. Some evidence points to the connection of the feast with Lug's marriage, though this has been allegorised into his wedding the "sovereignty of Erin." Perhaps we have here a hint of the rite of the sacred marriage, for the purpose of magically fertilising the fields against next year's sowing.

Due observance of the feast produced abundance of corn, fruit, milk, and fish. Probably the ritual observed included the preservation of the last sheaf as representing the corn-spirit, giving some of it to the cattle to strengthen them, and mingling it with next year's corn to impart to it the power of the corn-spirit. It may also have included the slaying of an animal or human incarnation of the corn-spirit, whose flesh and blood quickened the soil and so produced abundance next year, or, when partaken of by the worshippers, brought blessings to them. To neglect such rites, abundant instances of which exist in folk-custom, would be held to result in scarcity. This would also explain, as already suggested, why the festival was associated with the death of Tailtiu or of Carman. The euhemerised queen-goddess Tailtiu and the woman Carman had once been corn-goddesses, evolved from more primitive corn-spirits, and slain at the feast in their female representatives. The story of their death and burial at the festival was a dim memory of this ancient rite, and since the festival was also connected with the sun-god Lug, it was easy to bring him into relationship with the earlier goddess. Elsewhere the festival, in its memorial aspect, was associated with a king, probably because male victims had come to be representatives of a corn-god who had taken the place of the goddess.

Some of the ritual of these festivals is illustrated by scattered notices in classical writers, and on the whole they support our theory that the festivals originated in a female cult of spirits or goddesses of fertility. Strabo speaks of sacrifices offered to Demeter and Kore, according to the ritual followed at Samothrace, in an island near Britain, i.e. to native goddesses equated with them. He also describes the ritual of the Namnite women on an island in the Loire. They are called Bacchantes because they conciliated Bacchus with mysteries and sacrifices; in other words, they observed an orgiastic cult of a god equated with Bacchus. No man must set foot on the island, but the women left it once a year for intercourse with the other sex. Once a year the temple of the god was unroofed, and roofed again before sunset. If any woman dropped her load of materials (and it was said this always happened), she was torn in pieces and her limbs carried round the temple. 944 Dionysius Periegetes says the women were crowned with ivy, and celebrated their mysteries by night in honour of Earth and Proserpine with great clamour. 945 Pliny also makes a reference to British rites in which nude women and girls took part, their bodies stained with woad. 946

At a later time, S. Gregory of Tours speaks of the image of a goddess Berecynthia drawn on a litter through the streets, fields, and vineyards of Augustodunum on the days of her festival, or when the fields were threatened with scarcity. The people danced and sang before it. The image was covered with a white veil. 947 Berecynthia has been conjectured by Professor Anwyl to be the goddess Brigindu, worshipped at Valnay. 948

These rites were all directed towards divinities of fertility. But in harvest customs in Celtic Scotland and elsewhere two sheaves of corn were called respectively the Old Woman and the Maiden, the corn-spirit of the past year and that of the year to come, and corresponding to Demeter and Kore in early Greek agricultural ritual. As in Greece, so among the Celts, the primitive corn-spirits had probably become more individualised goddesses with an elaborate cult, observed on an island or at other sacred spots. The cult probably varied here and there, and that of a god of fertility may have taken the place of the cult of goddesses. A god was worshipped by the Namnite women, according to Strabo, goddesses according to Dionysius. The mangled victim was probably regarded as representative of a divinity, and perhaps part of the flesh was mixed with the seed-corn, like the grain of the Maiden sheaf, or buried in the earth. This rite is common among savages, and its presence in old European ritual is attested by survivals. That these rites were tabu to men probably points to the fact that they were examples of an older general custom, in which all such rites were in the hands of women who cultivated the earth, and who were the natural priestesses of goddesses of growth and fertility, of vegetation and the growing corn. Another example is found in the legend and procession of Godiva at Coventry—the survival of a pagan cult from which men were excluded. 949

Pliny speaks of the nudity of the women engaged in the cult. Nudity is an essential part of all primitive agricultural rites, and painting the body is also a widespread ritual act. Dressing with leaves or green stuff, as among the Namnite women, and often with the intention of personating the spirit of vegetation, is also customary. By unveiling the body, and especially the sexual organs, women more effectually represented the goddess of fertility, and more effectually as her representatives, or through their own powers, magically conveyed fertility to the fields. Nakedness thus became a powerful magico-religious symbol, and it is found as part of the ritual for producing rain. 950

There is thus abundant evidence of the cult of fertility, vegetation, and corn-spirits, who tended to become divinities, male or female. Here and there, through conservatism, the cult remained in the hands of women, but more generally it had become a ritual in which both men and women took part—that of the great agricultural festivals. Where a divinity had taken the place of the vaguer spirits, her image, like that of Berecynthia, was used in the ritual, but the image was probably the successor of the tree which embodied the vegetation-spirit, and was carried through the fields to fertilise them. Similar processions of images, often accompanied by a ritual washing of the image in order to invigorate the divinity, or, as in the similar May-day custom, to produce rain, are found in the Teutonic cult of Nerthus, the Phrygian of Cybele, the Hindu of Bhavani, and the Roman ritual of the Bona Dea. The image of Berecynthia was thus probably washed also. Washing the images of saints, usually to produce rain, has sometimes taken the place of the washing of a divine image, and similarly the relics of a saint are carried through a field, as was the tree or image. The community at Iona perambulated a newly sown field with S. Columba's relics in time of drought, and shook his tunic three times in the air, and were rewarded by a plentiful rain, and later, by a bounteous harvest. 951

Many of these local cults were pre-Celtic, but we need not therefore suppose that the Celts, or the Aryans as a whole, had no such cults. 952 The Aryans everywhere adopted local cults, but this they would not have done if, as is supposed, they had themselves outgrown them. The cults were local, but the Celts had similar local cults, and easily accepted those of the people they conquered. We cannot explain the persistence of such primitive cults as lie behind the great Celtic festivals, both in classical times and over the whole area of Europe among the peasantry, by referring them solely to a pre-Aryan folk. They were as much Aryan as pre-Aryan. They belong to those unchanging strata of religion which have so largely supplied the soil in which its later and more spiritual growths have flourished. And among these they still emerge, unchanged and unchanging, like the gaunt outcrops of some ancient rock formation amid rich vegetation and fragrant flowers.

Footnote 889: Pliny, xvi. 45; Cæsar, vi. 18. See my article "Calendar (Celtic)" in Hastings' Encyclopædia of Rel. and Ethics, iii. 78 f., for a full discussion of the problems involved.

Footnote 890: O'Donovan, Book of Rights, Intro. lii f.

Footnote 891: O'Donovan, li.; Bertrand, 105; Keating, 300.

Footnote 892: Samhain may mean "summer-end," from sam, "summer," and fuin, "sunset" or "end," but Dr. Stokes (US 293) makes samani- mean "assembly," i.e. the gathering of the people to keep the feast.

Footnote 893: Keating, 125, 300.

Footnote 894: See MacBain, CM ix. 328.

Footnote 895: Brand, i. 390; Ramsay, Scotland and Scotsmen in the Eighteenth Century, ii. 437; Stat. Account, xi. 621.

Footnote 896: Hazlitt, 297-298, 340; Campbell, Witchcraft, 285 f.

Footnote 897: Curtin, 72.

Footnote 898: Fitzgerald, RC vi. 254.

Footnote 899: See Chambers, Mediæval Stage, App. N, for the evidence from canons and councils regarding these.

Footnote 900: Tille, Yule and Christmas, 96.

Footnote 901: Chambers, Popular Rhymes, 166.

Footnote 902: Hutchinson, View of Northumberland, ii. 45; Thomas, Rev. de l'Hist. des Rel. xxxviii. 335 f.

Footnote 903: Patrol. Lot. xxxix. 2001.

Footnote 904: IT i. 205; RC v. 331; Leahy, i. 57.

Footnote 905: supra.

Footnote 906: The writer has himself seen such bonfires in the Highlands. See also Hazlitt, 298; Pennant, Tour, ii. 47; Rh[^y]s, HL 515, CFL i. 225-226. In Egyptian mythology, Typhon assailed Horus in the form of a black swine.

Footnote 907: Keating, 300.

Footnote 908: Joyce, SH ii. 556; RC x. 214, 225, xxiv. 172; O'Grady, ii. 374; CM ix. 209.

Footnote 909: See Mannhardt, Mythol. Forschung. 333 f.; Frazer, Adonis, passim; Thomas, Rev. de l'Hist. des Rel. xxxviii. 325 f.

Footnote 910: Hazlitt, 35; Chambers, Mediæval Stage, i. 261.

Footnote 911: Chambers, Book of Days, ii. 492; Hazlitt, 131.

Footnote 912: Hazlitt, 97; Davies, Extracts from Munic. Records of York, 270.

Footnote 913: supra; LL 16, 213.

Footnote 914: Chambers, Med. Stage, i. 250 f.

Footnote 915: Cormac, s.v. "Belltaine," "Bel"; Arch. Rev. i. 232.

Footnote 916: D'Arbois, ii. 136.

Footnote 917: Stokes, US 125, 164. See his earlier derivation, dividing the word into belt, connected with Lithuan. baltas, "white," and aine, the termination in sechtmaine, "week" (TIG xxxv.).

Footnote 918: Need-fire (Gael. Teinne-eiginn, "necessity fire") was used to kindle fire in time of cattle plague. See Grimm, Teut. Myth. 608 f.; Martin, 113; Jamieson's Dictionary, s.v. "neidfyre."

Footnote 919: Cormac, s.v.; Martin, 105, says that the Druids extinguished all fires until their dues were paid. This may have been a tradition in the Hebrides.

Footnote 920: Joyce, PN i. 216; Hone, Everyday Book, i. 849, ii. 595.

Footnote 921: Pennant, Tour in Scotland, i. 291.

Footnote 922: Hazlitt, 339, 397.

Footnote 923: Hone, Everyday Book, ii. 595. supra.

Footnote 924: Sinclair, Stat. Account, xi. 620.

Footnote 925: Martin, 105.

Footnote 926: For these usages see Ramsay, Scotland and Scotsmen in the Eighteenth Century, ii. 439 f.; Sinclair, Stat. Account, v. 84, xi. 620, xv. 517. For the sacramental and sacrificial use of similar loaves, see Frazer, Golden Bough 2, i. 94, ii. 78; Grimm, Teut. Myth. iii. 1239 f.

Footnote 927: New Stat. Account, Wigtownshire, 208; Hazlitt, 38, 323, 340.

Footnote 928: See Miss Owen, Folk-lore of the Musquakie Indians, 50; Frazer, Golden Bough 2, ii. 205.

Footnote 929: For notices of Beltane survivals see Keating, 300; Campbell, Journey from Edinburgh, i. 143; Ramsay, Scotland and Scotsmen, ii. 439 f.; Old Stat. Account, v. 84, xi. 620, xv. 517; Gregor, Folk-lore of N.E. of Scotland, 167. The paganism of the survivals is seen in the fact that Beltane fires were frequently prohibited by Scottish ecclesiastical councils.

Footnote 930: Meyrac, Traditions ... des Ardennes, 68.

Footnote 931: Bertrand, 119.

Footnote 932: Ibid. 407; Gaidoz, 21; Mannhardt, Baumkultus, 514, 523; Brand, i. 8, 323.

Footnote 933: Mannhardt, op. cit. 525 f.; Frazer, Golden Bough 2, iii. 319.

Footnote 934: supra.

Footnote 935: Frazer, op. cit. i. 74; Brand, i. 222, 237, 246, 318; Hone, Everyday Book, ii. 595; Mannhardt, op. cit. 177; Grimm, Teut. Myth. 621, 777 f.

Footnote 936: See my Childhood of Fiction, ch. v.

Footnote 937: Frazer, i. 82, ii. 247 f., 275; Mannhardt, 315 f.

Footnote 938: Martin, 117. The custom of walking deiseil round an object still survives, and, as an imitation of the sun's course, it is supposed to bring good luck or ward off evil. For the same rrrreason the right hand turn was of good augury. Medb's charioteer, as she departed for the war, made her chariot turn to the right to repel evil omens (LU 55). Curiously enough, Pliny (xxviii. 2) says that the Gauls preferred the left-hand turn in their religious rites, though Athenæus refers to the right-hand turn among them. Deiseil is from dekso-s, "right," and svel, "to turn."

Footnote 939: Hone, i. 846; Hazlitt, ii. 346.

Footnote 940: This account of the Midsummer ritual is based on notices found in Hone, Everyday Book; Hazlitt, ii. 347 f.; Gaidoz, Le Dieu Soleil; Bertrand; Deloche, RC ix. 435; Folk-Lore, xii. 315; Frazer, Golden Bough 2, iii. 266 f.; Grimm, Teut. Myth. ii. 617 f.; Monnier, 186 f.

Footnote 941: RC xvi. 51; Guiraud, Les Assemblées provinciales dans l'Empire Romain.

Footnote 942: D'Arbois, i. 215, Les Celtes, 44; Loth, Annales de Bretagne, xiii. No. 2.

Footnote 943: RC xvi. 51.

Footnote 944: Strabo, iv. 4. 6.

Footnote 945: Dion. Per. v. 570.

Footnote 946: Pliny, xxii. 1.

Footnote 947: Greg, de Glor. Conf. 477; Sulp. Sev. Vita S. Martini, 9; Pass. S. Symphor. Migne, Pat. Graec. v. 1463, 1466. The cult of Cybele had been introduced into Gaul, and the ritual here described resembles it, but we are evidently dealing here with the cult of a native goddess. See, however, Frazer, Adonis, 176.

Footnote 948: Anwyl, Celtic Religion, 41.

Footnote 949: See Hartland, Science of Fairy-Tales, 84 f.

Footnote 950: Professor Rh[^y]s suggests that nudity, being a frequent symbol of submission to a conqueror, acquired a similar significance in religious rites (AL 180). But the magical aspect of nudity came first in time.

Footnote 951: Adamnan, Vita S. Col. ii. 45.

Footnote 952: See Gomme, Ethnology in Folk-lore, 30 f., Village Community, 114.

CHAPTER XIX
ACCESSORIES OF CULT

TEMPLES

In primitive religion the place of worship is seldom a temple made with hands, but rather an enclosed space in which the symbol or image of the god stands. The sacredness of the god makes the place of his cult sacred. Often an open space in the forest is the scene of the regular cult. There the priests perform the sacred rites; none may enter it but themselves; and the trembling worshipper approaches it with awe lest the god should slay him if he came too near.

The earliest temples of the Gauls were sacred groves, one of which, near Massilia, is described by Lucan. No bird built in it, no animal lurked near, the leaves constantly shivered when no breeze stirred them. Altars stood in its midst, and the images of the gods were misshapen trunks of trees. Every tree was stained with sacrificial blood. The poet then describes marvels heard or seen in the grove—the earth groaning, dead yews reviving, trees surrounded with flame yet not consumed, and huge serpents twining round the oaks. The people feared to approach the grove, and even the priest would not walk there at midday or midnight lest he should then meet its divine guardian. 953 Dio speaks of human sacrifices offered to Andrasta in a British grove, and in 61 A.D. the woods of Mona, devoted to strange rites, were cut down by Roman soldiers. 954 The sacred Dru-nemeton of the Galatian Celts may have been a grove. 955 Place-names also point to the widespread existence of such groves, since the word nemeton, "grove," occurs in many of them, showing that the places so called had been sites of a cult. In Ireland, fid-nemed stood for "sacred grove." 956 The ancient groves were still the objects of veneration in Christian times, though fines were levied against those who still clung to the old ways. 957

Sacred groves were still used in Gallo-Roman times, and the Druids may have had a preference for them, a preference which may underlie the words of the scholiast on Lucan, that "the Druids worship the gods without temples in woods." But probably more elaborate temples, great tribal sanctuaries, existed side by side with these local groves, especially in Cisalpine Gaul, where the Boii had a temple in which were stored the spoils of war, while the Insubri had a similar temple. 958 These were certainly buildings. The "consecrated place" in Transalpine Gaul, which Cæsar mentions, and where at fixed periods judgments were given, might be either a grove or a temple. Cæsar uses the same phrase for sacred places where the spoils of war were heaped; these may have been groves, but Diodorus speaks of treasure collected in "temples and sacred places" ([Greek: en tois hierois chai temenesin]), and Plutarch speaks of the "temple" where the Arverni hung Cæsar's sword. 959 The "temple" of the Namnite women, unroofed and re-roofed in a day, must have been a building. There is no evidence that the insular Celts had temples. In Gallo-Roman times, elaborate temples, perhaps occupying sites of earlier groves or temples, sprang up over the Romano-Celtic area. They were built on Roman models, many of them were of great size, and they were dedicated to Roman or Gallo-Roman divinities. 960 Smaller shrines were built by grateful worshippers at sacred springs to their presiding divinity, as many inscriptions show. In the temples stood images of the gods, and here were stored sacred vessels, sometimes made of the skulls of enemies, spoils of war dedicated to the gods, money collected for sacred purposes, and war standards, especially those which bore divine symbols.

The old idea that stone circles were Druidic temples, that human sacrifices were offered on the "altar-stone," and libations of blood poured into the cup-markings, must be given up, along with much of the astronomical lore associated with the circles. Stonehenge dates from the close of the Neolithic Age, and most of the smaller circles belong to the early Bronze Age, and are probably pre-Celtic. In any case they were primarily places of sepulture. As such they would be the scene of ancestor worship, but yet not temples in the strict sense of the word. The larger circles, burial-places of great chiefs or kings, would become central places for the recurring rites of ghost-worship, possibly also rallying places of the tribe on stated occasions. But whether this ghost-worship was ever transmuted into the cult of a god at the circles is uncertain and, indeed, unlikely. The Celts would naturally regard these places as sacred, since the ghosts of the dead, even those of a vanquished people, are always dangerous, and they also took over the myths and legends 961 associated with them, such, e.g., as regarded the stones themselves, or trees growing within the circles, as embodiments of the dead, while they may also have used them as occasional places of secondary interment. Whether they were ever led to copy such circles themselves is uncertain, since their own methods of interment seem to have been different. We have seen that the gods may in some cases have been worshipped at tumuli, and that Lugnasad was, at some centres, connected with commemorative cults at burial-places (mounds, not circles). But the reasons for this are obscure, nor is there any hint that other Celtic festivals were held near burial mounds. Probably such commemorative rites at places of sepulture during Lugnasad were only part of a wider series occurring elsewhere, and we cannot assume from such vague notices that stone circles were Druidic temples where worship of an Oriental nature was carried on.

Professor Rh[^y]s is disposed to accept the old idea that Stonehenge was the temple of Apollo in the island of the Hyperboreans, mentioned by Diodorus, where the sun-god was worshipped. 962 But though that temple was circular, it had walls adorned with votive offerings. Nor does the temple unroofed yearly by the Namnite women imply a stone circle, for there is not the slightest particle of evidence that the circles were ever roofed in any way. 963 Stone circles with mystic trees growing in them, one of them with a well by which entrance was gained to Tír fa Tonn, are mentioned in Irish tales. They were connected with magic rites, but are not spoken of as temples. 964

ALTARS

Lucan describes realistically the awful sacrifices of the Gauls on cruel altars not a whit milder than those of Diana, and he speaks of "altars piled with offerings" in the sacred grove at Marseilles. 965 Cicero says that human victims were sacrificed on altars, and Tacitus describes the altars of Mona smeared with human blood. 966 "Druids' altars" are mentioned in the Irish "Expedition of Dathi," and Cormac speaks of indelba, or altars adorned with emblems. 967 Probably many of these altars were mere heaps of stone like the Norse horg, or a great block of stone. Some sacrifices, however, were too extensive to be offered on an altar, but in such cases the blood would be sprinkled upon it. Under Roman influence, Celtic altars took the form of those of the conquerors, with inscriptions containing names of native or Roman gods and bas-reliefs depicting some of these. The old idea that dolmens were Celtic altars is now abandoned. They were places of sepulture of the Neolithic or early Bronze Age, and were originally covered with a mound of earth. During the era of Celtic paganism they were therefore hidden from sight, and it is only in later times that the earth has been removed and the massive stones, arranged so as to form a species of chamber, have been laid bare.

IMAGES

The Gauls, according to Cæsar, possessed plurima simulacra of the native Mercury, but he does not refer to images of other gods. We need not infer from this that the Celts had a prejudice against images, for among the Irish Celts images are often mentioned, and in Gaul under Roman rule many images existed.

The existence of images among the Celts as among other peoples, may owe something to the cult of trees and of stones set up over the dead. The stone, associated with the dead man's spirit, became an image of himself, perhaps rudely fashioned in his likeness. A rough-hewn tree trunk became an image of the spirit or god of trees. On the other hand, some anthropomorphic images, like the palæolithic or Mycenæan figurines, may have been fashioned without the intermediary of tree-trunk or stone pillar. Maximus of Tyre says that the Celtic image of Zeus was a lofty oak, perhaps a rough-hewn trunk rather than a growing tree, and such roughly carved tree-trunks, images of gods, are referred to by Lucan in his description of the Massilian grove. 968 Pillar stones set up over the graves of the dead are often mentioned in Irish texts. These would certainly be associated with the dead; indeed, existing legends show that they were believed to be tenanted by the ghosts and to have the power of motion. This suggests that they had been regarded as images of the dead. Other stones honoured in Ireland were the cloch labrais, an oracular stone; the lia fail, or coronation stone, which shouted when a king of the Milesian race seated himself upon it; and the lia adrada, or stone of adoration, apparently a boundary stone. 969 The plurima simulacra of the Gaulish Mercury may have been boundary stones like those dedicated to Mercury or Hermes among the Romans and Greeks. Did Cæsar conclude, or was it actually the case, that the Gauls dedicated such stones to a god of boundaries who might be equated with Mercury? Many such standing stones still exist in France, and their number must have been greater in Cæsar's time. Seeing them the objects of superstitious observances, he may have concluded that they were simulacra of a god. Other Romans besides himself had been struck by the resemblance of these stones to their Hermai, and perhaps the Gauls, if they did not already regard them as symbols of a god, acquiesced in the resemblance. Thus, on the menhir of Kervadel are sculptured four figures, one being that of Mercury, dating from Gallo-Roman times. Beneath another, near Peronne, a bronze statuette of Mercury was discovered. 970 This would seem to show that the Gauls had a cult of pillar stones associated with a god of boundaries. Cæsar probably uses the word simulacrum in the sense of "symbol" rather than "image," though he may have meant native images not fully carved in human shape, like the Irish cérmand, cerstach, ornamented with gold and silver, the "chief idol" of north Ireland, or like the similarly ornamented "images" of Cromm Cruaich and his satellites. 971 The adoration of sacred stones continued into Christian times and was much opposed by the Church. 972 S. Samson of

Dol (sixth century) found men dancing round a simulacrum abominabile, which seems to have been a kind of standing stone, and having besought them to desist, he carved a cross upon it. 973 Several menhirion in France are now similarly ornamented. 974

The number of existing Gallo-Roman images shows that the Celts had not adopted a custom which was foreign to them, and they must have already possessed rude native images. The disappearance of these would be explained if they were made of perishable material. Wooden images of the Matres have been occasionally found, and these may be pre-Roman. Some of the images of the three-headed and crouching gods show no sign of Roman influences in their modelling, and they may have been copied from earlier images of wood. We also find divine figures on pre-Roman coins. 975 Certain passages in classical writings point to the existence of native images. A statue of a goddess existed in a temple at Marseilles, according to Justin, and the Galatian Celts had images of the native Juppiter and Artemis, while the conquering Celts who entered Rome bowed to the seated senators as to statues of the gods. 976 The Gauls placed rich ornaments on the images of the gods, and presumably these were native "idols."

"Idols" are frequently mentioned in Irish texts, and there is no doubt that these mean images. 977 Cormac mac Art refused to worship "idols," and was punished by the Druids. 978 The idols of Cromm Cruaich and his satellites, referred to in the Dindsenchas, were carved to represent the human form; the chief one was of gold, the others of stone. These were miraculously overthrown by S. Patrick; but in the account of the miracle the chief idol was of stone adorned with gold and silver, the others, numbering twelve, were ornamented with bronze. 979 They stood in Mag Slecht, and similar sacred places with groups of images evidently existed elsewhere, e.g. at Rath Archaill, "where the Druid's altars and images are." 980 The lady Cessair, before coming to Ireland, is said to have taken advice of her laimh-dhia, or "hand gods," perhaps small images used for divination. 981

For the British Celts the evidence is slender, but idolatry in the sense of "image-worship" is frequently mentioned in the lives of early saints. 982 Gildas also speaks of images "mouldering away within and without the deserted temples, with stiff and deformed features." 983 This pathetic picture of the forsaken shrines of forgotten gods may refer to Romano-Celtic images, but the "stiff and deformed features" suggest rather native art, the art of a people unskilful at reproducing the human form, however artistic they may have been in other directions.

If the native Celts of Ireland had images, there is no reason to suppose, especially considering the evidence just adduced, that the Gauls, or at least the Druids, were antagonistic to images. This last is M. Reinach's theory, part of a wider hypothesis that the Druids were pre-Celtic, but became the priests of the Celts, who till then had no priests. The Druids prohibited image-worship, and this prohibition existed in Gaul, ex hypothesi, from the end of palæolithic times. Pythagoras and his school were opposed to image-worship, and the classical writers claimed a connection between the Pythagoreans and the Druids. M. Reinach thinks there must have been some analogy between them, and that was hostility to anthropomorphism. But the analogy is distinctly stated to have lain in the doctrine of immortality or metempsychosis. Had the Druids been opposed to image-worship, classical observers could not have failed to notice the fact. M. Reinach then argues that the Druids caused the erection of the megalithic monuments in Gaul, symbols not images. They are thus Druidic, though not Celtic. The monuments argue a powerful priesthood; the Druids were a powerful priesthood; therefore the Druids caused the monuments to be built. This is not a powerful argument! 984

As has been seen, some purely Celtic images existed in Gaul. The Gauls, who used nothing but wood for their houses, probably knew little of the art of carving stone. They would therefore make most of their images of wood — a perishable material. The insular Celts had images, and if, as Cæsar maintained, the Druids came from Britain to Gaul, this points at least to a similarity of cult in the two regions. Youthful Gauls who aspired to Druidic knowledge went to Britain to obtain it. Would the Druids of Gaul have permitted this, had they been iconoclasts? No single text shows that the Druids had any antipathy to images, while the Gauls certainly had images of worshipful animals. Further, even if the Druids were priests of a pre-Celtic folk, they must have permitted the making of images, since many "menhir-statues" exist on French soil, at Aveyron, Tarn, and elsewhere. 985 The Celts were in constant contact with image-worshipping peoples, and could hardly have failed to be influenced by them, even if such a priestly prohibition existed, just as Israel succumbed to images in spite of divine commands. That they would have been thus influenced is seen from the number of images of all kinds dating from the period after the Roman conquest.

Incidental proofs of the fondness of the Celts for images are found in ecclesiastical writings and in late survivals. The procession of the image of Berecynthia has already been described, and such processions were common in Gaul, and imply a regular folk-custom. S. Martin of Tours stopped a funeral procession believing it to be such a pagan rite. 986 Councils and edicts prohibited these processions in Gaul, but a more effectual way was to Christianise them. The Rogation tide processions with crucifix and Madonna, and the carrying of S. John's image at the Midsummer festivals, were a direct continuation of the older practices. Images were often broken by Christian saints in Gaul, as they had been over-turned by S. Patrick in Ireland. "Stiff and deformed" many of them must have been, if one may judge from the Groah-goard or "Venus of Quinipily," for centuries the object of superstitious rites in Brittany. 987 With it may be compared the fetich-stone or image of which an old woman in the island of Inniskea, the guardian of a sacred well, had charge. It was kept wrapped up to hide it from profane eyes, but at certain periods it was brought out for adoration. 988

The images and bas-reliefs of the Gallo-Roman period fall mainly into two classes. In the first class are those representing native divinities, like Esus, Tarvos Trigaranos, Smertullos, Cernunnos, the horned and crouching gods, the god with the hammer, and the god with the wheel. Busts and statues of some water-goddesses exist, but more numerous are the representations of Epona. One of these is provided with a box pedestal in which offerings might be placed. The Matres are frequently figured, usually as three seated figures with baskets of fruit or flowers, or with one or more infants, like the Madonna. Images of triple-headed gods, supposed to be Cernunnos, have been found, but are difficult to place in any category. 989

To the images of the second class is usually attached the Roman name of a god, but generally the native Celtic name is added, but the images themselves are of the traditional Roman type. Among statues and statuettes of bronze, that of Mercury occurs most often. This may point to the fact that Cæsar's simulacra of the native Mercury were images, and that the old preference for representing this god continued in Roman times. Small figures of divinities in white clay have been found in large numbers, and may have been ex votos or images of household lararia. 990

SYMBOLS

Images of the gods in Gaul can be classified by means of their symbols — the mallet and cup (a symbol of plenty) borne by the god with the hammer, the wheel of the sun-god, the cornucopia and torque carried by Cernunnos. Other symbols occur on images, altars, monuments, and coins. These are the swastika and triskele, probably symbols of the sun; 991 single or concentric circles, sometimes with rays; 992 crosses; and a curious S figure. The triskele and the circles are sometimes found on faces figured on coins. They may therefore have been tattoo markings of a symbolic character. The circle and cross are often incised on bronze images of Dispater. Much speculation has been aroused by the S figure, which occurs on coins, while nine models of this symbol hang from a ring carried by the god with the wheel, but the most probable is that which sees in it a thunderbolt. 993 But lacking any old text interpreting these various symbols, all explanations of them must be conjectural. Some of them are not purely Celtic, but are of world-wide occurrence.

CULT OF WEAPONS

Here some reference may be made to the Celtic cult of weapons. As has been seen, a hammer is the symbol of one god, and it is not unlikely that a cult of the hammer had preceded that of the god to whom the hammer was given as a symbol. Esus is also represented with an axe. We need not repeat what has already been said regarding the primitive and universal cult of hammer or axe, 994 but it is interesting to notice, in connection with other evidence for a Celtic cult of weapons, that there is every reason to believe that the phrase sub ascia dedicare, which occurs in inscriptions on tombs from Gallia Lugdunensis, usually with the figure of an axe incised on the stone, points to the cult of the axe, or of a god whose symbol the axe was. 995 In Irish texts the power of speech is attributed to weapons, but, according to the Christian scribe, this was because demons spoke from them, for the people worshipped arms in those days. 996 Thus it may have been believed that spirits tenanted weapons, or that weapons had souls. Evidence of the cult itself is found in the fact that on Gaulish coins a sword is figured, stuck in the ground, or driving a chariot, or with a warrior dancing before it, or held in the hand of a dancing warrior. 997 The latter are ritual acts, and resemble that described by Spenser as performed by Irish warriors in his day, who said prayers or incantations before a sword stuck in the earth. 998 Swords were also addressed in songs composed by Irish bards, and traditional remains of such songs are found in Brittany. 999 They represent the chants of the ancient cult. Oaths were taken by weapons, and the weapons were believed to turn against those who lied. 1000 The magical power of weapons, especially of those over which incantations had been said, is frequently referred to in traditional tales and Irish texts. 1001 A reminiscence of the cult or of the magical power of weapons may be found in the wonderful "glaives of light" of Celtic folk-tales, and the similar mystical weapon of the Arthurian romances.

Footnote 953: Lucan, Pharsalia, iii. 399 f.

Footnote 954: Dio Cass. lxii. 7; Tac. Ann. xiv. 30.

Footnote 955: Strabo, xii. 51. Drunemeton may mean "great temple" (D'Arbois, Les Celtes, 203).

Footnote 956: Antient Laws of Ireland, i. 164.

Footnote 957: Holder, ii. 712. Cf. "Indiculus" in Grimm, Teut. Myth. 1739, "de sacris silvarum, quas nimidas (= nemeta) vocant."

Footnote 958: Livy, xxiii. 24; Polyb. ii. 32.

Footnote 959: Cæsar, vi. 13, 17; Diod. Sic. v. 27; Plutarch, Cæsar, 26.

Footnote 960: See examples in Dom Martin, i. 134 f.; cf. Greg. Tours, Hist. Franc. i. 30.

Footnote 961: See Reinach, "Les monuments de pierre brute dans le langage et les croyances populaires," Rev. Arch. 1893, i. 339; Evans, "The Roll-Right Stones," Folk-Lore, vi. 20 f.

Footnote 962: Rh[^y]s, HL 194; Diod. Sic. ii. 47.

Footnote 963: Rh[^y]s, 197.

Footnote 964: Joyce, OCR 246; Kennedy, 271.

Footnote 965: Lucan, i. 443, iii. 399f.

Footnote 966: Cicero, pro Fonteio, x. 21; Tac. Ann. xiv. 30. Cf. Pomp. Mela, iii. 2. 18.

Footnote 967: O'Curry, MS. Mat. 284; Cormac, 94. Cf. IT iii. 211, for the practice of circumambulating altars.

Footnote 968: Max. Tyr. Dissert. viii. 8; Lucan, iii. 412f.

Footnote 969: Antient Laws of Ireland, iv. 142.

Footnote 970: Rev. Arch. i. pl. iii-v.; Reinach, RC xi. 224, xiii. 190.

Footnote 971: Stokes, Martyr. of Oengus, 186-187.

Footnote 972: See the Twenty-third Canon of Council of Arles, the Twenty-third of the Council of Tours, 567, and ch. 65 of the Capitularia, 789.

Footnote 973: Mabillon, Acta, i. 177.

Footnote 974: Reinach, Rev. Arch. 1893, xxi. 335.

Footnote 975: Blanchet, i. 152-153, 386.

Footnote 976: Justin, xliii. 5; Strabo, xii. 5. 2; Plutarch, de Virt. Mul. xx.; Livy, v. 41.

Footnote 977: Cormac, 94.

Footnote 978: Keating, 356. See also Stokes, Martyr. of Oengus, 186; RC xii. 427, § 15; Joyce, SH 274 f.

Footnote 979: LL 213b; Trip. Life, i. 90, 93.

Footnote 980: O'Curry, MS. Mat. 284.

Footnote 981: Keating, 49.

Footnote 982: Jocelyn, Vita S. Kentig. 27, 32, 34; Ailred, Vita S. Ninian. 6.

Footnote 983: Gildas, § 4.

Footnote 984: For the whole argument see Reinach, RC xiii. 189 f. Bertrand, Rev. Arch. xv. 345, supports a similar theory, and, according to both writers, Gallo-Roman art was the result of the weakening of Druidic power by the Romans.

Footnote 985: L'Abbé Hermet, Assoc. pour l'avancement des Sciences, Compte Rendu, 1900, ii. 747; L'Anthropologie, v. 147.

Footnote 986: Corp. Scrip. Eccl. Lat. i. 122.

Footnote 987: Monnier, 362. The image bears part of an inscription ... LIT... and it has been thought that this read ILITHYIA originally. The name is in keeping with the rites still in use before the image. This would make it date from Roman times. If so, it is a poor specimen of the art of the period. But it may be an old native image to which later the name of the Roman goddess was given.

Footnote 988: Roden, Progress of the Reformation in Ireland, 51. The image was still existing in 1851.

Footnote 989: For figures of most of these, see Rev. Arch. vols. xvi., xviii., xix., xxxvi.; RC xvii. 45, xviii. 254, xx. 309, xxii. 159, xxiv. 221; Bertrand, passim; Courcelle-Seneuil, Les Dieux Gaulois d'apres les Monuments Figures, Paris, 1910.

Footnote 990: See Courcelle-Seneuil, op. cit.; Reinach, BF passim, Catalogue Sommaire du Musée des Ant. nat. 4 115-116.

Footnote 991: Reinach, Catal. 29, 87; Rev. Arch. xvi. 17; Blanchet, i. 169, 316; Huchet, L'art gaulois, ii. 8.

Footnote 992: Blanchet, i. 158; Reinach, BF 143, 150, 152.

Footnote 993: Blanchet, i. 17; Flouest, Deux Stèles (Append.), Paris, 1885; Reinach, BF 33.

Footnote 994: supra.

Footnote 995: Hirschfeld in CIL xiii. 256.

Footnote 996: RC xii. 107; Joyce, SH i. 131.

Footnote 997: Blanchet, i. 160 f.; Muret de la Tour, Catalogue, 6922, 6941, etc.

Footnote 998: View of the State of Ireland, 57.

Footnote 999: RC xx. 7; Martin, Études de la Myth. Celt. 164.

Footnote 1000: IT i. 206; RC ix. 144.

Footnote 1001: CM xiii. 168 f.; Miss Hull, 44, 221, 223.

CHAPTER XX
THE DRUIDS

Pliny thought that the name "Druid" was a Greek appellation derived from the Druidic cult of the oak ([Greek: drus]). 1002 The word, however, is purely Celtic, and its meaning probably implies that, like the sorcerer and medicine-man everywhere, the Druid was regarded as "the knowing one." It is composed of two parts—dru-, regarded by M. D'Arbois as an intensive, and vids, from vid, "to know," or "see." 1003 Hence the Druid was "the very knowing or wise one." It is possible, however, that dru- is connected with the root which gives the word "oak" in Celtic speech—Gaulish deruo, Irish dair, Welsh derw—and that the oak, occupying a place in the cult, was thus brought into relation with the name of the priesthood. The Gaulish form of the name was probably druis, the Old Irish was drai. The modern forms in Irish and Scots Gaelic, drui and draoi mean "sorcerer."

M. D'Arbois and others, accepting Cæsar's dictum that "the system (of Druidism) is thought to have been devised in Britain, and brought thence into Gaul," maintain that the Druids were priests of the Goidels in Britain, who imposed themselves upon the Gaulish conquerors of the Goidels, and that Druidism then passed over into Gaul about 200 B.C. 1004 But it is hardly likely that, even if the Druids were accepted as priests by conquering Gauls in Britain, they should have affected the Gauls of Gaul who were outside the reflex influence of the conquered Goidels, and should have there obtained that power which they possessed. Goidels and Gauls were allied by race and language and religion, and it would be strange if they did not both possess a similar priesthood. Moreover, the Goidels had been a continental people, and Druidism was presumably flourishing among them then. Why did it not influence kindred Celtic tribes without Druids, ex hypothesi, at that time? Further, if we accept Professor Meyer's theory that no Goidel set foot in Britain until the second century A.D., the Gauls could not have received the Druidic priesthood from the Goidels.

Cæsar merely says, "it is thought (existimatur) that Druidism came to Gaul from Britain." 1005 It was a pious opinion, perhaps his own, or one based on the fact that those who wished to perfect themselves in Druidic art went to Britain. This may have been because Britain had been less open to foreign influences than Gaul, and its Druids, unaffected by these, were thought to be more powerful than those of Gaul. Pliny, on the other hand, seems to think that Druidism passed over into Britain from Gaul. 1006

Other writers—Sir John Rh[^y]s, Sir G.L. Gomme, and M. Reinach—support on different grounds the theory that the Druids were a pre-Celtic priesthood, accepted by the Celtic conquerors. Sir John Rh[^y]s thinks that the Druidism of the aborigines of Gaul and Britain made terms with the Celtic conquerors. It was accepted by the Goidels, but not by the Brythons. Hence in Britain there were Brythons without Druids, aborigines under the sway of Druidism, and Goidels who combined Aryan polytheism with Druidism. Druidism was also the religion of the aborigines from the Baltic to Gibraltar, and was accepted by the Gauls. 1007 But if so, it is difficult to see why the Brythons, akin to them, did not accept it. Our knowledge of Brythonic religion is too scanty for us to prove that the Druids had or had not sway over them, but the presumption is that they had. Nor is there any historical evidence to show that the Druids were originally a non-Celtic priesthood. Everywhere they appear as the supreme and dominant priesthood of the Celts, and the priests of a conquered people could hardly have obtained such power over the conquerors. The relation of the Celts to the Druids is quite different from that of conquerors, who occasionally resort to the medicine-men of the conquered folk because they have stronger magic or greater influence with the autochthonous gods. The Celts did not resort to the Druids occasionally; ex hypothesi they accepted them completely, were dominated by them in every department of life, while their own priests, if they had any, accepted this order of things without a murmur. All this is incredible. The picture drawn by Cæsar, Strabo, and others of the Druids and their position among the Celts as judges, choosers of tribal chiefs and kings, teachers, as well as ministers of religion, suggests rather that they were a native Celtic priesthood, long established among the people.

Sir G.L. Gomme supports the theory that the Druids were a pre-Celtic priesthood, because, in his opinion, much of their belief in magic as well as their use of human sacrifice and the redemption of one life by another, is opposed to "Aryan sentiment." Equally opposed to this are their functions of settling controversies, judging, settling the succession to property, and arranging boundaries. These views are supported by a comparison of the position of the Druids relatively to the Celts with that of non-Aryan persons in India who render occasional priestly services to Hindu village communities. 1008 Whether this comparison of occasional Hindu custom with Celtic usage two thousand years ago is just, may be questioned. As already seen, it was no mere occasional service which the Druids rendered to the Celts, and it is this which makes it difficult to credit this theory. Had the Celtic house-father been priest and judge in his own clan, would he so readily have surrendered his rights to a foreign and conquered priesthood? On the other hand, kings and chiefs among the Celts probably retained some priestly functions, derived from the time when the offices of the priest-king had not been differentiated. Cæsar's evidence certainly does not support the idea that "it is only among the rudest of the so-called Celtic tribes that we find this superimposing of an apparently official priesthood." According to him, the power of the Druids was universal in Gaul, and had their position really corresponded to that of the pariah priests of India, occasional priests of Hindu villages, the determined hostility of the Roman power to them because they wielded such an enormous influence over Celtic thought and life, is inexplainable. If, further, Aryan sentiment was so opposed to Druidic customs, why did Aryan Celts so readily accept the Druids? In this case the receiver is as bad as the thief. Sir G.L. Gomme clings to the belief that the Aryans were people of a comparatively high civilisation, who had discarded, if they ever possessed, a savage "past." But old beliefs and customs still survive through growing civilisation, and if the views of Professor Sergi and others are correct, the Aryans were even less civilised than the peoples whom they conquered. 1009 Shape-shifting, magic, human sacrifice, priestly domination, were as much Aryan as non-Aryan, and if the Celts had a comparatively pure religion, why did they so soon allow it to be defiled by the puerile superstitions of the Druids?

M. Reinach, as we have seen, thinks that the Celts had no images, because these were prohibited by their priests. This prohibition was pre-Celtic in Gaul, since there are no Neolithic images, though there are great megalithic structures, suggesting the existence of a great religious aristocracy. This aristocracy imposed itself on the Celts. 1010 We have seen that there is no reason for believing that the Celts had no images, hence this argument is valueless. M. Reinach then argues that the Celts accepted Druidism en bloc, as the Romans accepted Oriental cults and the Greeks the native Pelasgic cults. But neither Romans nor Greeks abandoned their own faith. Were the Celts a people without priests and without religion? We know that they must have accepted many local cults, but that they adopted the whole aboriginal faith and its priests en bloc is not credible. M. Reinach also holds that when the Celts appear in history Druidism was in its decline; the Celt, or at least the military caste among the Celts, was reasserting itself. But the Druids do not appear as a declining body in the pages of Cæsar, and their power was still supreme, to judge by the hostility of the Roman Government to them. If the military caste rebelled against them, this does not prove that they were a foreign body. Such a strife is seen wherever priest and soldier form separate castes, each desiring to rule, as in Egypt.

Other writers argue that we do not find Druids existing in the Danube region, in Cisalpine territory, nor in Transalpine Gaul, "outside the limits of the region occupied by the Celtæ." 1011 This could only have weight if any of the classical writers had composed a formal treatise on the Druids, showing exactly the regions where they existed. They merely describe Druidism as a general Celtic institution, or as they knew it in Gaul or Britain, and few of them have any personal knowledge of it. There is no reason to believe that Druids did not exist wherever there were Celts. The Druids and Semnotheoi of the Celts and Galatæ referred to c. 200 B.C. were apparently priests of other Celts than those of Gaul, and Celtic groups of Cisalpine Gaul had priests, though these are not formally styled Druids. 1012 The argument ex silentio is here of little value, since the references to the Druids are so brief, and it tells equally against their non-Celtic origin, since we do not hear of Druids in Aquitania, a non-Celtic region. 1013

The theory of the non-Celtic origin of the Druids assumes that the Celts had no priests, or that these were effaced by the Druids. The Celts had priests called gutuatri attached to certain temples, their name perhaps meaning "the speakers," those who spoke to the gods. 1014 The functions of the Druids were much more general, according to this theory, hence M. D'Arbois supposes that, before their intrusion, the Celts had no other priests than the gutuatri. 1015 But the probability is that they were a Druidic class, ministers of local sanctuaries, and related to the Druids as the Levites were to the priests of Israel, since the Druids were a composite priesthood with a variety of functions. If the priests and servants of Belenos, described by Ausonius and called by him oedituus Beleni, were gutuatri, then the latter must have been connected with the Druids, since he says they were of Druidic stock. 1016 Lucan's "priest of the grove" may have been a gutuatros, and the priests (sacerdotes) and other ministers (antistites) of the Boii may have been Druids properly so called and gutuatri. 1017 Another class of temple servants may have existed. Names beginning with the name of a god and ending in gnatos, "accustomed to," "beloved of," occur in inscriptions, and may denote persons consecrated from their youth to the service of a grove or temple. On the other hand, the names may mean no more than that those bearing them were devoted to the cult of one particular god.

Our supposition that the gutuatri were a class of Druids is supported by classical evidence, which tends to show that the Druids were a great inclusive priesthood with different classes possessing different functions— priestly, prophetic, magical, medical, legal, and poetical. Cæsar attributes these to the Druids as a whole, but in other writers they are in part at least in the hands of different classes. Diodorus refers to the Celtic philosophers and theologians (Druids), diviners, and bards, as do also Strabo and Timagenes, Strabo giving the Greek form of the native name for the diviners, [Greek: ouateis], the Celtic form being probably vátis (Irish, fáith). 1018 These may have been also poets, since vátis means both singer and poet; but in all three writers the bards are a fairly distinct class, who sing the deeds of famous men (so Timagenes). Druid and diviner were also closely connected, since the Druids studied nature and moral philosophy, and the diviners were also students of nature, according to Strabo and Timagenes. No sacrifice was complete without a Druid, say Diodorus and Strabo, but both speak of the diviners as concerned with sacrifice. Druids also prophesied as well as diviners, according to Cicero and Tacitus. 1019 Finally, Lucan mentions only Druids and bards. 1020 Diviners were thus probably a Druidic sub-class, standing midway between the Druids proper and the bards, and partaking of some of the functions of both. Pliny speaks of "Druids and this race of prophets and doctors," 1021 and this suggests that some were priests, some diviners, while some practised an empiric medical science.

On the whole this agrees with what is met with in Ireland, where the Druids, though appearing in the texts mainly as magicians, were also priests and teachers. Side by side with them were the Filid, "learned poets," 1022 composing according to strict rules of art, and higher than the third class, the Bards. The Filid, who may also have been known as Fáthi, "prophets," 1023 were also diviners according to strict rules of augury, while some of these auguries implied a sacrifice. The Druids were also diviners and prophets. When the Druids were overthrown at the coming of Christianity, the Filid remained as a learned class, probably because they had abandoned all pagan practices, while the Bards were reduced to a comparatively low status. M. D'Arbois supposes that there was rivalry between the Druids and the Filid, who made common cause with the Christian missionaries, but this is not supported by evidence. The three classes in Gaul—Druids, Vates, and Bards—thus correspond to the three classes in Ireland—Druids, Fáthi or Filid, and Bards. 1024

We may thus conclude that the Druids were a purely Celtic priesthood, belonging both to the Goidelic and Gaulish branches of the Celts. The idea that they were not Celtic is sometimes connected with the supposition that Druidism was something superadded to Celtic religion from without, or that Celtic polytheism was not part of the creed of the Druids, but sanctioned by them, while they had a definite theological system with only a few gods. 1025 These are the ideas of writers who see in the Druids an occult and esoteric priesthood. The Druids had grown up pari passu with the growth of the native religion and magic. Where they had become more civilised, as in the south of Gaul, they may have given up many magical practices, but as a class they were addicted to magic, and must have taken part in local cults as well as in those of the greater gods. That they were a philosophic priesthood advocating a pure religion among polytheists is a baseless theory. Druidism was not a formal system outside Celtic religion. It covered the whole ground of Celtic religion; in other words, it was that religion itself.

The Druids are first referred to by pseudo-Aristotle and Sotion in the second century B.C., the reference being preserved by Diogenes Laertius: "There are among the Celtæ and Galatæ those called Druids and Semnotheoi." 1026 The two words may be synonymous, or they may describe two classes of priests, or, again, the Druids may have been Celtic, and the Semnotheoi Galatic (? Galatian) priests. Cæsar's account comes next in time. Later writers gives the Druids a lofty place and speak vaguely of the Druidic philosophy and science. Cæsar also refers to their science, but both he and Strabo speak of their human sacrifices. Suetonius describes their religion as cruel and savage, and Mela, who speaks of their learning, regards their human sacrifices as savagery. 1027 Pliny says nothing of the Druids as philosophers, but hints at their priestly functions, and connects them with magico-medical rites. 1028 These divergent opinions are difficult to account for. But as the Romans gained closer acquaintance with the Druids, they found less philosophy and more superstition among them. For their cruel rites and hostility to Rome, they sought to suppress them, but this they never would have done had the Druids been esoteric philosophers. It has been thought that Pliny's phrase, "Druids and that race of prophets and doctors," signifies that, through Roman persecution, the Druids were reduced to a kind of medicine-men. 1029 But the phrase rather describes the varied functions of the Druids, as has been seen, nor does it refer to the state to which the repressive edict reduced them, but to that in which it found them. Pliny's information was also limited.

The vague idea that the Druids were philosophers was repeated parrot-like by writer after writer, who regarded barbaric races as Rousseau and his school looked upon the "noble savage." Roman writers, sceptical of a future life, were fascinated by the idea of a barbaric priesthood teaching the doctrine of immortality in the wilds of Gaul. For this teaching the poet Lucan sang their praises. The Druids probably first impressed Greek and Latin observers by their magic, their organisation, and the fact that, like many barbaric priesthoods, but unlike those of Greece and Rome, they taught certain doctrines. Their knowledge was divinely conveyed to them; "they speak the language of the gods;" 1030 hence it was easy to read anything into this teaching. Thus the Druidic legend rapidly grew. On the other hand, modern writers have perhaps exaggerated the force of the classical evidence. When we read of Druidic associations we need not regard these as higher than the organised priesthoods of barbarians. Their doctrine of metempsychosis, if it was really taught, involved no ethical content as in Pythagoreanism. Their astronomy was probably astrological 1031 ; their knowledge of nature a series of cosmogonic myths and speculations. If a true Druidic philosophy and science had existed, it is strange that it is always mentioned vaguely and that it exerted no influence upon the thought of the time.

Classical sentiment also found a connection between the Druidic and Pythagorean systems, the Druids being regarded as conforming to the doctrines and rules of the Greek philosopher. 1032 It is not improbable that some Pythagorean doctrines may have reached Gaul, but when we examine the point at which the two systems were supposed to meet, namely, the doctrine of metempsychosis and immortality, upon which the whole idea of this relationship was founded, there is no real resemblance. There are Celtic myths regarding the rebirth of gods and heroes, but the eschatological teaching was apparently this, that the soul was clothed with a body in the other-world. There was no doctrine of a series of rebirths on this earth as a punishment for sin. The Druidic teaching of a bodily immortality was mistakenly assumed to be the same as the Pythagorean doctrine of the soul reincarnated in body after body. Other points of resemblance were then discovered. The organisation of the Druids was assumed by Ammianus to be a kind of corporate life—sodaliciis adstricti consortiis—while the Druidic mind was always searching into lofty things, 1033 but those who wrote most fully of the Druids knew nothing of this.

The Druids, like the priests of all religions, doubtless sought after such knowledge as was open to them, but this does not imply that they possessed a recondite philosophy or a secret theology. They were governed by the ideas current among all barbaric communities, and they were at once priests, magicians, doctors, and teachers. They would not allow their sacred hymns to be written down, but taught them in secret, 1034 as is usual wherever the success of hymn or prayer depends upon the right use of the words and the secrecy observed in imparting them to others. Their ritual, as far as is known to us, differs but little from that of other barbarian folk, and it included human sacrifice and divination with the victim's body. They excluded the guilty from a share in the cult—the usual punishment meted out to the tabu-breaker in all primitive societies.

The idea that the Druids taught a secret doctrine—monotheism, pantheism, or the like—is unsupported by evidence. Doubtless they communicated secrets to the initiated, as is done in barbaric mysteries everywhere, but these secrets consist of magic and mythic formulæ, the exhibition of Sacra, and some teaching about the gods or about moral duties. These are kept secret, not because they are abstract doctrines, but because they would lose their value and because the gods would be angry if they were made too common. If the Druids taught religious and moral matters secretly, these were probably no more than an extension of the threefold maxim inculcated by them according to Diogenes Laertius: "To worship the gods, to do no evil, and to exercise courage." 1035 To this would be added cosmogonic myths and speculations, and magic and religious formulæ. This will become more evident as we examine the position and power of the Druids.

In Gaul, and to some extent in Ireland, the Druids formed a priestly corporation—a fact which helped classical observers to suppose that they lived together like the Pythagorean communities. While the words of Ammianus—sodaliciis adstricti consortiis—may imply no more than some kind of priestly organisation, M. Bertrand founds on them a theory that the Druids were a kind of monks living a community life, and that Irish monasticism was a transformation of this system. 1036 This is purely imaginative. Irish Druids had wives and children, and the Druid Diviciacus was a family man, while Cæsar says not a word of community life among the Druids. The hostility of Christianity to the Druids would have prevented any copying of their system, and Irish monasticism was modelled on that of the Continent. Druidic organisation probably denoted no more than that the Druids were bound by certain ties, that they were graded in different ranks or according to their functions, and that they practised a series of common cults. In Gaul one chief Druid had authority over the others, the position being an elective one. 1037 The insular Druids may have been similarly organised, since we hear of a chief Druid, primus magus, while the Filid had an Ard-file, or chief, elected to his office. 1038 The priesthood was not a caste, but was open to those who showed aptitude for it. There was a long novitiate, extending even to twenty years, just as, in Ireland, the novitiate of the File lasted from seven to twelve years. 1039

The Druids of Gaul assembled annually in a central spot, and there settled disputes, because they were regarded as the most just of men. 1040 Individual Druids also decided disputes or sat as judges in cases of murder. How far it was obligatory to bring causes before them is unknown, but those who did not submit to a decision were interdicted from the sacrifices, and all shunned them. In other words, they were tabued. A magico-religious sanction thus enforced the judgments of the Druids. In Galatia the twelve tetrarchs had a council of three hundred men, and met in a place called Drunemeton to try cases of murder. 1041 Whether it is philologically permissible to connect Dru- with the corresponding syllable in "Druid" or not, the likeness to the Gaulish assembly at a "consecrated place," perhaps a grove (nemeton), is obvious. We do not know that Irish Druids were judges, but the Filid exercised judgments, and this may be a relic of their connection with the Druids. 1042

Diodorus describes the Druids exhorting combatants to peace, and taming them like wild beasts by enchantment. 1043 This suggests interference to prevent the devastating power of the blood-feud or of tribal wars. They also appear to have exercised authority in the election of rulers. Convictolitanis was elected to the magistracy by the priests in Gaul, "according to the custom of the State." 1044 In Ireland, after partaking of the flesh of a white bull, probably a sacrificial animal, a man lay down to sleep, while four Druids chanted over him "to render his witness truthful." He then saw in a vision the person who should be elected king, and what he was doing at the moment. 1045 Possibly the Druids used hypnotic suggestion; the medium was apparently clairvoyant.

Dio Chrysostom alleges that kings were ministers of the Druids, and could do nothing without them. 1046 This agrees on the whole with the witness of Irish texts. Druids always accompany the king, and have great influence over him. According to a passage in the Táin, "the men of Ulster must not speak before the king, the king must not speak before his Druid," and even Conchobar was silent until the Druid Cathbad had spoken. 1047 This power, resembling that of many other priesthoods, must have helped to balance that of the warrior class, and it is the more credible when we recall the fact that the Druids claimed to have made the universe. 1048 The priest-kingship may have been an old Celtic institution, and this would explain why, once the offices were separated, priests had or claimed so much political power.

That political power must have been enhanced by their position as teachers, and it is safe to say that submission to their powers was inculcated by them. Both in Gaul and in Ireland they taught others than those who intended to become Druids. 1049 As has been seen, their teachings were not written down, but transmitted orally. They taught immortality, believing that thus men would be roused to valour, buttressing patriotism with dogma. They also imparted "many things regarding the stars and their motions, the extent of the universe and the earth, the nature of things, and the power and might of the immortal gods." Strabo also speaks of their teaching in moral science. 1050 As has been seen, it is easy to exaggerate all this. Their astronomy was probably of a humble kind and mingled with astrology; their natural philosophy a mass of cosmogonic myths and speculations; their theology was rather mythology; their moral philosophy a series of maxims such as are found in all barbaric communities. Their medical lore, to judge from what Pliny says, was largely magical. Some Druids, e.g. in the south of Gaul, may have had access to classical learning, and Cæsar speaks of the use of Greek characters among them. This could hardly have been general, and in any case must have superseded the use of a native script, to which the use of ogams in Ireland, and perhaps also in Gaul, was supplementary. The Irish Druids may have had written books, for King Loegaire desired that S. Patrick's books and those of the Druids should be submitted to the ordeal by water as a test of their owners' claims. 1051

In religious affairs the Druids were supreme, since they alone "knew the gods and divinities of heaven." 1052 They superintended and arranged all rites and attended to "public and private sacrifices," and "no sacrifice was complete without the intervention of a Druid." 1053 The dark and cruel rites of the Druids struck the Romans with horror, and they form a curious contrast to their alleged "philosophy." They used divination and had regular formulæ of incantation as well as ritual acts by which they looked into the future. 1054 Before all matters of importance, especially before warlike expeditions, their advice was sought because they could scan the future.

Name-giving and a species of baptism were performed by the Druids or on their initiative. Many examples of this occur in Irish texts, thus of Conall Cernach it is said, "Druids came to baptize the child into heathenism, and they sang the heathen baptism (baithis geintlídhe) over the little child", and of Ailill that he was "baptized in Druidic streams". 1055 In Welsh story we read that Gwri was "baptized with the baptism which was usual at that time". 1056 Similar illustrations are common at name-giving among many races, 1057 and it is probable that the custom in the Hebrides of the midwife dropping three drops of water on the child in Nomine and giving it a temporary name, is a survival of this practice. The regular baptism takes place later, but this preliminary rite keeps off fairies and ensures burial in consecrated ground, just as the pagan rite was protective and admitted to the tribal privileges. 1058

In the burial rites, which in Ireland consisted of a lament, sacrifices, and raising a stone inscribed with ogams over the grave, Druids took part. The Druid Dergdamsa pronounced a discourse over the Ossianic hero Magneid, buried him with his arms, and chanted a rune. The ogam inscription would also be of Druidic composition, and as no sacrifice was complete without the intervention of Druids, they must also have assisted at the lavish sacrifices which occurred at Celtic funerals.

Pliny's words, "the Druids and that race of prophets and doctors", suggest that the medical art may have been in the hands of a special class of Druids though all may have had a smattering of it. It was mainly concerned with the use of herbs, and was mixed up with magical rites, which may have been regarded as of more importance than the actual medicines used. 1059 In Ireland Druids also practised the healing art. Thus when Cúchulainn was ill, Emer said, "If it had been Fergus, Cúchulainn would have taken no rest till he had found a Druid able to discover the cause of that illness." 1060 But other persons, not referred to as Druids, are mentioned as healers, one of them a woman, perhaps a reminiscence of the time when the art was practised by women. 1061 These healers may, however, have been attached to the Druidic corporation in much the same way as were the bards.

Still more important were the magical powers of the Druids—giving or withholding sunshine or rain, causing storms, making women and cattle fruitful, using spells, rhyming to death, exercising shape-shifting and invisibility, and producing a magic sleep, possibly hypnotic. They were also in request as poisoners. 1062 Since the Gauls went to Britain to perfect themselves in Druidic science, it is possible that the insular Druids were more devoted to magic than those of Gaul, but since the latter are said to have "tamed the people as wild beasts are tamed", it is obvious that this refers to their powers as magicians rather than to any recondite philosophy possessed by them. Yet they were clear-sighted enough to use every means by which they might gain political power, and some of them may have been open to the influence of classical learning even before the Roman invasion. In the next chapter the magic of the Druids will be described in detail.

The Druids, both in Gaul (at the mistletoe rite) and in Ireland, were dressed in white, but Strabo speaks of their scarlet and gold embroidered robes, their golden necklets and bracelets. 1063 Again, the chief Druid of the king of Erin wore a coloured cloak and had earrings of gold, and in another instance a Druid wears a bull's hide and a white-speckled bird headpiece with fluttering wings. 1064 There was also some special tonsure used by the Druids, 1065 which may have denoted servitude to the gods, as it was customary for a warrior to vow his hair to a divinity if victory was granted him. Similarly the Druid's hair would be presented to the gods, and the tonsure would mark their minister.

Some writers have tried to draw a distinction between the Druids of Gaul and of Ireland, especially in the matter of their priestly functions. 1066 But, while a few passages in Irish texts do suggest that the Irish Druids were priests taking part in sacrifices, etc., nearly all passages relating to cult or ritual seem to have been deliberately suppressed. Hence the Druids appear rather as magicians—a natural result, since, once the people became Christian, the priestly character of the Druids would tend to be lost sight of. Like the Druids of Gaul, they were teachers and took part in political affairs, and this shows that they were more than mere magicians. In Irish texts the word "Druid" is somewhat loosely used and is applied to kings and poets, perhaps because they had been pupils of the Druids. But it is impossible to doubt that the Druids in Ireland fulfilled functions of a public priesthood. They appear in connection with all the colonies which came to Erin, the annalists regarding the priests or medicine-men of different races as Druids, through lack of historic perspective. But one fact shows that they were priests of the Celtic religion in Ireland. The euhemerised Tuatha Dé Danann are masters of Druidic lore. Thus both the gods and the priests who served them were confused by later writers. The opposition of Christian missionaries to the Druids shows that they were priests; if they were not, it remains to be discovered what body of men did exercise priestly functions in pagan Ireland. In Ireland their judicial functions may have been less important than in Gaul, and they may not have been so strictly organised; but here we are in the region of conjecture. They were exempt from military service in Gaul, and many joined their ranks on this account, but in Ireland they were "bonny fechters," just as in Gaul they occasionally fought like mediæval bishops. 1067 In both countries they were present on the field of battle to perform the necessary religious or magical rites.

Since the Druids were an organised priesthood, with powers of teaching and of magic implicitly believed in by the folk, possessing the key of the other-world, and dominating the whole field of religion, it is easy to see how much veneration must have been paid them. Connoting this with the influence of the Roman Church in Celtic regions and the power of the Protestant minister in the Highlands and in Wales, some have thought that there is an innate tendency in the Celt to be priest-ridden. If this be true, we can only say, "the people wish to have it so, and the priests—pagan, papist, or protestant—bear rule through their means!"

Thus a close examination of the position and functions of the Druids explains away two popular misconceptions. They were not possessed of any recondite and esoteric wisdom. And the culling of mistletoe instead of being the most important, was but a subordinate part of their functions.

In Gaul the Roman power broke the sway of the Druids, aided perhaps by the spread of Christianity, but it was Christianity alone which routed them in Ireland and in Britain outside the Roman pale. The Druidic organisation, their power in politics and in the administration of justice, their patriotism, and also their use of human sacrifice and magic, were all obnoxious to the Roman Government, which opposed them mainly on political grounds. Magic and human sacrifice were suppressed because they were contrary to Roman manners. The first attack was in the reign of Augustus, who prohibited Roman citizens from taking part in the religion of the Druids. 1068 Tiberius next interdicted the Druids, but this was probably aimed at their human sacrifices, for the Druids were not suppressed, since they existed still in the reign of Claudius, who is said to have abolished Druidarum religionem dirae immanitatis. 1069 The earlier legislation was ineffective; that of Claudius was more thorough, but it, too, was probably aimed mainly at human sacrifice and magic, since Aurelius Victor limits it to the "notorious superstitions" of the Druids. 1070 It did not abolish the native religion, as is proved by the numerous inscriptions to Celtic gods, and by the fact that, as Mela informs us, human victims were still offered symbolically, 1071 while the Druids were still active some years later. A parallel is found in the British abolition of S[=a]ti in India, while permitting the native religion to flourish.

Probably more effective was the policy begun by Augustus. Magistrates were inaugurated and acted as judges, thus ousting the Druids, and native deities and native ritual were assimilated to those of Rome. Celtic religion was Romanised, and if the Druids retained priestly functions, it could only be by their becoming Romanised also. Perhaps the new State religion in Gaul simply ignored them. The annual assembly of deputies at Lugudunum round the altar of Rome and Augustus had a religious character, and was intended to rival and to supersede the annual gathering of the Druids. 1072 The deputies elected a flamen of the province who had surveillance of the cult, and there were also flamens for each city. Thus the power of the Druids in politics, law, and religion was quietly undermined, while Rome also struck a blow at their position as teachers by establishing schools throughout Gaul. 1073

M. D'Arbois maintains that, as a result of persecution, the Druids retired to the depths of the forests, and continued to teach there in secret those who despised the new learning of Rome, basing his opinion on passages of Lucan and Mela, both writing a little after the promulgation of the laws. 1074 . But neither Lucan nor Mela refer to an existing state of things, and do not intend their readers to suppose that the Druids fled to woods and caverns. Lucan speaks of them dwelling in woods, i.e. their sacred groves, and resuming their rites after Cæsar's conquest not after the later edicts, and he does not speak of the Druids teaching there. 1075 Mela seems to be echoing Cæsar's account of the twenty years' novitiate, but adds to it that the teaching was given in secret, confusing it, however, with that given to others than candidates for the priesthood. Thus he says: "Docent multa nobilissimos gentis clam et diu vicenis annis aut in specu aut in abditis saltibus," 1076 but there is not the slightest evidence that this secrecy was the result of the edicts. Moreover, the attenuated sacrificial rites which he describes were evidently practised quite openly. Probably some Druids continued their teaching in their secret and sacred haunts, but it is unlikely that noble Gauls would resort to them when Greco-Roman culture was now open to them in the schools, where they are found receiving instruction in 21 A.D. 1077 Most of the Druids probably succumbed to the new order of things. Some continued the old rites in a modified manner as long as they could obtain worshippers. Others, more fanatical, would suffer from the law when they could not evade its grasp. Some of these revolted against Rome after Nero's death, and it was perhaps to this class that those Druids belonged who prophesied the world-empire of the Celts in 70 A.D. 1078 The fact that Druids existed at this date shows that the proscription had not been complete. But the complete Romanising of Gaul took away their occupation, though even in the fourth century men still boasted of their Druidic descent. 1079

The insular Druids opposed the legions in Southern Britain, and in Mona in 62 A.D. they made a last stand with the warriors against the Romans, gesticulating and praying to the gods. But with the establishment of Roman power in Britain their fate must have resembled that of the Druids of Gaul. A recrudescence of Druidism is found, however, in the presence of magi (Druids) with Vortigern after the Roman withdrawal. 1080 Outside the Roman pale the Druids were still rampant and practised their rites as before, according to Pliny. 1081 Much later, in the sixth century, they opposed Christian missionaries in Scotland, just as in Ireland they opposed S. Patrick and his monks, who combated "the hard-hearted Druids." Finally, Christianity was victorious and the powers of the Druids passed in large measure to the Christian clergy or remained to some extent with the Filid. 1082 In popular belief the clerics had prevailed less by the persuasive power of the gospel, than by successfully rivalling the magic of the Druids.

Classical writers speak of Dryades or "Druidesses" in the third century. One of them predicted his approaching death to Alexander Severus, another promised the empire to Diocletian, others were consulted by Aurelian. 1083 Thus they were divineresses, rather than priestesses, and their name may be the result of misconception, unless they assumed it when Druids no longer existed as a class. In Ireland there were divineresses—ban-filid or ban-fáthi, probably a distinct class with prophetic powers. Kings are warned against "pythonesses" as well as Druids, and Dr. Joyce thinks these were Druidesses. 1084 S. Patrick also armed himself against "the spells of women" and of Druids. 1085 Women in Ireland had a knowledge of futurity, according to Solinus, and the women who took part with the Druids like furies at Mona, may have been divineresses. 1086 In Ireland it is possible that such women were called "Druidesses," since the word ban-drui is met with, the women so called being also styled ban-fili, while the fact that they belonged to the class of the Filid brings them into connection with the Druids. 1087 But ban-drui may have been applied to women with priestly functions, such as certainly existed in Ireland—e.g. the virgin guardians of sacred fires, to whose functions Christian nuns succeeded. 1088 We know also that the British queen Boudicca exercised priestly functions, and such priestesses, apart from the Dryades, existed among the continental Celts. Inscriptions at Arles speak of an antistita deae, and at Le Prugnon of a flaminica sacerdos of the goddess Thucolis. 1089 These were servants of a goddess like the priestess of the Celtic Artemis in Galatia, in whose family the priesthood was hereditary. 1090 The virgins called Gallizenæ, who practised divination and magic in the isle of Sena, were priestesses of a Gaulish god, and some of the women who were "possessed by Dionysus" and practised an orgiastic cult on an island in the Loire, were probably of the same kind. 1091 They were priestesses of some magico-religious cult practised by women, like the guardians of the sacred fire in Ireland, which was tabu to men. M. Reinach regards the accounts of these island priestesses as fictions based on the story of Circe's isle, but even if they are garbled, they seem to be based on actual observation and are paralleled from other regions. 1092

The existence of such priestesses and divineresses over the Celtic area is to be explained by our hypothesis that many Celtic divinities were at first female and served by women, who were possessed of the tribal lore. Later, men assumed their functions, and hence arose the great priesthoods, but conservatism sporadically retained such female cults and priestesses, some goddesses being still served by women—the Galatian Artemis, or the goddesses of Gaul, with their female servants. Time also brought its revenges, for when paganism passed away, much of its folk-ritual and magic remained, practised by wise women or witches, who for generations had as much power over ignorant minds as the Christian priesthood. The fact that Cæsar and Tacitus speak of Germanic but not of Celtic priestesses, can hardly, in face of these scattered notices, be taken as a proof that women had no priestly rôle in Celtic religion. If they had not, that religion would be unique in the world's history.

Footnote 1002: Pliny, HN xvi. 249.

Footnote 1003: D'Arbois, Les Druides, 85, following Thurneysen.

Footnote 1004: D'Arbois, op. cit. 12 f.; Deloche, Revue des Deux Mondes, xxxiv. 466; Desjardins, Geog. de la Gaule Romaine, ii. 518.

Footnote 1005: Cæsar, vi. 13.

Footnote 1006: Pliny, HN xxx. 1.

Footnote 1007: Rh[^y]s, CB 4 69 f.

Footnote 1008: Gomme, Ethnol. in Folk-lore, 58, Village Community, 104.

Footnote 1009: Sergi, The Mediterranean Race, 295.

Footnote 1010: Reinach, "L'Art plastique en Gaule et le Druidisme," RC xiii. 189.

Footnote 1011: Holmes, Cæsar's Conquest of Gaul, 15; Dottin, 270.

Footnote 1012: Diog. Laert. i. 1; Livy xxiii. 24.

Footnote 1013: Desjardins, op. cit. ii. 519; but cf. Holmes, 535.

Footnote 1014: Gutuatros is perhaps from gutu-, "voice" (Holder, i. 2046; but see Loth, RC xxviii. 120). The existence of the gutuatri is known from a few inscriptions (see Holder), and from Hirtius, de Bell. Gall. viii. 38, who mentions a gutuatros put to death by Cæsar.

Footnote 1015: D'Arbois, Les Druides, 2 f., Les Celtes, 32.

Footnote 1016: Ausonius, Professor. v. 7, xi. 24.

Footnote 1017: Lucan, iii. 424; Livy, xxiii. 24.

Footnote 1018: Diod. Sic. v. 31; Strabo, iv. 4. 4; Timagenes apud Amm. Marc. xv. 9.

Footnote 1019: Cicero, de Div. i. 41. 90; Tac. Hist. iv. 54.

Footnote 1020: Phars. i. 449 f.

Footnote 1021: HN xxx. i.

Footnote 1022: Filid, sing. File, is from velo, "I see" (Stokes, US 277).

Footnote 1023: Fáthi is cognate with Vates.

Footnote 1024: In Wales there had been Druids as there were Bards, but all trace of the second class is lost. Long after the Druids had passed away, the fiction of the derwydd-vardd or Druid-bard was created, and the later bards were held to be depositories of a supposititious Druidic theosophy, while they practised the old rites in secret. The late word derwydd was probably invented from derw, "oak," by some one who knew Pliny's derivation. See D'Arbois, Les Druides, 81.

Footnote 1025: For these views see Dottin, 295; Holmes, 17; Bertrand, 192-193, 268-269.

Footnote 1026: Diog. Laert. i. proem. 1. For other references see Cæsar, vi. 13, 14; Strabo, iv. 4. 4; Amm. Marc. xv. 9; Diod. Sic, v. 28; Lucan, i. 460; Mela, iii. 2.

Footnote 1027: Suet. Claud. 25; Mela, iii. 2.

Footnote 1028: Pliny, xxx. 1.

Footnote 1029: D'Arbois, Les Druides, 77.

Footnote 1030: Diod. Sic. v. 31. 4.

Footnote 1031: See Cicero, de Div. i. 41.

Footnote 1032: Diod. Sic. v. 28; Amm. Marc. xv. 9; Hippolytus, Refut. Hær. i. 22.

Footnote 1033: Amm. Marc. xv. 9.

Footnote 1034: Cæsar, vi. 14.

Footnote 1035: Diog. Laert. 6. Celtic enthusiasts see in this triple maxim something akin to the Welsh triads, which they claim to be Druidic!

Footnote 1036: Bertrand, 280.

Footnote 1037: Cæsar, vi. 13.

Footnote 1038: Trip. Life, ii. 325, i. 52, ii. 402; IT i. 373; RC xxvi. 33. The title rig-file, "king poet," sometimes occurs.

Footnote 1039: Cæsar, vi. 14.

Footnote 1040: Cæsar, vi. 13; Strabo, iv. 4. 4.

Footnote 1041: Strabo, xii. 5. 2.

Footnote 1042: Their judicial powers were taken from them because their speech had become obscure. Perhaps they gave their judgments in archaic language.

Footnote 1043: Diod. Sic. v. 31. 5.

Footnote 1044: Cæsar, vii. 33.

Footnote 1045: IT i. 213; D'Arbois, v. 186.

Footnote 1046: Dio, Orat. xlix.

Footnote 1047: LL 93.

Footnote 1048: Ancient Laws of Ireland, i. 22.

Footnote 1049: Cæsar, vi. 13, 14; Windisch, Táin, line 1070 f.; IT i. 325; Arch. Rev. i. 74; Trip. Life, 99; cf. O'Curry, MC ii. 201.

Footnote 1050: Cæsar, vi. 14; Strabo, iv. 4. 4.

Footnote 1051: Trip. Life, 284.

Footnote 1052: Lucan, i. 451.

Footnote 1053: Diod. v. 31. 4; cf. Cæsar, vi. 13, 16; Strabo, iv. 4. 5.

Footnote 1054: supra.

Footnote 1055: RC xiv. 29; Miss Hull, 4, 23, 141; IT iii. 392, 423; Stokes, Félire, Intro. 23.

Footnote 1056: Loth, i. 56.

Footnote 1057: See my art. "Baptism (Ethnic)" in Hastings' Encyclopædia of Religion and Ethics, ii. 367 f.

Footnote 1058: Carmichael, Carm. Gadel. i. 115.

Footnote 1059: supra.

Footnote 1060: IT i. 215.

Footnote 1061: O'Curry, MS. Mat. 221, 641.

Footnote 1062: RC xvi. 34.

Footnote 1063: Pliny, HN xvi. 45; Trip. Life, ii. 325; Strabo, iv. 275.

Footnote 1064: RC xxii. 285; O'Curry, MC ii. 215.

Footnote 1065: Reeves' ed. of Adamnan's Life of S. Col. 237; Todd, S. Patrick, 455; Joyce, SH i. 234. For the relation of the Druidic tonsure to the peculiar tonsure of the Celtic Church, see Rh[^y]s, HL 213, CB 4 72; Gougaud, Les Chrétientés Celtiques, 198.

Footnote 1066: See Hyde, Lit. Hist. of Ireland, 88; Joyce, SH i. 239.

Footnote 1067: Cæsar, vi. 14, ii. 10.

Footnote 1068: Suetonius, Claud. 25.

Footnote 1069: Pliny HN xxx. 1; Suet. Claud. 25.

Footnote 1070: de Cæsaribus, 4, "famosæ superstitiones"; cf. p. 328, infra.

Footnote 1071: Mela, iii. 2.

Footnote 1072: Mommsen, Rom. Gesch. v. 94.

Footnote 1073: Bloch (Lavisse), Hist. de France, i. 2, 176 f., 391 f.; Duruy, "Comment périt l'institution Druidique," Rev. Arch. xv. 347; de Coulanges, "Comment le Druidisme a disparu," RC iv. 44.

Footnote 1074: Les Druides, 73.

Footnote 1075: Phars. i. 453, "Ye Druids, after arms were laid aside, sought once again your barbarous ceremonials.... In remote forests do ye inhabit the deep glades."

Footnote 1076: Mela, iii. 2.

Footnote 1077: Tacit. iii. 43.

Footnote 1078: Ibid. iv. 54.

Footnote 1079: Ausonius, Prof. v. 12, xi. 17.

Footnote 1080: Nennius, 40. In the Irish version they are called "Druids." See p. 238, supra.

Footnote 1081: Pliny, xxx. 1.

Footnote 1082: Adamnan, Vita S. Col., i. 37. ii. 35, etc.; Reeves' Adamnan, 247 f.; Stokes, Three Homilies, 24 f.; Antient Laws of Ireland, i. 15; RC xvii. 142 f.; IT i. 23.

Footnote 1083: Lampridius, Alex. Sev. 60; Vopiscus, Numerienus, 14, Aurelianus, 44.

Footnote 1084: Windisch, Táin, 31, 221; cf. Meyer, Contributions to Irish Lexicog. 176 Joyce, SH i. 238.

Footnote 1085: IT i. 56.

Footnote 1086: Solinus, 35; Tac. Ann. xiv. 30.

Footnote 1087: RC xv. 326, xvi. 34, 277; Windisch, Táin, 331. In LL 75b we hear of "three Druids and three Druidesses."

Footnote 1088: supra; Keating, 331.

Footnote 1089: Jullian, 100; Holder, s.v. "Thucolis."

Footnote 1090: Plutarch, Vir. mul. 20.

Footnote 1091: Mela, iii. 6; Strabo, iv. 4. 6.

Footnote 1092: Reinach, RC xviii. 1 f. The fact that the rites were called Dionysiac is no reason for denying the fact that some orgiastic rites were practised. Classical writers usually reported all barbaric rites in terms of their own religion. M. D'Arbois (vi. 325) points out that Circe was not a virgin, and had not eight companions.

CHAPTER XXI
MAGIC

The Celts, like all other races, were devoted to magical practices, many of which could be used by any one, though, on the whole, they were in the hands of the Druids, who in many aspects were little higher than the shamans of barbaric tribes. But similar magical rites were also attributed to the gods, and it is probably for this reason that the Tuatha Dé Danann and many of the divinities who appear in the Mabinogion are described as magicians. Kings are also spoken of as wizards, perhaps a reminiscence of the powers of the priest king. But since many of the primitive cults had been in the hands of women, and as these cults implied a large use of magic, they may have been the earliest wielders of magic, though, with increasing civilisation, men took their place as magicians. Still side by side with the magic-wielding Druids, there were classes of women who also dealt in magic, as we have seen. Their powers were feared, even by S. Patrick, who classes the "spells of women" along with those of Druids, and, in a mythic tale, by the father of Connla, who, when the youth was fascinated by a goddess, feared that he would be taken by the "spells of women" (brichta ban). 1093 In other tales women perform all such magical actions as are elsewhere ascribed to Druids. 1094 And after the Druids had passed away precisely similar actions—power over the weather, the use of incantations and amulets, shape-shifting and invisibility, etc.—were, and still are in remote Celtic regions, ascribed to witches. Much of the Druidic art, however, was also supposed to be possessed by saints and clerics, both in the past and in recent times. But women remained as magicians when the Druids had disappeared, partly because of female conservatism, partly because, even in pagan times, they had worked more or less secretly. At last the Church proscribed them and persecuted them.

Each clan, tribe, or kingdom had its Druids, who, in time of war, assisted their hosts by magic art. This is reflected back upon the groups of the mythological cycle, each of which has its Druids who play no small part in the battles fought. Though Pliny recognises the priestly functions of the Druids, he associates them largely with magic, and applies the name magus to them. 1095 In Irish ecclesiastical literature, drui is used as the translation of magus, e.g. in the case of the Egyptian magicians, while magi is used in Latin lives of saints as the equivalent of the vernacular druides. 1096 In the sagas and in popular tales Druidecht, "Druidism," stands for "magic," and slat an draoichta, "rod of Druidism," is a magic wand. 1097 The Tuatha Dé Danann were said to have learned "Druidism" from the four great master Druids of the region whence they had come to Ireland, and even now, in popular tales, they are often called "Druids" or "Danann Druids." 1098 Thus in Ireland at least there is clear evidence of the great magical power claimed by Druids.

That power was exercised to a great extent over the elements, some of which Druids claimed to have created. Thus the Druid Cathbad covered the plain over which Deirdre was escaping with "a great-waved sea." 1099 Druids also produced blinding snow-storms, or changed day into night— feats ascribed to them even in the Lives of Saints. 1100 Or they discharge "shower-clouds of fire" on the opposing hosts, as in the case of the Druid Mag Ruith, who made a magic fire, and flying upwards towards it, turned it upon the enemy, whose Druid in vain tried to divert it. 1101 When the Druids of Cormac dried up all the waters in the land, another Druid shot an arrow, and where it fell there issued a torrent of water. 1102 The Druid Mathgen boasted of being able to throw mountains on the enemy, and frequently Druids made trees or stones appear as armed men, dismaying the opposing host in this way. They could also fill the air with the clash of battle, or with the dread cries of eldritch things. 1103 Similar powers are ascribed to other persons. The daughters of Calatin raised themselves aloft on an enchanted wind, and discovered Cúchulainn when he was hidden away by Cathbad. Later they produced a magic mist to discomfit the hero. 1104 Such mists occur frequently in the sagas, and in one of them the Tuatha Dé Danann arrived in Ireland. The priestesses of Sena could rouse sea and wind by their enchantments, and, later, Celtic witches have claimed the same power.

In folk-survivals the practice of rain-making is connected with sacred springs, and even now in rural France processions to shrines, usually connected with a holy well, are common in time of drought. Thus people and priest go to the fountain of Baranton in procession, singing hymns, and there pray for rain. The priest then dips his foot in the water, or throws some of it on the rocks. 1105 In other cases the image of a saint is carried to a well and asperged, as divine images formerly were, or the waters are beaten or thrown into the air. 1106 Another custom was that a virgin should clean out a sacred well, and formerly she had to be nude. 1107 Nudity also forms part of an old ritual used in Gaul. In time of drought the girls of the village followed the youngest virgin in a state of nudity to seek the herb belinuntia. This she uprooted, and was then led to a river and there asperged by the others. In this case the asperging imitated the falling rain, and was meant to produce it automatically. While some of these rites suggest the use of magic by the folk themselves, in others the presence of the Christian priest points to the fact that, formerly, a Druid was necessary as the rain producer. In some cases the priest has inherited through long ages the rain-making or tempest-quelling powers of the pagan priesthood, and is often besought to exercise them. 1108

Causing invisibility by means of a spell called feth fiada, which made a person unseen or hid him in a magic mist, was also used by the Druids as well as by Christian saints. S. Patrick's hymn, called Fâed Fiada, was sung by him when his enemies lay in wait, and caused a glamour in them. The incantation itself, fith-fath, is still remembered in Highland glens. 1109 In the case of S. Patrick he and his followers appeared as deer, and this power of shape-shifting was wielded both by Druids and women. The Druid Fer Fidail carried off a maiden by taking the form of a woman, and another Druid deceived Cúchulainn by taking the form of the fair Niamh. 1110 Other Druids are said to have been able to take any shape that pleased them. 1111 These powers were reflected back upon the gods and mythical personages like Taliesin or Amairgen, who appear in many forms. The priestesses of Sena could assume the form of animals, and an Irish Circe in the Rennes Dindsenchas called Dalb the Rough changed three men and their wives into swine by her spells. 1112 This power of transforming others is often described in the sagas. The children of Lir were changed to swans by their cruel stepmother; Saar, the mother of Oisin, became a fawn through the power of the Druid Fear Doirche when she rejected his love; and similarly Tuirrenn, mother of Oisin's hounds, was transformed into a stag-hound by the fairy mistress of her husband Iollann. 1113 In other instances in the sagas, women appear as birds. 1114 These transformation tales may be connected with totemism, for when this institution is decaying the current belief in shape-shifting is often made use of to explain descent from animals or the tabu against eating certain animals. In some of these Irish shape-shifting tales we find this tabu referred to. Thus, when the children of Lir were turned into swans, it was proclaimed that no one should kill a swan. The reason of an existing tabu seemed to be sufficiently explained when it was told that certain human beings had become swans. It is not impossible that the Druids made use of hypnotic suggestion to persuade others that they had assumed another form, as Red Indian shamans have been known to do, or even hallucinated others into the belief that their own form had been changed.

By a "drink of oblivion" Druids and other persons could make one forget even the most dearly beloved. Thus Cúchulainn was made to forget Fand, and his wife Emer to forget her jealousy. 1115 This is a reminiscence of potent drinks brewed from herbs which caused hallucinations, e.g. that of the change of shape. In other cases they were of a narcotic nature and caused a deep sleep, an instance being the draught given by Grainne to Fionn and his men. 1116 Again, the "Druidic sleep" is suggestive of hypnotism, practised in distant ages and also by present-day savages. When Bodb suspected his daughter of lying he cast her into a "Druidic sleep," in which she revealed her wickedness. 1117 In other cases spells are cast upon persons so that they are hallucinated, or are rendered motionless, or, "by the sleight of hand of soothsayers," maidens lose their chastity without knowing it. 1118 These point to knowledge of hypnotic methods of suggestion. Or, again, a spectral army is opposed to an enemy's force to whom it is an hallucinatory appearance—perhaps an exaggeration of natural hypnotic powers. 1119

Druids also made a "hedge," the airbe druad, round an army, perhaps circumambulating it and saying spells so that the attacking force might not break through. If any one could leap this "hedge," the spell was broken, but he lost his life. This was done at the battle of Cul Dremne, at which S. Columba was present and aided the heroic leaper with his prayers. 1120

A primitive piece of sympathetic magic used still by savages is recorded in the Rennes Dindsenchas. In this story one man says spells over his spear and hurls it into his opponent's shadow, so that he falls dead. 1121 Equally primitive is the Druidic "sending" a wisp of straw over which the Druid sang spells and flung it into his victim's face, so that he became mad. A similar method is used by the Eskimo angekok. All madness was generally ascribed to such a "sending."

Several of these instances have shown the use of spells, and the Druid was believed to possess powerful incantations to discomfit an enemy or to produce other magical results. A special posture was adopted—standing on one leg, with one arm outstretched and one eye closed, perhaps to concentrate the force of the spell, 1122 but the power lay mainly in the spoken words, as we have seen in discussing Celtic formulæ of prayer. Such spells were also used by the Filid, or poets, since most primitive poetry has a magical aspect. Part of the training of the bard consisted in learning traditional incantations, which, used with due ritual, produced the magic result. 1123 Some of these incantations have already come before our notice, and probably some of the verses which Cæsar says the Druids would not commit to writing were of the nature of spells. 1124 The virtue of the spell lay in the spoken formula, usually introducing the name of a god or spirit, later a saint, in order to procure his intervention, through the power inherent in the name. Other charms recount an effect already produced, and this, through mimetic magic, is supposed to cause its repetition. The earliest written documents bearing upon the paganism of the insular Celts contain an appeal to "the science of Goibniu" to preserve butter, and another, for magical healing, runs, "I admire the healing which Diancecht left in his family, in order to bring health to those he succoured." These are found in an eighth or ninth century MS., and, with their appeal to pagan gods, were evidently used in Christian times. 1125 Most Druidic magic was accompanied by a spell—transformation, invisibility, power over the elements, and the discovery of hidden persons or things. In other cases spells were used in medicine or for healing wounds. Thus the Tuatha Dé Danann told the Fomorians that they need not oppose them, because their Druids would restore the slain to life, and when Cúchulainn was wounded we hear less of medicines than of incantations used to stanch his blood. 1126 In other cases the Druid could remove barrenness by spells.

The survival of the belief in spells among modern Celtic peoples is a convincing proof of their use in pagan times, and throws light upon their nature. In Brittany they are handed down in certain families, and are carefully guarded from the knowledge of others. The names of saints instead of the old gods are found in them, but in some cases diseases are addressed as personal beings. In the Highlands similar charms are found, and are often handed down from male to female, and from female to male. They are also in common use in Ireland. Besides healing diseases, such charms are supposed to cause fertility or bring good luck, or even to transfer the property of others to the reciter, or, in the case of darker magic, to cause death or disease. 1127 In Ireland, sorcerers could "rime either a man or beast to death," and this recalls the power of satire in the mouth of File or Druid. It raised blotches on the face of the victim, or even caused his death. 1128 Among primitive races powerful internal emotion affects the body in curious ways, and in this traditional power of the satire or "rime" we have probably an exaggerated reference to actual fact. In other cases the "curse of satire" affected nature, causing seas and rivers to sink back. 1129 The satires made by the bards of Gaul, referred to by Diodorus, may have been believed to possess similar powers. 1130 Contrariwise, the Filid, on uttering an unjust judgment, found their faces covered with blotches. 1131

A magical sleep is often caused by music in the sagas, e.g. by the harp of Dagda, or by the branch carried by visitants from Elysium. 1132 Many "fairy" lullabies for producing sleep are even now extant in Ireland and the Highlands. 1133 As music forms a part of all primitive religion, its soothing powers would easily be magnified. In orgiastic rites it caused varying emotions until the singer and dancer fell into a deep slumber, and the tales of those who joined in a fairy dance and fell asleep, awaking to find that many years had passed, are mythic extensions of the power of music in such orgiastic cults. The music of the Filid had similar powers to that of Dagda's harp, producing laughter, tears, and a delicious slumber, 1134 and Celtic folk-tales abound in similar instances of the magic charm of music.

We now turn to the use of amulets among the Celts. Some of these were symbolic and intended to bring the wearer under the protection of the god whom they symbolised. As has been seen, a Celtic god had as his symbol a wheel, probably representing the sun, and numerous small wheel discs made of different materials have been found in Gaul and Britain. 1135 These were evidently worn as amulets, while in other cases they were offered to river divinities, since many are met with in river beds or fords. Their use as protective amulets is shown by a stele representing a person wearing a necklace to which is attached one of these wheels. In Irish texts a Druid is called Mag Ruith, explained as magus rotarum, because he made his Druidical observations by wheels. 1136 This may point to the use of such amulets in Ireland. A curious amulet, connected with the Druids, became famous in Roman times and is described by Pliny. This was the "serpents' egg," formed from the foam produced by serpents twining themselves together. The serpents threw the "egg" into the air, and he who sought it had to catch it in his cloak before it fell, and flee to a running stream, beyond which the serpents, like the witches pursuing Tam o' Shanter, could not follow him. This "egg" was believed to cause its owner to obtain access to kings or to gain lawsuits, and a Roman citizen was put to death in the reign of Claudius for bringing such an amulet into court. Pliny had seen this "egg." It was about the size of an apple, with a cartilaginous skin covered with discs. 1137 Probably it was a fossil echinus, such as has been found in Gaulish tombs. 1138 Such "eggs" were doubtless connected with the cult of the serpent, or some old myth of an egg produced by serpents may have been made use of to account for their formation. This is the more likely, as rings or beads of glass found in tumuli in Wales, Cornwall, and the Highlands are called "serpents' glass" (glain naidr), and are believed to be formed in the same way as the "egg." These, as well as old spindle-whorls called "adder stones" in the Highlands, are held to have magical virtues, e.g. against the bite of a serpent, and are highly prized by their owners. 1139

Pliny speaks also of the Celtic belief in the magical virtues of coral, either worn as an amulet or taken in powder as a medicine, while it has been proved that the Celts during a limited period of their history placed it on weapons and utensils, doubtless as an amulet. 1140 Other amulets—white marble balls, quartz pebbles, models of the tooth of the boar, or pieces of amber, have been found buried with the dead. 1141 Little figures of the boar, the horse, and the bull, with a ring for suspending them to a necklet, were worn as amulets or images of these divine animals, and phallic amulets were also worn, perhaps as a protection against the evil eye. 1142

A cult of stones was probably connected with the belief in the magical power of certain stones, like the Lia Fail, which shrieked aloud when Conn knocked against it. His Druids explained that the number of the shrieks equalled the number of his descendants who should be kings of Erin. 1143 This is an ætiological myth accounting for the use of this fetich-stone at coronations. Other stones, probably the object of a cult or possessing magical virtues, were used at the installation of chiefs, who stood on them and vowed to follow in the steps of their predecessors, a pair of feet being carved on the stone to represent those of the first chief. 1144 Other stones had more musical virtues—the "conspicuous stone" of Elysium from which arose a hundred strains, and the melodious stone of Loch Láig. Such beliefs existed into Christian times. S. Columba's stone altar floated on the waves, and on it a leper had crossed in the wake of the saint's coracle to Erin. But the same stone was that on which, long before, the hero Fionn had slipped. 1145

Connected with the cult of stones are magical observances at fixed rocks or boulders, regarded probably as the abode of a spirit. These observances are in origin pre-Celtic, but were practised by the Celts. Girls slide down a stone to obtain a lover, pregnant women to obtain an easy delivery, or contact with such stones causes barren women to have children or gives vitality to the feeble. A small offering is usually left on the stone. 1146 Similar rites are practised at megalithic monuments, and here again the custom is obviously pre-Celtic in origin. In this case the spirits of the dead must have been expected to assist the purposes of the rites, or even to incarnate themselves in the children born as a result of barren women resorting to these stones. 1147 Sometimes when the purpose of the stones has been forgotten and some other legendary origin attributed to them, the custom adapts itself to the legend. In Ireland many dolmens are known, not as places of sepulture, but as "Diarmaid and Grainne's beds"—the places where these eloping lovers slept. Hence they have powers of fruitfulness and are visited by women who desire children. The rite is thus one of sympathetic magic.

Holed dolmens or naturally pierced blocks are used for the magical cure of sickness both in Brittany and Cornwall, the patient being passed through the hole. 1148 Similar rites are used with trees, a slit being often made in the trunk of a sapling, and a sickly child passed through it. The slit is then closed and bound, and if it joins together at the end of a certain time, this is a proof that the child will recover. 1149 In these rites the spirit in stone or tree was supposed to assist the process of healing, or the disease was transferred to them, or, again, there was the idea of a new birth with consequent renewed life, the act imitating the process of birth. These rites are not confined to Celtic regions, but belong to that universal use of magic in which the Celts freely participated.

Since Christian writers firmly believed in the magical powers of the Druids, aided however by the devil, they taught that Christian saints had miraculously overcome them with their own weapons. S. Patrick dispelled snow-storms and darkness raised by Druids, or destroyed Druids who had brought down fire from heaven. Similar deeds are attributed to S. Columba and others. 1150 The moral victory of the Cross was later regarded also as a magical victory. Hence also lives of Celtic saints are full of miracles which are simply a reproduction of Druidic magic—controlling the elements, healing, carrying live coals without hurt, causing confusion by their curses, producing invisibility or shape-shifting, making the ice-cold waters of a river hot by standing in them at their devotions, or walking unscathed through the fiercest storms. 1151 They were soon regarded as more expert magicians than the Druids themselves. They may have laid claim to magical powers, or perhaps they used a natural shrewdness in such a way as to suggest magic. But all their power they ascribed to Christ. "Christ is my Druid"—the true miracle-worker, said S. Columba. Yet they were imbued with the superstitions of their own age. Thus S. Columba sent a white stone to King Brude at Inverness for the cure of his Druid Broichan, who drank the water poured over it, and was healed. 1152 Soon similar virtues were ascribed to the relics of the saints themselves, and at a later time, when most Scotsmen ceased to believe in the saints, they thought that the ministers of the kirk had powers like those of pagan Druid and Catholic saint. Ministers were levitated, or shone with a celestial light, or had clairvoyant gifts, or, with dire results, cursed the ungodly or the benighted prelatist. They prophesied, used trance-utterance, and exercised gifts of healing. Angels ministered to them, as when Samuel Rutherford, having fallen into a well when a child, was pulled out by an angel. 1153 The substratum of primitive belief survives all changes of creed, and the folk impartially attributed magical powers to pagan Druid, Celtic saints, old crones and witches, and Presbyterian ministers.

Footnote 1093: IT i. 56; D'Arbois, v. 387.

Footnote 1094: See, e.g., "The Death of Muirchertach," RC xxiii. 394.

Footnote 1095: HN xxx. 4, 13.

Footnote 1096: Zimmer, Gloss. Hibern. 183; Reeves, Adamnan, 260.

Footnote 1097: Kennedy, 175; cf. IT i. 220.

Footnote 1098: See RC xii. 52 f.; D'Arbois, v. 403-404; O'Curry, MS. Mat. 505; Kennedy, 75, 196, 258.

Footnote 1099: D'Arbois, v. 277.

Footnote 1100: Stokes, Three Middle Irish Homilies, 24; IT iii. 325.

Footnote 1101: RC xii. 83; Miss Hull, 215; D'Arbois, v. 424; O'Curry, MC ii. 215.

Footnote 1102: Keating, 341; O'Curry, MS. Mat. 271.

Footnote 1103: RC xii. 81.

Footnote 1104: Miss Hull, 240 f.

Footnote 1105: Maury, 14.

Footnote 1106: Sébillot, ii. 226 f., i. 101, ii. 225; Bérenger-Féraud, Superstitions et Survivances, iii. 169 f.; Stat. Account, viii. 52.

Footnote 1107: Rev. des Trad. 1893, 613; Sébillot, ii. 224.

Footnote 1108: Bérenger-Féraud, iii. 218 f.; Sébillot, i. 100, 109; RC ii. 484; Frazer, Golden Bough 2, i. 67.

Footnote 1109: D'Arbois, v. 387; IT i. 52; Dixon, Gairloch, 165; Carmichael, Carm. Gad. ii. 25.

Footnote 1110: RC xvi. 152; Miss Hull, 243.

Footnote 1111: D'Arbois, v. 133; IT ii. 373.

Footnote 1112: Mela, iii. 6; RC xv. 471.

Footnote 1113: Joyce, OCR 1 f.; Kennedy, 235.

Footnote 1114: Bird-women pursued by Cúchulainn; D'Arbois, v. 178; for other instances see O'Curry, MS. Mat. 426; Miss Hull, 82.

Footnote 1115: D'Arbois, v. 215.

Footnote 1116: Joyce, OCR 279.

Footnote 1117: Ibid. 86.

Footnote 1118: RC xxiii. 394; Jocelyn, Vita S. Kent. c. 1.

Footnote 1119: RC xv. 446.

Footnote 1120: O'Conor, Rer. Hib. Scrip. ii. 142; Stokes, Lives of Saints, xxviii.

Footnote 1121: RC xv. 444.

Footnote 1122: supra.

Footnote 1123: O'Curry, MS. Mat. 240.

Footnote 1124: supra; Cæsar, vi. 14.

Footnote 1125: Zimmer, Gloss. Hiber. 271. Other Irish incantations, appealing to the saints, are found in the Codex Regularum at Klosternenburg (RC ii. 112).

Footnote 1126: Leahy, i. 137; Kennedy, 301.

Footnote 1127: Sauvé, RC vi. 67 f.; Carmichael, Carm. Gadel., passim; CM xii. 38; Joyce, SH i. 629 f.; Camden, Britannia, iv. 488; Scot, Discovery of Witchcraft, iii. 15.

Footnote 1128: For examples see O'Curry, MS. Met. 248; D'Arbois, ii. 190; RC xii. 71, xxiv. 279; Stokes, TIG xxxvi. f.

Footnote 1129: Windisch, Táin, line 3467.

Footnote 1130: Diod. Sic. v. 31.

Footnote 1131: D'Arbois, i. 271.

Footnote 1132: RC xii. 109; Nutt-Meyer, i. 2; D'Arbois, v. 445.

Footnote 1133: Petrie, Ancient Music of Ireland, i. 73; The Gael, i. 235 (fairy lullaby of MacLeod of MacLeod).

Footnote 1134: O'Curry, MS. Mat. 255.

Footnote 1135: Archæologia, xxxix. 509; Proc. Soc. Ant. iii. 92; Gaidoz, Le Dieu Gaul. du Soleil, 60 f.

Footnote 1136: IT iii. 409; but see Rh[^y]s, HL 215.

Footnote 1137: Pliny, HN xxix. 3. 54.

Footnote 1138: Rev. Arch. i. 227, xxxiii. 283.

Footnote 1139: Hoare, Modern Wiltshire, 56; Camden, Britannia, 815; Hazlitt, 194; Campbell, Witchcraft, 84. In the Highlands spindle-whorls are thought to have been perforated by the adder, which then passes through the hole to rid itself of its old skin.

Footnote 1140: Pliny, xxxii. 2. 24; Reinach, RC xx. 13 f.

Footnote 1141: Rev. Arch. i. 227; Greenwell, British Barrows, 165; Elton, 66; Renel, 95f., 194f.

Footnote 1142: Reinach, BF 286, 289, 362.

Footnote 1143: O'Curry, MS Mat. 387. See a paper by Hartland, "The Voice of the Stone of Destiny," Folk-lore Journal, xiv. 1903.

Footnote 1144: Petrie, Trans. Royal Irish Acad. xviii. pt. 2.

Footnote 1145: O'Curry, MS. Mat. 393 f.

Footnote 1146: Sébillot, i. 334 f.

Footnote 1147: Trollope, Brittany, ii. 229; Bérenger-Féraud, Superstitions et Survivances, i. 529 f.; Borlase, Dolmens of Ireland, iii. 580, 689, 841 f.

Footnote 1148: Rev. des Trad. 1894, 494; Bérenger-Féraud, i. 529, ii. 367; Elworthy, Evil Eye, 70.

Footnote 1149: Bérenger-Féraud, i. 523; Elworthy, 69, 106; Reinach, L'Anthropologie, iv. 33.

Footnote 1150: Kennedy, 324; Adamnan, Vita S. Col. ii. 35.

Footnote 1151: Life of S. Fechin of Fore, RC xii. 333; Life of S. Kieran, O'Grady, ii. 13; Amra Cholumbchille, RC xx. 41; Life of S. Moling, RC xxvii. 293; and other lives passim. See also Plummer, Vitæ Sanctorum Hiberniæ.

Footnote 1152: Adamnan, ii. 34. This pebble was long preserved, but mysteriously disappeared when the person who sought it was doomed to die.

Footnote 1153: Wodrow, Analecta, passim; Walker, Six Saints of the Covenant, ed. by Dr. Hay Fleming.

CHAPTER XXII
THE STATE OF THE DEAD

Among all the problems with which man has busied himself, none so appeals to his hopes and fears as that of the future life. Is there a farther shore, and if so, shall we reach it? Few races, if any, have doubted the existence of a future state, but their conceptions of it have differed greatly. But of all the races of antiquity, outside Egypt, the Celts seem to have cherished the most ardent belief in the world beyond the grave, and to have been preoccupied with its joys. Their belief, so far as we know it, was extremely vivid, and its chief characteristic was life in the body after death, in another region. 1154 This, coupled with the fact that it was taught as a doctrine by the Druids, made it the admiration of classical onlookers. But besides this belief there was another, derived from the ideas of a distant past, that the dead lived on in the grave—the two conceptions being connected. And there may also have been a certain degree of belief in transmigration. Although the Celts believed that the soul could exist apart from the body, there seems to be no evidence that they believed in a future existence of the soul as a shade. This belief is certainly found in some late Welsh poems, where the ghosts are described as wandering in the Caledonian forest, but these can hardly be made use of as evidence for the old pagan doctrine. The evidence for the latter may be gathered from classical observers, from archæology and from Irish texts.

Cæsar writes: "The Druids in particular wish to impress this on them that souls do not perish, but pass from one to another (ab aliis ... ad alios) after death, and by this chiefly they think to incite men to valour, the fear of death being overlooked." Later he adds, that at funerals all things which had been dear to the dead man, even living creatures, were thrown on the funeral pyre, and shortly before his time slaves and beloved clients were also consumed. 1155 Diodorus says: "Among them the doctrine of Pythagoras prevailed that the souls of men were immortal, and after completing their term of existence they live again, the soul passing into another body. Hence at the burial of the dead some threw letters addressed to dead relatives on the funeral pile, believing that the dead would read them in the next world." 1156 Valerius Maximus writes: "They would fain make us believe that the souls of men are immortal. I would be tempted to call these breeches-wearing folk fools, if their doctrine were not the same as that of the mantle-clad Pythagoras." He also speaks of money lent which would be repaid in the next world, because men's souls are immortal. 1157 These passages are generally taken to mean that the Celts believed simply in transmigration of the Pythagorean type. Possibly all these writers cite one common original, but Cæsar makes no reference to Pythagoras. A comparison with the Pythagorean doctrine shows that the Celtic belief differed materially from it. According to the former, men's souls entered new bodies, even those of animals, in this world, and as an expiation. There is nothing of this in the Celtic doctrine. The new body is not a prison-house of the soul in which it must expiate its former sins, and the soul receives it not in this world but in another. The real point of connection was the insistence of both upon immortality, the Druids teaching that it was bodily immortality. Their doctrine no more taught transmigration than does the Christian doctrine of the resurrection. Roman writers, aware that Pythagoras taught immortality via a series of transmigrations, and that the Druids taught a doctrine of bodily immortality, may have thought that the receiving of a new body meant transmigration. Themselves sceptical of a future life or believing in a traditional gloomy Hades, they were bound to be struck with the vigour of the Celtic doctrine and its effects upon conduct. The only thing like it of which they knew was the Pythagorean doctrine. Looked at in this light, Cæsar's words need not convey the idea of transmigration, and it is possible that he mistranslated some Greek original. Had these writers meant that the Druids taught transmigration, they could hardly have added the passages regarding debts being paid in the other world, or letters conveyed there by the dead, or human sacrifices to benefit the dead there. These also preclude the idea of a mere immortality of the soul. The dead Celt continued to be the person he had been, and it may have been that not a new body, but the old body glorified, was tenanted by his soul beyond the grave. This bodily immortality in a region where life went on as on this earth, but under happier conditions, would then be like the Vedic teaching that the soul, after the burning of the body, went to the heaven of Yama, and there received its body complete and glorified. The two conceptions, Hindu and Celtic, may have sprung from early "Aryan" belief.

This Celtic doctrine appears more clearly from what Lucan says of the Druidic teaching. "From you we learn that the bourne of man's existence is not the silent halls of Erebus, in another world (or region, in orbe alio) the spirit animates the members. Death, if your lore be true, is but the centre of a long life." For this reason, he adds, the Celtic warrior had no fear of death. 1158 Thus Lucan conceived the Druidic doctrine to be one of bodily immortality in another region. That region was not a gloomy state; rather it resembled the Egyptian Aalu with its rich and varied existence. Classical writers, of course, may have known of what appears to have been a sporadic Celtic idea, derived from old beliefs, that the soul might take the form of an animal, but this was not the Druidic teaching. Again, if the Gauls, like the Irish, had myths telling of the rebirth of gods or semi-divine beings, these may have been misinterpreted by those writers and regarded as eschatological. But such myths do not concern mortals. Other writers, Timagenes, Strabo, and Mela, 1159 speak only of the immortality of the soul, but their testimony is probably not at variance with that of Lucan, since Mela appears to copy Cæsar, and speaks of accounts and debts being passed on to the next world.

This theory of a bodily immortality is supported by the Irish sagas, in which ghosts, in our sense of the word, do not exist. The dead who return are not spectres, but are fully clothed upon with a body. Thus, when Cúchulainn returns at the command of S. Patrick, he is described exactly as if he were still in the flesh. "His hair was thick and black ... in his head his eye gleamed swift and grey.... Blacker than the side of a cooking spit each of his two brows, redder than ruby his lips." His clothes and weapons are fully described, while his chariot and horses are equally corporeal. 1160 Similar descriptions of the dead who return are not infrequent, e.g. that of Caoilte in the story of Mongan, whom every one believes to be a living warrior, and that of Fergus mac Roich, who reappeared in a beautiful form, adorned with brown hair and clad in his former splendour, and recited the lost story of the Táin. 1161 Thus the Irish Celts believed that in another world the spirit animated the members. This bodily existence is also suggested in Celtic versions of the "Dead Debtor" folk-tale cycle. Generally an animal in whose shape a dead man helps his benefactor is found in other European versions, but in the Celtic stories not an animal but the dead man himself appears as a living person in corporeal form. 1162 Equally substantial and corporeal, eating, drinking, lovemaking, and fighting are the divine folk of the síd or of Elysium, or the gods as they are represented in the texts. To the Celts, gods, síde, and the dead, all alike had a bodily form, which, however, might become invisible, and in other ways differed from the earthly body.

The archæological evidence of burial customs among the Celts also bears witness to this belief. Over the whole Celtic area a rich profusion of grave-goods has been found, consisting of weapons, armour, chariots, utensils, ornaments, and coins. 1163 Some of the interments undoubtedly point to sacrifice of wife, children, or slaves at the grave. Male and female skeletons are often in close proximity, in one case the arm of the male encircling the neck of the female. In other cases the remains of children are found with these. Or while the lower interment is richly provided with grave-goods, above it lie irregularly several skeletons, without grave-goods, and often with head separated from the body, pointing to decapitation, while in one case the arms had been tied behind the back. 1164 All this suggests, taken in connection with classical evidence regarding burial customs, that the future life was life in the body, and that it was a replica of this life, with the same affections, needs, and energies. Certain passages in Irish texts also describe burials, and tell how the dead were interred with ornaments and weapons, while it was a common custom to bury the dead warrior in his armour, fully armed, and facing the region whence enemies might be expected. Thus he was a perpetual menace to them and prevented their attack. 1165 Possibly this belief may account for the elevated position of many tumuli. Animals were also sacrificed. Hostages were buried alive with Fiachra, according to one text, and the wives of heroes sometimes express their desire to be buried along with their dead husbands. 1166

The idea that the body as well as the soul was immortal was probably linked on to a very primitive belief regarding the dead, and one shared by many peoples, that they lived on in the grave. This conception was never forgotten, even in regions where the theory of a distant land of the dead was evolved, or where the body was consumed by fire before burial. It appears from such practices as binding the dead with cords, or laying heavy stones or a mound of earth on the grave, probably to prevent their egress, or feeding the dead with sacrificial food at the grave, or from the belief that the dead come forth not as spirits, but in the body from the grave. This primitive conception, of which the belief in a subterranean world of the dead is an extension, long survived among various races, e.g. the Scandinavians, who believed in the barrow as the abiding place of the dead, while they also had their conception of Hel and Valhalla, or among the Slavs, side by side with Christian conceptions. 1167 It also survived among the Celts, though another belief in the orbis alius had arisen. This can be shown from modern and ancient folk-belief and custom.

In numerous Celtic folk-tales the dead rise in the body, not as ghosts, from the grave, which is sometimes described as a house in which they live. They perform their ordinary occupations in house or field; they eat with the living, or avenge themselves upon them; if scourged, blood is drawn from their bodies; and, in one curious Breton tale, a dead husband visits his wife in bed and she then has a child by him, because, as he said, "sa compte d'enfants" was not yet complete. 1168 In other stories a corpse becomes animated and speaks or acts in presence of the living, or from the tomb itself when it is disturbed. 1169 The earliest literary example of such a tale is the tenth century "Adventures of Nera," based on older sources. In this Nera goes to tie a withy to the foot of a man who has been hung. The corpse begs a drink, and then forces Nera to carry him to a house, where he kills two sleepers. 1170 All such stories, showing as they do that a corpse is really living, must in essence be of great antiquity. Another common belief, found over the Celtic area, is that the dead rise from the grave, not as ghosts, when they will, and that they appear en masse on the night of All Saints, and join the living. 1171

As a result of such beliefs, various customs are found in use, apparently to permit of the corpse having freedom of movement, contrary to the older custom of preventing its egress from the grave. In the west of Ireland the feet of the corpse are left free, and the nails are drawn from the coffin at the grave. In the Hebrides the threads of the shroud are cut or the bindings of feet, hands, and face are raised when the body is placed in the coffin, and in Brittany the arms and feet are left free when the corpse is dressed. 1172 The reason is said to be that the spirit may have less trouble in getting to the spirit world, but it is obvious that a more material view preceded and still underlies this later gloss. Many stories are told illustrating these customs, and the earlier belief, Christianised, appears in the tale of a woman who haunted her friends because they had made her grave-clothes so short that the fires of Purgatory burnt her knees. 1173

Earlier customs recorded among the Celts also point to the existence of this primitive belief influencing actual custom. Nicander says that the Celts went by night to the tombs of great men to obtain oracles, so much did they believe that they were still living there. 1174 In Ireland, oracles were also sought by sleeping on funeral cairns, and it was to the grave of Fergus that two bards resorted in order to obtain from him the lost story of the Táin. We have also seen how, in Ireland, armed heroes exerted a sinister influence upon enemies from their graves, which may thus have been regarded as their homes—a belief also underlying the Welsh story of Bran's head.

Where was the world of the dead situated? M. Reinach has shown, by a careful comparison of the different uses of the word orbis, that Lucan's words do not necessarily mean "another world," but "another region," i.e. of this world. 1175 If the Celts cherished so firmly the belief that the dead lived on in the grave, a belief in an underworld of the dead was bound in course of time to have been evolved as part of their creed. To it all graves and tumuli would give access. Classical observers apparently held that the Celtic future state was like their own in being an underworld region, since they speak of the dead Celts as inferi, or as going ad Manes, and Plutarch makes Camma speak of descending to her dead husband. 1176 What differentiated it from their own gloomy underworld was its exuberant life and immortality. This aspect of a subterranean land presented no difficulty to the Celt, who had many tales of an underworld or under-water region more beautiful and blissful than anything on earth. Such a subterranean world must have been that of the Celtic Dispater, a god of fertility and growth, the roots of things being nourished from his kingdom. From him men had descended, 1177 probably a myth of their coming forth from his subterranean kingdom, and to him they returned after death to a blissful life.

Several writers, notably M. D'Arbois, assume that the orbis alius of the dead was the Celtic island Elysium. But that Elysium never appears in the tales as a land of the dead. It is a land of gods and deathless folk who are not those who have passed from this world by death. Mortals may reach it by favour, but only while still in life. It might be argued that Elysium was regarded in pagan times as the land of the dead, but after Christian eschatological views prevailed, it became a kind of fairyland. But the existing tales give no hint of this, and, after being carefully examined, they show that Elysium had always been a place distinct from that of the departed, though there may have arisen a tendency to confuse the two.

If there was a genuine Celtic belief in an island of the dead, it could have been no more than a local one, else Cæsar would not have spoken as he does of the Celtic Dispater. Such a local belief now exists on the Breton coast, but it is mainly concerned with the souls of the drowned. 1178 A similar local belief may explain the story told by Procopius, who says that Brittia (Britain), an island lying off the mouth of the Rhine, is divided from north to south by a wall beyond which is a noxious region. This is a distorted reminiscence of the Roman wall, which would appear to run in this direction if Ptolemy's map, in which Scotland lies at right angles to England, had been consulted. Thither fishermen from the opposite coast are compelled to ferry over at dead of night the shades of the dead, unseen to them, but marshalled by a mysterious leader. 1179 Procopius may have mingled some local belief with the current tradition that Ulysses' island of the shades lay in the north, or in the west. 1180 In any case his story makes of the gloomy land of the shades a very different region from the blissful Elysium of the Celts and from their joyous orbis alius, nor is it certain that he is referring to a Celtic people.

Traces of the idea of an underworld of the dead exist in Breton folk-belief. The dead must travel across a subterranean ocean, and though there is scarcely any tradition regarding what happens on landing, M. Sébillot thinks that formerly "there existed in the subterranean world a sort of centralisation of the different states of the dead." If so, this must have been founded on pagan belief. The interior of the earth is also believed to be the abode of fabulous beings, of giants, and of fantastic animals, and there is also a subterranean fairy world. In all this we may see a survival of the older belief, modified by Christian teaching, since the Bretons suppose that purgatory and hell are beneath the earth and accessible from its surface. 1181

Some British folk-lore brought to Greece by Demetrius and reported by Plutarch might seem to suggest that certain persons—the mighty dead—were privileged to pass to the island Elysium. Some islands near Britain were called after gods and heroes, and the inhabitants of one of these were regarded as sacrosanct by the Britons, like the priestesses of Sena. They were visited by Demetrius, who was told that the storms which arose during his visit were caused by the passing away of some of the "mighty" or of the "great souls." It may have been meant that such mighty ones passed to the more distant islands, but this is certainly not stated. In another island, Kronos was imprisoned, watched over by Briareus, and guarded by demons. 1182 Plutarch refers to these islands in another work, repeating the story of Kronos, and saying that his island is mild and fragrant, that people live there waiting on the god who sometimes appears to them and prevents their departing. Meanwhile they are happy and know no care, spending their time in sacrificing and hymn-singing or in studying legends and philosophy.

Plutarch has obviously mingled Celtic Elysium beliefs with the classical conception of the Druids. 1183 In Elysium there is no care, and favoured mortals who pass there are generally prevented from returning to earth. The reference to Kronos may also be based partly on myths of Celtic gods of Elysium, partly on tales of heroes who departed to mysterious islands or to the hollow hills where they lie asleep, but whence they will one day return to benefit their people. So Arthur passed to Avalon, but in other tales he and his warriors are asleep beneath Craig-y-Ddinas, just as Fionn and his men rest within this or that hill in the Highlands. Similar legends are told of other Celtic heroes, and they witness to the belief that great men who had died would return in the hour of their people's need. In time they were thought not to have died at all, but to be merely sleeping and waiting for their hour. 1184 The belief is based on the idea that the dead are alive in grave or barrow, or in a spacious land below the earth, or that dead warriors can menace their foes from the tomb.

Thus neither in old sagas, nor in Märchen, nor in popular tradition, is the island Elysium a world of the dead. For the most part the pagan eschatology has been merged in that of Christianity, while the Elysium belief has remained intact and still survives in a whole series of beautiful tales.

The world of the dead was in all respects a replica of this world, but it was happier. In existing Breton and Irish belief—a survival of the older conception of the bodily state of the dead—they resume their tools, crafts, and occupations, and they preserve their old feelings. Hence, when they appear on earth, it is in bodily form and in their customary dress. Like the pagan Gauls, the Breton remembers unpaid debts, and cannot rest till they are paid, and in Brittany, Ireland, and the Highlands the food and clothes given to the poor after a death, feed and clothe the dead in the other world. 1185 If the world of the dead was subterranean,—a theory supported by current folk-belief, 1186 —the Earth-goddess or the Earth-god, who had been first the earth itself, then a being living below its surface and causing fertility, could not have become the divinity of the dead until the multitude of single graves or barrows, in each of which the dead lived, had become a wide subterranean region of the dead. This divinity was the source of life and growth; hence he or she was regarded as the progenitor of mankind, who had come forth from the underworld and would return there at death. It is not impossible that the Breton conception of Ankou, death personified, is a reminiscence of the Celtic Dispater. He watches over all things beyond the grave, and carries off the dead to his kingdom. But if so he has been altered for the worse by mediæval ideas of "Death the skeleton". 1187 He is a grisly god of death, whereas the Celtic Dis was a beneficent god of the dead who enjoyed a happy immortality. They were not cold phantasms, but alive and endowed with corporeal form and able to enjoy the things of a better existence, and clad in the beautiful raiment and gaudy ornaments which were loved so much on earth. Hence Celtic warriors did not fear death, and suicide was extremely common, while Spanish Celts sang hymns in praise of death, and others celebrated the birth of men with mourning, but their deaths with joy. 1188 Lucan's words are thus the truest expression of Celtic eschatology—"In another region the spirit animates the members; death, if your lore be true, is but the passage to enduring life."

There is no decisive evidence pointing to any theory of moral retribution beyond the grave among the pagan Celts. Perhaps, since the hope of immortality made warriors face death without a tremor, it may have been held, as many other races have believed, that cowards would miss the bliss of the future state. Again, in some of the Irish Christian visions of the otherworld and in existing folk-belief, certain characteristics of hell may not be derived from Christian eschatology, e.g. the sufferings of the dead from cold. 1189 This might point to an old belief in a cold region whither some of the dead were banished. In the Adventures of S. Columba's Clerics, hell is reached by a bridge over a glen of fire, 1190 and a narrow bridge leading to the other world is a common feature in most mythologies. But here it may be borrowed from Scandinavian sources, or from such Christian writings as the Dialogues of S. Gregory the Great. 1191 It might be contended that the Christian doctrine of hell has absorbed an earlier pagan theory of retribution, but of this there is now no trace in the sagas or in classical references to the Celtic belief in the future life. Nor is there any reference to a day of judgment, for the passage in which Loegaire speaks of the dead buried with their weapons till "the day of Erdathe," though glossed "the day of judgment of the Lord," does not refer to such a judgment. 1192 If an ethical blindness be attributed to the Celts for their apparent lack of any theory of retribution, it should be remembered that we must not judge a people's ethics wholly by their views of future punishment. Scandinavians, Greeks, and Semites up to a certain stage were as unethical as the Celts in this respect, and the Christian hell, as conceived by many theologians, is far from suggesting an ethical Deity.

Footnote 1154: Skene, i. 370.

Footnote 1155: Cæsar, vi. 14, 19.

Footnote 1156: Diod. Sic. v, 28.

Footnote 1157: Val. Max. vi. 6. 10.

Footnote 1158: Phars. i. 455 f.

Footnote 1159: Amm. Marc. xv. 9; Strabo, iv. 4; Mela, iii. 2.

Footnote 1160: Miss Hull, 275.

Footnote 1161: Nutt-Meyer, i. 49; Miss Hull, 293.

Footnote 1162: Larminie, 155; Hyde, Beside the Fire, 21, 153; CM xiii. 21; Campbell, WHT, ii. 21; Le Braz2, i. p. xii.

Footnote 1163: Von Sacken, Das Grabfeld von Hallstatt; Greenwell, British Barrows; RC x. 234; Antiquary, xxxvii. 125; Blanchet, ii. 528 f.; Anderson, Scotland in Pagan Times.

Footnote 1164: L'Anthropologie, vi. 586; Greenwell, op. cit. 119.

Footnote 1165: Nutt-Meyer, i. 52; O'Donovan, Annals, i. 145, 180; RC xv. 28. In one case the enemy disinter the body of the king of Connaught, and rebury it face downwards, and then obtain a victory. This nearly coincides with the dire results following the disinterment of Bran's head (O'Donovan, i. 145; cf. p. 242, supra).

Footnote 1166: LU 130a; RC xxiv. 185; O'Curry, MC i. p. cccxxx; Campbell, WHT iii. 62; Leahy, i. 105.

Footnote 1167: Vigfusson-Powell, Corpus Poet. Boreale, i. 167, 417-418, 420; and see my Childhood of Fiction, 103 f.

Footnote 1168: Larminie, 31; Le Braz2, ii. 146, 159, 161, 184, 257 (the rôle of the dead husband is usually taken by a lutin or follet, Luzel, Veillées Bretons, 79); Rev. des Trad. Pop. ii. 267; Ann. de Bretagne, viii. 514.

Footnote 1169: Le Braz2, i. 313. Cf. also an incident in the Voyage of Maelduin.

Footnote 1170: RC x. 214f. Cf. Kennedy, 162; Le Braz2, i. 217, for variants.

Footnote 1171: Curtin, Tales, 156; supra.

Footnote 1172: Curtin, Tales, 156; Campbell, Superstitions, 241; Folk-Lore, xiii. 60; Le Braz2, i. 213.

Footnote 1173: Folk-Lore, ii. 26; Yeats, Celtic Twilight, 166.

Footnote 1174: Tertullian, de Anima, 21.

Footnote 1175: Reinach, RC xxii. 447.

Footnote 1176: Val. Max. vi. 6; Mela, iii. 2. 19; Plut. Virt. mul 20.

Footnote 1177: supra.

Footnote 1178: Le Braz2, i. p. xxxix. This is only one out of many local beliefs (cf. Sébillot, ii. 149).

Footnote 1179: Procop. De Bello Goth. vi. 20.

Footnote 1180: Claudian, In Rufin. i. 123.

Footnote 1181: Sébillot, i. 418 f.

Footnote 1182: de Defectu Orac. 18. An occasional name for Britain in the Mabinogion is "the island of the Mighty" (Loth, i. 69, et passim). To the storm incident and the passing of the mighty, there is a curious parallel in Fijian belief. A clap of thunder was explained as "the noise of a spirit, we being near the place in which spirits plunge to enter the other world, and a chief in the neighbourhood having just died" (Williams, Fiji, i. 204).

Footnote 1183: de Facie Lun[oe], 26.

Footnote 1184: See Hartland, Science of Fairy Tales, 209; Macdougall, Folk and Hero Tales, 73, 263; Le Braz2, i. p. xxx. Mortals sometimes penetrated to the presence of these heroes, who awoke. If the visitor had the courage to tell them that the hour had not yet come, they fell asleep again, and he escaped. In Brittany, rocky clefts are believed to be the entrance to the world of the dead, like the cave of Lough Dearg. Similar stories were probably told of these in pagan times, though they are now adapted to Christian beliefs in purgatory or hell.

Footnote 1185: Le Braz2, i. p. xl, ii. 4; Curtin, 10; MacPhail, Folk-Lore, vi. 170.

Footnote 1186: supra, and Logan, Scottish Gael, ii. 374; Folk-Lore, viii. 208, 253.

Footnote 1187: Le Braz2, i. 96, 127, 136f., and Intro, xlv.

Footnote 1188: Philostratus, Apoll. of Tyana, v. 4; Val. Max. ii. 6. 12.

Footnote 1189: Le Braz1, ii. 91; Curtin, Tales, 146. The punishment of suffering from ice and snow appears in the Apocalypse of Paul and in later Christian accounts of hell.

Footnote 1190: RC xxvi. 153.

Footnote 1191: Bk. iv. ch. 36.

Footnote 1192: Erdathe, according to D'Arbois, means (1) "the day in which the dead will resume his colour," from dath, "colour"; (2) "the agreeable day," from data, "agreeable" (D'Arbois, i. 185; cf. Les Druides, 135).

CHAPTER XXIII
REBIRTH AND TRANSMIGRATION

In Irish sagas, rebirth is asserted only of divinities or heroes, and, probably because this belief was obnoxious to Christian scribes, while some MSS. tell of it in the case of certain heroic personages, in others these same heroes are said to have been born naturally. There is no textual evidence that it was attributed to ordinary mortals, and it is possible that, if classical observers did not misunderstand the Celtic doctrine of the future life, their references to rebirth may be based on mythical tales regarding gods or heroes. We shall study these tales as they are found in Irish texts.

In the mythological cycle, as has been seen, Etain, in insect form, fell into a cup of wine. She was swallowed by Etar, and in due time was reborn as a child, who was eventually married by Eochaid Airem, but recognized and carried off by her divine spouse Mider. Etain, however, had quite forgotten her former existence as a goddess. 1193

In one version of Cúchulainn's birth story Dechtire and her women fly away as birds, but are discovered at last by her brother Conchobar in a strange house, where Dechtire gives birth to a child, of whom the god Lug is apparently the father. In another version the birds are not Dechtire and her women, for she accompanies Conchobar as his charioteer. They arrive at the house, the mistress of which gives birth to a child, which Dechtire brings up. It dies, and on her return from the burial Dechtire swallows a small animal when drinking. Lug appears to her by night, and tells her that he was the child, and that now she was with child by him (i.e. he was the animal swallowed by her). When he was born he would be called Setanta, who was later named Cúchulainn. Cúchulainn, in this version, is thus a rebirth of Lug, as well as his father. 1194

In the Tale of the Two Swineherds, Friuch and Rucht are herds of the gods Ochall and Bodb. They quarrel, and their fighting in various animal shapes is fully described. Finally they become two worms, which are swallowed by two cows; these then give birth to the Whitehorn and to the

Black Bull of Cuailgne, the animals which were the cause of the Táin. The swineherds were probably themselves gods in the older versions of this tale. 1195

Other stories relate the rebirth of heroes. Conchobar is variously said to be son of Nessa by her husband Cathbad, or by her lover Fachtna. But in the latter version an incident is found which points to a third account. Nessa brings Cathbad a draught from a river, but in it are two worms which he forces her to swallow. She gives birth to a son, in each of whose hands is a worm, and he is called Conchobar, after the name of the river into which he fell soon after his birth. The incident closes with the words, "It was from these worms that she became pregnant, say some." 1196 Possibly the divinity of the river had taken the form of the worms and was reborn as Conchobar. We may compare the story of the birth of Conall Cernach. His mother was childless, until a Druid sang spells over a well in which she bathed, and drank of its waters. With the draught she swallowed a worm, "and the worm was in the hand of the boy as he lay in his mother's womb; and he pierced the hand and consumed it." 1197

The personality of Fionn is also connected with the rebirth idea. In one story, Mongan, a seventh-century king, had a dispute with his poet regarding the death of the hero Fothad. The Fian Caoilte returns from the dead to prove Mongan right, and he says, "We were with thee, with Fionn." Mongan bids him be silent, because he did not wish his identity with Fionn to be made known. "Mongan, however, was Fionn, though he would not let it be told." 1198 In another story Mongan is son of Manannan, who had prophesied of this event. Manannan appeared to the wife of Fiachna when he was fighting the Saxons, and told her that unless she yielded herself to him her husband would be slain. On hearing this she agreed, and next day the god appeared fighting with Fiachna's forces and routed the slain. "So that this Mongan is a son of Manannan mac Lir, though he is called Mongan son of Fiachna." 1199 In a third version Manannan makes the bargain with Fiachna, and in his form sleeps with the woman. Simultaneously with Mongan's birth, Fiachna's attendant had a son who became Mongan's servant, and a warrior's wife bears a daughter who became his wife. Manannan took Mongan to the Land of Promise and kept him there until he was sixteen. 1200 Many magical powers and the faculty of shape-shifting are attributed to Mongan, and in some stories he is brought into connection with the síd. 1201 Probably a myth told how he went to Elysium instead of dying, for he comes from "the Land of Living Heart" to speak with S. Columba, who took him to see heaven. But he would not satisfy the saints' curiosity regarding Elysium, and suddenly vanished, probably returning there. 1202

This twofold account of Mongan's birth is curious. Perhaps the idea that he was a rebirth of Fionn may have been suggested by the fact that his father was called Fiachna Finn, while it is probable that some old myth of a son of Manannan's called Mongan was attached to the personality of the historic Mongan.

About the era of Mongan, King Diarmaid had two wives, one of whom was barren. S. Finnen gave her holy water to drink, and she brought forth a lamb; then, after a second draught, a trout, and finally, after a third, Aed Slane, who became high king of Ireland in 594. This is a Christianised version of the story of Conall Cernach's birth. 1203

In Welsh mythology the story of Taliesin affords an example of rebirth. After the transformation combat of the goddess Cerridwen and Gwion, resembling that of the swine-herds, Gwion becomes a grain of wheat, which Cerridwen in the form of a hen swallows, with the result that he is reborn of her as Taliesin. 1204

Most of these stories no longer exist in their primitive form, and various ideas are found in them—conception by magical means, divine descent through the amour of a divinity and a mortal, and rebirth.

As to the first, the help of magician or priest is often invoked in savage society and even in European folk-custom in case of barrenness. Prayers, charms, potions, or food are the means used to induce conception, but perhaps at one time these were thought to cause it of themselves. In many tales the swallowing of a seed, fruit, insect, etc., results in the birth of a hero or heroine, and it is probable that these stories embody actual belief in such a possibility. If the stories of Conall Cernach and Aed Slane are not attenuated instances of rebirth, say, of the divinity of a well, they are examples of this belief. The gift of fruitfulness is bestowed by Druid and saint, but in the story of Conall it is rather the swallowing of the worm than the Druid's incantation that causes conception, and is the real motif of the tale.

Where the rebirth of a divinity occurs as the result of the swallowing of a small animal, it is evident that the god has first taken this form. The Celt, believing in conception by swallowing some object, and in shape-shifting, combined his information, and so produced a third idea, that a god could take the form of a small animal, which, when swallowed, became his rebirth. 1205 If, as the visits of barren women to dolmens and megalithic monuments suggest, the Celts believed in the possibility of the spirit of a dead man entering a woman and being born of her or at least aiding conception,—a belief held by other races, 1206 —this may have given rise to myths regarding the rebirth of gods by human mothers. At all events this latter Celtic belief is paralleled by the American Indian myths, e.g. of the Thlinkeet god Yehl who transformed himself now into a pebble, now into a blade of grass, and, being thus swallowed by women, was reborn.

In the stories of Etain and of Lud, reborn as Setanta, this idea of divine transformation and rebirth occurs. A similar idea may underlie the tale of Fionn and Mongan. As to the tales of Gwion and the Swineherds, the latter the servants of gods, and perhaps themselves regarded once as divinities, who in their rebirth as bulls are certainly divine animals, they present some features which require further consideration. The previous transformations in both cases belong to the Transformation Combat formula of many Märchen, and obviously were not part of the original form of the myths. In all such Märchen the antagonists are males, hence the rebirth incident could not form part of them. In the Welsh tale of Gwion and in the corresponding Taliesin poem, the ingenious fusion of the Märchen formula with an existing myth of rebirth must have taken place at an early date. 1207 This is also true of The Two Swineherds, but in this case, since the myth told how two gods took the form of worms and were reborn of cows, the formula had to be altered. Both remain alive at the end of the combat, contrary to the usual formula, because both were males and both were reborn. The fusion is skilful, because the reborn personages preserve a remembrance of their former transformations, 1208 just as Mongan knows of his former existence as Fionn. In other cases there is no such remembrance. Etain had forgotten her former existence, and Cúchulainn does not appear to know that he is a rebirth of Lug.

The relation of Lug to Cúchulainn deserves further inquiry. While the god is reborn he is also existing as Lug, just as having been swallowed as a worm by Dechtire, he appears in his divine form and tells her he will be born of her. In the Táin he appears fighting for Cúchulainn, whom he there calls his son. There are thus two aspects of the hero's relationship to Lug; in one he is a rebirth of the god, in the other he is his son, as indeed he seems to represent himself in The Wooing of Emer, and as he is called by Laborcham just before his death. 1209 In one of the birth-stories he is clearly Lug's son by Dechtire. But both versions may simply be different aspects of one belief, namely, that a god could be reborn as a mortal and yet continue his divine existence, because all birth is a kind of rebirth. The men of Ulster sought a wife for Cúchulainn, "knowing that his rebirth would be of himself," i.e. his son would be himself even while he continued to exist as his father. Examples of such a belief occur elsewhere, e.g. in the Laws of Manu, where the husband is said to be reborn of his wife, and in ancient Egypt, where the gods were called "self-begotten," because each was father to the son who was his true image or himself. Likeness implied identity, in primitive belief.

Thus the belief in mortal descent from the gods among the Celts may have involved the theory of a divine avatar. The god became father of a mortal by a woman, and part of himself passed over to the child, who was thus the god himself.

Conchobar was also a rebirth of a god, but he was named from the river whence his mother had drawn water containing the worms which she swallowed. This may point to a lost version in which he was the son of a river-god by Nessa. This was quite in accordance with Celtic belief, as is shown by such names as Dubrogenos, from dubron, "water," and genos, "born of"; Divogenos, Divogena, "son or daughter of a god," possibly a river-god, since deivos is a frequent river name; and Rhenogenus, "son of the Rhine." 1210 The persons who first bore these names were believed to have been begotten by divinities. Mongan's descent from Manannan, god of the sea, is made perfectly clear, and the Welsh name Morgen = Morigenos, "son of the sea," probably points to a similar tale now lost. Other Celtic names are frequently pregnant with meaning, and tell of a once-existing rich mythology of divine amours with mortals. They show descent from deities—Camulogenus (son of Camulos), Esugenos (son of Esus), Boduogenus (son of Bodva); or from tree-spirits—Dergen (son of the oak), Vernogenus (son of the alder); or from divine animals—Arthgen (son of the bear), Urogenus (son of the urus). 1211 What was once an epithet describing divine filiation became later a personal name. So in Greece names like Apollogenes, Diogenes, and Hermogenes, had once been epithets of heroes born of Apollo, Zeus, and Hermes.

Thus it was a vital Celtic belief that divinities might unite with mortals and beget children. Heroes enticed away to Elysium enjoyed the love of its goddesses—Cúchulainn that of Fand; Connla, Bran, and Oisin that of unnamed divinities. So, too, the goddess Morrigan offered herself to Cúchulainn. The Christian Celts of the fifth century retained this belief, though in a somewhat altered form. S. Augustine and others describe the shaggy demons called dusii by the Gauls, who sought the couches of women in order to gratify their desires. 1212 The dusii are akin to the incubi and fauni, and do not appear to represent the higher gods reduced to the form of demons by Christianity, but rather a species of lesser divinities, once the object of popular devotion.

These beliefs are also connected with the Celtic notions of transformation and transmigration—the one signifying the assuming of another shape for a time, the other the passing over of the soul or the personality into another body, perhaps one actually existing, but more usually by actual rebirth. As has been seen, this power of transformation was claimed by the Druids and by other persons, or attributed to them, and they were not likely to minimise their powers, and would probably boast of them on all occasions.

Such boasts are put into the mouths of the Irish Amairgen and the Welsh Taliesin. As the Milesians were approaching Ireland, Amairgen sang verses which were perhaps part of a ritual chant:

> "I am the wind which blows over the sea,
> I am the wave of the ocean,
> I am the bull of seven battles,
> I am the eagle on the rock...
> I am a boar for courage,
> I am a salmon in the water, etc." 1213

Professor Rh[^y]s points out that some of these verses need not mean actual transformation, but mere likeness, through "a primitive formation of predicate without the aid of a particle corresponding to such a word as 'like.'" 1214 Enough, however, remains to show the claim of the magician. Taliesin, in many poems, makes similar claims, and says, "I have been in a multitude of shapes before I assumed a consistent form" — that of a sword, a tear, a star, an eagle, etc. Then he was created, without father or mother. 1215 Similar pretensions are common to the medicine-man everywhere. But from another point of view they may be mere poetic extravagances such as are common in Celtic poetry. 1216 Thus Cúchulainn says: "I was a hound strong for combat ... their little champion ... the casket of every secret for the maidens," or, in another place, "I am the bark buffeted from wave to wave ... the ship after the losing of its rudder ... the little apple on the top of the tree that little thought of its falling." 1217 These are metaphoric descriptions of a comparatively simple kind. The full-blown bombast appears in the Colloquy of the Two Sages, where Nede and Fercertne exhaust language in describing themselves to each other. 1218 Other Welsh bards besides Taliesin make similar boasts to his, and Dr. Skene thinks that their claims "may have been mere bombast." 1219 Still some current belief in shape-shifting, or even in rebirth, underlies some of these boastings and gives point to them. Amairgen's "I am" this or that, suggests the inherent power of transformation; Taliesin's "I have been," the actual transformations. Such assertions do not involve "the powerful pantheistic doctrine which is at once the glory and error of Irish philosophy," as M. D'Arbois claims, 1220 else are savage medicine-men, boastful of their shape-shifting powers, philosophic pantheists. The poems are merely highly developed forms of primitive beliefs in shape-shifting, such as are found among all savages and barbaric folk, but expressed in the boastful language in which the Celt delighted.

How were the successive shape-shiftings effected? To answer this we shall first look at the story of Tuan Mac Caraill, who survived from the days of Partholan to those of S. Finnen. He was a decrepit man at the coming of Nemed, and one night, having lain down to sleep, he awoke as a stag, and lived in this form to old age. In the same way he became a boar, a hawk, and a salmon, which was caught and eaten by Cairell's wife, of whom he was born as Tuan, with a perfect recollection of his different forms. 1221

This story, the invention of a ninth or tenth century Christian scribe to account for the current knowledge of the many invasions of Ireland, 1222 must have been based on pagan myths of a similar kind, involving successive transformations and a final rebirth. Such a myth may have been told of Taliesin, recounting his transformations and his final rebirth, the former being replaced at a later time by the episode of the Transformation Combat, involving no great lapse of time. Such a series of successive shapes — of every beast, a dragon, a wolf, a stag, a salmon, a seal, a swan — were ascribed to Mongan and foretold by Manannan, and Mongan refers to some of them in his colloquy with S. Columba — "when I was a deer ... a salmon ... a seal ... a roving wolf ... a man." 1223 Perhaps the complete story was that of a fabulous hero in human form, who assumed different shapes, and was finally reborn. But the transformation of an old man, or an old animal, into new youthful and vigorous forms might be regarded as a kind of transmigration — an extension of the transformation idea, but involving no metempsychosis, no passing of the soul into another body by rebirth. Actual transmigration or rebirth occurs only at the end of the series, and, as in the case of Etain, Lug, etc., the pre-existent person is born of a woman after being swallowed by her. Possibly the transformation belief has reacted on the other, and obscured a belief in actual metempsychosis as a result of the soul of an ancestor passing into a woman and being reborn as her next child. Add to this that the soul is often thought of as a tiny animal, and we see how a point d'appui for the more materialistic belief was afforded. The insect or worms of the rebirth stories may have been once forms of the soul. It is easy also to see how, a theory of conception by swallowing various objects being already in existence, it might be thought possible that eating a salmon — a transformed man — would cause his rebirth from the eater.

The Celts may have had no consistent belief on this subject, the general idea of the future life being of a different kind. Or perhaps the various beliefs in transformation, transmigration, rebirth, and conception by unusual means, are too inextricably mingled to be separated. The nucleus of the tales seems to be the possibility of rebirth, and the belief that the soul was still clad in a bodily form after death and was itself a material thing. But otherwise some of them are not distinctively Celtic, and have been influenced by old Märchen formulæ of successive changes adopted by or forced upon some person, who is finally reborn. This formulæ is already old in the fourteenth century B.C. Egyptian story of the Two Brothers.

Such Celtic stories as these may have been known to classical authors, and have influenced their statements regarding eschatology. Yet it can hardly be said that the tales themselves bear witness to a general transmigration doctrine current among the Celts, since the stories concern divine or heroic personages. Still the belief may have had a certain currency among them, based on primitive theories of soul life. Evidence that it existed side by side with the more general doctrines of the future life may be found in old or existing folk-belief. In some cases the dead have an animal form, as in the Voyage of Maelduin, where birds on an island are said to be souls, or in the legend of S. Maelsuthain, whose pupils appear to him after death as birds. 1224 The bird form of the soul after death is still a current belief in the Hebrides. Butterflies in Ireland, and moths in Cornwall, and in France bats or butterflies, are believed to be souls of the dead. 1225 King Arthur is thought by Cornishmen to have died and to have been changed into the form of a raven, and in mediæval Wales souls of the wicked appear as ravens, in Brittany as black dogs, petrels, or hares, or serve their term of penitence as cows or bulls, or remain as crows till the day of judgment. 1226 Unbaptized infants become birds; drowned sailors appear as beasts or birds; and the souls of girls deceived by lovers haunt them as hares. 1227

These show that the idea of transmigration may not have been foreign to the Celtic mind, and it may have arisen from the idea that men assumed their totem animal's shape at death. Some tales of shape-shifting are probably due to totemism, and it is to be noted that in Kerry peasants will not eat hares because they contain the souls of their grandmothers. 1228 On the other hand, some of these survivals may mean no more than that the soul itself has already an animal form, in which it would naturally be seen after death. In Celtic folk-belief the soul is seen leaving the body in sleep as a bee, butterfly, gnat, mouse, or mannikin. 1229 Such a belief is found among most savage races, and might easily be mistaken for transmigration, or also assist the formation of the idea of transmigration. Though the folk-survivals show that transmigration was not necessarily alleged of all the dead, it may have been a sufficiently vital belief to colour the mythology, as we see from the existing tales, adulterated though these may have been.

The general belief has its roots in primitive ideas regarding life and its propagation—ideas which some hold to be un-Celtic and un-Aryan. But Aryans were "primitive" at some period of their history, and it would be curious if, while still in a barbarous condition, they had forgotten their old beliefs. In any case, if they adopted similar beliefs from non-Aryan people, this points to no great superiority on their part. Such beliefs originated the idea of rebirth and transmigration. 1230 Nevertheless this was not a characteristically Celtic eschatological belief; that we find in the theory that the dead lived on in the body or assumed a body in another region, probably underground.

Footnote 1193: For textual details see Zimmer, Zeit. für Vergl. Sprach. xxviii. 585 f. The tale is obviously archaic. For a translation see Leahy, i. 8 f.

Footnote 1194: IT i. 134 f.; D'Arbois, v. 22. There is a suggestion in one of the versions of another story, in which Setanta is child of Conchobar and his sister Dechtire.

Footnote 1195: IT iii. 245; RC xv. 465; Nutt-Meyer, ii. 69.

Footnote 1196: Stowe MS. 992, RC vi. 174; IT ii. 210; D'Arbois, v. 3f.

Footnote 1197: IT iii. 393. Cf. the story of the wife of Cormac, who was barren till her mother gave her pottage. Then she had a daughter (RC xxii. 18).

Footnote 1198: Nutt-Meyer, i. 45 f., text and translation.

Footnote 1199: Ibid. 42 f.

Footnote 1200: Ibid. 58. The simultaneous birth formula occurs in many Märchen, though that of the future wife is not common.

Footnote 1201: Nutt-Meyer, i. 52, 57, 85, 87.

Footnote 1202: ZCP ii. 316 f. Here Mongan comes directly from Elysium, as does Oisin before meeting S. Patrick.

Footnote 1203: IT iii. 345; O'Grady, ii. 88. Cf. Rees, 331.

Footnote 1204: Guest, iii. 356 f.; supra.

Footnote 1205: In some of the tales the small animal still exists independently after the birth, but this is probably not their primitive form.

Footnote 1206: See my Religion: Its Origin and Forms, 76-77.

Footnote 1207: Skene, i. 532. After relating various shapes in which he has been, the poet adds that he has been a grain which a hen received, and that he rested in her womb as a child. The reference in this early poem from a fourteenth century MS. shows that the fusion of the Märchen formula with a myth of rebirth was already well known. See also Guest, iii. 362, for verses in which the transformations during the combat are exaggerated.

Footnote 1208: Skene, i. 276, 532.

Footnote 1209: Miss Hull, 67; D'Arbois, v. 331.

Footnote 1210: For various forms of geno-, see Holder, i. 2002; Stokes, US 110.

Footnote 1211: For all these names see Holder, s.v.

Footnote 1212: S. Aug. de Civ. Dei, xv. 23; Isidore, Orat. viii. 2. 103. Dusios may be connected with Lithuanian dvaese, "spirit," and perhaps with [Greek: Thehos] (Holder, s.v.). D'Arbois sees in the dusii water-spirits, and compares river-names like Dhuys, Duseva, Dusius (vi. 182; RC xix. 251). The word may be connected with Irish duis, glossed "noble" (Stokes, TIG 76). The Bretons still believe in fairies called duz, and our word dizzy may be connected with dusios, and would then have once signified the madness following on the amour, like Greek [Greek: nympholeptos], or "the inconvenience of their succubi," described by Kirk in his Secret Commonwealth of the Elves.

Footnote 1213: LL 12b; TOS v. 234.

Footnote 1214: Rh[^y]s, HL 549.

Footnote 1215: Skene, i. 276, 309, etc.

Footnote 1216: Sigerson, Bards of the Gael, 379.

Footnote 1217: Miss Hull, 288; Hyde, Lit. Hist. of Ireland, 300.

Footnote 1218: RC xxvi. 21.

Footnote 1219: Skene, ii. 506.

Footnote 1220: D'Arbois, ii. 246, where he also derives Erigena's pantheism from Celtic beliefs, such as he supposes to be exemplified by these poems.

Footnote 1221: LU 15a; D'Arbois, ii. 47 f.; Nutt-Meyer, ii. 294 f.

Footnote 1222: Another method of accounting for this knowledge was to imagine a long-lived personage like

Fintan who survived for 5000 years. D'Arbois, ii. ch. 4. Here there was no transformation or rebirth.

Footnote 1223: Nutt-Meyer, i. 24; ZCP ii. 316.

Footnote 1224: O'Curry, MS. Mat. 78.

Footnote 1225: Wood-Martin, Pagan Ireland, 140; Choice Notes, 61; Monnier, 143; Maury, 272.

Footnote 1226: Choice Notes, 69; Rees, 92; Le Braz2, ii. 82, 86, 307; Rev. des Trad. Pop. xii. 394.

Footnote 1227: Le Braz2, ii. 80; Folk-lore Jour. v. 189.

Footnote 1228: Folk-Lore, iv. 352.

Footnote 1229: Carmichael, Carm. Gadel. ii. 334; Rh[^y]s, CFL 602; Le Braz2, i. 179, 191, 200.

Footnote 1230: Mr. Nutt, Voyage of Bran, derived the origin of the rebirth conception from orgiastic cults.

CHAPTER XXIV
ELYSIUM

The Celtic conception of Elysium, the product at once of religion, mythology, and romantic imagination, is found in a series of Irish and Welsh tales. We do not know that a similar conception existed among the continental Celts, but, considering the likeness of their beliefs in other matters to those of the insular Celts, there is a strong probability that it did. There are four typical presentations of the Elysium conception. In Ireland, while the gods were believed to have retired within the hills or síd, it is not unlikely that some of them had always been supposed to live in these or in a subterranean world, and it is therefore possible that what may be called the subterranean or síd type of Elysium is old. But other types also appear — that of a western island Elysium, of a world below the waters, and of a world co-extensive with this and entered by a mist.

The names of the Irish Elysium are sometimes of a general character — Mag Mór, "the Great Plain"; Mag Mell, "the Pleasant Plain"; Tír n'Aill, "the Other-world"; Tir na m-Beo, "the Land of the Living"; Tír na n-Og, "the Land of Youth"; and Tír Tairngiri, "the Land of Promise" — possibly of Christian origin. Local names are Tír fa Tonn, "Land under Waves"; I-Bresail and the Land of Falga, names of the island Elysium. The last denotes the Isle of Man as Elysium, and it may have been so regarded by Goidels in Britain at an early time. 1231 To this period may belong the tales of Cúchulainn's raid on Falga, carried at a later time to Ireland. Tír Tairngiri is also identified with the Isle of Man. 1232

A brief résumé of the principal Elysium tales is necessary as a preliminary to a discussion of the problems which they involve, though it can give but little idea of the beauty and romanticism of the tales themselves. These, if not actually composed in pagan times, are based upon story-germs current before the coming of Christianity to Ireland.

1. The síd Elysium. — In the story of Etain, when Mider discovered her in her rebirth, he described the land whither he would carry her, its music and its fair people, its warm streams, its choice mead and wine. There is eternal youth, and love is blameless. It is within Mider's síd, and Etain

accompanies him there. In the sequel King Eochaid's Druid discovers the síd, which is captured by the king, who then regains Etain. 1233 Other tales refer to the síd in similar terms, and describe its treasures, its food and drink better than those of earth. It is in most respects similar to the island Elysium, save that it is localised on earth.

2. The island Elysium.—The story of the voyage of Bran is found fragmentarily in the eleventh century LU, and complete in the fourteenth and sixteenth century MSS. It tells how Bran heard mysterious music when asleep. On waking he found a silver branch with blossoms, and next day there appeared a mysterious woman singing the glory of the land overseas, its music, its wonderful tree, its freedom from pain and death. It is one of thrice fifty islands to the west of Erin, and there she dwells with thousands of "motley women." Before she disappears the branch leaps into her hand. Bran set sail with his comrades and met Manannan crossing the sea in his chariot. The god told him that the sea was a flowery plain, Mag Mell, and that all around, unseen to Bran, were people playing and drinking "without sin." He bade him sail on to the Land of Women. Then the voyagers went on and reached the Isle of Joy, where one of their number remained behind. At last they came to the Land of Women, and we hear of their welcome, the dreamlike lapse of time, the food and drink which had for each the taste he desired. Finally the tale recounts their home-sickness, the warning they received not to set foot on Erin, how one of their number leaped ashore and turned to ashes, how Bran from his boat told of his wanderings and then disappeared for ever. 1234

Another story tells how Connla was visited by a goddess from Mag Mell. Her people dwell in a síd and are called "men of the síd." She invites him to go to the immortal land, and departs, leaving him an apple, which supports him for a month without growing less. Then she reappears and tells Connla that "the Ever-Living Ones" desire him to join them. She bids him come with her to the Land of Joy where there are only women. He steps into her crystal boat and vanishes from his father and the Druid who has vainly tried to exercise his spells against her. 1235 In this tale there is a confusion between the síd and the island Elysium.

The eighteenth century poem of Oisin in Tír na n-Og is probably based on old legends, and describes how Niam, daughter of the king of Tír na n-Og, placed geasa on Oisin to accompany her to that land of immortal youth and beauty. He mounted on her steed, which plunged forwards across the sea, and brought them to the land where Oisin spent three hundred years before returning to Ireland, and there suffering, as has been seen, from the breaking of the tabu not to set foot on the soil of Erin. 1236

In Serglige Conculaind, "Cúchulainn's Sickness," the goddess Fand, deserted by Manannan, offers herself to the hero if he will help her sister's husband Labraid against his enemies in Mag Mell. Labraid lives in an island frequented by troops of women, and possessing an inexhaustible vat of mead and trees with magic fruit. It is reached with marvellous speed in a boat of bronze. After a preliminary visit by his charioteer Laeg, Cúchulainn goes thither, vanquishes Labraid's foes, and remains a month with Fand. He returns to Ireland, and now we hear of the struggle for him between his wife Emer and Fand. But Manannan suddenly appears, reawakens Fand's love, and she departs with him. The god shakes his cloak between her and Cúchulainn to prevent their ever meeting again. 1237 In this story Labraid, Fand, and Liban, Fand's sister, though dwellers on an island Elysium, are called síd-folk. The two regions are partially confused, but not wholly, since Manannan is described as coming from his own land (Elysium) to woo Fand. Apparently Labraid of the Swift Hand on the Sword (who, though called "chief of the síde", is certainly a war-god) is at enmity with Manannan's hosts, and it is these with whom Cúchulainn has to fight. 1238

In an Ossianic tale several of the Fians were carried off to the Land of Promise. After many adventures, Fionn, Diarmaid, and others discover them, and threaten to destroy the land if they are not restored. Its king, Avarta, agrees to the restoration, and with fifteen of his men carries the Fians to Erin on one horse. Having reached there, he bids them look at a certain field, and while they are doing so, he and his men disappear. 1239

3. Land under Waves.—Fiachna, of the men of the síd, appeared to the men of Connaught, and begged their help against Goll, who had abducted his wife. Loegaire and his men dive with Fiachna into Loch Naneane, and reach a wonderful land, with marvellous music and where the rain is ale. They and the síd-folk attack the fort of Mag Mell and defeat Goll. Each then obtains a woman of the síde, but at the end of a year they become homesick. They are warned not to descend from horseback in Erin. Arrived among their own people, they describe the marvels of Tír fa Tonn, and then return there, and are no more seen. 1240 Here, again, the síd Elysium and Land under Waves are confused, and the divine tribes are at war, as in the story of Cúchulainn.

In a section of the Ossianic tale just cited, Fionn and his men arrive on an island, where Diarmaid reaches a beautiful country at the bottom of a well. This is Tír fa Tonn, and Diarmaid fights its king who has usurped his nephew's inheritance, and thus recovers it for him. 1241

4. Co-extensive with this world.—An early example of this type is found in the Adventures of Cormac. A divine visitant appeared to Cormac and gave him in exchange for his wife, son, and daughter, his branch of

golden apples, which when shaken produced sweetest music, dispelling sorrow. After a year Cormac set out to seek his family, and as he journeyed encountered a mist in which he discovered a strange house. Its master and mistress—Manannan and his consort—offered him shelter. The god brought in a pig, every quarter of which was cooked in the telling of a true tale, the pig afterwards coming to life again. Cormac, in his tale, described how he had lost his family, whereupon Manannan made him sleep, and brought in his wife and children in. Later he produced a cup which broke when a lie was told, but became whole again when a true word was spoken. The god said Cormac's wife had now a new husband, and the cup broke, but was restored when the goddess declared this to be a lie. Next morning all had disappeared, and Cormac and his family found themselves in his own palace, with cup and branch by their side. 1242 Similarly, in The Champion's Ecstasy, a mysterious horseman appears out of a mist to Conn and leads him to a palace, where he reveals himself as the god Lug, and where there is a woman called "the Sovereignty of Erin." Beside the palace is a golden tree. 1243 In the story of Bran, Mag Mell is said to be all around the hero, though he knows it not—an analogous conception to what is found in these tales, and another instance is that of the mysterious house entered by Conchobar and Dechtire. 1244 Mag Mell may thus have been regarded as a mysterious district of Erin. This magic mist enclosing a marvellous dwelling occurs in many other tales, and it was in a mist that the Tuatha Déa came to Ireland.

A certain correspondence to these Irish beliefs is found in Brythonic story, but here the Elysium conception has been influenced by Christian ideas. Elysium is called Annwfn, meaning "an abyss," "the state of the dead," "hell," and it is also conceived of as is elfydd, "beneath the earth." 1245 But in the tales it bears no likeness to these meanings of the word, save in so far as it has been confused by their Christian redactors with hell. It is a region on the earth's surface or an over-or under-sea world, in which some of the characteristics of the Irish Elysium are found—a cauldron, a well of drink sweeter than wine, and animals greatly desired by mortals, while it is of great beauty and its people are not subject to death or disease. Hence the name Annwfn has probably taken the place of some earlier pagan title of Elysium.

In the tale of Pwyll, the earliest reference to Annwfn occurs. It is ruled by Arawn, at war with Hafgan. Arawn obtains the help of Pwyll by exchanging kingdoms with him for a year, and Pwyll defeats Hafgan. It is a beautiful land, where merriment and feasting go on continuously, and its queen is of great loveliness. It has no subterranean character, and is conceived apparently as contiguous to Pwyll's kingdom. 1246 In other tales it is the land whence Gwydion and others obtain various animals. 1247 The later folk-conception of the demoniac dogs of Annwfn may be based on an old myth of dogs with which its king hunted. These are referred to in the story of Pwyll. 1248

Annwfn is also the name of a land under waves or over sea, called also Caer Sidi, "the revolving castle," about which "are ocean's streams." It is "known to Manawyddan and Pryderi," just as the Irish Elysium was ruled by Manannan. 1249 Another "Caer of Defence" is beneath the waves. 1250 Perhaps the two ideas were interchangeable. The people of this land are free from death and disease, and in it is "an abundant well, sweeter than white wine the drink in it." There also is a cauldron belonging to the lord of Annwfn, which was stolen by Arthur and his men. Such a cauldron is the property of people belonging to a water world in the Mabinogion. 1251

The description of the isle of Avallon (later identified with Glastonbury), whither Arthur was carried, completes the likeness to the Irish Elysium. No tempest, excess of heat or cold, nor noxious animal afflicts it; it is blessed with eternal spring and with fruit and flowers growing without labour; it is the land of eternal youth, unvisited by death or disease. It has a regia virgo lovelier than her lovely attendants; she cured Arthur of his wounds, hence she is the Morgen of other tales, and she and her maidens may be identified with the divine women of the Irish isle of women. Morgen is called a dea phantastica, and she may be compared with Liban, who cured Cúchulainn of his sickness. 1252

The identification of Avallon with Glastonbury is probably post-pagan, and the names applied to Glastonbury—Avallon, Insula Pomonum, Insula vitrea—may be primitive names of Elysium. William of Malmesbury derives Insula Pomonum in its application to Glastonbury from a native name Insula Avallonioe, which he connects with the Brythonic avalla, "apples," because Glastenig found an apple tree there. 1253 The name may thus have been connected with marvellous apple trees, like those of the Irish Elysium. But he also suggests that it may be derived from the name of Avalloc, living there with his daughters. Avalloc is evidently the "Rex Avallon" (Avallach) to whose palace Arthur was carried and healed by the regia virgo. 1254 He may therefore have been a mythic lord of Elysium, and his daughters would correspond to the maidens of the isle. William also derives "Glastonbury" from the name of an eponymous founder Glastenig, or from its native name Ynesuuitron, "Glass Island." This name reappears in Chretien's Eric in the form "l'isle de verre." Giraldus explains the name from the glassy waters around Glastonbury, but it may be an early name of Elysium. 1255 Glass must have appealed to the imagination of Celt, Teuton, and Slav, for we hear of Merlin's glass house, a glass fort discovered by Arthur, a glass tower attacked by the Milesians, Etain's glass grianan, and a boat of glass which conveyed Connla to Elysium. In Teutonic and Slavonic myth and Märchen, glass mountains, on which dwell mysterious personages, frequently occur.

The origin of the Celtic Elysium belief may be found in universal myths of a golden age long ago in some distant Elysian region, where men had lived with the gods. Into that region brave mortals might still penetrate, though it was lost to mankind as a whole. In some mythologies this Elysium is the land whither men go after death. Possibly the Celtic myth of man's early intercourse with the gods in a lost region took two forms. In one it was a joyful subterranean region whither the Celt hoped to go after death. In the other it was not recoverable, nor was it the land of the dead, but favoured mortals might reach it in life. The Celtic Elysium belief, as known through the tales just cited, is always of this second kind. We surmise, however, that the land of the dead was a joyous underworld ruled over by a god of fertility and of the dead, and from that region men had originally come forth. The later association of gods with the síd was a continuation of this belief, but now the síd are certainly not a land of the dead, but Elysium pure and simple. There must therefore have been at an early period a tendency to distinguish between the happy region of the dead, and the distant Elysium, if the two were ever really connected. The subject is obscure, but it is not impossible that another origin of the Elysium idea may be found in the phenomenon of the setting sun: it suggested to the continental Celts that far off there was a divine land where the sun-god rested. When the Celts reached the coast this divine western land would necessarily be located in a far-off island, seen perhaps on the horizon. Hence it would also be regarded as connected with the sea-god, Manannan, or by whatsoever name he was called. The distant Elysium, whether on land or across the sea, was conceived in identical terms, and hence also whenever the hollow hills or síd were regarded as an abode of the gods, they also were described just as Elysium was.

The idea of a world under the waters is common to many mythologies, and, generally speaking, it originated in the animistic belief that every part of nature has its indwelling spirits. Hence the spirits or gods of the waters were thought of as dwelling below the waters. Tales of supernatural beings appearing out of the waters, the custom of throwing offerings therein, the belief that human beings were carried below the surface or could live in the region beneath the waves, are all connected with this animistic idea. Among the Celts this water-world assumed many aspects of Elysium, and it has names in common with it, e.g. it is called Mag Mell. Hence in many popular tales it is hardly differentiated from the island Elysium; oversea and under-waves are often synonymous. Hence, too, the belief that such water-worlds as I-Bresail, or Welsh fairy-lands, or sunken cities off the Breton coast, rise periodically to the surface, and would remain there permanently, like an island Elysium, if some mortal would fulfil certain conditions. 1256

The Celtic belief in Tír fa Tonn is closely connected with the current belief in submerged towns or lands, found in greatest detail on the Breton coast. Here there are many such legends, but most prominent are those which tell how the town of Is was submerged because of the wickedness of its people, or of Dahut, its king's daughter, who sometimes still seeks the love of mortals. It is occasionally seen below the waves or even on their surface. 1257 Elsewhere in Celtic regions similar legends are found, and the submersion is the result of a curse, of the breaking of a tabu, or of neglect to cover a sacred well. 1258 Probably the tradition of actual cataclysms or inroads of the sea, such as the Celts encountered on the coasts of Holland, may account for some of these legends, which then mingled with myths of the divine water-world.

The idea that Elysium is co-extensive with this world and hidden in a mist is perhaps connected with the belief in the magical powers of the gods. As the Druids could raise a mist at will, so too might the gods, who then created a temporary Elysium in it. From such a mist, usually on a hill, supernatural beings often emerged to meet mortals, and in Märchen fairyland is sometimes found within a mist. 1259 It was already believed that part of the gods' land was not far off; it was invisibly on or within the hills on whose slopes men saw the mist swirling mysteriously. Hence the mist may simply have concealed the síd of the gods. But there may also have been a belief that this world was actually interpenetrated by the divine world, for this is believed of fairyland in Welsh and Irish folk-lore. Men may unwittingly interfere with it, or have it suddenly revealed to them, or be carried into it and made invisible. 1260

In most of the tales Elysium is a land without grief or death, where there is immortal youth and peace, and every kind of delight. But in some, while the sensuous delights are still the same, the inhabitants are at war, invite the aid of mortals to overcome their foes, and are even slain in fight. Still in both groups Elysium is a land of gods and supernatural folk whither mortals are invited by favour. It is never the world of the dead; its people are not mortals who have died and gone thither. The two conceptions of Elysium as a land of peace and deathlessness, and as a land where war and death may occur, may both be primitive. The latter may have been formed by reflecting back on the divine world the actions of the world of mortals, and it would also be on a parallel with the conception of the world of the dead where warriors perhaps still fought, since they were buried with their weapons. There were also myths of gods warring with each other. But men may also have felt that the gods were not as themselves, that their land must be one of peace and deathlessness. Hence the idea of the peaceful Elysium, which perhaps found most favour with the people. Mr. Nutt thought that the idea of a warlike Elysium may have resulted from Scandinavian influence acting on existing tales of a peaceful Elysium, 1261 but we know that old myths of divine wars already existed. Perhaps this conception arose among the Celts as a warlike people, appealing to their warrior instincts, while the peaceful Elysium may have been the product of the Celts as an agricultural folk, for we have seen that the Celt was now a fighter, now a farmer. In its peaceful aspect Elysium is "a familiar, cultivated land," where the fruits of the earth are produced without labour, and where there are no storms or excess of heat or cold — the fancies which would appeal to a toiling, agricultural people. There food is produced magically, yet naturally, and in agricultural ritual men sought to increase their food supply magically. In the tales this process is, so to speak, heightened. 1262

Some writers have maintained that Elysium is simply the land of the dead, although nothing in the existing tales justifies this interpretation. M. D'Arbois argues for this view, resting his theory mainly on a passage in the story of Connla, interpreted by him in a way which does not give its real meaning. 1263 The words are spoken by the goddess to Connla, and their sense is — "The Ever-Living Ones invite thee. Thou art a champion to Tethra's people. They see thee every day in the assemblies of thy fatherland, among thy familiar loved ones." 1264 M. D'Arbois assumes that Tethra, a Fomorian, is lord of Elysium, and that after his defeat by the Tuatha Déa, he, like Kronos, took refuge there, and now reigns as lord of the dead. By translating ar-dot-chiat ("they see thee," 3rd plur., pres. ind.) as "on t'y verra," he maintains that Connla, by going to Elysium, will be seen among the gatherings of his dead kinsfolk. But the words, "Thou art a champion to Tethra's people," cannot be made to mean that Tethra is a god of the dead. It means simply that Connla is a mighty warrior, one of those whom Tethra, a war-god, would have approved. The phrase, "Tethra's mighty men," used elsewhere, 1265 is a conventional one for warriors. The rest of the goddess's words imply that the Immortals from afar, or perhaps "Tethra's mighty men," i.e. warriors in this world, see Connla in the assemblies of his fatherland in Erin, among his familiar friends. Dread death awaits them, she has just said, but the Immortals desire Connla to escape that by coming to Elysium. Her words do not imply that he will meet his dead ancestors there, nor is she in any sense a goddess of death. If the dead went to Elysium, there would be little need for inviting a living person to go there. Had Connla's dead ancestors or Tethra's people (warriors) been in Elysium, this would contradict the picture drawn by the goddess of the land whither she desires him to go — a land of women, not of men. Moreover, the rulers of Elysium are always members of the Tuatha Dé Danann or the síd-folk, never a Fomorian like Tethra. 1266

M. D'Arbois also assumes that "Spain" in Nennius' account of the Irish invasions and in Irish texts means the land of the dead, and that it was introduced in place of some such title as Mag Mór or Mag Mell by "the euhemerising process of the Irish Christians." But in other documents penned by Irish Christians these and other pagan titles of Elysium remain unchanged. Nor is there the slightest proof that the words used by Tuan MacCaraill about the invaders of Ireland, "They all died," were rendered in an original text, now lost according to M. D'Arbois, "They set sail for Mag Mór or Mag Mell," a formula in which Nennius saw indications of a return to Spain. 1267 Spain, in this hypothetical text, was the Land of the Dead or Elysium, whence the invaders came. This "lost original" exists in M. D'Arbois imagination, and there is not the slightest evidence for these alterations. Once, indeed, Tailtiu is called daughter of Magh Mór, King of Spain, but here a person, not a place, is spoken of. 1268 Sir John Rh[^y]s accepts the identification of Spain with Elysium as the land of the dead, and finds in every reference to Spain a reference to the Other-world, which he regards as a region ruled by "dark divinities." But neither the lords of Elysium nor the Celtic Dispater were dark or gloomy deities, and the land of the dead was certainly not a land of darkness any more than Elysium. The numerous references to Spain probably point to old traditions regarding a connection between Spain and Ireland in early times, both commercial and social, and it is not impossible that Goidelic invaders did reach Ireland from Spain. 1269 Early maps and geographers make Ireland and Spain contiguous; hence in an Irish tale Ireland is visible from Spain, and this geographical error would strengthen existing traditions. 1270 "Spain" was used vaguely, but it does not appear to have meant Elysium or the Land of the Dead. If it did, it is strange that the Tuatha Dé Danann are never brought into connection with it.

One of the most marked characteristics of the Celtic Elysium is its deathlessness. It is "the land of the living" or of "the Ever-Living Ones," and of eternal youth. Most primitive races believe that death is an accident befalling men who are naturally immortal; hence freedom from such an accident naturally characterises the people of the divine land. But, as in other mythologies, that immortality is more or less dependent on the eating or drinking of some food or drink of immortality. Manannan had immortal swine, which, killed one day, came alive next day, and with their flesh he made the Tuatha Dé Danann immortal. Immortality was also conferred by the drinking of Goibniu's ale, which, either by itself or with the flesh of swine, formed his immortal feast. The food of Elysium was inexhaustible, and whoever ate it found it to possess that taste which he preferred. The fruit of certain trees in Elysium was also believed to confer immortality and other qualities. Laeg saw one hundred and fifty trees growing in Mag Mell; their nuts fed three hundred people. The apple given by the goddess to Connla was inexhaustible, and he was still eating it with her when Teigue, son of Cian, visited Elysium. "When once they had partaken of it, nor age nor dimness could affect them." 1271 Apples, crimson nuts, and rowan berries are specifically said to be the food of the gods in the tale of Diarmaid and Grainne. Through carelessness one of the berries was dropped on earth, and from it grew a tree, the berries of which had the effect of wine or mead, and three of them eaten by a man of a hundred years made him youthful. It was guarded by a giant. 1272 A similar tree growing on earth—a rowan guarded by a dragon, is found in the tale of Fraoch, who was bidden to bring a branch of it to Ailill. Its berries had the virtue of nine meals; they healed the wounded, and added a year to a man's life. 1273 At the wells which were the source of Irish rivers were supposed to grow hazel-trees with crimson nuts, which fell into the water and were eaten by salmon. 1274 If these were caught and eaten, the eater obtained wisdom and knowledge. These wells were in Erin, but in some instances the well with its hazels and salmon is in the Other-world, 1275 and it is obvious that the crimson nuts are the same as the food of the gods in Diarmaid and Grainne.

Why should immortality be dependent on the eating of certain foods? Most of man's irrational ideas have some reason in them, and probably man's knowledge that without food life would come to an end, joined to his idea of deathlessness, led him to believe that there was a certain food which produced immortality just as ordinary food supported life. On it gods and deathless beings were fed. Similarly, as water cleansed and invigorated, it was thought that some special kind of water had these powers in a marvellous degree. Hence arose the tales of the Fountain of Youth and the belief in healing wells. From the knowledge of the nourishing power of food, sprang the idea that some food conferred the qualities inherent in it, e.g. the flesh of divine animals eaten sacramentally, and that gods obtained their immortality from eating or drinking. This idea is widespread. The Babylonian gods had food and water of Life; Egyptian myth spoke of the bread and beer of eternity which nourished the gods; the Hindus and Iranians knew of the divine soma or haoma; and in Scandinavian myth the gods renewed their youth by tasting Iduna's golden apples.

In Celtic Elysium tales, the fruit of a tree is most usually the food of immortality. The fruit never diminishes and always satisfies, and it is the food of the gods. When eaten by mortals it confers immortality upon them; in other words, it makes them of like nature to the gods, and this is doubtless derived from the widespread idea that the eating of food given by a stranger makes a man of one kin with him. Hence to eat the food of gods, fairies, or of the dead, binds the mortal to them and he cannot leave their land. This might be illustrated from a wide range of myth and folk-belief. When Connla ate the apple he at once desired to go to Elysium, and he could not leave it once he was there; he had become akin to its people. In the stories of Bran and Oisin, they are not said to have eaten such fruit, but the primitive form of the tales may have contained this incident, and this would explain why they could not set foot on earth unscathed, and why Bran and his followers, or, in the tale of Fiachna, Loegaire and his men who had drunk the ale of Elysium, returned thither. In other tales, it is true, those who eat food in Elysium can return to earth—Cormac and Cúchulainn; but had we the primitive form of these tales we should probably find that they had refrained from eating. The incident of the fruit given by an immortal to a mortal may have borrowed something from the wide folk-custom of the presentation of an apple as a gage of love or as a part of the marriage rite. 1276 Its acceptance denotes willingness to enter upon betrothal or marriage. But as in the Roman rite of confarreatio with its savage parallels, the underlying idea is probably that which has just been considered, namely, that the giving and acceptance of food produces the bond of kinship.

As various nuts and fruits were prized in Ireland as food, and were perhaps used in some cases to produce an intoxicant, 1277 it is evident that the trees of Elysium were, primarily, a magnified form of earthly trees. But all such trees were doubtless objects of a cult before their produce was generally eaten; they were first sacred or totem-trees, and their food eaten only occasionally and sacramentally. If so, this would explain why they grew in Elysium and their fruit was the food of the gods. For whatever man eats or drinks is generally supposed to have been first eaten and drunk by the gods, like the soma. But, growing in Elysium, these trees, like the trees of most myths of Elysium, are far more marvellous than any known on earth. They have branches of silver and golden apples; they have magical supplies of fruit, they produce wonderful music which sometimes causes sleep or oblivion; and birds perch in their branches and warble melody "such that the sick would sleep to it." It should be noted also that, as Miss Hull points out, in some tales the branch of a divine tree becomes a talisman leading the mortal to Elysium; in this resembling the golden bough plucked by Æneas before visiting the underworld. 1278 This, however, is not the fundamental characteristic of the tree, in Irish story. Possibly, as Mr. A.B. Cook maintains, the branch giving entrance to Elysium is derived from the branch borne by early Celtic kings of the wood, while the tree is an imaginative form of those which incarnated a vegetation spirit. 1279 Be this as it may, it is rather the fruit eaten by the mortal which binds him to the Immortal Land.

The inhabitants of Elysium are not only immortal, but also invisible at will. They make themselves visible to one person only out of many present with him. Connla alone sees the goddess, invisible to his father and the Druid. Mananuan is visible to Bran, but there are many near the hero whom he does not see; and when the same god comes to Fand, he is invisible to Cúchulainn and those with him. So Mider says to Etain, "We behold, and are not beheld." 1280 Occasionally, too, the people of Elysium have the power of shape-shifting—Fand and Liban appear to Cúchulainn as birds.

The hazel of knowledge connects wisdom with the gods' world, and in Celtic belief generally civilisation and culture were supposed to have come from the gods. The things of their land were coveted by men, and often stolen thence by them. In Welsh and Irish tales, often with reference to the Other-world, a magical cauldron has a prominent place. Dagda possessed such a cauldron and it was inexhaustible, and a vat of inexhaustible mead is described in the story of Cúchulain's Sickness. Whatever was put into such cauldrons satisfied all, no matter how numerous they might be. 1281 Cúchulainn obtained one from the daughter of the king of Scath, and also carried off the king's three cows. 1282 In an analogous story, he stole from Cúroi, by the connivance of his wife Bláthnat, her father Mider's cauldron, three cows, and the woman herself. But in another version Cúchulainn and Cúroi go to Mider's stronghold in the Isle of Falga (Elysium), and steal cauldron, cows, and Bláthnat. These were taken from Cúchulainn by Cúroi; hence his revenge as in the previous tale. 1283 Thus the theft was from Elysium. In the Welsh poem "The Spoils of Annwfn," Arthur stole a cauldron from Annwfn. Its rim was encrusted with pearls, voices issued from it, it was kept boiling by the breath of nine maidens, and it would not boil a coward's food. 1284

As has been seen from the story of Gwion, he was set to watch a cauldron which must boil until it yielded "three drops of the grace of inspiration." It belonged to Tegid Voel and Cerridwen, divine rulers of a Land under the Waters. 1285 In the Mabinogi of Branwen, her brother Bran received a cauldron from two beings, a man and a huge woman, who came from a lake. This cauldron was given by him to the king of Erin, and it had the property of restoring to life the slain who were placed in it. 1286

The three properties of the cauldron—inexhaustibility, inspiration, and regeneration—may be summed up in one word, fertility; and it is significant that the god with whom such a cauldron was associated, Dagda, was a god of fertility. But we have just seen it associated, directly or indirectly, with goddesses—Cerridwen, Branwen, the woman from the lake—and perhaps this may point to an earlier cult of goddesses of fertility, later transferred to gods. In this light the cauldron's power of restoring to life is significant, since in early belief life is associated with what is feminine. Woman as the fruitful mother suggested that the Earth, which produced and nourished, was also female. Hence arose the cult of the Earth-mother who was often also a goddess of love as well as of fertility. Cerridwen, in all probability, was a goddess of fertility, and Branwen a goddess of love. 1287 The cult of fertility was usually associated with orgiastic and indiscriminate love-making, and it is not impossible that the cauldron, like the Hindu yoni, was a symbol of fertility. 1288 Again, the slaughter and cooking of animals was usually regarded as a sacred act in primitive life. The animals were cooked in enormous cauldrons, which were found as an invariable part of the furniture of every Celtic house. 1289 The quantities of meat which they contained may have suggested inexhaustibility to people to whom the cauldron was already a symbol of fertility. Thus the symbolic cauldron of a fertility cult was merged with the cauldron used in the religious slaughter and cooking of animal food. The cauldron was also used in ritual. The Cimri slaughtered human victims over a cauldron and filled it with their blood; victims sacrificed to Teutates were suffocated in a vat (semicupium); and in Ireland "a cauldron of truth" was used in the ordeal of boiling water. 1290 Like the food of men which was regarded as the food of the gods, the cauldron of this world became the marvellous cauldron of the Other-world, and as it then became necessary to explain the origin of such cauldrons on earth, myths arose, telling how they had been stolen from the divine land by adventurous heroes, Cúchulainn, Arthur, etc. In other instances, the cauldron is replaced by a magic vessel or cup stolen from supernatural beings by heroes of the Fionn saga or of Märchen. 1291 Here, too, it may be noted that the Graal of Arthurian romance has affinities with the Celtic cauldron. In the Conte du Graal of pseudo-Chrétien, a cup comes in of itself and serves all present with food. This is a simple conception of the Graal, but in other poems its magical and sacrosanct character is heightened. It supplies the food which the eater prefers, it gives immortal youth and immunity from wounds. In these respects it presents an unmistakable likeness to the cauldron of Celtic myth. But, again, it was the vessel in which Christ had instituted the Blessed Sacrament; it contained His Blood; and it had been given by our Lord to Joseph of Arimathea. Thus in the Graal there was a fusion of the magic cauldron of Celtic paganism and the Sacred Chalice of Christianity, with the product made mystic and glorious in a most wonderful manner. The story of the Graal became immensely popular, and, deepening in ethical, mystical, and romantic import as time went on, was taken up by one poet after another, who "used it as a type of the loftiest goal of man's effort." 1292

In other ways myth told how the gifts of civilisation came from the gods' world. When man came to domesticate animals, it was believed in course of time that the knowledge of domestication or, more usually, the animals themselves had come from the gods, only, in this case, the animals were of a magical, supernatural kind. Such a belief underlies the stories in which Cúchulainn steals cows from their divine owners. In other instances, heroes who obtain a wife from the síd-folk, obtain also cattle from the síd. 1293 As has been seen the swine given to Pryderi by Arawn, king of Annwfn, and hitherto unknown to man, are stolen from him by Gwydion, Pryderi being son of Pwyll, a temporary king of Annwfn, and in all probability both were lords of Elysium. The theft, in the original form of the myth, must thus have been from Elysium, though we have a hint in "The Spoils of Annwfn" that Gwydion (Gweir) was unsuccessful and was imprisoned in Annwfn, to which imprisonment the later blending of Annwfn with hell gave a doleful aspect. 1294 In a late Welsh MS., a white roebuck and a puppy (or, in the Triads, a bitch, a roebuck, and a lapwing) were stolen by Amæthon from Annwfn, and the story presents archaic features. 1295 In some of these tales the animals are transferred to earth by a divine or semi-divine being, in whom we may see an early Celtic culture-hero. The tales are attenuated forms of older myths which showed how all domestic animals were at first the property of the gods, and an echo of these is still heard in Märchen describing the theft of cattle from fairyland. In the most primitive form of the tales the theft was doubtless from the underworld of gods of fertility, the place whither the dead went. But with the rise of myths telling of a distant Elysium, it was inevitable that some tales should connect the animals and the theft with that far-off land. So far as the Irish and Welsh tales are concerned, the thefts seem mainly to be from Elysium. 1296

Love-making has a large place in the Elysium tales. Goddesses seek the love of mortals, and the mortal desires to visit Elysium because of their enticements. But the love-making of Elysium is "without sin, without crime," and this phrase may perhaps suggest the existence of ritual sex-unions at stated times for magical influence upon the fertility of the earth, these unions not being regarded as immoral, even when they trespassed on customary tribal law. In some of the stories Elysium is composed of many islands, one of which is the "island of women." 1297 These women and their queen give their favours to Bran and his men or to Maelduin and his company. Similar "islands of women" occur in Märchen, still current among Celtic peoples, and actual islands were or still are called by that name — Eigg and Groagez off the Breton coast. 1298 Similar islands of women are known to Chinese, Japanese, and Ainu folk-lore, to Greek mythology (Circe's and Calypso's islands), and to ancient Egyptian conceptions of the future life.

1299 They were also known elsewhere, 1300 and we may therefore assume that in describing such an island as part of Elysium, the Celts were using something common to universal folk-belief. But it may also owe something to actual custom, to the memory of a time when women performed their rites in seclusion, a seclusion perhaps recalled in the references to the mysterious nature of the island, its inaccessibility, and its disappearance once the mortal leaves it. To these rites men may have been admitted by favour, but perhaps to their detriment, because of their temporary partner's extreme erotic madness. This is the case in the Chinese tales of the island of women, and this, rather than home-sickness, may explain the desire of Bran, Oisin, etc., to leave Elysium. Celtic women performed orgiastic rites on islands, as has been seen. 1301 All this may have originated the belief in an island of beautiful divine women as part of Elysium, while it also heightened its sensuous aspect.

Borrowed from the delight which the Celt took in music is the recurring reference to the marvellous music which swelled in Elysium. There, as the goddess says to Bran, "there is nothing rough or harsh, but sweet music striking on the ear." It sounded from birds on every tree, from the branches of trees, from marvellous stones, and from the harps of divine musicians. And this is recalled in the ravishing music which the belated traveller hears as he passes fairy-haunted spots—"what pipes and timbrels, what wild ecstasy!" The romantic beauty of Elysium is described in these Celtic tales in a way unequalled in all other sagas or Märchen, and it is insisted on by those who come to lure mortals there. The beauty of its landscapes—hills, white cliffs, valleys, sea and shore, lakes and rivers,—of its trees, its inhabitants, and its birds,—the charm of its summer haze, is obviously the product of the imagination of a people keenly alive to natural beauty. The opening lines sung by the goddess to Bran strike a note which sounds through all Celtic literature:

"There is a distant isle, around which sea-horses glisten,

...

A beauty of a wondrous land, whose aspects are lovely,

Whose view is a fair country, incomparable in its haze.

It is a day of lasting weather, that showers silver on the land;

A pure white cliff on the range of the sea,

Which from the sun receives its heat."

So Oisin describes it: "I saw a country all green and full of flowers, with beautiful smooth plains, blue hills, and lakes and waterfalls." All this and more than this is the reflection of nature as it is found in Celtic regions, and as it was seen by the eye of Celtic dreamers, and interpreted to a poetic race by them.

In Irish accounts of the síd, Dagda has the supremacy, wrested later from him by Oengus, but generally each owner of a síd is its lord. In Welsh tradition Arawn is lord of Annwfn, but his claims are contested by a rival, and other lords of Elysium are known. Manannan, a god of the sea, appears to be lord of the Irish island Elysium which is called "the land of Manannan," perhaps because it was easy to associate an oversea world "around which sea-horses glisten" with a god whose mythic steeds were the waves. But as it lay towards the sunset, and as some of its aspects may have been suggested by the glories of the setting sun, the sun-god Lug was also associated with it, though he hardly takes the place of Manannan.

Most of the aspects of Elysium appear unchanged in later folk-belief, but it has now become fairyland—a place within hills, mounds, or síd, of marvellous beauty, with magic properties, and where time lapses as in a dream. A wonderful oversea land is also found in Märchen and tradition, and Tír na n-Og is still a living reality to the Celt. There is the fountain of youth, healing balsams, life-giving fruits, beautiful women or fairy folk. It is the true land of heart's desire. In the eleventh century MSS. from which our knowledge of Elysium is mainly drawn, but which imply a remote antiquity for the materials and ideas of the tales, the síd-world is still the world of divine beings, though these are beginning to assume the traits of fairies. Probably among the people themselves the change had already begun to be made, and the land of the gods was simply fairyland. In Wales the same change had taken place, as is seen by Giraldus' account of Elidurus enticed to a subterranean fairyland by two small people. 1302

Some of the Elysium tales have been influenced by Christian conceptions, and in a certain group, the Imrama or "Voyages," Elysium finally becomes the Christian paradise or heaven. But the Elysium conception also reacted on Christian ideas of paradise. In the Voyage of Maelduin, which bears some resemblance to the story of Bran, the Christian influence is still indefinite, but it is more marked in the Voyage of Snedgus and MacRiagla. One island has become a kind of intermediate state, where dwell Enoch and Elijah, and many others waiting for the day of judgment. Another island resembles the Christian heaven. But in the Voyage of Brandan the pagan elements have practically disappeared; there is an island of hell and an island of paradise. 1303 The island conception is the last relic of paganism, but now the voyage is undertaken for the purpose of revenge or penance or pilgrimage. Another series of tales of visionary journeys to hell or heaven are purely Christian, yet the joys of heaven have a sensuous aspect which recalls those of the pagan

Elysium. In one of these, The Tidings of Doomsday, 1304 there are two hells, and besides heaven there is a place for the boni non valde, resembling the island of Enoch and Elijah in the Voyage of Snedgus. The connection of Elysium with the Christian paradise is seen in the title Tir Tairngiri, "The Land of Promise," which is applied to the heavenly kingdom or the land flowing with milk and honey in early glosses, e.g. on Heb. iv. 4, vi. 15, where Canaan and the regnum c[oe]lorum are called Tír Tairngiri, and in a gloss to 1 Cor. x. 4, where the heavenly land is called Tír Tairngiri Innambéo, "The Land of Promise of the Living Ones," thus likening it to the "Land of the Living" in the story of Connla.

Sensuous as many of the aspects of Elysium are, they have yet a spiritual aspect which must not be overlooked. The emphasis placed on its beauty, its music, its rest and peace, its oblivion, is spiritual rather than sensual, while the dwelling of favoured mortals there with divine beings is suggestive of that union with the divine which is the essence of all religion. Though men are lured to seek it, they do not leave it, or they go back to it after a brief absence, and Laeg says that he would prefer Elysium to the kingship of all Ireland, and his words are echoed by others. And the lure of the goddess often emphasises the freedom from turmoil, grief, and the rude alarms of earthly life. This "sweet and blessed country" is described with all the passion of a poetical race who dreamed of perfect happiness, and saw in the joy of nature's beauty, the love of women, and the thought of unbroken peace and harmony, no small part of man's truest life. Favoured mortals had reached Elysium, and the hope that he, too, might be so favoured buoyed up the Celt as he dreamed over this state, which was so much more blissful even than the future state of the dead. Many races have imagined a happy Other-world, but no other race has so filled it with magic beauty, or so persistently recurred to it as the Celts. They stood on the cliffs which faced the west, and as the pageant of sunset passed before them, or as at midday the light shimmered on the far horizon and on shadowy islands, they gazed with wistful eyes as if to catch a glimpse of Elysium beyond the fountains of the deep and the halls of the setting sun. In all this we see the Celtic version of a primitive and instinctive human belief. Man refuses to think that the misery and disappointment and strife and pain of life must always be his. He hopes and believes that there is reserved for him, somewhere and at some time, eternal happiness and eternal love.

Footnote 1231: Nutt-Meyer, i. 213.

Footnote 1232: Joyce, OCR 431.

Footnote 1233: D'Arbois, ii. 311; IT i. 113 f.; O'Curry, MC iii. 190.

Footnote 1234: Nutt-Meyer, i. 1 f., text and translation.

Footnote 1235: LU 120a; Windisch, Irische Gramm. 120 f.; D'Arbois, v. 384 f.; Gaelic Journal, ii. 307.

Footnote 1236: TOS iv. 234. See also Joyce, OCR 385; Kennedy, 240.

Footnote 1237: LU 43 f.; IT i. 205 f.; O'Curry, Atlantis, ii., iii.; D'Arbois, v. 170; Leahy, i. 60 f.

Footnote 1238: "From Manannan came foes."

Footnote 1239: Joyce, OCR 223 f.

Footnote 1240: O'Grady, ii. 290. In this story the sea is identified with Fiachna's wife.

Footnote 1241: Joyce, OCR 253 f.

Footnote 1242: IT iii. 211 f.; D'Arbois, ii. 185.

Footnote 1243: O'Curry, MS. Mat. 388.

Footnote 1244: A similar idea occurs in many Fian tales.

Footnote 1245: Evans, Welsh Dict. s.v. "Annwfn"; Anwyl, 60; Gaidoz, ZCP i. 29 f.

Footnote 1246: Loth, i. 27 f.; see p. 111, supra.

Footnote 1247: supra.

Footnote 1248: Guest, iii. 75; Loth, i. 29 f.

Footnote 1249: Skene, i. 264, 276. Cf. the Ille tournoiont of the Graal romances and the revolving houses of Märchen. A revolving rampart occurs in "Maelduin" (RC x. 81).

Footnote 1250: Skene, i. 285.

Footnote 1251: supra.

Footnote 1252: Chretien, Eric, 1933 f.; Geoffrey, Vita Merlini, 41; San Marte, Geoffrey, 425. Another Irish Liban is called Muirgen, which is the same as Morgen. See Girald. Cambr. Spec. Eccl. Rolls Series, iv. 48.

Footnote 1253: William of Malmesbury, de Ant. Glaston. Eccl.

Footnote 1254: San Marte, 425.

Footnote 1255: Op. cit. iv. 49.

Footnote 1256: Joyce, OCR 434; Rh[^y]s, CFL i. 170; Hardiman, Irish Minst. i. 367; Sébillot, ii. 56 f.; Girald. Cambr. ii. 12. The underworld is sometimes reached through a well (cf. , supra; TI iii. 209).

Footnote 1257: Le Braz 2, i. p. xxxix, ii. 37 f.; Albert le Grand, Vies de Saints de Bretagne, 63.

Footnote 1258: A whole class of such Irish legends is called Tomhadna, "Inundations." A typical instance is that of the town below Lough Neagh, already referred to by Giraldus Cambrensis, Top. Hib. ii. 9; cf. a Welsh instance in Itin. Cambr. i. 2. See Rh[^y]s, CFL, passim; Kennedy, 282; Rev. des Trad. Pop. ix. 79.

Footnote 1259: Scott. Celt. Rev. i. 70; Campbell, WHT Nos. 38, 52; Loth, i. 38.

Footnote 1260: Curtin, Tales, 158; Rh[^y]s, CFL i. 230.

Footnote 1261: Nutt-Meyer, i. 159.

Footnote 1262: In the Vedas, Elysium has also a strong agricultural aspect, probably for the same reasons.

Footnote 1263: D'Arbois, ii. 119, 192, 385, vi. 197, 219; RC xxvi. 173; Les Druides, 121.

Footnote 1264: For the text see Windisch, Ir. Gram. 120: "Totchurethar bii bithbi at gérait do dáinib Tethrach. ar-dotchiat each dia i n-dálaib tathardai eter dugnathu inmaini." Dr. Stokes and Sir John Rh[^y]s have both privately confirmed the interpretation given above.

Footnote 1265: "Dialogue of the Sages," RC xxvi. 33 f.

Footnote 1266: Tethra was husband of the war-goddess Badb, and in one text his name is glossed badb (Cormac, s.v. "Tethra"). The name is also glossed muir, "sea," by O'Cleary, and the sea is called "the plain of Tethra" (Arch. Rev. i. 152). These obscure notices do not necessarily denote that he was ruler of an oversea Elysium.

Footnote 1267: Nennius, Hist. Brit. § 13; D'Arbois, ii. 86, 134, 231.

Footnote 1268: LL 8b; Keating, 126.

Footnote 1269: Both art motifs and early burial customs in the two countries are similar. See Reinach, RC xxi. 88; L'Anthropologie, 1889, 397; Siret, Les Premiere Ages du Metal dans le Sud. Est. de l'Espagne.

Footnote 1270: Orosius, i. 2. 71; LL 11b.

Footnote 1271: D'Arbois, v. 384; O'Grady, ii. 385.

Footnote 1272: TOS iii. 119; Joyce, OCR 314. For a folk-tale version see Folk-lore, vii. 321.

Footnote 1273: Leahy, i. 36; Campbell, LF 29; CM xiii. 285; Dean of Lismore's Book, 54.

Footnote 1274: O'Curry, MC ii. 143; Cormac, 35.

Footnote 1275: supra; IT iii. 213.

Footnote 1276: See Gaidoz, "La Requisition de l'Amour et la Symbolisme de la Pomme," Ann. de l'École Pratique des Hautes Études, 1902; Fraser, Pausanias, iii. 67.

Footnote 1277: Rh[^y]s, HL 359.

Footnote 1278: "The Silver Bough in Irish Legend," Folk-Lore, xii. 431.

Footnote 1279: Cook, Folk-Lore, xvii. 158.

Footnote 1280: IT i. 133.

Footnote 1281: O'Donovan, Battle of Mag Rath, 50; D'Arbois, v. 67; IT i. 96. Dagda's cauldron came from Murias, probably an oversea world.

Footnote 1282: Miss Hull, 244. Scath is here the Otherworld, conceived, however, as a dismal abode.

Footnote 1283: O'Curry, MC ii. 97, iii. 79; Keating, 284 f.; RC xv. 449.

Footnote 1284: Skene, i. 264; cf. RC xxii. 14.

Footnote 1285: supra.

Footnote 1286: Guest, iii. 321 f.

Footnote 1287: supra.

Footnote 1288: For the use of a vessel in ritual as a symbol of deity, see Crooke, Folk-Lore, viii. 351 f.

Footnote 1289: Diod. Sic. v. 28; Athen. iv. 34; Joyce, SH ii. 124; Antient Laws of Ireland, iv. 327. The cauldrons of Irish houses are said in the texts to be inexhaustible (cf. RC xxiii. 397).

Footnote 1290: Strabo, vii. 2. 1; Lucan, Usener's ed., p. 32; IT iii. 210; Antient Laws of Ireland, i. 195 f.

Footnote 1291: Curtin, HTI 249, 262.

Footnote 1292: See Villemarqué, Contes Pop. des anciens Bretons, Paris, 1842; Rh[^y]s, AL; and especially Nutt, Legend of the Holy Grail, 1888.

Footnote 1293: "Adventures of Nera," RC x. 226; RC xvi. 62, 64.

Footnote 1294: supra.

Footnote 1295: supra.

Footnote 1296: For parallel myths see Rig-Veda, i. 53. 2; Campbell, Travels in South Africa, i. 306; Johnston, Uganda Protectorate, ii. 704; Ling Roth, Natives of Sarawak, i. 307; and cf. the myth of Prometheus.

Footnote 1297: This is found in the stories of Bran, Maelduin, Connla, in Fian tales (O'Grady, ii. 228, 238), in the "Children of Tuirenn," and in Gaelic Märchen.

Footnote 1298: Martin, 277; Sébillot, ii. 76.

Footnote 1299: Burton, Thousand Nights and a Night, x. 239; Chamberlain, Aino Folk-Tales, 38; L'Anthropologie, v. 507; rrrMaspero, Hist. anc. des peuples de l'Orient, i. 183. The lust of the women of these islands is fatal to their lovers.

Footnote 1300: An island near New Guinea is called "the land of women." On it men are allowed to land temporarily, but only the female offspring of the women are allowed to survive (L' Anthrop. v. 507). The Indians of Florida had a tradition of an island in a lake inhabited by the fairest women (Chateaubriand, Autob. 1824, ii. 24), and Fijian mythology knows of an Elysian island of goddesses, near the land of the gods, to which a few favoured mortals are admitted (Williams, Fiji, i. 114).

Footnote 1301: supra. Islands may have been regarded as sacred because of such cults, as the folk-lore reported by Plutarch suggests (p. 343, supra). Celtic saints retained the veneration for islands, and loved to dwell on them, and the idea survives in folk-belief. Cf. the veneration of Lewismen for the Flannan islands.

Footnote 1302: Gir. Camb. Itin. Camb. i. 8.

Footnote 1303: Translations of some of these Voyages by Stokes are given in RC, vols. ix. x. and xiv. See also Zimmer, "Brendan's Meerfahrt," Zeits. für Deut. Alt. xxxiii.; cf. Nutt-Meyer, ch. 4, 8.

Footnote 1304: RC iv. 243.

INDEX

Abnoba
Adamnan
Aed Abrat
Aed Slane
Aeracura
Afanc
Agricultural rites. See Festivals.
Aife
Aillén
Aine
Aitherne
Albiorix
All Saints' Day
All Souls' Day
Allat
Alpine race
Altars
Amæthon
Amairgen
Ambicatus
Amours with mortals, divine.
Amulets
Ancestor worship
Andarta
Andrasta
Anextiomarus
Animal gods, anthropomorphic

Animal worship.
Animals, burial of
Animals, descent from
Animals, domestic, from the gods' land
Animals, dressing as
Animals, sacramental eating of
Animals, slaughter of
Animals, tabooed
Animism
Ankou
Annwfn.
Anu
Anwyl, Prof. note
Apollo
Arawn
Archæology
Arduinna
Arianrhod
Artemis
Artaios
Arthur.
Arthurian cycle
Artor
Arvalus
Astrology
Augustus
Auto-suggestion
Avagddu
Avallon
Bacchus
Badb.
Badbcatha
Balor note
Banba

Banfeinnidi
Bangaisgedaig
Baptism note
Bards
Barintus
Barrex
Barri, S.
Bear, cult of
Beddoe, Dr.
Belatucadros
Belenos
Belgæ
Beli
Belinuntia
Belinus
Belisama
Bellovesus
Beltane.
Bericynthia
Bertrand, M.
Bile
Bile
Bird gods
Birth
Black Annis' Bower
Blathnat
Blodeuwedd.
Blood
Blood, Brotherhood
Boand
Boar, cult of
Bodb
Bodb Dearg
Bormana

Borvo
Boudicca
Boughs
Boundary stones
Braciaca
Bran .
Branwen.
Braziers, god of
Brennius
Brennus
Bres
Brian
Bride, S.
Bridge
Bridge of Life
Brigantia
Brigindo
Brigit
Brigit, St.. note
Broca
Bronze Age
Brother-sister unions
Brown Bull
Brownie
Brug. See Síd
Brythons
Brythons, gods of.
Buanann
Bull, cult of.
Burial rites
Caer Sidi
Cæsar.
Cakes
Calatin

Calendar
Camulos
Candlemas
Cannibalism
Caoilte
Caractacus
Carman
Carpenters, god of
Cassiterides
Cassivellaunus
Castor and Pollux
Caswallawn
Cathbad
Cathubodua
Caturix
Cauldron
Celtæ
Celtiberians
Celtic and Teutonic religion
Celtic empire
Celtic origins
Celtic people, types of
Celtic religion, evolution of
Celtic religion, higher aspects of
Celtic religion, homogeneity of
Celtic religion, Roman influence on
Celts, gods of
Celts, religiosity of
Celts, temperament of
Cenn Cruaich note.
Cera
Cernunnos..
Cerridwen.
Cessair

Cethlenn
Cetnad
Charms
Church and paganism
Cian
Clairvoyance
Cleena
Clota
Clutoida
Cocidius
Cock
Columba, S. note.
Combats, ritual
Comedovæ
Comyn, M.
Conaire
Conall Cernach
Conan
Conception, magical
Conchobar
Conn
Conncrithir
Connla
Conservatism in belief
Coral
Coranians
Cordelia
Cormac
Corn-spirit
Corotacus
Cosmogony
Couvade
Crafts, gods of
Cranes

Craniology
Creation
Creiddylad
Creidne
Creirwy
Crom Dubh
Crom Eocha
Cromm Cruaich
Cross
Cross-roads
Cruithne
Cúchulainn
Cúchulainn saga.
Culann
Culture goddesses
Culture gods and heroes note
Cumal
Cúroi
Cursing wells
Dagda.
Damona
Dance, ritual
Danu.
Daoine-sidhe
D'Arbois, M.
Day of Judgment
Dead, condition and cult of
Dead Debtor
Dead, land of, and Elysium
Dead living in grave.
Debility of Ultonians
Dechelette, M.
Dechtire.
Deiseil

Dei Terreni
Demeter
Demons.
Devorgilla
Diana
Diancecht
Diarmaid
Dii Casses
Diodorus Siculus
Dionysus
Dioscuri
Dirona
Dirra
Disablot
Disir
Dispater
Distortion
Divination
Divine descent
Divine kings
Divineresses
Diviners
Divining rod
Dolmens
Domestication
Dominæ
Domnu note
Dôn
Donnotaurus
Dragon
Drink of oblivion
Druidesses
Druidic Hedge
Druidic sending

Druids
Druids and Filid
Druids and magic
Druids and medicine
Druids and monasticism
Druids and Pythagoras
Druids and Rome
Druids, classical references to
Druids, dress of
Druids, origin of
Druids, poems of
Druids, power of
Druids, teaching of
Druids, varieties of
Drunemeton
Dualism
Dumias
Dusii
Dwelling of gods. See Gods, abode of
Dylan
Each uisge
Earth and Under-earth
Earth cults
Earth divinities. note
Eclipses
Ecne
Ecstasy
Egg, serpent's
Elatha
Elcmar
Elements, cult of
Elphin
Elves note
Elysium
Elysium, and Paradise

Elysium, characteristics off
Elysium, lords of
Elysium, names of
Elysium, origin of
Elysium, varieties of
Emer
Enbarr
Eochaid
Eochaid Ollathair
Eochaid O'Flynn
Eogabail
Epona
Eri
Eridanus
Eriu
Esus
Etain
Etair
Ethics
Ethne note
Euhemerisation.
Eurosswyd
Evans, Dr
Evil eye
Evnissyen
Exogamy
Ex votos
Fachan
Fairies.. note.
Fairyland
Fáith
Falga
Fand
Ferdia
Fergus

Fertility cults
Festivals
Festivals of dead
Fetich
Fiachna
Fians
Filid
Findbennach
Finnen, S
Finntain
Fionn
Fionn saga
Fir Dea
Fir Domnann
Fir Síde
Firbolgs
Fires.
Fires, sacred
Fish, sacred
Flann Manistrech
Flood
Fomorians
Food of immortality
Food as bond of relationship
Forest divinities
Fotla
Foundation sacrifices
Fountains
Fountains of youth
Fraoch
Friuch
Frazer, Dr. J.G
Fuamnach
Funeral sacrifices
Future life

Galatæ
Galli
Gallizenæ. See Priestesses
Galioin
Garbh mac Stairn
Gargantua note
Garman
Gauls
Gavida
Geasa.. See Tabu
Geoffrey of Monmouth
Ghosts
Ghosts in trees
Gildas
Gilla Coemain
Gilvæthwy
Glass
Glastonbury
Goborchin
God of Connaught
God of Druidism
God of Ulster
Goddesses and mortals
Goddesses, preeminence of
Godiva
Gods, abode of
Gods, children of
Gods, fertility and civilisation from land of
Gods uniting with mortals
Goibniu
Goidels
Goll mac Morna
Gomme, Sir G.L
Goose
Govannon

Graal
Grainne
Grannos
Gregory of Tours
Groves
Growth, divinities of
Gruagach
Guinevere
Gurgiunt
Gutuatri
Gwawl
Gweir
Gwion
Gwydion
Gwyn
Gwythur
Hades
Hafgan
Hallowe'en
Hallstatt
Hallucinations
Hammer as divine symbol
Hammer, God with
Haoma
Hare
Harvest
Head-hunting
Heads, cult of
Healing plants
Healing ritual
Healing springs
Hearth as altar
Heaven and earth
Hen
Hephaistos

Heracles
Heroes in hills
Hills
Holder, A
Horned helmets
Horns, gods with
Horse
Hu Gadarm note
Hyde, Dr
Hyperboreans
Hypnotism
Iberians
Icauna
Iconoclasm
Igerna
Images
Imbas Forosnai
Immortality
Incantations
Incest
Indech
Inspiration
Invisibility
Is
Iuchar, Iucharbar
Janus
Joyce, Dr
Juno
Junones
Jullian
Juppiter
Kalevala
Keane
Keating
Kei

Keres
Kieva
King and fertility
Kings, divine
Kings, election of
Kore
Kronos
La Tène
Labraid
Lakes
Lammas
Land under waves
Lear
Ler, Lir note
Lia Fail
Liban
Libations
Ligurians
Llew
Lludd Llawereint
Llyr
Lochlanners
Lodens
Loegaire
Lonnrot
Loth, M
Love
Lucan
Luchtine
Lucian
Lug note note..
Lugaid
Lugnasad
Lugoves
Lugus

Lycanthropy
Mabinogion
Mabon
MacBain, Dr
MacCuill, MacCecht, and MacGrainne
Macha
MacIneely
MacPherson
Madonna
Maelduin
Maelrubha, S.
Magic
Magic, agricultural note
Magico-medical rites
Magonia
Magtured
Man, origin of
Manannan note ..
Manawyddan
Mannhardt
Maponos
Märchenormulæ
Marriage, sacred
Mars
Martin
Martinmas
Math
Matholwych
Matres
Matriarchate
Matronæ
May-day
May-queen
Medb
Medicine

Mediterranean race
Medros
Megaliths . See Stonehenge
Men, cults of
Mercury
Merlin
Mermaids
Metempsychosis
Meyer, Prof
Miach
Mider
Midsummer
Mile
Milesians
Minerva
Miracles
Mistletoe
Mithraism
Moccus
Modranicht
Modron
Mogons
Mongan
Moon
Morgen
Morrigan
Morvran
Mounds
Mountain gods
Mountains
Mowat, M
Muireartach
Muirne
Mule
Mullo

Music
Mythological school
Name
Name-giving
Nantosvelta
Nature divinities and spirits
Needfire
Nemaind
Neman
Nemedians
Nemeton
Nemetona
Nennius
Neo-Druidic heresy note
Neptune
Nera
Nessa
Nét
Neton
New Year
Night
Niskas
Nodons
Norse influence
Nuada.
Nuada Necht
Nudd
Nudd Hael
Nudity
Nutt, Mr
Nymphs
Nynnyaw
Oak
Oaths
O'Curry

O'Davoren
Oengus
Oghams
Ogma
Ogmíos
Oilill Olom
Oisin
Omens
Oracles
Oran
Orbis alius
Orbsen
Ordeals
Orgiastic rites
Osiris
Paradise
Partholan
Pastoral stage
Patrick, S...
Peanfahel
Peisgi
Penn Cruc
Pennocrucium
Perambulation
Persephone
Picts
Pillar of sky
Place-names note
Plants
Pliny
Plutarch
Pluto
Plutus
Poeninus
Poetry, divinities of

Pollux
Polyandry
Polygamy
Prayer
Pre-Celtic cults
Priesthood. See Druids.
Priestesses.
Priest-kings
Procopius
Prophecy
Pryderi
Pwyll
Pythagoras
Quadriviæ
Ragnarok
Rain-making
Rebirth
Reinach, M. note
Relics
Retribution
Rhiannon
Rh[^y]s, Sir J..
Rigantona
Rigisama
River divinities
Rivers, cult of
Rivers, names of
Roman and Celtic gods
Romans and Druids
Ruadan
Ruad-rofhessa
Rucht
Rudiobus
Saar
Sacramental rites

Sacrifice of aged
Sacrifice of animals
Sacrifice, foundation
Sacrifice, human
Sacrifice to dead
Sacrificial offerings
Sacrificial survivals
Saints.. note
Saints and wells
Saints' days and pagan festivals
Salmon of knowledge
Samhain
Satire
Saturn
Scandinavia and Ireland
Scathach
Scotti
Sea
Sébillot
Segomo
Segovesus
Selvanus
Semnotheoi
Sequana
Sergi, Prof
Serpent
Serpent with ram's head
Serpent's egg
Serpent's glass
Setanta
Shape-shifting
Síd note
Silvanus
Sinend
Sinnan

Sirona
Skene, Dr
Slain gods and human victims
Sleep, magic
Smertullos
Smiths, god of
Smiths, magic of
Solar hero
Soma
Soul as animal
Soul, separable
Spain
Spells
Squatting gods
Sreng
Stag
Stanna
Stokes, Dr.
Stone circles
Stonehenge
Stones, cult of
Sualtaim
Submerged towns
Sucellos
Suicide
Sul
Suleviæ
Sun
Sun myths
Swan-maidens
Swastika
Swine
Swineherds, The Two
Symbols
Tabu ... See Geasa

Tadg
Taghairm
Tailtiu
Táin bó Cuailgne
Taliesin
Taran
Taranis
Taranos
Tarbh Uisge
Tarvos Trigaranos
Tattooing
Tegid Voel
Teinm Laegha
Tempestarii
Temples
Tethra
Teutates
Teyrnon
Three-headed gods
Thumb of knowledge
Thurnam, Dr
Tír na n-Og
Tombs as sacred places
Tonsure
Torque
Totatis
Totemism
Toutatis
Transformation. See Shapeshifting
Transformation Combat
Transmigration
Tree cults.
Tree descent from

Trees of Elysium
Trees of Immortality
Triads.. note
Triple goddesses
Tristram
Tuan MacCairill
Tuatha Dé Danann..
Tutelar divinities
Tuag
Twrch Trwyth
Tyr
Underworld
Urien
Urwisg
Uthyr
Valkyries
Vegetation cults
Vegetation gods and spirits.
Venus of Quinipily
Vera
Vesta
Vierges noires
Vintius
Virgines
Viviane
Vortigern
Vosegus
Votive offerings
Vulcan
War chants
War goddesses
War gods
Warrior, ideal

Warrior, power of dead
Washer at the Ford
Water bull
Water fairies note
Water, guardians of
Water horse
Water world note
Waves, fighting the
Waves, nine
Weapons
Wells
Wells, origin of
Wheel, god with
Wheel symbol
White women
Wind
Windisch, Prof
Wisdom
Wisdom from eating animal note
Wolf god
Witch
Women and magic
Women as first civilisers
Women as warriors
Women, cults of.
Women, islands of
World catastrophe
World, origin of
Wren
Yama
Year, division of
Yule log
Zeus
Zimmer